We Were *Walimu* Once and Young

The Teacher — Paul Nzalamba

We Were *Walimu* Once and Young

Snapshots of Teaching in East Africa
—
Adventure and Discovery in
Kenya, Tanzania, and Uganda
—
E. Brooks Goddard, Editor

Copyright © 2017 by E. Brooks Goddard
(Introduction, section introductions, reference material, and compilation of the collective works.)

The stories in this collection are copyrighted by the individual authors.

First Edition, June 2017
Print ISBN: 978-1939423856

Published by Jugum Press
505 Broadway East #237
Seattle, Washington USA
Find eBook editions at www.jugumpress.com
Contact: JugumPress@outlook.com

Library of Congress Control Number: 2017906409
Jugum Press, Seattle, Washington USA

Back cover and frontispiece: "The Teacher," © Paul Nzalamba; used by permission of the artist.

Photographs of students on the front and back covers by Jim Blair and Brooks Goddard.

"Memories of Kenyan Independence," from *Mau Mau's Children: The Making of Kenya's Postcolonial Elite* by David P. Sandgren. Reprinted by permission of the University of Wisconsin Press. ©2012 by the Board of Regents of the University of Wisconsin System.

This book is provided for your personal enjoyment only. All rights reserved. This book, or any parts of it, may not be reproduced without permission, except for common re-use purposes such as reviews and minimal, acknowledged quotations.

Contents

Introduction • 1

Maps of East Africa • 3

Have We Forgotten? • 7

I: Key Moments and Experiences • 9

II: Teaching and School Life • 129

III: Trips and Travel • 243

IV: Surprise • 323

V: Politics and Politicians • 349

VI: Tributes • 383

TEA-Alumni Authors • 415

TEA and TEEA History • 427

Acknowledgments • 429

Author Index • 431

Title Index • 439

Topic Index • 441

We Were *Walimu* Once and Young

"They must be professionally first rate or capable of becoming so through the training that will be provided for them. They must be personally resourceful and imaginative in surmounting the unexpected, the difficult or the routine. They must be capable of relating themselves to new situations, new associates and new friends. With no trace of paternalism, they must be able to cooperate with Africa in educating itself. They must be animated by a spirit of service that is realistic, not sentimental, that is durable, not romantic. They must be knowledgeable about American life and education and ready to learn understandingly about the people and cultures of other lands."

R. Freeman (Jay) Butts
New York Times
February 5, 1961

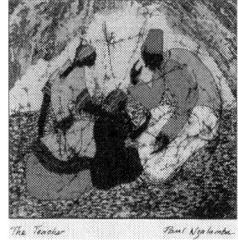

Introduction

Several international education visionaries met in Princeton, New Jersey, USA, in the first week of December, 1960, anticipating the needs of the future countries of Kenya, Tanzania, and Uganda. They decided to form with their counterparts in the UK a program for supplying secondary school teachers and ultimately teacher educators beginning in 1961.

Prompted by Karl Bigelow and Freeman Jay Butts of Teachers College, Columbia University, and inspired both by John Kennedy's inaugural address of January 20, 1961, and by Julius Nyerere, incoming president of Tanganyika (later Tanzania), Teachers for East Africa (TEA) and Teacher Education for East Africa (TEEA) were launched.

Out into such postings as Gulu, Kampala, Kapenguria, Narok, Iringa, and Arusha went the first of 575 Americans and 200 Brits, most single, some with families. They went through training of six weeks to nine months, taught in the educational system of their hosts for two years or more, and returned home. The programs ended in 1972. TEA was launched just weeks after Kennedy's address, and for most of these idealistic people, it was the tour of a lifetime. All have vivid memories, and many returned for visits. They were the *walimu*, their students were *wanafuzi*.

This book is a collection of memories from those days when mission, profession, and adventure engagingly coalesced. For many "facing Mount Kenya" was real. Most of the schools were boarding schools, because colonial governments educated only about five percent of secondary school-aged children (eighty percent of the students were boys) and thought to do so in schools that provided accommodation, food, and books. Today, independent governments educate about sixty percent of the eligible population (forty percent of the students are girls), most in schools within a reasonable walking distance of their students' homes and many still in boarding environments.

In 1999 Ed Schmidt gathered the names of those teachers. Nine days after the 9/11 terrorist attacks in 2001, 130 people from TEA and TEEA, organized by Frank Ballance, gathered at the Jurys Hotel in DuPont Circle in Washington, DC, and formed Teachers for East Africa Alumni (TEA-Alumni), which went on to reunite every other year until its last in 2017. Money was raised for East African school support, 190 grants totaling $270,000, and organized groups went back to the countries in 2003, 2005, and 2011. Individuals returned on their own, some to see their "old" schools, some representing TEA-Alumni to review needs, and some to greet the families of their former students.

These stories are divided into six sections for organizational purposes. There are roughly 200 stories by 100 authors. All in different lengths, different voices. Some were written while the authors were at work in East Africa, but most are recent memoirs. Entries for this book closed in March 2017, but new stories can still be submitted to:

www.tea-a.org, Story Project

These tales, compiled and reviewed with the usual caveats, form a splendid salute to a proud program. You can read these stories and others at http://bit.ly/teaaki.

Dunia ni maarifa

E. Brooks Goddard, editor

Maps of East Africa

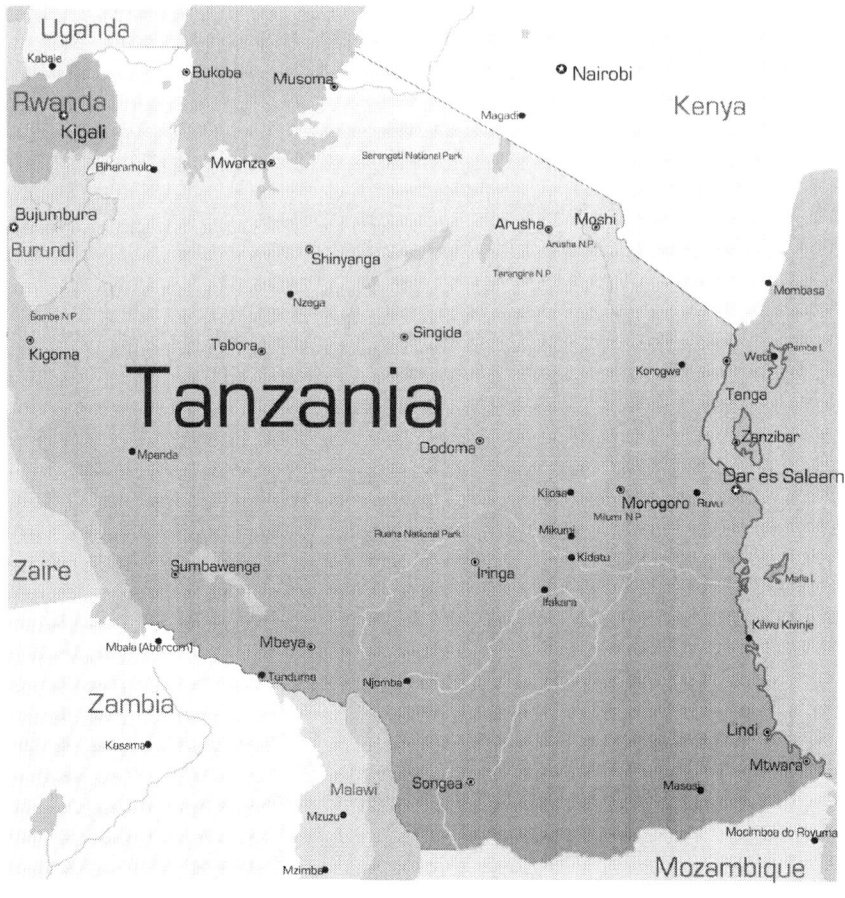

Have We Forgotten?

Moses L. Howard

The teachers who were the initial participants in the Teachers for East Africa project of the 1960s were all Americans (UK participation began in 1962), but we are each quite different. We came from different parts of America. We came with our own unique stories, backgrounds, and mythologies. We came with our prejudices but packed them away, hid them. But they were always with us.

I came from Mississippi. When I left there in 1961, policemen were using dogs to herd young school children into cattle pens in the fairgrounds in Jackson, Mississippi, because these children were black and were marching down to the bus station to see the Freedom Riders and the sit-ins instead of going to school in segregated classrooms.

Back then we heard about the "culture shock" of going into a new country where the rules are different. You no longer feel restricted by the social rules that govern you at home, but you don't yet feel responsible for the rules of your host country.

I witnessed a young housewife from America openly experiencing a bit of culture shock in the Airline Curio Shoppe at the airport in Kano, Nigeria. I was in back of her as she stood by her husband with a little blonde child on her hip. She watched the black stewardesses and pilots as they walked out to board their planes along with most of the passengers, who were also black. She gently elbowed her husband in his side and said, "Honey!" He answered, "Yeah?" and she said in a slightly bewildered voice, "Everyone here is black!" He looked at her, smiled, and said, "Well, dear, it is Africa..."

In describing our coming to Africa, we had to deal with culture shock. What was proper to do? What mores were we expected to respect? We had to answer questions about whom we loved, about how much we drank, and about how late to stay out on school nights. How do we treat the local people? What determined our moral compass? We were free to choose!

We had the British as a standard for teaching and for treating "native" servants. We had to decide whether to follow their lead or to change slowly what they had in place. What we did then says something about our character. Yet no one knew about our choices and actions but us. Did we question? Did we reflect? Did we teach more to memorize or did we mix our teaching with problem solving? Did we have to remember that we were always teachers, that even when we were not in the classrooms, whenever we acted, we were teaching?

What did we see? Did we notice that the upper level economy was not in the hands of Africans? Did we notice that most of the students we taught had parents who were mostly house servants, drivers, or yard-care workers or small-unit farmers? What did we think of that? Were we invited to the Europeans-only clubs? What did we do when we were asked to join?

As I write this, I am just asking, not accusing. We are all Americans and we are all in this together. We were passionate about living in Africa, and we still are. We gleaned the substance of our stories from our teaching experience and our interactions with the people of the towns and villages where we taught at that particular time.

The reason for interest in our writing is because the independence of the three East African countries remains associated with the years of our coming to teach. We Americans came to teach at their celebration of freedom, which came almost two hundred years after we attained our own independence from the same country that held them in bondage.

We taught the students who saw their countries gain their independence. We taught the students who became the first free leaders and government officials, the first free teachers who grew up in a free Uganda, a free Kenya, and a free Tanzania. ☐

I: Key Moments and Experiences

Half a century down the road, several authors express the power of the TEA experience in directing their lives. Thus Clarence Hunter, in his *Search for Self in the Motherland*, calls his five-year stay in Uganda "the defining moment of my life."

Arguably the most dramatic changes of direction occurred for those who, like Dagmar Telfer Muthamia, married a Kenyan or an Ugandan, like Gloria Lindsey Alibaruho. Specific responsibilities, both outside and within the classroom, as well as remarkable experiences and momentous events off campus, made Carol Heath's *TEA Time* an important "maturing time in my life" and "vastly expanded my world view."

In just *Three Hundred* TEA *Words*, Lloyd Sherman relates experiences that were "the grist for a life seeking the answers to fundamental questions about the conditions that made a difference in learning which have energized my professional life ever since." Brief but memorable, Nat Frothingham's entry, *You Are My Son*, is the touching story of a "chance meeting" on a path near his school.

In this section:

Donald Adams	*Much Forgotten, Much Regained* • 12
Gloria Lindsey Alibaruho	*Kibo and Paradise* • 14
Jay Anderson	*A Clean Well-Pressed Shirt* • 15
Jerry Barr	*Stopping Fires in the Bush* • 16 *Introducing Basketball* • 17
John Bing	*Testing for a Driver's License* • 19
Jim Blair	*TEA Reflections* • 20
Kay Borkowski	*A Life-defining Experience* • 21
Jay Butts	*Career Memories* • 22
Bill Cahill	*A Humbling Experience* • 24
Betty Castor	*Operation Uganda and More* • 25
Betty Coxson	*Africa in My Life* • 27
Ann Russell Dickinson	*Memories Come in All Sizes* • 30
Audrey Van Cleve Dickson	*Bukoba, Tanzania, 1963* • 31
Linda Lenhardt Donaldson	*Visits to My Students' Homes* • 32
John Dwyer	*Three Letters Home* • 38
David Evans	*The Famed Flight to Entebbe via Kano* • 53
Nat Frothingham	*You Are My Son* • 54
Brooks Goddard	*That First Night at Makerere* • 55 *Sports* • 56
Charles Good	*Life-long Close Connections* • 57
Bob Gurney	*The Hills of Kampala in Three Acts* • 58
Henry Hamburger	*Unwelcome* • 59 *TEA Successes, Then and Now* • 60
Carol Heath	*TEA Time* • 61
Ted Heaton	*Attending a Circumcision Ceremony* • 62
Rod Hinkle	*Life-changing Event* • 64 *Transition to Peace Corps* • 65
Moses L. Howard	*David Bruce's Microscope* • 65 *No Entry Permit* • 66 *Empakos* • 68 *India and African Life* • 69

Edward Hower	*Careers Out of Africa* • 72
Jack Humbles	*Female Circumcision* • 73
Clarence Hunter	*The Search for Self in the Motherland* • 74
Marty McCall Lemke	*First Wave Romance* • 78
Clive Mann	*Malaria and Me* • 79 *The Joys of Ajon* • 81 *Pets in Uganda* • 82 *Pets in Kenya* • 84 *Wild Animal Tales from Kapsabet* • 87
Eugene Marschall	*The Mpemba Effect* • 89
Mary Jo McMillin	*Double, Double, Toil and Trouble* • 90 *November 1963, Songea, Tanganyika* • 91 *Cooking All the Time* • 93
Patricia (Schmitt) Mische	*From the Minnesota River Valley to the Peaks of Kilimanjaro* • 94 *The Time I Gave Away My Watch* • 98
Frank Mitchell	*My East Africa Story* • 100
Peter Moock	*Journey in My Ford Anglia to Visit Maasai Well* • 103
Eva Murray-Scelzo	*Scenes from a Tropical Hiatus* • 105
Jack Paarlberg	*My Greatest Gift* • 106
Kate Parry	*Uganda Voluntary Work Camps* • 108
George Pollock	*Why Africa is Always on My Mind* • 109
Joel Reuben	*Getting Posted to the Right School* • 111
Lloyd Sherman	*Three Hundred TEA Words* • 113
Harold Scheub	*TEA Changed My Life* • 115 *Two Remarkable Flights* • 119
Reed Stewart	*Learning from Future Teachers* • 121
Ron Stockton	*Kenya Nostalgia* • 122
George Urch	*Memories* • 124
Jim Wallace	*Dukas, Dear Dukas* • 125
Joel Watne	*Culture Shock* • 126

Much Forgotten, Much Regained

Donald Adams

I remember, when student teaching at the Gayaza Girls School, that the headmistress had broken her arm before my arrival there, and the old science building burning while there. I had forgotten that the headmistress became very concerned about electrical wires that ran past the burning classroom, and I managed to cut electrical power off by standing on top of a Land Rover and pulling the transformer switch.

I'd forgotten also, that Professor Lucas drove Mary Ann Jackson and me out to Gayaza on October 2, 1961, for our two-week assignment, only two days after Group 1C first arrived in Uganda. Also forgotten was the first night in my room at the University Farm, Kabanyola with spring bed and thin mattress devoid of pillow, sheet, or blanket (having been reassured before departure from Kampala that bedding was provided) and the resultant head cold for much of my student teaching at Gayaza.

During my two-week stay at Kabanyola, I was befriended and accepted by African agricultural students. One student in particular, Matthew Okai, from northern Buganda helped me to adjust to life at the University Farm. Now curious as to what might have become of Matthew, I searched the web, finding that he had taught at Makerere University and other colleges, authored books, and served as a member of the board of directors of the Bank of Uganda. I now wish that I had read my diary earlier and had sent Matthew a note of belated thanks, as he passed away in 2008.

Forgotten was the fact that Bob Hobkirk and I, both staying in University Hall, had to sign in a book at the entrance to the Hall should we arrive there after 11:30 p.m. Although never presented with the Hall rules or regulations, after we signed in a couple of times, we received a warning note from Warden Allen. Later, Jerry Barr and I would be threatened with dismissal by Warden Allen for leaving University Hall and Campus, while taking excursions into northern Uganda, without his permission.

I also remember TEA members participating in basketball, baseball, and volleyball on the athletic fields of Makerere University. One of the volleyball memories was of a team being selected to go to Kenya to participate in a demonstration game there, of having traveled to Kenya with Jerry Barr for the game, only to learn that it had again been cancelled. We ended up sleeping on the door step of a college apartment, no doubt scaring occupants by our unannounced presence. Forgotten was the fact that Bob Maxon, Bob Hobkirk, Charles Good, and Dale Otto were also on that team which had practiced several times for this ill-fated event, and that Charles, who had broken his finger trying to catch a soft ball, hit by me, had to cancel out of the proposed match.

Another forgotten event was a dance competition held in celebration of Kabaka returning from England, a competition with a goat to be awarded to the winning team. American students were invited to compete and Sue Geiger, Linda Kunz, Dick Ramsdell, Don MacMaster, Richard Hawkins, and several others competed as a team. One member of each group was then selected based upon dancing skill to participate in an African Dance; Linda was selected from our group and danced quite well with that select group. Mitchell Hall won the goat.

Writing in the diary includes places forgotten: Canteen, City Club, The White Nile, Top Life Club. Also, the numerous social interactions of our group during swimming, table tennis, bridge, hearts, chess, movies, and so, which brought us together even closer as a family. Whenever lonely, we guys would go to Mary Stuart Hall and be welcomed by TEA ladies who would accompany us to movies or on a trip to a club. Until reading the diary, I had forgotten how much I had missed these social interactions when I left by car for my assignment in Malangali, some 700 air miles south of Kampala.

I also had no idea of the impact that the TEA group had on life in Kampala and Makerere University until reading from *Birth of a Dream Weaver*, where the shock of British and American cultures colliding in East Africa resulted in changes in both lifestyle and cultural expectations. ☐

Kibo and Paradise

Gloria Lindsey Alibaruho

In 1962, I was posted to Machame Girls' School at an altitude of approximately 6,000 feet on Mt. Kilimanjaro. I saw many people attempt to go up the mountain; some made it and others did not due to the impact of the atmospheric pressure on them. I took many drinks for Americans and friends going up the 'Mountain' and administered meds for blisters and air sickness for those coming down.

Every morning when I got up, I would go to my window to see if the peaks were still there. It was an automatic reaction, the same as I do every morning here in Uganda since I live on a slight plateau facing Lake Victoria, visible from three windows in my residence.

When I returned to the US after my tour of duty, my automatic response in the morning was to go to the window subconsciously expecting to see Kibo or the saddle in between or even the clouds shrouding the 'Mountain.' It was always so awesome just as are the sail boats that waver in the sun on Sundays here in Uganda.

It was on Kilimanjaro that I heard about the assassination of President John F. Kennedy. I remember vividly descending the 'Mountain' on my way to Moshi town at the foot of Kilimanjaro where Chagga people, villagers who lived on the slopes, lined the sides of the road and turned their faces in sympathy as I drove down in my small blue Anglia car.

Believe it or not, there are occasions when I still have nostalgic feelings about 'Kilimanjaro' and, like Hemingway's leopard, want to go there. I think East Africa is the closest I will ever be to paradise. □

A Clean Well-Pressed Shirt

Jay Anderson

I was sitting at my desk reading and correcting a mound of student essays. The topic they were writing on was in a Nigerian book, *Things Fall Apart* by Chinua Achebe: the death of a young African boy. The essays were very good. My "house boy" Charles, actually a grown man and father of four, interrupted me.

"There is a man at the door for you."

The man was old, African, and serious. Charles translated. I was needed at the school's swimming pool. As the swimming "master," I was responsible for the pool.

"What does he want?"

Charles said only that I was needed and that only a white man would do. So I left my essays on death and walked with the serious old man and Charles down to the pool.

After our walk through the Ugandan forest, we arrived. I saw in the pool with its clear green water, lying face down, the body of a young drowned girl, perhaps three or four years old. She was as still as a floating leaf. On the hillsides around the pool were many Ugandan men, women, and children sitting silently. They waited patiently for me to bring her to them.

Charles whispered to me, "Only a *Mzungu* (white person, non-African) can touch a dead body that's drowned. It's our tradition." So I slipped into the cold shallow water and crossed over to her and lifted her up. She was stiff but still warm and light as some dead birds I have carried to their graves. I walked up the steps out of the pool, laid her on the bright green grass on the hillside, then took off my white shirt and lay it over her. Suddenly, the wailing began. Cries, screams, moans, like the heavens breaking in a thunderstorm of African grief. Charles and I left.

A month, perhaps later, Charles called me again. There is a man for you at the door. I went. It was the same old serious man. He held out his hands and gave me back my now clean, well-pressed shirt. □

Stopping Fires in the Bush

Jerry Barr

It was my second weekend as a mathematics teacher at Sir Samuel Baker Senior Secondary School in Sambaker, twenty miles from Gulu, Uganda. In 1961, Gulu was a small dusty town, no movies or any other recreation that a twenty-two-year-old from Chicago was used to. There was just a few *dukas* run by the same Mr. Patel. Those Patels must have been a big family. Now my duties at Sambaker included five days a week teaching and voluntary extra activates including sports after teaching. So what to do on the weekends?

As a boy, I was involved with the Boy Scouts. Camping, fishing, and hunting were my pleasure, and I had made the rank of Eagle Scout at thirteen years old. So now, located more than two hundred miles from the pleasures of large cities and in the bush of northern Uganda in 1961, I was in camping heaven. So camping became one of my weekend activities. I had a small but comfortable two-man tent, cots and sleeping bags, and other camping equipment plus fishing and rifle equipment for my own "safaris." I was ready.

So now, on my second weekend at Sambaker, I decided to drive to Murchison Falls National Park and do some animal watching. The park was only a three-hour drive from my house, so a friend and I loaded up the camping gear and went "on safari."

There was a lovely hotel called Paraa Safari Lodge right near the actual falls, complete with comfortable rooms, balconies, a restaurant and complete bar, but we would be camping! Our destination was going to be the Paraa Lodge camping area.

As was the norm in Northern Uganda, the road was *murram* gravel, barely two-lanes wide with plenty of potholes and washboard. Traveling two hours went well, but as we got to the road bordering the park and near the entrance, we came upon what we believed was the start of a wild fire. Did my Boy Scout training jump into action! We parked the Land Rover, and with wet towels and shovels, we spent more than one hour putting out the fire. Of course, tired and thirsty, we were covered in black soot from the burning bushes and grass. There was no such thing as carrying ice on safari. We surely needed a cold Bell or Tusker.

We jumped back into the Land Rover, got to Paraa Lodge, and went right to the bar for that tall cold Tusker. Of course, the bar was filled with customers including many English bureaucrats taking the weekend off, with the gin and tonics flowing. There we were, faces and clothes black with soot and proud of our accomplishment, putting out what appeared to be the beginning of a major fire.

Of course, the folks at the bar asked what had happened, and proudly, we announced our success to all who would listen. The entire bar full of patrons went up for grabs in laughter. We as rank American rookies got the news: these fires were set on purpose to burn off the ten-foot-tall elephant grass during the dry season. This was a common practice, especially in the Murchison Falls National Park, better for tourists to see the animals.

At least the Tusker beers were cold. □

Introducing Basketball

Jerry Barr

When I first arrived in Uganda to attend teacher training at Makerere College in Kampala in October, 1961, as a member of the first TEA group, I was twenty-two years old and a sports enthusiast with a great interest in basketball. During this time, I met Larry Olds, a great friend and great basketball player. With others, we had great fun playing basketball while at Makerere.

My sports background came out of Banning Union High School in southern California where I played for the Banning High School basketball team. Banning, a town of 6,000 with 250 students in the school, was located on the high desert in southern California, twenty-two miles from Palm Springs. My senior year, as a forward and co-captain on our school team, we had a great year and ended up winning the California high school championship in 1957, beating schools with thousands of students and great players. I was honored to be chosen as a first-string forward on the All-California state team. In my college years, I played on the Ripon College basketball team. So, I was well versed in playing basketball.

After completing the TEA requirements at Makerere, I was assigned to teach maths at Sir Samuel Baker Senior Secondary School in Northern Uganda. On my arrival there, I was well received, assigned housing, and since it was a boarding school, I was expected to participate in after-school activities. I had no problem with this, and of course, as a young and enthusiastic athlete, I was ready.

Since there was no basketball at Sambaker, the students suggested I come out on the football field to play football (what I called soccer) and see what I could do. I had never played this game but it did not seem complicated. Oh, did I find otherwise! The students ran around me with ease! With no shoes they dribbled the soccer ball around me, in front of me, behind me and over me! Feeling like a fish out of water, I knew this was not going to work for me.

So I thought, why not set up a basketball program at Sambaker and I suggested this to the headmaster. I got the okay from him but without any funds, and told me that I would have to do all the work. We decided on the location of the court and I pegged out the boundaries. Again, because of the lack of funds, we decided that the surface would be. *Murram* was a fine red gravel that was hard and smooth (and cheap!). So, with the school tractor, I leveled out the area.

Murram was added and packed down. The school carpenter built the backboards out of locally available mahogany, and they were supported on telephone poles on each side of the court.

In the meantime, my folks in the US sent me rims and basketballs to get ready for the fun. We were ready to go! Our student athletes were ready to try something new! And so was I—this was my forte! So they came with enthusiasm to learn a new sport and I did my best to show them the ins and outs of basketball. We practiced and set up games with our neighboring schools—including our nearest school with our most honored and talented friend, Mr. Basketball, Larry Olds.

We had plenty of students who became basketball enthusiasts and I knew the sport at Sambaker and Uganda was there to stay. ☐

Testing for a Driver's License
John Bing

After two classes and a coffee break in the morning, we went into town in the afternoon to get a driver's license. The officer in charge, a smiling British type with meerschaum pipe and blond mustache and shirt untucked around an ample waist, told us that our America licenses weren't any good and that there was a two-month wait for appointments. However, he said he would try to work with me that afternoon if I got all the necessary papers. Hunt's Motors would know how to go about this, he claimed, and sent me over there, neglecting to give directions.

After wandering in the wrong direction for fifteen minutes, we asked, turned around, picked up a copy of the Uganda Driving Code, and went to Hunt's Motors. There they were happy to oblige and gave us a chauffeured car.

They gave the driver directions to pick up what we needed. We went to the wrong building first and then to the right one. We paid five shillings and got a temporary license. We drove back to the college where I got my Polaroid camera to take the three pictures of myself needed. Returning the car at about 1:00, we said we'd pick it up at about 2:00 p.m. for the test at 2:30 p.m. and had lunch at the Imperial Hotel, reading our book between courses.

I got up before the meal was completely finished to pick up the car, telling the waiter that my friend was staying. Our waiter thought that this meant that we were staying at the hotel and tore up our bill and made out a separate one. The manager investigated, and Pat told me afterwards that they finally straightened it out. I walked the mile or so down to where the car was and picked it up with driver, practiced a little, and went down to the driving test building. I then found that we still needed yet another form, so we drove to another building and got the form—ten shillings.

Finally, back at the test building, I got into the car with the pleasant Englishman and drove around town. I didn't look carefully at one intersection and almost got rammed, but otherwise thought I did okay. Before we left, the inspector had asked the Hunt's driver how I was and he had replied great or something like that.

On returning, the inspector asked Pat if he'd ever driven with me on the left-hand side of the road. On entering the building, he said I'd flunked, that I wasn't sure enough of shifting with my left hand and to come back after I'd practiced more. So I took the car off, practiced for forty-five minutes, and returned to Hunt's Motors. Result: a forty shilling charge for the car, fifteen shillings for papers, and no license. □

TEA Reflections

Jim Blair

What did TEA do for me? Honestly, it shaped and changed my whole life. I was never much of a student. I went to college on athletic scholarships and did just enough work to remain eligible. I never participated in classroom discussions. When I applied to TEA, I could not name one country in East Africa. I was married and we had a one-year-old son. I was overwhelmed by the talents and intellect of the other members of my group (3C) at Columbia. I doubted that I would be able to teach African kids anything.

I arrived at Magamba Secondary School in Lushoto, Tanzania, and found a new school with all new students. There were no lesson plans. The headmaster showed me my classroom and told me I was to teach history and geography to Forms 1, 2, and 3. That was my total indoctrination. So I just did it. I found that I had unrealized talent. I could teach. Once I realized that I could accomplish whatever I put my mind to, I never looked back.

When my tour ended, I applied to law school even though my college grades were not good enough to allow me to be admitted and I could not take the LSAT exam. Solely because of a wonderful reference letter from TEA, I was admitted on probation. After the first semester, I was off probation and was given a scholarship. I completed law school in twenty-seven months and went to Alaska as an assistant district attorney. I discovered that I had a talent as a trial lawyer. I tried twelve felony cases my first year out of law school. I was elected president of the Alaska Bar Association when I was thirty-four years old, and I was appointed to the Superior Court bench at thirty-five. I retired from judging at forty-eight and joined a large law firm as a trial lawyer. I retired completely at fifty-five. Without my TEA experience, I would never have had such an interesting life. □

A Life-defining Experience

Kay Borkowski

It's August 11, 2011, and here in our little Mexican village on the north shore of Lake Chapala, I'm finally searching for words to describe how TEA affected my life. I—who claimed as an undergraduate at Vanderbilt, "I will not teach!"—have spent most of my life teaching because of TEA. From Uganda and Kenya, to western Australia, to the US, back to Kenya (evaluating math skills for a technical college established by the Danes), back to the US, to Malaysia (establishing a new university), back to the US, and finally to the United Arab Emirates (establishing a new university for women in Dubai) where I married Danny Borkowski, "retired" from teaching and joined him in Saudi Arabia. TEA was a life-defining experience for me.

From the way I teach to how I have handled and continue to handle the difficulties life is sure to bring to us all, I've been positively influenced by TEA. TEA provided the opportunity for life-long friendships, people with whom I join to celebrate and to commiserate.

TEA also influenced the life of the countries where we taught. When I was working again in Kenya, 1980–83, my then nine-year-old daughter and I were shopping in Nakuru. I heard a voice say, "Miss Strain, *Miss Strain!*" Now that was a voice from the past!

It was a former student from Machakos Girls' School shopping with one of her children. She had completed at least one university degree and was married to the equivalent of the governor of the province. She shared news of students from Machakos, many of whom had received PhDs.

Also, the grandson of one of "my" Machakos girls danced at our wedding in Ras al Khamiah, UAE, in June of 1999 when I married Danny Borkowski. His father was a pilot for Kenya Airways. How's that for a "small world" story? □

Career Memories

Jay Butts

You may not believe it, but it was just last Friday in 1999 that the final decorating of my new unit here at Carmel Valley Manor was finished. And for the first time, I have had put up on the wall several framed photographs of key events and some awards I have received over the years. Two of them deal with international events, in which I was privileged to be photographed with presidents of two countries.

The first is a somewhat fuzzy (and unplanned) photo of me introducing Julius Nyerere to Dave Scanlon as Nyerere finished speaking to the final orientation session for the first Groups A and B on the eve of their departure for Kampala on July 12, 1961. Dave and I had gone down to an open hearing at the UN finalizing Tanzania's independence. We sent a note down to Nyerere on the platform asking him to come up to Teachers College on the off chance that he would come to speak to the group—and sure enough, he agreed and drove me up in his limousine where Dave and the rest of the group was waiting. Do you remember that?

The other shows Jim Perkins, president of Cornell, introducing me to Lyndon Johnson on the occasion of an International Conference on the World Crisis in Education at Williamsburg in October 1967. Johnson had proposed the International Education Act of 1967 to promote international studies in American schools. But, the act was never funded as the national revolt against Vietnam was elevating. But it still was a good idea, unfortunately never consummated.

And I have just turned up a photo of me with a third president, which I probably will never frame. It was taken in the lecture hall of the Department of Education at Makerere where the African Association for Teacher Education was meeting in March, 1971. It shows the vice chancellor of Makerere introducing President Idi Amin who gave a short speech of welcome written by Carl Graham to the association. And I am shown on the other side of the table waiting to give the keynote speech of which Idi had preempted half. It should be noted that the Makerere faculty had greeted Amin's overthrow of Milton Obote in January as a "man of the people."

But, enough of recollection of the ups and downs of the 1960s and 1970s. Let's hope we have all learned from our failures as well as from our successes. And TEA/TEEA must surely be counted as one of our most cherished successes, even if it benefited us more than it did our counterparts.

In case you are wondering where I came in, it was because I was thrust into the picture as Director of International Studies at Teachers

College just in time to go with Dave Scanlon and Gray Cowan of Columbia's African Studies to each of the East African countries in February 1961. We got signed undertakings that they wanted Teachers College to do the job under USAID. We arrived home exhilarated and exhausted on February 28, only to wake up the next morning to find that JFK had appointed Shriver to be head of a Peace Corps that would send teachers all over the world. No wonder USAID had moved so fast! ☐

A Humbling Experience
Bill Cahill

In the latter part of 1964, during the period in which I had been dragooned into becoming Acting Headmaster of Chewoyet "Boys" Secondary School in Kapenguria and while I was composing another of my 'get-me-out-of-this-administrative-position!" missives to Don Knies, word came down to our little brick house with the view of Mt. Elgon that a vehicle had arrived at the school with a film crew in it.

Winter break had started and few students were around. I hurried up to my office and found a three-man Russian documentary film crew and their Kenyan driver. The driver explained to me that they had come to Chewoyet to film the place where Jomo Kenyatta, Bildad Kaggia, et al., had been tried in connection with the Mau Mau Rebellion of the mid1950s. The driver also explained to me that the three Russians did not speak English. The driver himself did not speak Russian. Did I speak Russian? Well, no.

The Russians were a congenial, friendly bunch. They figured that, as an educated person, I must speak French. Well, no. German? Well, sort of. I had had two years of college German, ending in 1959, so we tried that. The problem was that, while I still had the grammar, much of my German vocabulary was already beyond the grasp of unprompted memory. And when grasping for a word, I would come up with something in Latin (high school memories) or in Swahili (thank you, Sharifa Zawawi).

No matter how gutturally you pronounce them, words like *agricolae* and *madirisha* do not function well in spoken German sentences.

Then there was another humiliation. I was the Headmaster, the expert, so I must know exactly in which room the trial had been held, right? The Russians knew the English word "right." And where the defendants and the judge had sat, right? And some other interesting facts or anecdotes about the trial, right? Wrong, wrong, and wrong. I suspect I ended up in their film footage as comedy relief. "Just listen to this man's very strange German!"

When they finished the filming, they bade me a jovial farewell and gave me a bottle of vodka. I needed it.

And if you over see that famous photo of Jomo Kenyatta and the others standing in front of the long brick building that temporarily functioned as a courthouse, the window next to the brick arch in the background was mine for a while, the Headmaster's office window. Acting Headmaster Judson Jones (TEA Wave 2) preceded me. It was Jud's office window, too.

Truth is stranger than fiction. □

Operation Uganda and More

Betty Castor (Elizabeth Bowe)

My interest in East Africa preceded my joining TEA. As a college student at Glassboro State College, New Jersey, in the early sixties, our international relations club jumped enthusiastically into an effort to send books and school supplies to the newly independent African country. Why would we focus on Uganda? Conveniently, it was becoming independent in 1962. Operation Uganda was a student-led effort to engage not only our college but also schools and communities around southern New Jersey.

For over a year we collected books and scientific equipment. The bounty was stored in a house on campus dubbed the "Uganda House." Surprisingly, our efforts gained some attention. We were soon invited to the United Nations to meet the prospective Prime Minister, Milton Obote, and other VIPs, including U Thant, Secretary General of the United Nations. Naturally, we thought we were all ambassadors!

The fact that our faculty advisor was Dr. Livingston (Marius, that is) also added to the interest. Meanwhile, we were receiving thousands of books and other equipment—with no sure way to transport them to Mombasa. We finally enlisted the help of the Commander of the US Navy. The first shipment of boxes was on its way courtesy of the military!

Meanwhile a most unbelievable invitation came our way when President Kennedy invited one of us—that would be me- to join his official delegation to the Independence Day ceremony and celebration in Kampala. Imagine traveling on Air Force One, joining Senator Smith (D) Massachusetts and other dignitaries on this amazing trip. We stopped for an overnight and reception at the US Embassy in Rome. For this senior who had never been out of the country, it was an awesome experience.

When I arrived in Kampala, I stayed with an American couple who were teaching at a school that was receiving our books, Kibuli Secondary School. Books, books were everywhere. However, the highlight of this short one-week visit was attending the actual independence ceremony at Kololo Stadium. I well remember, the Union Jack being replaced by a flag of Uganda. With a celebratory mixture of bands, tribal dancing, the King's African Rifles and many dignitaries, the Duke of Kent presided over the formal transfer of power.

Meanwhile, back at Glassboro, the college celebrated, too. The Uganda Ambassador to the United Nations, Apollo Kironda, and local and state politicians were on hand under a great tent donated by the

Hunt circus. We had arranged a transatlantic telephone call between Kampala and Glassboro—big technology for the day.

My trip back on Air Force One was filled with wonderful memories and a strong desire to return and teach. Although I was thinking of the Peace Corps, I was contacted by the office of Freeman Butts at Teachers College. The rest is history so to speak. I learned about the program, met many like-minded teachers, and had a life-changing experience teaching and living in East Africa.

So much has happened in the short history of independent Uganda. We're fortunate to have enjoyed it at such an idyllic period. ☐

Africa in My Life

Betty Coxson

I think my interest in Africa was first ignited by my eighth grade history teacher at William Penn Nixon Grammar School in Chicago, Illinois. I remember being intrigued by the pyramids, the sphinx, the Rosetta Stone, the pharaohs, and mummies. I had also been introduced to Egypt in various Sunday School lessons featuring Joseph and his brothers, the good years and the bad years, the plagues, and Baby Moses set adrift in the Nile in a pitch-lined basket to save him from the pharaoh's baby killers. Exodus records the waters parting to allow the Israelites to cross safely on dry land. It wasn't called Africa at that time. It was just Egypt, as if the rest of Africa didn't exist.

This teacher touched on other events in history such as World War I, then called the Great War. She talked about the starvation in Europe and Herbert Hoover's efforts to ease the suffering. We also learned about President Wilson's deep disappointment that the US was unwilling to ratify the League of Nations as a means of stopping any further wars. I was lucky in both middle school and high school to have good teachers who made history come to life.

Many years later Africa began to emerge in my consciousness as a place. I heard about a young man from Malawi who wanted to go to school in the United States. Without any knowledge of distances or difficulties, he started walking and eventually ended up at the American Embassy in Sudan where he was fixed up with clothes, a passport, and a plane ticket to a small-town college in Skagit Valley, Washington. He was featured in a small article in *Time*. Legson Kayira was his name. He died in 2012 after a career as a teacher and writer. Legson lived in fear of the dictator Hastings Banda, but Banda is now dead and Legson's wife Julie journeyed safely back to Malawi to bury his ashes there.

If the "Dark Continent" could inspire such passionate interest in education as Legson exhibited, I was ready to pack my bags when President John F. Kennedy hurled out his challenge to "Ask not what your country can do for you, but what you can do for your country." I volunteered and went to Nigeria. After two years I went home but signed up for another group (TEEA) that was going to East Africa, Uganda in my case, to train teachers under the Agency for International Development.

It was a very special time, and those of us who took advantage of the opportunities afforded now look back with gratitude that we were at the right place at the right time, and smart enough to recognize such a golden opportunity. Our goal was to work ourselves out of jobs in Africa and replace ourselves with trained African teachers. The TEA and TEEA programs ended in the early seventies. Peace Corps is still giving young Americans the chances we had in the early sixties.

I graduated from Luther College, a small school in Decorah, Iowa. I was trained as a teacher, but wasn't sure that was what I really wanted to do. My six years in Nigeria and Uganda helped me put aside my doubts. I taught English and journalism but also saw a crying need for libraries. I organized books and trained student librarians in Aba, Nigeria. When I got to Uganda, I organized and developed two libraries, one at Kinyamasika, Fort Portal, and the other at Lady Irene, Ndejji.

Since the school in Ndejji was surrounded by several other schools, I set out to raise money to build a library accessible to all the nearby schools. I solicited funds from the school district where I had been teaching and got additional funds from the Agency for International Development. Uganda volunteer students came to our campus on weekends to make cement blocks. The library was called Mukwano, "friendship," because it was a cooperative effort.

I obtained my master's degree from Long Beach State University in 1961. I taught in high schools in Orange County in California and Twenty Nine Palms and Yucca Valley in the Morongo Unified School District until I retired. Then I became an adjunct faculty member at Copper Mountain Community College in Joshua Tree, California, where I taught English and journalism.

In 1990 I heard about a program called Educational Services Exchange with China (ESEC). It was a summer program so I applied and was accepted. We were organized into small teams to teach English at schools all over China. I taught in a university about a one hour bus trip from Shanghai. In 1993 I signed up for another stint in Changchun in Northern China.

In 1998 I retired and moved to the small town Buffalo Center, Iowa, where I purchased a home for $7,500. I helped conduct a writing contest in the middle school for thirteen years. We published students' work in a magazine called Middle Musings. I am still helping with reading at the Timely Mission Care Center and also the Middle School. I am secretary of the newly formed Historical Society and we have charge of our new museum. That's where I am today. □

Memories Come in All Sizes

Ann Russell Dickinson

My mind swirls with memories from different aspects of my time. Makerere means for me teatime with brown bread and orange marmalade in Makerere's cafeteria. You couldn't walk down the Makerere hill to Wandagaya without seeing the fruit bats blackening the entire sky at sunset. And once in town I still remember the pleasant odor of the evening cooking fires of Kampala.

The landscape of Rosary College in Mwanza was dominated by enormous rock formations flung about the landscape. We had to cancel classes on the mornings that the baboons came down from those rocks and camped on the outside hallways of the school. On feast days, the students circling around bonfires and showed off their tribal dances.

We used to fly back and forth between Kampala and Mwanza in a single-engine plane over Lake Victoria. The pilots would stuff handkerchiefs under their earphones and read a book, and then look up part way through the trip to land on a dirt runway in Bukoba to deliver the mail.

Then there was the time when I was napping with fellow Serengeti safari mates under an acacia tree, only to be woken up circled by large animals and two vultures on the treetop.

On another occasion some friends and I were terrorized in Queen Elizabeth Park by an elephant with a torn ear and broken tusk who charged out of the bush at four of us standing by his watering hole. We ran, jumped into our car, swerved frantically to find the road, and screamed in fear until we picked up speed and the *tembo* gave up the chase.

Finally and more in present time, the TEA-Alumni's Tanzania trip in 2005 was very special. I visited six former Rosary students still in the work force as elementary and secondary school teachers, nurses, and social workers. These grandmothers were needed because AIDS had taken so many of the younger generation. So meeting my former students convinced me that our TEA work in the 1960s was not in vain. ☐

Bukoba, Tanzania, 1963

Audrey Van Cleve Dickson

You could get stuck in this town
Be careful with your entry
False-fronted shops, almost empty
Murram streets flanked by deep retainers
Veils of lake flies, drape verandas and corners.

Indian fusion blares from windows left ajar
Over there I saw the cremation, watching from afar
Man laid out on bed of fire, flames flapping upwards
He sat erect before burning to ashes
As huge hippos snorted in the inlet.

February rains will come, it is foretold
Chickens will put laying on hold again
The dock over there will flood
Cutting us off from boat and road
Isolated, shoes will grow mold.

This is the open air market
Tin roof, din of rain, rain, rain
Cattle driven on hoof
Round Lake Victoria, tough as hide
Meat spread out beside the millet
Every mound two shillings a pound
Buy the fillet.

Down by the lake is the British Club
Where expats drink whisky and beer
Play billiards and golf in teams
Complain that hippos ruin the greens
They talk of leaving here.

There is the dispensary, treatment for dysentery
Drink salty IVs to save you pain
Hope antibiotics are not dead to cure
Denatured by heat or moisture
From weeks of rain, rain, rain.

Lucky to survive a clawing place
We are young and full of rosiness
This town burns in our beings forever
You, visitor, go quickly. Do not linger.
The incessant rain will start
You will not escape for months, maybe never. ☐

Visits to My Students' Homes

Linda Lenhardt Donaldson

I was driving down the escarpment from Limuru into the Rift Valley on my way to the home of one of my students at Loreto Convent High School for Girls. I'd been teaching in Kenya for eight months and had already experienced a few adventures traveling around the country. Some were short weekend trips, others such as the trip to Mombasa during the December term break lasted around two weeks.

I often put as much energy and sense of discovery into my travels over term breaks as I did into preparation and teaching of science and English classes to my eager students, spending every night and most weekends preparing lessons according to the syllabi of the Cambridge Overseas Exams, a thoroughly foreign institution to an American, but one for which I had been well tutored by Teachers College at Columbia University before I arrived in Kenya.

Now I was about to spend almost a week visiting four of the many students who had begged me to spend time at their homes in the bush. I had directions from both the students and the head mistress, Mother Superior, who seemed to know where all of her students lived. Looking back I wonder if I chose the first home as a way to ease myself into the rural conditions I would be experiencing, but at the time I think I was just a young, eager traveler wanting to arrive at the nearest home first, not knowing what to expect.

I stopped a few times to check directions once I turned off the main road to Naivasha. I was closer now to Mt. Longonot, which could be seen in the distance from the top of the escarpment road near Limuru. So I knew I was near. Finally I asked a woman walking to market with bunches of bananas in a basket on her head. She appeared to be dressed in the Kikuyu tribeswoman garb, so I tried to communicate in the limited Kikuyu I had picked up from the Form 1 students who had arrived at Loreto knowing limited English or Swahili. None of the rural tribes spoke Swahili in this area. When I said the name of my student's father, the woman broke into a smile, and drew directions in the dusty road. I was only twenty minutes or so down two more narrow roads to the family compound. Soon I would begin to experience the daily life of another culture.

I don't know who was more surprised, my student and the three women with her who rushed to see my red roadster MGTD, with the top down, gifts in the small back, or me, seeing not one but two cement block houses instead of the typical thatched roof hut I'd expected. After hugs, wide smiles and greetings in English, Kikuyu and Swahili–everyone knew *Jambo*, *Habari Gani*, and *Nzuri*.

After introducing me to her mother, the oldest of the women, my student, Wangui, led me into the larger of the two homes, insisting I enter first, the start of the honored teacher treatment I would receive throughout my visits, no matter my protests. We were in the home of Wangui's mother, the first wife of Wangui's father, whom I learned was one of the few Kikuyu in the area who owned land which some of his tribe, mostly women, helped him farm. He was an elder and a tribal chief. Hence he could afford the dowries for more than one wife, three in all. They now sat on a bench across from Wangui and me, seated on two wood chairs next to a square table. The only other furniture in the room were two more chairs behind the table and a larger wood arm chair that looked like it could have once been in an English settler's home.

With Wangui acting as translator, we talked about Loreto Convent, about the school activities Wangui enjoyed, especially field hockey, which I coached. (When I'd arrived the previous September, the head, Mother Superior, laughed at my astonishment at hearing they played hockey in Limuru, near the equator, informing me it was field hockey, unbeknownst to one who graduated from a college in St Paul, Minnesota, a home of ice hockey).

Soon we began talking about topics of interest to the women especially, including the differences between their culture and ours. They began quizzing me about my family, finally asking if my father was rich enough to have many wives. Wangui was embarrassed, but even she did not know the answer to that one. I explained that having more than one wife was neither culturally acceptable nor legal in the US. Wangui's mother, first wife, became quite animated saying she wished women in Kenya had such status, sounding bitter that her husband had taken two more wives.

The younger women said little, but did remind her that there were not enough men to go around and that they helped her with everything, did more work on the farm and shared the smaller home. I could only note that someday perhaps women would be able to change their now independent country. Wangui remained silent, a dutiful daughter, nodding in agreement at times, then said, "When I finish my education I will visit America and I will live as Americans live. I hope my country will change someday!"

That evening I met her father as he sat down at the table for dinner, mugs of the juice and fat of the meat that had been cooking all day placed in front of the two of us. I thought this would be for all, but as he drank his, I was told to do the same. Four of us were then served by the two younger wives a meat stew with *ngima/ugali*, a somewhat flat dumpling like mixture made of maize flour, which we dipped into the stew.

The two women had also cooked a vegetable mixture of greens and some beans and maize, *githeri*, and stewed a chicken for the "honored" guest. Normally, I thought, and Wangui later confirmed, these would not all be served at the same meal.

We finished this feast with a sweet milky tea and her father sat in the large wooden chair, his, as I'd suspected, asking me questions about Wangui's studies and work habits, much like many fathers would do. We'd begun dinner at their usual hour of 8:00, so by now it was quite late. After I said *asante sana*, thank you, to all, Wangui took me to her room, furnished only with a few books and clothes on two shelves and a bed which she proudly showed me, saying it would be mine that night.

That night I slept soundly until their rooster woke me at daybreak, around 6:30 the next morning. Shortly after Wangui knocked on the bedroom door with a cup of hot tea and milk, served as the school did in the morning. Like the students, I added sugar. Then, unlike the Loreto students who for breakfast ate bread and butter and *ngima* cooked to a porridge consistency, I was served fried eggs with bread and fried bananas. Again, my only choice was to graciously accept and eat with enthusiasm.

After more lively conversation between Wangui's mother and me, Wangui again translating, one of the other wives, both of whom had gone out at daybreak to work in the fields, brought me a crude crate holding not one but two live chickens. For me! How could I accept such a generous gift? Again, I had no choice but was glad that at least they all asked for me to send photos I had taken of everyone home with Wangui at the next term's end and her mother promised to ride along with Wangui's father and have tea with me when they brought their daughter back to school.

I felt that was a large victory for her mother's desired place in her world. She did come then and we did have tea, and American cookies which I made for the occasion. I left midmorning filled with smiles, a new understanding of the young women I was teaching and the back of my small MG with sacks of potatoes, maize, and bananas as well as the crate of chickens. I hoped the clouds that appeared were not filled with rain as the canvas car top was buried under the gifts.

Getting to the next home I planned to visit would be trickier. The previous week, the second of this month long term holiday, I had received a letter from the student, Njeeri, giving me directions and instructions. After heading to Naivasha to fill up my gas tank, I set off on the first of many very narrow dirt roads to the place about two hours away where I was to meet her uncle who taught elementary school in that area. We would park in a field off the road about halfway between the school and her family compound.

Though I was young and usually confident, at this point I was concerned that if he did not appear, I would only have about three hours of daylight left before the sunset and darkness set in quickly. I might not have time to backtrack to Naivasha before I was alone in the bush in the dark. I had to trust Njeeri and that her uncle would be there. Not to worry.

When I arrived at 3:30 p.m., there he was waiting for me with his four-door sedan in what looked to me the middle of the bush where the road I had traveled met a dirt track. He said he had left school early and then explained I would have to leave my car there as the tires would not make it down the muddy track and into the more muddy compound. So I had to set aside the thought that I might never see my car again, and we transferred the chickens, produce, and my luggage to his car before putting the top up on mine.

He asked if he could drive it to his school when we returned with me driving his car. Yes, I agreed, thinking, if it is here. Twenty or so minutes later we arrived at a compound as different from the one I had left as the schools to which my TEA colleagues and I had been assigned. The cement block buildings housing the dorm and schoolrooms of Loreto, its nearness to Nairobi—about an hour down a mostly tarmac road to the city—were as much a contrast to the isolated primitive schools and housing where some of my fellow teachers taught and lived as was this collection of small huts with thatched roofs to the cement block homes of the student's family I had just left.

Small children here were playing with crude wooden toys or in the mud, the younger one without diapers, the older toddlers running toward us. Her uncle translated their cries of welcome. Njeeri came towards us also, with her mother and sisters. Greetings and introductions began. Thanks for the gifts from me, protests that they must not take her classmate's gifts to me, and finally hugs ensued.

I was shown around the compound, with the first stop her grandmother's larger cooking hut where we would also sit and visit and eat. The smoke from the fire mostly went up the center of the thatched round hut, but some had already started filling the inside with a haze which would be thicker by the time we ate.

The next hut to see was that of her parents sleeping quarters which consisted of a platform a tiny bit wider than a twin bed and a bit shorter. This would be where I would sleep, again the room and hut of honor. Njeeri and her sisters including the toddler slept in a larger sleeping hut on floor mats. Her uncle, an older brother out working still and the young boys shared another hut.

That night I was again treated to the local food, similar but tasting differently from the previous meal I'd had. And this time we all ate around and ate together. It wasn't as late or as fancy as the evening before, but it was equally interesting and enjoyable. Her uncle led us in telling stories, with he and Njeeri translating.

Even the grandmother joined in, her delight at seeing my interest and laughter obvious. As with most older Kikuyu women, I suspected she was not as old as she looked. Hard work and sun caused wrinkles and aging to set in early. Even though the smoke in the hut was getting thicker, I was having a great time, trying not to cough too much or too loudly. I was glad for the smoke, as after their recent rain, the mosquitoes were thick.

Suddenly Njeeri and her uncle said it is time to go! I thought they meant bed and though it was early, about 8:00 p.m., I was ready for sleep. But he proclaimed that they head a surprise for me.

Grandmother said loudly, "No, don't go. The gods will be sorry."

Njeeri, translated, adding that her grandmother loved telling stories and was very old fashioned. Then she, her two sisters and two brothers and I all piled into the uncle's car. We seemed to drive for at least an hour, in a different direction from which I had come. Soon I could see the lights of the edge of a large village; as they blame brighter I thought a city.

In a short time it seemed we were on the far outskirts of Nairobi! I was confused, my sense of direction gone. Njeeri's uncle said that the family compound was near Thika, which I hadn't realized as I had driven the rural roads from Wangui's home to Njeeri's. From their home tonight we had wound around to Thika Road which brought us to the outskirts of Nairobi.

Then he exclaimed, ah, we are here. "Here" was an outdoor movie theatre. I was more than amazed, I was flabbergasted. I had no idea such a place existed in Kenya. This was the surprise. Of course, I was quietly disappointed; outdoor movie theaters were still common then in America. I had come to Kenya, visited my students' homes for anything but an American experience.

This was their way of showing me that they too had technical progress. For them it was also cultural progress, as before independence only the colonialists were allowed into this drive in. Now all Kenyans could enjoy it. This surprise was for me a humbling lesson. Kenyans wanted to be as advanced as any country, wanted to be westernized; it was why my students were sent to boarding schools at great expense to their families, the pride of their tribes, why they studied so hard.

Much as I enjoyed my journeys within their land and culture, I need to remember always why I was there. ☐

Three Letters Home

John Dwyer

It can be awkward terrain to edit letters written fifty-five years ago and trickier when the author cannot inform the editing, but I found these letters so compelling that I could not exclude them. These letters were written to John's intended, the woman he married in 1964 when he returned to the States. They were married for forty-one years before her death in 2005, when John and I were roommates during Dar05. Jan Kerr accompanied John on EA11, and they were married in 2015. John is now in a nursing home in northern Virginia. John's daughter Nelia and Jan gave permission to use these letters.

Monday, 3 September 1962
St. Aloysius College, Nyapea, Private Bag
P.O. Arua, Uganda

Dear Lia,

One day I will bring you here, to this astoundingly beautiful continent. We will sit, on another planet, it seems, and watch the day ebb away into night in the very short time it takes here on the equator. There is no twilight, but we will watch a sunset in which you can see far more than any fireplace: mountains, lakes, rivers—all formed in flames which will continuously change color until they are gone. Supervising the spectacle, like C. B. DeMille in his boom chair, is the evening star, Venus: the first and only spectator in the West.

Turning our eyes to the East, we will see, not darkness, not Technicolor, but brilliant lighting creating the blue-black-yellow background of El Greco's "Toledo during a Storm" every ten seconds. The clouds so illuminated will not be above us, but across the river or over the mountains; there will be no accompanying thunder or rain, but just the mysterious light. A mystery, but oh, so real!

I had been spoiled and sheltered in Kampala during those ten days of "orientation" until I saw these other things which make up the real Africa. My first trip was west and south of Kampala, to Fort Portal and Queen Elizabeth National Park. (See the map of Uganda on page 5.) Fort Portal reminds me of a little village in Vermont: clean, manicured lawns and shrubs, nestled in the shadows of the Mountains of the Moon.

I drove up into these, heading for the famous pigmy country on the Congo side. The road is dirt and narrow, hanging on the side of each mountain. At every curve you look straight north through the valley into an expanding plain miles beyond. You turn west through a winding pass at the northern extreme and look far down into a valley of villages beside a snake-like river, and beyond to the 10,000-foot peaks in the Congo.

At this point, I think I told you on a post card, I had a flat tire miles from anywhere, which taxed my adventuresome spirit, and I headed back, praying for my spare to last. It did, and I made my way southward to the above-mentioned game park. There were the famous animals of Africa, sometimes nearer than I wanted them to be. A friend, whom I met there, and I went out early the next morning, when we saw the most game, and saw the snow-capped tip of Mt. Stanley, which, we were told, only comes out of the clouds ten times a year!

The following night I stayed at a little lodge which is on the escarpment overlooking the park. Up early that next morning, I could see, with my new binoculars, herds of elephant and buffalo far down in the valley. I came back that day to Kampala through Mbarara, the capital of the Ankole district of Uganda.

I stopped to talk to quite a few Africans on this trip, and, although there was a language barrier, I found them all very friendly. Even those carrying spears! The Polaroid is what excites them beyond belief. Most have never seen themselves in a mirror, let alone a picture, so they sometimes have difficulty recognizing themselves in a group! I gave a copy to them, usually, and one little boy went screaming off to his friends with it, as though a miracle had happened! Well, it had!

I headed up here from Kampala on Thursday, August 30 with all my earthly belongings it seems, plus one new one: a six-month-old mongrel puppy!

On to Nyapea (fifty miles south of Arua) on the thirty-first, Friday, and here I've been in Shangri-La since. The school and adjacent mission form an oasis in the West Nile wilderness. Beautiful freshly-mown lawns, tropical trees and flowers, clean stucco buildings. I share a house with a seemingly nice chap named John Magner from Gardner, Mass. It's a three-bedroom ranch-type, with hot-and-cold running water, electricity until 10:30 p.m., a houseboy and garden boy who do all the cooking, cleaning and laundry: all very cheap! So, except for the isolation, there is none of the "hardship" I expected. The brothers are mostly American, the rest African, and are very nice. The headmaster, Brother Howard, has been here since 1939!

2 November 1962

Dear Lia,

I've just finished dinner (Nile perch: delicious and boneless) coffee, brandy (Courvoisier, plain glass snifter) and a large and delicious cigar. I spent this time, with Spanish guitar music from the "wireless" in the background. Decision: so as not to destroy your faith in my logical, orderly (and somewhat unromantic?) mind, I shall start at the beginning, for here, too, "...the sun also riseth, and Vanity! Vanity! All is vanity and chasing of the wind..."

So, let me ramble, I know not where, read what is worth reading, and count the rest as mere digital calisthenics, but know that I do it all with the firm conviction that somehow we are together, even as Donne says: "They who one another keep Alive, ne'er parted be."

Our African neighbors keep chickens but without a pen or "coop." They "wander lonely as a cloud," pecking and clucking, but somehow always know where they belong. The proud rooster greets the African dawn with as fierce a cry as was ever known on a nineteenth century New England farm, and this, invariably, is what wakes us. Occasionally, however, Hilario, the houseboy, will precede the crowing by a matter of seconds, a tray of hot tea in hand, saying the happy Swahili greeting: "*Jambo, Habari, Mzuri!*" It is the dawn of the sea, the dawn of fiction, the dawn an American never sees due to the intervention of trees, concrete, or sleep.

Like the sun's retirement on the other end of the day, it is beyond the powers of the ordinary mortal to describe; not having Bartlett at hand yet, however, I am not able to refer to comments of the poets on the spectacle. So, unprofessionally: See the dawn. It is Gold. It is Red. It is Yellow. It is all these colors. It is beautiful. It makes you wonder why everyone doesn't get up at this time just to see this wonderful spectacle. I am happy. I am awake. And then tea.

This grass, greener even than that "in the other fellow's yard," stretches around the house at a distance of eighty yards or so on all sides, and is punctuated at irregular intervals by poinsettia trees, their perennial scarlet blossoms rivaled only by the sun. The spaces between them are usually occupied by the chickens which presents a hideous contrast with which to end this paragraph.

Breakfast might yet be preceded by attendance at Mass in the boys' chapel. You would want to see an occasional representation of African worship and the weekday Mass is different from the one we attend on Sunday, as I will describe later. It is a short walk across the wet lawn, through the tall evergreen hedge which separates our quarters from the "quad" (they don't call it that, but I like to preserve a bit of my Ivy League heritage outside of the bullshit I sling them in class about Yale), in between the class room buildings and over to the front of the small chapel from which emit the pre-Mass prayers of the boys.

We meet the Brothers gathered there, and we all go in to our seats in the back, where there are a few *prie-dieus* for the softer civilized race; the boys have hard row benches. The Mass proper is preceded by the burning of incense such as the world has ever seen since the coronation of Gregory VII in the eleventh century. Every available chalice, urn, candle, and vestment is exposed to the odor, along with the offended nostrils of many of the participants. High Mass or no the ceremony is accompanied with the most enthusiastic hymn singing this side of a revival meeting in St. Mary's, Georgia. I love it and bellow along with the rest of them:

> *Kyrie, eléison. Christe, eléison...*
> *Gloria in Excelsis Deo...*
> *Tantum Ergo...*
> Holy God, We Praise They Name.

Someday I might even try to convince them that "Jesus Calls Us 'Ore the Tumult" ("Life at Home is Sad and Dreary") is a Catholic hymn!

The boys themselves lead the prayers, and it is delightful to hear, with an unaccustomed ear, the voice of an African boy taking the place of an authoritative priest and saying, "For the Propagation of the Faith, Hail Mary…" One of the boys also accompanies the singing of the organ, one of the many incongruous instruments one finds here. His taste runs not to the pious dirge, but usually to the gay gavotte, Roman style. Since he is playing right behind your ear, it takes some will power not to get up and sneak a dance while the boys aren't looking.

Let's go back for breakfast. Yes, there is well done bacon! It took a couple of days to teach the boy, but now I'm convinced that I can get it anywhere in the world. I'm even so used to it now that I allow him to alternate it with well-done sausage every other day. He's not so good on the eggs; they're invariably overdone. His next lesson will be in poached eggs, but I'm wary: even the best cook can't keep those soft. You will balk at the lack of fresh citrus juice, but what the hell, you're in Africa! Canned V-8! The coffee is magnificent. I always knew I was smart to drink it black; you have your choice between goat's milk and evaporated from a can.

Drinking is a subject for a whole dissertation in itself. Mine is almost wholly limited to beer and brandy. Bourbon can be had in some spots in Kampala, but it is pretty expensive. You soon get over wanting ice. Gin-and-tonic material (here it can be a year-round drink) is available in Arua. The beer is stronger but not so dry as in the States, and it comes in liter bottles for about 28¢. The best beer is Stanor, which is smuggled over from the Congo at reasonably competitive prices. It's worth the extra few cents, both in taste and the excitement of possessing illicit goods.

So, during the week, usually a beer in the late afternoon, brandy after dinner, and another beer later on. On the weekends in Arua, drinking is a little heavier, but still mostly beer. John Gouffini, our weekend host, makes a helluva drink for Sunday lunch, though: he calls it a John Collins, and the ingredients are secret. I've been able to get this much out of him: the glass is sugared, it contains gin, lemon juice (from trees in his own back yard), and—get this—altar wine! Ought to call it Father John Collins.

I left out lunch, but it's much the same as dinner except that the latter includes soup (from a package). The meat dish is alternately goat or beef, and Hilario is good in cooking it in a variety of ways. White potatoes are not available often, so we get sweet: mashed, boiled, baked and French-fried. Vegetables are mostly from the brothers' garden, and include peas, carrots, cauliflower, eggplant, and beets. He's wonderful at pies (especially apple), cakes, and puddings. He's even got me eating desserts! But the most (to be continued)....

21 January 1963

And now, the trip! Settle down for a couple more pages of enthusiasm about East Africa! We didn't see all we wanted to see, of course, and I'll never even get all in that we did see, but I'll try to include all the highlights.

I left here on the eighth of December, and went to Arua for a day to play golf. I had to go that way anyway, because the ferry across the Nile which we would normally use at Pakwach was flooded out. From Aura, I went north and saw that section of the West Nile and Madi Districts for the first time. Being so close to the Sudan, the Lugbara and Madi tribes are from more purely Nilotic stock: a taller, more majestic appearance than the ordinary Bantu, but more primitive also. I think I've told you that the women wear only leaves fore-n-aft. I had the first roll of color film in the new camera at this point, too, and got some good shots of an impressive mountain that overlooks the ferry landing at Laropi.

Since this was now the only crossing over the Nile, and it is the cotton harvesting season, John Magher, my housemate, had had to wait for three hours to get across the day before. I was travelling on a Sunday, though, and only had to wait about an hour. It was a very hot day, and the last one hundred miles to Gulu on the Acholi side were uneventful, except for the more noticeable friendliness of this tribe. I spent the next week at Sir Samuel Baker School in Gulu, correcting the Junior Secondary Leaving examinations in geography (the same ones I had supervised at Goli, when we had to ride bicycles).

This was tedious work of the worst kind, but it will mean some good money (and I'm now broke!) if the ministry ever gets around to sending the check. While there, I stayed with Bob Smart, one of the group that I came over with, and we had some pleasant evenings with other interesting faculty members. Bob and I also took a side trip one day when we were finished over to Fatiko, Sir Samuel Baker's camp. Baker was a British explorer of the mid-nineteenth century, who discovered Lake Albert and Murchison Falls. This camp, built in one of the few rock formations of the area, is actually a fort, as Baker came out on his second trip to suppress the slave trade.

I left Gulu on the following Sunday, the sixteenth, for Kampala where I met John, who had not felt like correcting exams. Caught up on a few movies and found some bourbon to drink, collected assorted souls, and headed east.

Jinja is located on Lake Victoria at the point out of which the Nile flows. Ripon Falls was the old source, but these have disappeared since the great Owen Falls hydroelectric dam was completed there in 1954. Down the river, however, about eight miles north, there still remains the Bujugali Falls, which Bob Smart and I had discovered in August. I wanted to go back to get some color shots, which we did. The falls themselves are not as spectacular as the surrounding area: you drive to them and overlook them from a cliff and you can see the Nile stretching away for miles in either direction. When you walk down a long, winding path to the water's edge, you can literally feel the power of this great river right there at its origin.

From there we drove to Tororo and Mbale. The former has a very unusual 'rock' which sticks up from the surrounding flatlands like a sore thumb; the latter has a commanding view of Mt. Elgon, which straddles the Uganda–Kenya border. After a beer or two back at the Rock Hotel in Tororo, we headed for the Kenya border. Except for the detour to the falls, we had been on paved roads all the way from Kampala. But at the Kenya border it turns back to *murram*. Not too bad, though, and we covered the ninety miles to Eldoret fairly quickly. Stopped at a pleasant hotel there.

The next day, Thursday, the twentieth, we headed south down a back road through some very pretty country. The road, however, was miserable, and on one bad turn I hit a rock which I couldn't see, and put a hole in the crankcase and ruined the sump-pump. We were able to limp to Kericho, however, and had plenty of time to investigate that uninteresting little town while the car was being repaired. A new road to Kericho, however, and we made it to Pat Brown's at Kericho in time for dinner that night.

We decided to make Friday a one-day round trip and come back to Pat's again that night. So, off through some of the most beautiful sections of the White Highlands (the area of Kenya settled by European farmers; since they own the land, this is one of the greatest stumbling blocks to Kenya's independence; Uganda has never had a white settler problem) to Nakuru. Beer and lunch at the Stag's Head Hotel, and off to see the flocks of pink flamingoes on the adjacent lake. They were disappointingly few in number that day (I'm told that sometimes there are millions) and we couldn't get close enough for good pictures, but they are quite a sight.

Then off north in the afternoon to Thompson's Falls, between the edge of the Rift Valley escarpment and the Aberdare Mountains. They are very high falls, perhaps 200 feet, but there is not the great rush of water that you find at Murchison. Rather, a thin stream glides over some very beautiful rocks into a pool below. A little African boy was there to guide us down to the bottom over a steep trail. There was a hotel right there at the site, so we enjoyed a couple of beers before heading back to Kericho.

We added Pat to the entourage the next day, and headed for Nairobi, stopping off at the Menengai Crater, one of the largest in the world. Nairobi is a modern city in every sense of the word, and has a larger

European population (there are only three types of people in the world referred to in Africa: Europeans, Asians, and Africans) than Kampala, so I felt for a moment that I was back in New York, or perhaps Atlanta.

We spent the long Christmas weekend there at the YMCA, which had a swimming pool and did a lot of prowling around the city, including the game park which is five miles out of town. The animals are quite tame there, and although we didn't see a lion or rhino, I got a good picture of a giraffe and of a baboon on the hood of the car! On Sunday night we got tickets to a concert by Miriam Makeba, a Xhosa singer from South Africa, who has made a big hit in the States. She makes this strange and wonderful 'click' sound while punctuating her songs. She is the most exciting singer I've seen on the stage since Odetta, and I came away short of breath.

Christmas was a fair, pleasant day in the mid-seventies, but somehow, we just didn't feel like being in Africa then. Going to church wasn't even quite right because it was so crowded we had to stand outside and couldn't hear the sermon. Again, the crowd was very interesting, because the Catholic population of Nairobi is largely made up of Goans, Asians from a tiny Portuguese colony on the West Coast of India. The YMCA put on a Christmas dinner that tried hard but failed. Some of the bowl of the fruit punch, some cookies, and an old Margaret Rutherford movie, and failed even more positively. We adjourned to the nearest bar for a surer form of Christmas cheer.

December 26, in the British Empire that was and the Commonwealth that is, is also a public holiday, Boxing Day. It is surprising to me the number of Britishers who are unable to explain to a 'Yank' the origin of the name, but simply accept it as a logical excuse for not going to work on the day after Christmas. I finally found out that it derives from a quaint old custom among the landed gentry of England, whereby unwanted gifts were tied up again in the boxes and opened by them early on the morning of the Nativity, and distributed among the faithful servants of the manor. I don't know if this is true or not, but it does explain why so many of the Nairobi shops were closed when we were looking for staples to take with us on our trip south that morning.

We finally found a *duka*, whose owner either did not know of or did not believe in this hallowed tradition of the West, bought some fruit and film, and got on our way. This was perhaps the most interesting part of the trip, because we passed through the land of the famous but decadent Maasai warriors. This is a tribe which has resisted all attempts by the British or other Africans to educate them or change their nomadic, cattle-raising and rustling existence. The young warriors smear their hair in red ochre, or clay, wear nothing but a loosely-wrapped blanket, and carry spears, clubs, and other light weapons while their women-folk carry enormous loads of wood and other essentials.

I had become captivated by one of their weapons, called a *rungu*. It is simply a stick what that appears to be a large ball of wood fitted over the end; not unlike a bandleader's twirling baton at a high school football game. Actually, it is one piece of wood, and the round part is the root of the plant, and the stick being the stalk. This also is covered with red ochre, and is used as a throwing weapon, both for defense and for hunting. At any rate, I was able to talk one youngster out of his for the measly price of about fifty cents.

Our destination was south to Moshi and Arusha: the Mt. Kilimanjaro area. To get there, of course, we had to cross into Tanganyika. Now East Africa is one area of the world where you can pass from one country to another with a minimum of difficulty because the three countries have so much in common. There had been no barrier when crossing from Uganda to Kenya, and we didn't expect one on going into Tanganyika; as a matter of fact we were looking forward to tarmac roads again.

No such luck. There was a cross bar over the road at the border, and a little house manned by two uniformed Africans who had the radio on full blast and were doing the twist. They were insistent upon seeing our passports. Tanganyika, they informed us (as if we didn't already know), was not only a newly-independent country, but also a newly-proclaimed republic.

We protested that we were all respectable *walimu* (teachers) from Uganda, and that our passports were buried under piles of luggage. (We were actually trying to cover up for Pat, who had not brought his with him.) Finally, after much haggling, they agreed to let us through 'because we are human beings' on the condition that we report at the first opportunity to an immigration officer.

There are two towns in Tanganyika in the Kilimanjaro area: Moshi and Arusha. There isn't much in either of them except an occasional good view of the mountain when it comes out of the clouds. We had tea in Arusha, and then went on to Moshi for a couple of days, browsing around, visiting a school where Keith thought he was going to be posted, and seeing a couple of movies.

We left there on the morning of Friday the twenty-eighth, and headed southeast to Mombasa. We had to cross into Kenya again at this point, and although there was no trouble with border guards, we were back on a terrible road, which proceeded to knock the hell out of the tires. Kenya, by the way, is the only country in the world which does not have a main road connecting its major city with the coast. We had to buy a new tire in Voi, the half-way point, and another in the same garage on the way back a week later!

We were going through Tsavo National Park, but didn't see much other than a few antelope of various species, too far away to photograph. Arrived in Mombasa late that afternoon. Since the city is on an island, we had to cross a bridge to get there, and we could see some large ships in the harbor.

Checked in at the infamous New Bristol Hotel, ten shillings a night bed-and-breakfast ($1.50), bathed, had a drink, and went out to see the town. Found a good restaurant that served lobster (my first since arrival!) and then went to one of the city's pleasure domes. Mombasa is a port city in the classic sense: when the ships are in the population doubles. All the city's economic energy is directed towards these (and all) visitors, so it's a wide open town.

The Asians, who control almost all the business in East Africa, keep a very tight hand on the prostitution in the city, and the African girls here are far more interesting than in Kampala and Nairobi. (You can think what you like, but we just talked to them!) They aren't allowed to leave the bars until closing, they are all inspected weekly and carry cards around with them, and they are very entertaining to be with, and, from what I could gather, very well paid, both by their customers and by their employers.

The next day we headed out to find Gene Ashby's place. He is the American teacher who was planning to throw the New Year's party for anyone who happened to be in town. He teaches at a school about ten miles north of Mombasa, which is located on an inlet off the Indian Ocean, a gorgeous site. We weren't planning to impose, but since he already had a crowd there, we decided to add our sleeping bags to the ones already on the long porch, and save a few shillings. So we moved out that afternoon, and spent the next few days lounging around the beach resort just a mile down the road from his place.

What a change from the rest of Africa: white sands, warm water, palm trees, just like Fernandina! We usually went in town for dinner at night, and then either prowling or a flick. New Year's Eve was welcomed in with grand style, with forty or so travelers in attendance. Still, it was a night when no one really wanted to be in Africa. We topped off the show at about 4:00 a.m. with a concert on African drums of various sizes, trying to accompany Gene's houseboy, who was singing and playing guitar.

We recuperated the next day on the beach, and then on the second took a day hop to the famous resort at Malindi, seventy miles north on the coast. The biggest attraction there was supposed to be the surf, of which there ain't any at Mombasa, due to a large reef. Well, it turned out that there was surf, but that's about all. The town itself was not very interesting, sort of what a resort colony looks like the States during the off-season, except that this was supposed to be the on-season.

The Arab population is much larger on the coast, however, and we did have a chance to talk to quite a few of them as we walked along the beach. The best part of the day though was on the way up, when we stopped to inspect the ruins of an ancient Arab city (fourteenth century) at Gedi, just south of Malindi. Interesting carvings adorned the walls of the harems, and wells of depths up to sixty feet were scattered around the compound. I could imagine doomed maidens, waiting the sacrifice, poised on the lip of each of these as I peered down, looking for skeletons. There weren't any. I guess the Arabs didn't go in for that sort of thing.

Gedi's setting was unusual also: not on the coast, but four miles inland, in real jungly growth which lent an eerie atmosphere to some of the pictures I got. We stayed in a bar in Malindi until well after dark, so the best part of the return trip was the ferry we had to cross. Most of the ferries in East Africa (you have to cross two coming to Nyapea from Kampala) close at dark, but this one is open twenty-four hours. It was the first time I had been on a boat in the dark since August 9, and the few drinks I had had leant to pleasant reveries. Might I also arouse your curiosity by telling you that our picture appears in color on page 87 of the November 1962 issue of *Playboy?*

When we got back to Gene's that night, I found myself in the second bridge game I'd played in Africa, and it went on until 5:15 a.m. This did not make for bright eyes in this old head three hours later when we had planned to leave.

But up we got, saw some more sights of Mombasa, Fort Jesus, and the Arab *dhows* in the harbor, and pushed off at noon on January 3. Since we could not afford to get down to Zanzibar, Dar es Salaam, or lower Tanganyika on this trip, the journey home retraced most of the same path.

On the way back, we picked up our second tire in the same garage in Voi, as I mentioned, and the third one on the following day in Moshi, where we had better pictures of the mountain, and saw another movie. We were in somewhat of a hurry to get back to Nairobi, for *Beyond the Fringe,* which we hadn't been able to see on the way down, was closing the next night. The acting was top-notch; I was amazed because I thought they were local amateurs, but I found out later that it was a London company.

While in Nairobi, I better tell you about the Thorn Tree, a sidewalk café, of sorts, in front of the New Stanley Hotel: Nairobi's biggest. It is a place of which it is said, "If you sit there long enough, you'll soon see everyone you know in East Africa." I accepted this as a somewhat justified exaggeration, until Saturday morning coffee (almost beer) time, when along walked three of the brothers from Nyapea in company with our new headmaster! (The Sacred Heart Brothers have three locations in East Africa.) We also ran into the two guys we had met in Kampala in October who are hitch-hiking around the world, just back from South Africa; they might be up here for a visit in a few days.

On Sunday, the sixth, Pat, John, and I (the others, out of money, went back to Kampala) went north to Nyeri to visit a friend, in John's group from last year, whom we had met in Mombasa. Went to his "club" that night and learned to play Liar's Dice, which with beer, kept us up until 5:30 a.m. I didn't think that any game but bridge could get that kind of hold on me. Relaxed most of the next day under the shadow of Mt. Kenya, and headed back to Kericho via Nairobi and Nakuru on Tuesday, the eighth. Left Pat off, and Wednesday morning John and I headed for Kampala.

We stopped to Tororo again, and got to the City Bar (the veritable nerve center of Kampala) about 7:00 p.m. Visited some people I had missed on the way through, had dinner at the Brubakers (the couple who were with us on the trip), saw a couple of days' worth of flicks and went up to Gulu on Saturday, the twelfth.

Unfortunate experience on that leg of the trip. After waiting about two hours to get across the Arua ferry, there is a small bridge to cross north of it, where a lorry (truck) had overturned into the river. The tarpaulin was over the back, and two boys were caught inside and drowned.

Stayed at Bob's that night (he wasn't there, but I know his houseboy now), and then back here, with three shillings in my pocket and no food in the house on Sunday, January 13.

End of tiring, but wonderful trip. □

The Famed Flight to Entebbe via Kano
David Evans

As a member of the very first TEA group, I have vivid memories of the trip to Entebbe. About ninety TEA teachers were crammed into an old Lockheed Constellation that TEA had chartered to take us to Africa. The plane was so full that one of the lavatories was packed with luggage and unusable. During preflight take off, the stewardess could be heard giving the pilot instructions on where the switch was to turn on the fasten seat belt signs—this did not inspire confidence in the crew!

The flight refueled in West Africa (I don't remember where) and then took off for Kano in northern Nigeria. The temperature in the plane was well over ninety degrees, and we were sweltering. The pilot came on the intercom and said the air conditioning wasn't working and that the plane was too heavy to fly higher where it would be cooler. Eventually, after he burned enough fuel, he was able to move to a higher altitude.

When we landed in Kano around 2:00 in the morning, we blew a tire. There were no parts available, so we had to wait while a new tire was brought in on a flight from Paris.

After much palaver, an arrangement was reached which allowed us to leave the airport and visit a nearby village which was our first taste of the real Africa.

When the plane was finally ready, we were told that there would be more delay because the airport in Entebbe was not open until the next morning. We finally arrived in Entebbe on Sunday morning, having left JFK on the previous Thursday evening. TEA did not use that charter company again! ☐

You Are My Son

Nat Frothingham

I taught English at an African secondary school for boys not far from Nairobi, Kenya. The school had its own compound of buildings, playing fields, and houses for teachers. Beyond the compound was what was then called the Kikuyu Reserve, an African settlement of thatched houses and small *shambas*.

One day I took a walk with a schoolboy along a very narrow track outside of the school grounds. Coming toward us from a distance along this track were two Kikuyu women. When our paths crossed, we stopped to talk. We exchanged greetings and my schoolboy friend translated their Kikuyu greeting into English for me and translated my greeting in English into Kikuyu for them. After we had exchanged greetings, one woman made a surprising declaration.

"What did she say?" I asked my schoolboy friend.

"She says you are her son," he replied.

I think I laughed and objected.

"No," she said, "you are my son. If my son was in your country, you would be his father and he would be your son. But you are in our country, and I am your mother and you are my son."

I had to think about what she said. This African woman was telling me about our basic human solidarity beyond the differences of language, customs, histories, skin color, or the flags of our nationalities.

Since that chance meeting, I have been continuously touched by the generosity of that woman's remark and the tenderness of her powerful acceptance. □

That First Night at Makerere
Brooks Goddard

New Hall at Makerere University College was, indeed, new and new to me. But I silently said, "Hey, I can do this" and went to bed. I awoke at 2:00 a.m. and looked out of my dorm room window at the dark and wondered about the ten lit rooms.

"Brooks," I said to myself, "What have you done? You're 10,000 miles from home and only one day into a three-year commitment. What were you thinking?" I went down to the bathroom to splash water on my face, looked out the window again and again, and ultimately went back to sleep. I never had another waking night while in East Africa.

That night in 1964 was a watershed moment in my life, because it marked the edge of my indecision. I was in that room in that institution in that country because I had chosen it and because I had survived momentary doubt. That night, in some way, defined me, not so much because of the doubt but because I went forward without doubt.

I then taught and traveled without compunction and with great joy and interest. I began to explore what I now realize was my life and my way of being in the world. The bookend of that night in 1964 was a morning in 1968 when I awoke in New York City wondering why I wasn't back in Kenya. That morning led to the first of several bouts with depression I have had over the ensuing years and was powerful to me in the moment. But in memory the event that stays with me is still that night in 1964 at Makerere.

I suspect that the overwhelming feeling of positive engagement in my TEA teaching experience and the equally powerful experiences I had while traveling home in the first five months of 1968 (from Kenya to Ethiopia to India to overland to Europe) helped me to become a better teacher. Marrying my wife Jeanie in 1970 certainly made me become a better human being. Who is to say that the first didn't lead to the second?

By a strange coincidence I just finished reading Mary Bateson's *Composing a Further Life*, which documents what I (and we) am living: how do we re-create engagement in this newly-coined life stage of "adulthood II"? Thus the engagement I feel with TEA-Alumni is really an outgrowth of the engagement I made in 1964 and again in 1970 and explains why I look back on the three TEA-Alumni East Africa trips of 2003, 2005, and 2011 with fondness that belies the difficulties of those journeys.

I feel that I am in the midst of the ultimate existential life circumstance and look forward expectantly to whatever engagement is out there in whatever night I shall awake to. ☐

Sports

Brooks Goddard

After arriving at Makerere in October of 1964 and having found the tennis courts, I was playing with some unsuspecting soul when I substituted a ball from the vacuum can I had brought with me for the unpressurized balls we were playing with. My first serve bounced twenty feet and was unhittable!

Under more prosaic conditions I played a lot of tennis in Uganda and Kenya. I played many days at Lugogo Stadium with Bob Greenwood, a Brit TEAer who was a Cambridge blue. We even played in the Uganda Open in 1965, an exhibition against Donald Dell and Allan Fox at Jinja, and a few other tournaments. I had more success with doubles than with singles. Most of the players were Asian or European. When my parents visited in August of 1966 we saw Laver and Rosewall play in Nairobi. Bob and I have continued our friendship, but I missed seeing him in EA11 when he decided at the last minute not to venture forth from his Diani Beach (Mombasa) residence.

I also played squash with a small team organized by T. A. Brett of the UK. Our best player was a thirty-something woman who had once been world ranked. She said that her parents had come out to Kenya in the 1920s and walked up to Nanyuki behind an oxcart to start what became the Silverbeck Hotel whose bar, if I recall properly, was right on the equator. We played a few clubs in Kampala, Kisumu, and Nairobi. It was my introduction to the international game which had different court dimensions and different scoring. It's where I learned to lob since the outdoor courts generally didn't have a ceiling (no dummy, me). Coincidentally, I came across Bwana Brett eight years ago on the internet.

One of my fond Makerere memories was the University Games of 1965. On our basketball team, I believe the lanky Robin Wilkins was in the pivot and Ward Heneveld played power forward. Jerry Atkin may have been the shooting guard. I think I also played volleyball. I also played some basketball in Nairobi on a team playing opposite Peace Corps volunteers. One of my most instructive times was learning to play field hockey in Makerere physical education classes. I damn near got killed and developed then and there a very healthy respect for those who play the game. It is definitely not a game for sissies.

Like travel, food, and music, sport is a great transcultural experience. ☐

Life-long Close Connections

Charles Good

My TEA 1961-63 experience and my posting to Lubiri Secondary School (SS) in Mengo-Kampala, Uganda, ranks as the most important and seminal experience of my early adult life. It set me up for a wonderful career and life-long, close connections with Africans and Africa, in the US as well as Africa. Fortunately, my East African and other African experience did not end in 1963.

I was able to rack up about more than six years' total residence in Uganda, Kenya, Tanzania, and Malawi between 1967 and 2013, largely through varied research work in medical geography, traditional ethnomedical systems in Uganda and Kenya, community-based HIV/AIDS studies in Tanzania, and the historical/cultural geography of the introduction and attempts to create a Western mission-based health care system in colonial Nyasaland/Malawi, 1989–2004.

Since 2003 I have been worked with resettlement of Somali Bantu in Blacksburg, Virginia, and with the Presbyterian Church in on-going health and education programs in Malawi. ☐

The Hills of Kampala in Three Acts
Bob Gurney

I lived for a while in a huge house in Buganda. It had the biggest picture window I have ever seen. You could see for miles across the trees. It must have been a supermarket window. It had no curtains. I quite like my privacy. I was in a local market and saw rolls of a light brown material which was very cheap. It was bark cloth. I went back with it and hung it up, not very expertly but it did the job.

A feeling of relaxation came over me as I sat, in the evenings, enjoying my privacy, instead of being on view on top of the hill like a tailor's dummy. People started to look at me with sad expressions. They seemed to be keeping away. I wondered if they were sad at missing the evening spectacle. Eventually one of the locals plucked up courage and asked if there had been a death.

"No, no, we're fine, thank you," I replied, puzzled.

"Only, we wrap dead bodies up in bark cloth here," the gentleman explained.

I think the curtains soon came down. I am not sure though because I left for a flat in Kampala shortly afterwards.

—

I don't remember a heat as intense as that which filled the valley I had to cross each day in Kampala. I had to pause in the shade of every tree. It was like entering an oven. Later, at dusk, the sky would darken with bats and the air would become cold.

—

I got back late. There was a curfew in Kampala. There were soldiers on the road outside my flat on top of Nakasero Hill. They had said on television that anyone out after ten would be shot. It was five to ten. The streetlights were out. There was just a crescent moon.

Then I saw it, curled up, on the top step, by the door: the snake. I heard a rifle being cocked. What was it to be, the soldiers or the snake? Would they shoot? They won't kill me. They will kill me. Were they from the north? Should I call out, tell them who I am? Would they speak Swahili, Luganda, English, or something else, like Lugbara?

My knowledge of snakes was sketchy. A bite could be fatal. Key in hand I jumped over the snake and was inside in a flash, locking the door behind me. Through the mosquito screen that covered the kitchen window I saw the soldiers ambling back towards their barracks inside Lugard's Fort. ☐

Unwelcome

Henry Hamburger

Judith and I hustled back from a brief honeymoon in time for the six-week TEA training at Teachers College. As a graduate student in African Studies, she came to East Africa not to teach but to carry out research for a PhD dissertation. As background to that, she began to make the acquaintance of various people of current or likely future significance to the power structure in Kakamega, the regional capital where we lived and I taught.

About six weeks into our time there, a movie was to be shown at the country club that I did not wish to see, and so she proceeded to attend it with the local magistrate, Fida Abdullah. Though the name may sound Arabic, he had ancestors from India who had come to Kenya in 1790, or so I heard. In any case, I was called aside the next morning by the headmaster, Mr. Stewart, who informed me that "those fellows" (his terminology) were not welcome at the Club and I was not to allow any such thing to happen again.

Two months later Judith and I went to Nairobi to watch as the Union Jack descended, the flag of the new nation rose, Jomo Kenyatta triumphantly waved his fly-whisk, the multitudes cheered, and the days of segregation at the Kakamega Country Club drew to a close. □

TEA Successes, Then and Now

Henry Hamburger

August, 1963, Nairobi.
I am in TEA. It is four months until Uhuru. We have trained for six weeks at Teachers College in New York and for ten days in Nairobi. During the latter two incidents, a colonist second cousin tells me that Africans will not learn math from me because they have only recently descended from the trees. And the program assigns me to teach white British colonial girls in this major urban center.

I say I came to Africa to teach Africans and I'm taking the next plane home. They relent. I go to Kakamega, thirty miles from Lake Victoria, where Africans not only learn math from me, they learn advanced level math and some pass with distinction on exams created at Cambridge University, pride of the metropole. One rises to become Dean of the Faculty of Science at Kenyatta University and in 2010 is honored by them as a pioneer dean. This I learn from searching the web where my second cousin is not mentioned.

1999, Bethesda, Maryland, USA

I have been back in the US for thirty-four years. Ed Schmidt calls. He is finding us all, us ex-TEA people. Reunion talk starts. We schedule a reunion in Washington for November 20, 2001, nine days after what becomes "9/11."

We go forward anyway. Two East African ambassadors to the US join us. Inspiring things get said about the old days. We still want to help. We think we have something to give. Even just to do that and especially to have anything useful to say, we need to go back, so some of us do that, in 2003.

We meet principals, teachers, students, education officers, even ministers of education. We find a school in Uganda to assist. We develop criteria. I go back in 2004 to find a school in Kenya to assist. Ultimately we will find many more. In 2005 another gang of us travel and visit schools in Tanzania. One of us knew Benjamin Mkapa when they were at Makerere, and invites him. He consents to address us in Dar and the press is all over it! □

TEA Time

Carol Heath

Spending over two years at Bwiru Girls School in Tanzania with TEA in the early 1960s was both exciting and sobering for me. Bwiru is just outside Mwanza on the shores of Lake Victoria; it was a lazy, quiet town but it had many schools and young teachers and professionals from around the world. We shared American holidays like Thanksgiving, were asked to a Guy Fawkes Bonfire by the British, attended a henna ceremony for one of the African teachers who was to be married. We took school breaks to travel as far as Victoria Falls one time and weekends off to visit the nearby Serengeti.

And there was a palpable hope and lots of energy for this soon to be free country. Everyone felt it. Julius Nyerere (a hero who visited our school more than once) was to be president, and the girls at the school were aware of their privilege and most of them desperately wanted to learn. It was a twenty-two-year-old's dream place to be if you wanted to experience new things. And it changed and vastly expanded my world view.

It was also a maturing time in my life. We were given not only the responsibility of teaching, but also monitoring many African girls at a boarding school: late night walks with the watchman who carried a lantern to make sure all was well in the dormitories; infrequent but necessary trips to the town hospital; being aware of the "uncles" who came to visit a girl; learning how to live in a house that came with a cook and a gardener who needed sugar and payment for their work. The death of a fellow teacher in a car accident on the road to Dar was very painful. I grew up and had a wonderful time doing it. □

Attending a Circumcision Ceremony
Ted Heaton

We left our house at three-thirty and got to the student's home in time for supper: very good *posho* and chicken. We got to the ceremony at eight, and people were already dancing around the six boys who were to be circumcised.

The boys have to do a lot of preparation before the ceremony: they have to run along the road all the time ringing bells in each hand and run to relatives' homes inviting them to the ceremony. On the day before they are to be circumcised, they go to their maternal uncle, and he kills a cow. They wear a huge piece of meat around their necks as they go back home.

At about 7:00 that evening, they are placed in the center of dancing people and they ring their bells, making rhythmic movements all night until dawn. If they stop, people will think they are weak and not fully determined to be circumcised. We were taken right up to the boys so we could see. They keep up their movements and bell ringing, sweat pouring down their faces, and they look like they are in a trance or hypnotized. Their faces are expressionless; they don't smile. If they show one bit of fear, they will not be circumcised. All the time, people are dancing around them—doing any kind of movement as long as they keep the time—singing, whistling, shouting.

We watched this for a while, and then decided to go to bed at eleven. We slept in our car. We were going to get up at four, but it was really raining and the boys and dancers had moved inside a house. At about seven that morning, the boys were given some roasted meat to eat and then taken to the river. Then, an interesting thing happened: a father took his son away by force, refusing to have him circumcised, because the boy's oldest brother hadn't been circumcised; therefore, apparently, the younger brother couldn't be either. They locked this boy in a hut, but a little later he broke out and ran to the river, fully determined to be circumcised. They let him go: they didn't deny him.

At the river, they stripped naked; then their heads and noses were covered with mud. We were put right up front, enabling us to see everything. They stood in position, in a row, all the time expressionless. The actual operation was over in a flash and was very gruesome. There were three circumcisers: the first put some medicine on a boy's penis and pulled the foreskin way down over the head of the penis; the second did the cutting, and the third did the trimming.

As I said, it is all done in a flash, thank heavens, or I couldn't have lasted through much more. I just don't see how the boys stood all of it: it must have been very painful. And since none of them even winced or blinked, they were all given money by the people—coins were stuck in the mud on their heads. It was a most fascinating ceremony, very much the custom of this tribe, and all I can say is I'm glad our son won't be confronted with it. ☐

Life-changing Event

Rod Hinkle

Few decisions one makes are life changing, but joining TEA in 1961, was just that for me. I had finished college and law school and one year teaching social studies in Newton, Massachusetts, but had no clear life goal. But, upon returning from TEA, I decided to pursue an EdD degree in International Education with Drs. Butts and Scanlon.

One day a call came from Syracuse University, the entity that had won a contract to train Peace Corps upper primary school teachers for Tanganyika. They wanted a former TEAer to ease the transition in Tanganyika from USAID teachers to Peace Corps teachers. Recently married to fellow TEAer Margaret Polga, who had taught at neighboring Marian College in Morogoro, we returned to Tanganyika not knowing Margaret was pregnant. Our first child, Marin, was born at Aga Khan Hospital in Dar. Because of wars in neighboring countries, at that time, it was risky traveling to visit Peace Corps teachers.

I will always prize a letter written in 1965 by the Regional Commissioner of Mtwara region—a neighboring region to war torn Mozambique—which I always carried in case of capture. It read:

> "Mr. R. Hinkle.
> The above named person is a Leader of the American Peace Corps. He is visiting this Region in Connection with Peace Corps duties. Grateful for any help you can give him if in need."

Thankfully, I never needed the help of the regional commissioner. But I still prize that letter, and now it is safely contained in a scrapbook of my life's adventures along with the address and picture of our Dar es Salaam house in case Marin ever wants to see her first home. ☐

Transition to Peace Corps
Rod Hinkle

In 1965–67, I was the Contractor's Overseas Rep for Syracuse University which had won the contract to train the Peace Corps teachers for Tanzania to replace the TEA teachers. Margaret Rose (Polga) was my wife then, and our first child, Marin, was born there.

My job was a little vague but, basically, as an ex-TEAer from Mzumbe Secondary School in Morogoro, Tanzania, I was supposed to ease the transition from TEA to Peace Corps because the East African ministries were not pleased to replace the older and more experienced TEA teachers with Peace Corps volunteers. (I used to joke that Sargent Shriver finally got to his brother-in-law, pointing to a world map showing only East Africa using non-Peace Corps teachers to make the switch.) As a further step to show the "bona fides" of Peace Corps' intent to work with the Tanzanian government, I was housed in the Inspectorate Division of the Ministry of Education and not the Peace Corps office in Dar es Salaam.

I visited schools, observed teachers, ran a few meetings and conferences, but basically was a trouble shooter for the ministry if and when one of those "inexperienced Peace Corps teachers" ran into trouble. Thankfully, that happened very infrequently, and looking back on the experience, the transition from TEA to Peace Corps went smoothly. □

David Bruce's Microscope
Moses L. Howard

In 1965, on loan to UNESCO at Uganda Technical College, I helped to train the country's first locally trained-onsite laboratory technicians. Until then, laboratory technicians were trained and examined in London by the City and Guilds of London and other United Kingdom examining bodies. These trainees studied locally and were examined locally.

We had well-equipped chemistry and biology laboratories with the exception of adequate microscopes. Raiding some high school labs, we found fifteen passable microscopes. Most had low magnification and unsatisfactory resolving power. It was a busy year with teacher and students collecting and testing the country's milk, blood, infective tissues, microbes, and fungi of every type. From classrooms, we went to the Fisheries Department and Viral Institute at Entebbe.

Most trainees passed, and UNESCO examiners were satisfied. The examiners, however, criticized our lack of good microscopes. But I went to our best one and called an examiner over to have a look. It was a magnificent black-and-gold instrument with a large barrel and clear lenses. I watched him focus and refocus it, running an appreciative hand up and down the barrel of it and calling to his fellow examiners that we had indeed made a discovery. I wanted to look into the microscope to see what he had discovered, but it was the microscope itself to which he referred. On the barrel was printed *DK Bruce FRS*— that is, David K. Bruce, Fellow in the Royal Society.

The examiner pronounced it to be the same microscope that David K. Bruce had used in South Africa in 1901 to prove that trypanosomes carried by the tsetse fly caused *nagana* in cows and horses. He used it again in Uganda in 1903 to prove that trypanosomes carried by tsetse flies, *glossina*, cause sleeping sickness in humans.

It was significant: our first trained-onsite technicians were using that same microscope. ☐

No Entry Permit

Moses L. Howard

I first came to Entebbe, Uganda as a Fulbright scholar and teacher in 1961 on a BOAC flight from London. My trip had taken me, an African American lecturer at a community college in Mississippi, to the Foreign

Service School in Georgetown University, then to the Foreign Service office in London, and soon, I hoped, to Ntare School in Mbarara, Uganda.

On the flight, I could identify the nationalities of many of the passengers: British, African, Belgians, Germans, and French. I think I was the only American among them, and certainly the only African American, or so-called American Negro, onboard. So imagine everyone's shock when I was detained at the port of entry. The airport officials could not stamp my entry visa. The appropriate offices had issued me all the necessary traveling documents except one. I had a visa but no entry permit. I was detained for four hours while an officer wired London for further instructions regarding my permission to enter Africa.

After four hours, I was summoned and told I was to be given a temporary entry permit and had to swear to an affidavit that I was, indeed, who I said I was. They photographed me numerous times in specific positions and attached three photos to the affidavit, making a copy which they said I had to carry at all times. They also confiscated my passport and said they would contact me within ten days at the place I was posted.

It was in those circumstances that I contemplated that ages ago my ancestors had been kidnapped, taken forcibly from Africa, and now, when their son returned, others could enter without problems while he had to have a special permit to do so.

I went to my post, and six weeks later my passport arrived at the nearest post office. I signed my name and then was finger printed and given the passport. I checked the pages and found that the British Consulate and the American Embassy had stamped it. I was finally in Africa legally. A descendent of slaves, a son of Africa, had returned three hundred years later and had been given a permit to enter. □

Empakos

Moses L. Howard

When I first came to Uganda and was a divorced young lecturer at Ntare School, I used to hang out and drink tea with a young nurse who worked at Mbarara Hospital. Her name was Lisa Kawumara.

On the occasion of our first cup of tea, she asked me my name, and I told her my name was Moses. She reflected for a moment, sipping her tea, then puffing her face and pointing at me with her small pert nose, she said, "*Yawe! Musa!* No. You're a Moses, but I am calling you Akiiki." And as we sat, she kept looking at me and referring to me when she had a question about America or my students at Ntare. "And so, Akiiki, what forms are you teaching?" And I would tell her I was teaching Forms 5 and 6. And so after that, she left notes at my house addressed to Akiiki or she told other nurses that Akiiki was sure to stop by and to give me a message that she had left for me. Once she told me to call her Aboowli.

When I asked her about these names, she said they were *empako*. Upon further questioning, she said, "They are like nicknames or pet names, you know, terms of endearment." I wanted to know why she had selected these—the *empako* for me and the one for herself—and she said there were more, but these fit us. I wanted to know why, and when I would not relent, she told me there were many such names and they differed across tribes, but she would just give me a few. As far as I can remember, these are the names and the meanings she gave to me:

> *Abooli* means a cat or quiet person.
> *Atwooki* considered a naughty person.
> *Abooki* means like a horn or fat or quiet.
> *Apuuli* means a baby boy or little nice dog.
> *Abbala* means keeper of cattle.
> *Acaali* means dog.
> *Araali* means thunder or lightning.
> *Amooti, Akiiki,* and *Okali* are names given to very special people.

Lisa Kawumara-Aboowli told me there were twelve or more *empakos*. She did not know the meanings of all of them, because some were names of evil spirits and should never be pronounced. ☐

India and African Life
Moses L. Howard

In 1961 throughout towns in East Africa were many Indians. Locally, they were called Asians. They had originated in India but may have recently emigrated from other countries that had an affiliation with the British Commonwealth. They were Sikhs, Hindi, and Muslims who followed the Agha Khan or were members of other ethnic groups of the Indian subcontinent. Some young Indians came to school with Africans, especially in the technical colleges and the teacher training colleges, and they talked about their customs and religious beliefs.

African names sound different: Mukasa, Sentongo, Kajubi, Nagenda. Indian names were Patel, Surrender Panzer, Desai, Sumitri. Even the places from which they came sound different to an African: India, Calcutta, Bengal, Gujarat, Dharma, and different countries such as Fiji, Columbia, Peru. There were even a few from Canada.

The British colonial rulers brought in the Asians. Some of them had British citizenship. A few had maneuvered their way into African citizenship, but most of them were stateless. British colonialists allowed them in and gave them preference over Africans in competing for civil service jobs, especially if they qualified. For example, Mr. Sumitir Joshi was a business graduate, and Mr. Summitry Chandra had a master's degree in chemistry and was head of department at the teacher training college where I taught.

Many of the Asians had better education qualification than the Africans. They qualified for jobs in the civil service that allowed them to clerk in offices. They worked in car dealerships and ran shops in the towns.

They also generally lived in those towns: for example, in Uganda, towns such as Kampala, Mbarara, Masaka, Mubendi, and Jinja; in Kenya, in Nairobi, Mombasa, and Nyeri; in Tanzania, Moshi, Dar es Salaam. In 1961, in contrast only a relatively small number of Africans lived in the towns. Africans for the most part lived in villages or on small farms near the towns.

Africans trekked into towns in the early morning every day. They lined the roadways and streets coming to work in the houses of the British civil servants or in the shops of the Asians. In the evening, the streets and roadways were again crowded with Africans hurrying back to their homes in villages miles away. In the morning, they walked or rode bicycles loaded with bananas, corn, tomatoes, beans, peas, chickens, or pineapples. Some arrived driving goats or packing all kinds of goods from their farms to be sold in the towns during the day. Some might ride buses or taxis, but very many more walked, laden with all kinds of farm produce to sell in the towns.

The bicycles, loaded with goods for sale in the mornings, became taxis carrying passengers back to farm villages in the evening. They were used as taxis to transport people home. Africans might have worked in shops in the town or in the homes of Asians or British expatriates. They cooked food, shopped for groceries, and kept house for their employers. A few of them had substandard homes in an unlit part of the town. Indian people, on the other hand, worked in government offices and administered the postal service, or worked for the public works or water departments on roads, streets, and the electric system. The Asians' houses were well constructed of cement blocks and finished inside with plaster.

There were schools near the town for British children. Indians often had their own private schools, but they also attended African and British schools. School masters above junior high school were mostly British or Asian. Africans could attend if they could afford the very high fees. Most British children were sent to boarding schools in Kenya or back to England, Ireland, or Scotland. Africans who were rich enough to afford the fees sent their children to boarding schools.

During weekdays, people worked from seven o'clock in the morning to around noon when they had one and a half hours of free time during the hottest part of the day. Most of the streets were empty at that time as people quietly found a place to escape the heat. During those week days Asian families were rarely seen; they remained behind the doors and fences of their compounds. But on Saturdays and especially on Sundays, when the town was almost clear of Africans, when the Africans were mostly at their homes and farms in the rural villages away from the towns, it was then that the Indian women appeared, always attractively dressed in colorful saris and long beautiful dresses, leisurely walking and conversing in the town streets or entering the one movie house from which wafted the stirring music of a sitar. Their hair was done in long black strands and shone and gave off a perfume. Girls with long hair all nicely done and the boys in short khaki pants and shirts masterfully ironed by African servants came out of their homes and flooded streets and byways of entire towns.

They paraded up and down the streets, sat out in front of stores which were always closed on Sundays. The women greeted each other and exchanged the week's gossip. Children exchanged the news from their schools. Boys looked at older girls and talked sports. Girls seemed not to notice the boys, but they collected in groups under the jacaranda trees and whispered about them. The men sat or stood in small groups talking about the week's business and making new deals for the coming weeks.

If you strolled near the talking men, you heard names like Patel, Dias, or Adatia, and you heard talk about the sugar cane plantation or the cement factory or coffee trading or tea industry. If you came near women, there was talk of the children and school, of marriage, and of who had made a big coup in business or who had been promoted.

Most Indian families ran some kind of business such as small shops, for instance, that sold tea, sugar, rice, beans, crackers, hair oil, combs, aspirin, flour, charcoal, cooking oil, kerosene, cooking pots, dishes, spoons, hoes, shovels, and *pangas*. For important, well-paying jobs in the British services like those in the public works—water, roads, streets, traffic supervisors—Indian men were made overseers. These jobs were given to Indians rather than Africans. Men who worked these jobs found ways to make more money through making deals and charging people extra for getting jobs done quickly. People in these jobs could make money quickly and become rich. People who found work as teachers and low-level clerks were stuck with their salaries and did not have leverage to get ahead financially. ☐

Careers Out of Africa

Edward Hower

I can trace a lot of the best things I've done back to the three years I spent in Uganda and Kenya with TEA, from 1963 to 1965. My first teaching experience, at age twenty-two, was in a refugee camp in Bombo, Uganda, while I was getting my Dip. Ed. at Makerere. My students were from the southern Sudan; they'd protested the mandatory use of Arabic in their schools and had to flee when northern Sudanese soldiers had massacred their families. I've never forgotten these students' stories, which I'm sure influenced me to become a counselor for five years with at-risk kids back in the States.

While living in Nairobi, I developed the meager skills I'd learned as a folk-singer in Greenwich Village coffee houses and became a star of Sunday Star Time on *Voice of Kenya* TV, which put me in touch with all the entertainers in the city. They became great friends; we had many unforgettable parties and night club jams. In those days, anyone who could play an instrument could be a star. My career fizzled when I got back to New York, but I've kept performing for fun.

Africa fascinated me, and I returned to graduate school to get a master's degree in anthropology. Though I never taught it, the degree helped me get two Fulbright grants to India years later. I used my field work skills to gather folk tales for a book (*The Pomegranate Princess* is still in print) and lecture on folklore at colleges in South Asia and the US.

In Africa, I found that I loved teaching and have made it one of my careers working in inner city programs and later at universities in the United States and abroad. Mainly, Africa got me focused on a writing career I'd started in college. My first novel, *The New Life Hotel* (also still in print), was set in Kimilili, on the Kenya side of Mt. Elgon where I did my practice teaching at a Kamusinga Friends School. I'm still writing, finishing my tenth book, and see no reason to ever stop. One of the first stories I published, "The Educated Billy-Goats" is about a young American teacher visiting one of his students in a rural village, an experience I had many times. The story, which became part of the novel is included in my collection, *Voices in the Water*. Thank you, TEA, for starting me off on so many fascinating careers. ☐

Female Circumcision

Jack Humbles

It was late April when I took a bus from Moshi for Arusha in the evening. One of my Maasai students, Richard Koila, wanted me to visit him near Arusha during a school break. I arrived at Monduli late that night. Monduli is a Maasai town of about 3,000 people and Richard's brother-in-law is the area commissioner, so I stayed at his house. The house is very nice but no electricity but also no mosquitoes. Richard was not there, but his sister was expecting me.

The next day the commissioner's driver took me to a Maasai *boma* where Richard was visiting. They were having a circumcision ceremony for a young girl about twelve years old. According to local custom, the girl's future husband had to be present with a friend. Richard was the friend. The operation was Saturday morning. Before the operation, she had to walk in the cold rain about eight miles without any clothes on. This was to make her numb before the procedure so she would feel less pain.

Afterwards various young men took turns trying to pick her up, but she refused them all until Richard's friend tried. Then she let him pick her up.

We were still celebrating the next day and had honey beer, which we drank from a cow's horn, with about two hundred people standing around. Soon the young warriors started dancing. They danced for hours. Much to my surprise, several of them who could speak English asked me why I didn't have a camera with me.

After drinking a lot of beer, they decided we should eat some food. The young men are allowed to eat only meat, soured milk, and cattle blood. Luckily they gave me only milk. It was not good but Richard said that it was his favorite food. I managed to drink one glass. Fresh milk is placed in long, narrow gourds and shaken often while souring. Just before serving, the milk is shaken again. It still has lumps in it and is very thick. □

The Search for Self in the Motherland

Clarence Hunter

"Africa, I lay my hand upon your swarthy belly-
And keep it there till death stubs his toe
against my manhood in the night"
O Africa, Where I Baked My Bread
—Lance Jeffers

Night falls suddenly in the African hinterland. One moment there is a brilliant sunset with a fusion of colors—blue, gray, purple, and gold—splashed against the sky as on a painter's canvas. The next moment there is a blackened sky devoid of any color. The nights in the hinterland are eerie, as animals both large and small creep out of their holes and lairs in search of food, preying on the wild and tame, emitting sounds which can cause fear yet bring a sense of comfort as one feels the balance of nature. I gained this sense of overpowering forces of the African night as I hastened to find shelter as evening closed in on me.

I was on my way to visit a student who lived at the foot of the Ruwenzori Mountains in a small village in western Uganda. This would be the last time that I would be able to see my student/friend, as the forces of Idi Amin were imposing stringent restrictions on travel. My passport meant little to his forces, and I had learned from my long stay in Uganda that an African-American travelling by bus was just another member of a different tribe. I had been travelling all day from Kampala with the hope of reaching Fort Portal by nightfall.

Along the way continuous breakdowns, washed out roads, army checkpoints and other assorted matters forced me to seek other means of transportation before night closed in around me. I did not have any great fear, as I had been in Uganda for some time, coming with the first contingent of Teachers for East Africa. I had been threatened but never really abused. I was considered an oddity in the village of Kisubi, near the school where I taught, and many had referred to me as the "African who does not speak the mother tongue." Yet this was the first time I found myself in the hinterland with night approaching quickly.

Luckily for me a long-haul driver heading for Zaire came along while I was standing on the road and took me to a small community—nothing more than a *duka*, a small transient hotel and a restaurant. Together we shared a meal of curried goat and *matoke*, drank some *pombe*, and talked about the state of the world in general, before we both went to bed to listen to the world around us.

Since I had been in Uganda, I had seen the history of East Africa unfold before my very eyes: the coming of the independence of Uganda; the rise and fall of my good friend, Benedicto Kiwanuka; the overthrow of Kabaka Mutesa II; the rise of Milton Obote, the first Prime Minister and President of Uganda; and the rise of Idi Amin. In my travels throughout East Africa I had seen both the beauty and the savagery of nature and man's inhumanity to man. I had tired of the death and destruction. I wanted to leave Uganda and return home, yet I had to get clear in my mind who I was and why I had come to Africa in the first place.

In 1961 East Africa was in the midst of momentous changes. Tanganyika (Tanzania), guided by Julius Nyerere, was on the threshold of independence. Kenya, still seething from the Mau Mau emergency was in turmoil as the demands grew for Jomo Kenyatta to be released from jail. Uganda was moving toward self-government, and it appeared that the "Pearl of Africa" would peacefully gain its true independence from Britain. This was not to happen.

In the United States things were different for me. Despite the Brown decision of 1954, I was still relegated to teach in the segregated system that I had been assigned to since release from my service in Korea. In addition the winds of change in American society had been blowing for some time as black Americans had become frustrated with the slow movement toward a free society progressed through the courts and the continuous demonstrations. As a boy I was told about Africa as the Motherland, the land of our deliverance from the oppression of the white society—our promised land. So when Teachers College, Columbia, asked for teachers for East Africa, I answered the call with the hope I would gain that for which I was searching. I was not aware of the tribalism, the religious division created by the British, and what I would have to do and say as a black American.

It was into this maelstrom that I came as a naive black American determined to assist my African brothers and sisters in nation building. To my students I was a novelty, someone that they had read about in the newspapers or magazines. To the people of the village I was an enigma. I closely resembled any average Muganda, but I could not speak Luganda, and when I tried my limited Swahili, I was looked upon as African from another tribe with a different language or dialect. It was not long before the euphoria of being in the Motherland vanished. The whole experience confused me. All Africans belonged to some tribe and their name would identify their origin. Every African therefore had a name that was uniquely theirs. My name stamped me as being an African without identity. My close African friends were sympathetic to my dilemma and insisted that my problem originated from the fact that I was born of slave parents.

I immediately tried to fit in and my students helped me. They gave me an adopted name of Mukasa—a very standard Baganda name. They invited me to their homes, where I learned to greet in true Baganda fashion, a greeting so long that you were advised not begin it unless you had a year in your life to give to greetings alone. The Civil Rights crisis that was developing in the States gave me the opportunity to discuss the attitudes of the white ruling class in the South and the need to resist tyranny wherever it was found.

Many of my students felt that if tyranny was not met in Uganda at its beginning of independence, then the nation would suffer for years to come. Tyranny did come to the nation, and many of my students and friends were casualties of the resistance to it. Even today as I see Mathias Kiwanuka play for the New York football Giants, the image of his grandfather Benedicto flashes through my mind. I should have avoided any political involvement, but I could not avoid the friendships which Kiwanuka and other members of his party afforded me.

In 1966 I formally left Uganda and TEA. The journey through those years had been rewarding. There were happy moments and humorous moments. I could recall nearly being arrested by the Kabaka's police for non-payment of poll tax. They would later explain that I looked like any other Muganda. It was scary then, but my friends and I could laugh about it later. Through all of this misidentification, I had a feeling of belonging. No one could place me with a tribe, but all I met during my stay knew that somewhere in the history of the continent my ancestors were dragged from their homes and sold into slavery. I was taught by Carter G. Woodson early in my life not to forsake Africa but to embrace it. He emphasized that it was the land that gave you soul. This was so true. And through the years, as I recall my stay in the "pearl of Africa," I know that this period was the defining moment of my life. ☐

First Wave Romance

Marty McCall Lemke

Dick and I fell in love at the Makerere pool, courted at LaQuinta and the City Bar, celebrated our engagement in Mombasa, and married in Bukoba on March 10, 1961. Moira Harbottle came down on the lake steamer, Harry came a week later with flowers in the steamer's kitchen cooler for my bouquet, and Sharon Lybeck, my maid of honor, arrived just in time for the wedding. Thrice married in one day! At 10:00 a.m., after a very brief ceremony in his office, the soon-to-be-gone British district commissioner signed a paper saying we were civilly married, although he technically no longer had any legal authority.

Since I was at Kahororo, a Lutheran mission school, the missionaries decided we should get married in the "eyes of God" in a little chapel they bedecked with flowers. At 2:00 p.m., a Norwegian missionary married us—although he spoke little English and had no authority to marry *wazungu*. After a reception at the Lake Hotel, we retired to our little house at Kahororo.

Just as it was getting dark, a ring of fire sprang up around our house, burning away all evil spirits from the union, and my school boys began to serenade us with the help of some Scandinavian and American friends. After a couple of hours, they pounded on the door, asking if I had been satisfied with this man. If I answered yes, I would become a woman of his village. If I answered no, I could return home with them, and it would be as if this never happened.

I said, "*Yes!*" □

Malaria and Me
Clive Mann

As a biologist I knew a lot about malaria before going to Makerere. That didn't stop me from contracting this really awful disease on three occasions in East Africa. The day before I was due to be inspected by Prof. Lucas at Makerere College School I began to feel quite ill, and during that evening and night it got worse. This was before our first proper teaching practice, which in my case was to be at Tororo Boys' High School.

Pain seemed to emanate from every part of my body, and the principal (there were a number) hallucination was that my body was breaking into tiny parts that then went off in every direction and then came together in pairs. I must have been thinking about termite *alates* ["swarmers"] at some point. I was incredibly cold at times and at others burning hot. My sheets were drenched in sweat. My head was banging.

Somehow the next morning I managed to get a message to Lucas, whose response was something along the lines of

"Oh, is he? I've seen malingerers before. I'll soon settle this."

He banged on my door and almost immediately barged in.

"Good God, you really are ill," he said, and left before I could speak. Someone called a doctor, and of course I recovered none the worse for the experience. However, I did vow to be more careful over prophylaxis.

I guess I wasn't careful enough. A couple of years later after a day-long wedding reception in Soroti, my Punjabi mechanic mate Aslam and I decided to drive the seventy miles to Mbale. He had drunk more than me, so I drove my Saab. After about ten miles, at Awoja swamp, I decided I needed to sleep. Aslam had already passed out. I took a track that I knew into the swamp and parked. Before going to sleep I checked all windows were closed. I then got out to relieve myself and on return didn't shut the door properly so the courtesy light remained on as an added advertisement to the mosquitoes. In the morning there were so many bloated mosquitoes in the car it was like smog, and the ceiling was red with blood smears from their crushed bodies.

That was probably how I got my second bout of malaria. I was terribly ill and losing weight, because I couldn't keep anything down, not even water. Perhaps not as painful as the Kampala bout, but much more nauseous. Out of the blue a New Zealand photographer friend, Moira, from Dar es Salaam, turned up and was alarmed at my gaunt appearance.

"Don't you fancy eating anything?" she said.

Suddenly I thought of lemon meringue pie! She went off to town to get the ingredients and cooked two huge pies for me. I ate both, one straight after the other: the first food (or liquid) I had been able to keep down for about a week. Two days later I had recovered sufficiently to take her to Karamoja where she wanted to do some photography.

From then on I was careful with prophylaxis, and discovered a newish drug called Resochen. This is chloroquine-based and also effective against intestinal amoebae. When I lived in Kenya, the altitude was too great for malaria, at least that was the received wisdom. I always took Resochen when spending time in the lowlands. Some of our pupils came from lower country and, I guess, managed to import both the parasite plasmodium and the mosquito vector Anopheles up to Kapsabet. One of my pupils died of cerebral malaria, and he had not been in low country.

This should have been a warning to me. However, a few months later I went down with my third, and hopefully last, bout. What I remember chiefly about this were the violent headaches and tremendous fevers. I recovered of course, and from then on always took Resochen, even for a couple of weeks after returning to UK. I had seen a friend from Tanzania, who had never knowingly had malaria, collapse at a party in London with the disease. He had stopped the prophylaxis on leaving Africa! □

The Joys of Ajon

Clive Mann

I had sampled a number of so-called "African beers" and didn't feel positively impressed. Some reminded me of a mixture of warm vinegar and Weetabix. A Chagga brew that I had at Tengeru, near Arusha, was quite pleasant. However, on moving to Soroti, I soon discovered the joys of the Teso *ajon* made from sorghum. I suppose it would be described as an acquired taste, but it didn't take me long to acquire it. Some *wazungu* hated it, others took to it like ducks to water.

In Soroti I had large servants' quarters but no servants. Some of the pupils at my day school had up to twenty miles to cycle to school, and the same back again, every day. I allowed a number, never knew quite how many, to live in these quarters provided they did a few chores for which I paid them. Two I remember in particular were Justin Ogilut, at one time school captain, and John Okoboi, both excellent pupils, great characters, friends, and true gentlemen.

The first time Justin asked me to visit his village we set off on my BSA 500cc motorbike. After a short while he wanted to stop, and he asked me if it was necessary to keep his foot on the footrest. I explained that it was dangerous not to as his foot might go in the wheel. He complained that one foot was getting very hot, and I realized I could smell burning. He was resting one foot on the exhaust pipe! I showed him the footrest, and we continued.

A message must have been sent on ahead because when we arrived the whole village, mostly relatives of Justin, greeted us with a dance. I was introduced to everyone, and as I shook hands with some it was obvious that the *ajon* party had already begun. The imbibers sit around a communal earthenware pot and drink through long straws of varying lengths, but many around 70–100cm long. I can't remember what the straw is made from, but certainly natural material, and at one end it has a tiny basket-like filter to prevent particles from being sucked up. The straws are passed round, and every so often they have to be shaken to dislodge the trapped solids. At times the pot is topped up with hot water from a kettle. Drinking parties can go on for some time.

The boys in my servants' quarters used to organize such a party in my garden at the end of each term. Among the guests were usually the two Dutch Catholic priests of the area, Franz Hilders and Franz Hoefnagels. Apart from us three, I think everyone else was African. Towards the end of my stay, a tall, stately Itesot nurse, Margaret, moved into the house next door. Margaret called on me and asked if I would like to partake of some *ajon*, as she had recently been to her village and brought back "the makings" which were now fermenting, and it would be ready tomorrow. I jumped at the chance, and discovered the best *ajon* I had tasted.

Sometime after I left Soroti, Margaret married Roger Wigglesworth (TEA 4B, Teso College). They later turned up not far from me in Kenya, and again in Brunei. Whenever Margaret went to Uganda, she would return with the makings of her superb *ajon*.

Both she and Roger are now sadly dead. I went to both their funerals in Shrewsbury, England, about ten years apart. At Margaret's funeral I mentioned to a nephew that she produced a superb brew. He agreed with me emphatically and told me that she was considered "Ajon Queen" throughout Teso. ☐

Pets in Uganda

Clive Mann

I did not intentionally acquire any pets when I lived in East Africa. Because I traveled so much I thought it unfair on the animals, even on cats and dogs. However, I did in fact have quite a variety over the years.

My first was a nestling Barn Owl. It was given to me by a student who had no idea of its provenance so I could not return it to its nest. It soon became very friendly, and I fed it with bits of raw meat covered with small pieces of chicken feathers. He—if it was a male—used to perch on my shoulder as I walked around the garden and the neighborhood. When he was fully fledged I tried to get him to fly away but to no avail. My closest neighbor at the time worked for the Game Department and had one wife living with him. She got used to this strange sight of an *mzungu* with an owl on his shoulder.

One day as I walked in the garden I heard a shriek. This came from another wife of my neighbor whom I'd never met. She stared and pointed at the owl, laughing and letting out exclamations of surprise. We had a chat about it and she asked why it didn't fly away. I said I didn't really know, but my experience of owls in the past is that they will latch on to a human who brings them up, and become very friendly. At that moment, he took flight and kept going in a straight line. I rushed to get my binoculars and followed his progress in the direction of Arapai. He did not stop, and eventually disappeared from sight, never to be seen again.

Some months after I lost my barn owl, a student brought me a baby female patas monkey. His father's lorry driver had acquired this on a trip to Karamoja, but the family decided they didn't want it. "Hairy Mary" when very small would cling to my shoulder and getting hungry would suck my earlobe until a bottle of milk appeared. As she got older she had the free run of my quite considerable garden where there were plenty of trees. Sometimes she would doze on my lap as I sat on the veranda; if I was dozing, she would carefully open one of my eyes and look closely. On occasion she would take an interest in my nostrils and rapidly poke a finger up my nose causing me to shout because of the shock, whereupon she would jump onto the table knocking over cups, glasses etc. Her eyesight was amazing and she would stare at a tree trunk in the distance and make it obvious she wanted me to take her there. This could be at a distance of fifty meters or so, and on arrival would find that she was watching a termite column she hoped to feed on.

I always took her into the house at night, and if I forgot she would not come down from a tree she may have climbed, and I would have to climb up to fetch her. She was friendly to most human males, but could be pugnacious towards females. When I left Uganda, I gave her to

Martin Wyatt at Makerere School who already had a large male patas. I used to stay with Martin when I visited Kampala from Kenya so I got to see Hairy Mary on a number of occasions. She was kept on a running leash long enough so that she and Boy could torment Martin's Alsatian. Once a girl was crossing the garden and Hairy Mary launched herself on her leash at the poor girl's head. I rushed over and did a miraculous save, catching her in midair.

For a short time I had a giant pouched rat that somehow got itself into a brick shed-like structure in my garden. It was two stories, the upper part basically being a "room" completely surrounded by metal mosquito netting. He was a friendly creature, quite a lot bigger than a brown rat, and with a tail partly white. He was completely vegetarian. Hairy Mary was fascinated by him but never tried to touch him. I left the door slightly open so he could come and go. After a few months he disappeared. Hairy Mary used to go and look for him, turning over the straw bedding, seemingly puzzled by his absence. ☐

Pets in Kenya

Clive Mann

As I showed in my story "Pets in Uganda," pets acquired me rather than vice versa. When I lived in Kabarnet a pleasant-looking, friendly *shenzi* dog was often seen roaming around near my house and I gave her an occasional scrap to eat. She took to following me into the house and just sitting down by the fire. I bought some dog food from KFA in Eldoret and fed her on a regular basis.

A German working for an aid organization came to my house and said that he wanted a dog for his children and heard that I had one that I might like to off-load. I was quite pleased that she would now get a more stable home. A few days later the dog re-appeared at my house and moved back in. After another couple of days I was sitting on my veranda when the dog pricked up her ears and then rushed into the house and hid under my bed. She had heard the characteristic sound of the German's VW camper, which was now approaching the house. He jumped out and stormed towards me, carrying a stick. "Vere iss my dok? Vy haf you taken it?"

I now realized that she had run away because of ill treatment. I told him what I thought, and said I did not expect to see him again. Now I had a dog. I named her Trixie. She dug a den in the garden, and it was obvious she was about to give birth. I got a box, filled it with old clothing for her to give birth in, and confined her to quarters. She dragged the box under my bed and that's where her first litter was born in the middle of the night. She had two litters of pups in all, totaling twenty-four, until I had her spayed. I kept two, a female "Sumuni," and a male "Scrofa." The others I gave to a farmer friend, Jasse, much to the delight of his younger siblings.

—

When I lived in Kapsabet, I used to spend at least one weekend each month studying birds in Kakamega Forest. In January 1971, I found a nest of African grass owls on the ground in a large glade. Owls do not easily desert their nests, but I was very careful on approaching the nest so I would not reveal it to someone else. When the two nestlings were large enough, I ringed (banded) them.

On my next trip to the forest I came across an African wheeling his bike towards me. Dangling from the handlebars were the nestling owls attached by string. Of course I had to ignore my usual advice to friends, and I bought them from him, after he told me they were for the pot. They could not be returned to their nest for obvious reasons. I took them home, planning to release them when ready. As there were two, they did not become tame and pet-like. However, just before they were due for release my servant, Saul, poisoned them.

A young blue monkey was also obtained through misplaced pity by purchase from a local's handlebars. I wondered about its strange behavior, and quickly released it was blind. The sad creature lived about two years before also being poisoned along with the owls. That poison was the cause was confirmed by the local vet.

—

On the school compound at Kapsabet, and viewable from my teaching laboratory, a pair of African wood owls nested in a tree-hole and had one nestling. I ringed this when it was old enough. I did my best not to advertise the nest. Coming back after a few days away, I was surprised to find him—"Woodford," as he became—was sitting on a perch in my aviary. My servant Thomas said that a schoolboy, assuming that the bird was my property, had brought it.

I put it back in its nest, and a few days later, now fully-fledged, he was back in the aviary again. He became very tame and, having no small inmates in the aviary, I removed a section of netting. He then could come and go. At first he seemed reluctant to leave, and I cut down on the food. Gradually he spent more and more nights away, but returning to roost during daylight. Eventually he disappeared, hopefully to lead a normal life in the wild.

At times friends left animals with me when they went on long leave, so my house did become somewhat (Gerald) "Durrellian." An English couple at the agricultural station asked me to mind a young duiker and a gray-crested crane. I never managed to identify the species of antelope, but researching it recently I think it may have been "Peter's Duiker." Although the crane wasn't a problem, the duiker did have a difficulty. The doors of my house were normally open in daylight hours and things wandered in an out. My servant Thomas used to polish the floors with red "Cardinal." By using bits of sheepskin as skates, he skid around until the floors were like ice. I couldn't always keep my feet myself, but the poor duiker found it impossible to stand. I must have read somewhere about the solution to this which is to put strips of rough-backed "Elastoplast" on its hooves. This I did, and it worked a treat.

—

One of my neighbors, an Englishman and deputy head, and his wife who was Turkana, had a mini-farm in their garden. When they left Kenya for UK, they gave me the farm animals, about a dozen white rabbits, three turkeys, a few ducks, and numerous chickens. Apart from some eggs, I ate only two rabbits. They made delicious beer casseroles, but then I found I could not kill any more of them. They were so trusting, I felt very bad ending their lives. I managed to give some away as pets.

On one occasion I was away over the Christmas period for about three weeks. This was during the regime of my first servant in Kapsabet, Saul. When I returned, I found the grass owls poisoned and all the farm animals gone. According to Saul, they had all been taken by hyenas. Although hyenas were regular in my garden in Soroti, I never saw or heard them at Kapsabet, and nor did anyone else!

A big problem with having pets when living away from your home country is the difficulty of finding new homes for them when you eventually repatriate yourself, and the great sadness of leaving them. When it was time for me to leave Kenya, I contacted the KSPCA in Nairobi and gave details of my cat and dogs to a very helpful lady. Within no time, she had found a good home for Trixie and Sumuni together, but no one wanted Scrofa. I had to leave him with her when I left Kenya. We had a farewell in his pen, and I had a large lump in my throat. The KSPCA lady said she thought she would not find a home for Sheba, because he was an un-castrated male, but said I could leave him with her.

When I got back to UK a few months later, there was an aerogramme waiting for me from this lady. The Finnish ambassador had taken Scrofa. Her other piece of good news was that Sheba's testes had not descended and he had not matured, so she decided to keep him herself. At times I wondered whimsically if giving him a female-sounding name was the cause of him not becoming a mature male. □

Wild Animal Tales from Kapsabet

Clive Mann

The Kapsabet area of Kenya was not well-endowed with mammals, and what were there were mostly small. A few species of mongoose and squirrel, couple of species of monkeys, a few species of small antelopes rarely encountered, bats, and rodents. Therefore, it was quite easy to remember the few occasions when something unusual happened. Soroti in Uganda was more exciting in that spotted hyenas regularly came to my dustbins, and other gardens had been visited by a lion and a leopard during my time there, although I did not see them.

Mole-rats (rodents that live underground) were common at Kapsabet, and their molehill-like mounds of soil could be seen on any grassy area. Because they ate roots, they could create havoc in some crops. The local people tried to kill them when they could. The usual method was to place a noose in one of their tunnels beneath a soil mound. The noose was attached to a springy sapling which was bent down and held in place by stick which was the "trigger." If a mole-rat put his head into the noose and continued onwards, this would pull out the "trigger" and the sapling would spring erect pulling up the noose with the unfortunate creature's neck in it. Sometimes when I was teaching I would be disturbed by the sound of a trap being sprung, especially as at times it would be accompanied by squeals from the rodent.

At the bottom of the garden of my first house at Kapsabet I had an aardvark's burrow and sometimes I was lucky enough to see him above ground, but rarely. One night returning late to school I saw an aardvark at the side of the *murram* road just before the eastern entrance to the school apparently trying to go through a stout wire fence in order to escape from my vehicle.

I got out of my Land Rover and walked very slowly towards him. When I got within about four meters, he reared up and showed me his formidable fore-paws adapted for digging. These could have done some damage to me so I backed away. I realized that he didn't actually require any help and could easily have dug under the fence. Perhaps he was one of the family that lived in my garden. Khassogo Owa Namwamba, who has adopted me as his uncle, says that there are now aardvark holes all over the Kapsabet area which I don't think was the case when I lived there.

Once at my second house, I got up at 3:00 a.m. to leave early for Kaptagat Forest. I had a couple of friends from Siaya staying, and we were going to spend two days and a night there to study the birds. I opened my veranda door and my three dogs shot inside, hair standing on end, tails between their legs and facial skin pulled back giving them a hideous visage, and hid behind furniture.

This had never happened before so I went out to investigate and could hear a leopard somewhere in the hedge at the bottom of the garden. I woke Thomas, my servant, and asked him to warn other folk on the compound, and to keep his wife and children indoors or very close to him. Knowing my dogs, once the initial fear had been forgotten they would be back out on the hunt. So I instructed Thomas to keep them in the house. When I came back the next day people were so relieved I was alive. A rumor had been spread that the leopard had killed me, and that was why no one could find me. □

The Mpemba Effect

Eugene Marschall

I was a physics and chemistry teacher at Mkwawa High School in Iringa, Tanzania, from July 1965 to April 1967. One of my students was Erasto Mpemba. One of the subjects in the A level physics syllabus was Newton's law of cooling. The law basically states that the rate of cooling of a hot body is proportional to the difference between the temperature of the hot body and its surrounding temperature. According to the law, it should not matter at which temperature a hot body starts to cool since all such bodies should go through the same temperature trajectory.

However, Erasto was able to show that a warmer body cools or freezes faster than a cooler one does. When Erasto brought this to my notice, I at first did not believe it. Urged on by the class and Erasto himself, we did the experiment and, lo and behold, he was right: a warmer body does freeze faster than a colder body. I was at least honest enough to admit that I could give no explanation. This happened quite early on in my teaching period in Mkwawa High School, so my aura as a teacher who could not fail suffered as a result. Erasto Mpemba was a very enthusiastic student, and I am glad to say he passed the A level exams.

I saw him once later in Dar es Salaam, and he told me that he had a good government job, which was what most students in those days were aiming for.

In 1967, I went to the MBA course at INSEAD in Fontainebleau, France. A local French business publication cited the case of the Mpemba Effect as an example of how one should not always trust the received wisdom. One of our professors on the course used this article as an example and to the astonishment of the other students, I was able to reveal that I was the teacher who did not (initially) believe Mpemba! Moral of this story: be careful to believe what others say is the truth.

> For more about the Mpemba Effect, see
> http://bit.ly/mpemba-1. □

Double, Double, Toil and Trouble

Mary Jo McMillin

Joseph burst in this morning exclaiming, "Oh, Memsaab, do you know what I've been hearing many people say in the town?"

Witchcraft was brewing in the bush; we'd heard it first from Pillay. Now the townspeople as well as schoolboys are dazed. Two weeks after headmaster Paul Mhaiki's return to Songea, acting headmaster Mbenna, greedy for power, decided to turn to black magic. The story is that Mbenna and one of the African teachers had brought a black rooster to a *mganga*, a witch doctor, late one night.

The ritual took place near Matagoro Mountain, high on a granite cliff where deformed newly born babies were once left for the gods.

Hidden in darkness, the *mganga* killed, bled, and stewed the rooster into a potion with herbs and roots. Mbenna drank the broth and fell into a trance under incantations and the sorcerer's ceremonial feathers, blood, and beads. The *mganga* put a hex on Mhaiki: he would either die, fall seriously ill, or be transferred to another school. Mbenna would again become headmaster.

Some say the story leaked after a TANU youth leader heard a rumor and, hidden, observed the ceremony. Others say the friend accompanying Mbenna feared for his own life when he heard the death oath pronounced and told the authorities. The black magic had taken place about a month earlier, and the witch doctor was now in prison. The regional commissioner pressed charges, and the witch doctor eventually confessed. The education officer went to Dar to resolve the problem, and no one knows what will happen.

We felt concern for Mhaiki; he was terribly frightened. Mhaiki and Mbenna, both Catholics, have counseled with one of the mission priests to make a settlement, but in East Africa talking does not abolish fear. The battle lines remained. A hex was a hex. □

November 1963, Songea, Tanganyika

Mary Jo McMillin

In southern Tanganyika in the back and beyond of Songea, Bob finishes correcting final exams and changes the oil in the car before he has it greased in town. We'll safari out tomorrow and won't be back till early January. We'll carry gallon jugs of gas, sleeping bags, and plenty of boiled water. I fill two of the five-pound powdered milk tins with peanut butter cookies and graham crackers for snacks with bananas. I wrap spice cakes, coconut wafers, and orange hermits to leave with friends along the way. We'll be packed tightly but plan to make room for one schoolboy who needs a lift to Njombe. If we get stuck on muddy roads, we're hoping there'll be public works (PWD) workers along the roads to help. By seven a.m. tomorrow we plan to be headed toward Kenya and ultimately as far as the Ruwenzori Mountains in Uganda. Just two or three days to *ice cream!*

Odom, a husky schoolboy, knocks at our door about 6:30 a.m., and the three of us leave the mud puddles of Songea in a cloud of mist following a rainy night. The haze so densely covers the hills we can't see the trees that nearly touch our front porch. The umbrella branches and grasses look jungle-like. Birds dart ahead of us; one is summer-squash yellow with charcoal wings and a red band at its throat. Beyond the eroding humped hills surrounding Songea we drive atop woodless crests, making our way up the Lukumburu escarpment. Although we slither and skid, I hold my breath as Bob keeps his foot on the accelerator. We slide through waves of mud and make record time, barreling through 182 miles to Njombe in five hours.

On the morning of November 23, we sit at a white linen-covered table in the dining room at Iringa's White Horse Inn and stare into saucers of grapefruit. The seedy white centers have been neatly cored and heaped with sugar. As we're spooning the segments, the Greek hotel proprietor rushes to our table. He tells us the news he's just heard on his ham radio. Napkins in hand, we follow him into his office, and in disbelief, thousands of miles from home, listen to the announcement that President Kennedy has been assassinated. Our host grasps our shoulders. I feel far away and wonder why we're here.

We push on toward Dodoma, and join the Great North Road to Arusha. In one day we motor past sun-beaten plains, sand-swept valleys, and lush forests. Near Arusha the landscape stretches into a green carpet dotted with wide-leaved banana plants and immense hardwoods. We drive by sisal fields, where giant tractors creep over plantations. The plains feed into vast grasslands before the rising pyramid of Mt. Meru. Three giraffes graze ahead, our first sighting of big game. By late afternoon we stop at a hotel in Arusha, a fair-sized town with high-rise buildings and three movie theaters. In the city center bead-bejeweled Maasai wander among Asians and Europeans. We notice a snack stand selling hamburgers, hot dogs and doughnuts, but no *ice cream.*

Sunday afternoon we step quietly beneath the tolling bell tower of the Evangelical Lutheran Church for a memorial service for President Kennedy. Heavy silence fills the packed stucco sanctuary where we stand arm to arm black, white, tan—people of the world. The air echoes with Bach and "Lord, have mercy." We return to the African sun with eyes downcast and learn the suspected assassin has been shot. ☐

Cooking All the Time

Mary Jo McMillin

Though I was a kind of hanger-on TEAer since it was my then husband, Robert Wendel, who was selected for the 1963–65 wave, I was actively there at all stages, from Columbia to the last drive to Dar, and participated wholly in our remote post (the most remote in southwest Tanganyika). I taught on local terms for our school, Songea Secondary, prepared numerous tea parties and suppers for school boys, plus elaborate celebration dinners for staff and ministry inspectors.

I was cooking all the time and brought home a repertoire of Indian cuisine learned from wives of shopkeepers. (Even tonight, I rolled chapatis with the stubby pin, a gift from the Punjabi wife of our postmaster and ground mint for raita in a stone mortar.)

As I've made my career in the culinary world, what I experienced in East Africa honed skills I've used through a lifetime and the world viewed through those months opened my eyes like no other educational experience. Little did I know then, more than fifty years ago, that I was walking in the footsteps of Elspeth Huxley, Karen Blixen, and Hemingway. Eventually, all their stories took on new light, and now when I read Alexandra Fuller, I totally know what she's saying. ☐

From the Minnesota River Valley to the Peaks of Kilimanjaro

Patricia (Schmitt) Mische

Minnesota, where I grew up, is blessed with beautiful lakes, rivers, woods, hills and valleys, but no mountains. Yet, without ever seeing them, mountains possessed me. In high school, I fantasized about snow-capped peaks and described them in poetry as if I had actually been there. The first opportunity to turn fantasy into reality came when, as part of TEA in 1961, I was sent to study at the London Institute of Education.

While there, four of us took a weekend trip to Wales to climb Mt. Snowden. I thought I was physically fit and experienced enough from country hiking to walk up Snowden in my sneakers. Half way up, I sank in exhaustion, my ankle twisted and my feet and legs throbbing, while my companions, experienced climbers, raced ahead to the summit. A Welsh grandmother, wearing a skirt and sensible walking shoes, and her six-year old grandson, passed me on their Sunday stroll up the trail and smiled with pity at my plight. Then and there I decided to turn humiliation into victory. When I got to East Africa I would climb Kilimanjaro; but I would be physically fit, mentally prepared, and come to the mountain with respect, humility, and sturdy shoes.

As it happened, after a semester at Makerere University in Uganda, I was posted to Mukumu Girls Secondary School, near Kakamega, Kenya, far from Kilimanjaro and not at an altitude that would acclimatize my lungs to Kilimanjaro's 19,000 foot altitude. To test my readiness, I joined some friends in climbing nearby Mt. Elgon, which had no snow-capped peaks, but enough crags, crevices, and ascending challenges to forewarn that I needed more training. So, to the amusement of my students, teaching colleagues, and Baluyia neighbors living along the equator, I began running every day up and down the pathways and rocky hillsides. People thought this behavior crazy.

"Why are you doing this, miss?"

How could I explain it? What reasonable person would run in the African sun to prepare for a mountain? In fact, why would a reasonable person want to climb a mountain? "Because it is there," was not accepted as a reasonable response.

I no longer remember how I got from Kakamega in Kenya to Moshi on the Tanzanian side of Kilimanjaro, whether I took local buses, hitchhiked (as I sometimes did in those days), rode in a car with friends, or some combination of all three. But in August of 1963, there I was, at a hotel at the base of the mountain, signing up to join a guided five-day trek: three days up and two days down the mountain.

The trip up to the first and second base camps was not that difficult: it was mind over matter, one foot after the other up an incline that wound through forests and around villages. We started before dawn so that we could get to the next base camp before dark, with enough time to wash, eat, and sleep on wooden bunks. On the way up, there was time to greet people living on the slopes, admire the beautiful views of the snow-covered peak as it emerged around bends, to turn back to see villages shrinking behind and below us, examine changing flora and fauna at different elevations, marveling all the while at the beauty of life on Earth.

Every step on the journey brought some discovery or insight. For me, entering into the contours of the mountain was to enter into the journeying of the cosmos and the Earth, all that emanated from the big bang and its spawning of galaxies and planets, evolving through geological and biological phenomena that included shifting and colliding Earth plates and volcanic eruptions, the appearance of living cells and the flowering and foresting of planet Earth, and the emergence of human beings and their spread around the planet. To enter the mountain was to enter the mystery of life's oneness and diversity. It was all here, marked in the mountain.

There was, too, the camaraderie of making the climb with others, people who came as strangers, entered into this journey across language barriers, and, although not likely to meet again, became forever bound together. At the second base camp, where nothing much grew and the air was thin and crisp, we sipped hot soup and were advised not to eat or drink anything more before attempting the final ascent.

Beyond this point, an elevation of 15,000 feet, the altitude would make us nauseous. We were also advised to sleep early because we had to rise at midnight if we were to climb to the top by sunrise and return before clouds circled and made the descent perilous. Kilimanjaro's highest peak is an extinct volcano and the top rim around the crater is narrow. One misstep in low visibility can be fatal.

I didn't sleep that night. I was too cold and hungry, but also excited and determined. Our group had already been greatly reduced in number. Half had turned back at the first base camp. By the second base camp, more had turned back; one had heart palpitations and required medical assistance. So, at midnight, with only moon and star light to see our way, only five of us started out. I was the only woman and the only English-speaker.

As we headed up the rocky slope, I quickly understood why we had to start at midnight. For every three steps step forward we slid back two. We were walking up a steep incline of shifting scree—loose stones and gravel. The air grew thinner and thinner. Hours passed this way. Three steps forward, two back. Then we came to snow and ice and two more people turned back. Now there were only three: our Chagga guide, a German botanist, and me. We did not speak. Not only did we not know each other's languages, we needed all our energy for the climb and just to breathe. The need for ski poles was clear. We had to plunge in the pick and leverage each step forward to avoid sliding back down.

Finally, just as the first sun rays could be seen rising behind us to the east, we took the last step to the top of the rim. There was the flag of the newly independent Tanzania, fastened firmly to a pole embedded into the mountain top, but flying free in a biting wind. There in front and below us was the seemingly bottomless crater. There behind us was the world from which we had come, small and far away. We stood in the wind, feet anchored to the top of the Earth on a very narrow rim, head in the now blue sky, with beams of blinding light bouncing off the ice-covered mountain.

I wanted to sing Beethoven's "Ode to Joy." Instead, I pulled an orange from my pocket and peeled it, resting the ski pole under my arm. Hungry and thirsty, this orange, though seedy and tough, was the best I ever ate. Then, I threw up—into the crater. In the angst of the moment, I began to lose my balance, grabbed for my pole, and instead of grasping it, knocked it flying. It went bouncing down, down, down into the crater. It was going to be a hard descent without it, just how hard I did not yet realize.

I had prepared myself for the climb up, but had not even considered that the descent would require a different set of muscles and skills, and shoes with cushions in different places. Not only did I slide down ice and scree, falling more than once. But even after we came to firmer ground and clear paths, every downward step threw my toes with full force into the front of my shoes. By the time we reached the first base camp my toes were a mass of blisters and blood. When we reached the hotel, I could barely walk. Thus did I go from incredible joy to the painful reality of loving a mountain.

Before climbing Kilimanjaro, I had been reading Teilhard de Chardin's evolutionary account in *The Phenomenon of Man*, a work and author that at the time was forbidden to Catholics like myself, but which, having overridden the constraints, opened to me the far reaches of the past. Here in East Africa, the Leakeys had recently found oldest human fossil record of our human ancestors, more evidence of our past evolutionary journey.

At Mukumu and other schools throughout East Africa, a new generation of Africans was being prepared to lead in nation-building. When I arrived, Tanzania had just become independent. Uganda's independence came a year later, and I cheered with others as the new Ugandan flag was raised in Kampala. Soon it would be Kenya's turn. This process was going on throughout Africa. Surely this was the age of nation-states.

But this was only a small part of the transformation underway. Just down the road from Mukumu, where we still had no electricity, satellite monitoring stations had been erected to monitor Glenn's earth orbit. We were entering a future of space-age communications and increasing global interdependence. In a few months I would be returning to the US.

Kilimanjaro had been a culminating experience through which I could touch and integrate in deeper ways the far past of Earth history, the present human challenges, and new possibilities for the Earth and humanity in an emerging future. Fifty years later, I still feel awe and gratitude for those five days on the mountain. □

The Time I Gave Away My Watch
Patricia (Schmitt) Mische

I was prepared to experience culture shock in East Africa. But that didn't happen until I returned to the US. Instead, the unexpected happened. My sense of time exploded—backward, forward, and inward. In Tanzania's Olduvai Gorge, Mary and Louis Leakey were discovering the oldest human fossil forms and re-setting the date of human origins millions of years earlier than previously assumed. In Kenya, near the equator where I was teaching, satellite-monitoring stations were erected to track the first human orbit of the Earth. Our concepts of the future were rocketing into space. And I was reading *The Phenonmenon of Man* by Teilhard de Chardin, who traced more than 13 million years of cosmic and planetary evolution. My mind was being stretched in all directions by new macro views of time.

The micro view was no less explosive. In rural Kenya, people did not measure time in hours or minutes but by the rising and setting of the sun, by patterns of light and darkness, by sounds of birds and insects, by the feel of dry and wet seasons. At Mukumu, we had no electricity, no telephones, no radios. My students were signaled when to rise, eat, attend class, or play games, not by clocks but the sound of school bells. They knew who won the track meet by the sound of beating drums relaying news across the countryside. But I still wore my watch, a gift from my family who measured time and virtue by punctual performance of duties. And so my life in Kenya proceeded in a parallel universe of time conception. I lived by the rhythm of a different beat than the people around me.

Then one day. I was assigned to administer the Cambridge exams at another school. It was paramount that exam administrators arrive at their assigned school early, make sure that the exams were untampered, and prepare the exam room. That morning I arose at 5:00 a.m. It would take an hour to get to this school, longer if it rained and the dirt roads were muddy. A driver had been hired to get me there with time to spare. At 5:30, the appointed time of departure, the driver had not appeared. At 6:00, no driver. At 6:30, no driver. Then at 7:00, he appeared with the rising sun, all smiles. I was furious and shouted in anger. He drove like hell through mud and bounced over ruts while I fumed.

When we arrived, quite late, the waiting students were filled with anxiety; their future depended on this exam. I don't know how those students did, and whether or not they secured a place in higher education. But I do know that I felt ashamed at losing my temper and becoming disjointed from the community I had come to serve. My sense of time was a source of tension.

That day I decided to give away my watch. I gave it to one of my Form 4 students for whom I had arranged a college scholarship in the US. She was going to need that watch to fit in on the other side of an evolving world. On my new side of the world I wanted to learn to hear, see, know time differently, to make room for setbacks, human error, spontaneity, and the unexpected. ☐

My East Africa Story

Frank Mitchell

My mom Grace Mitchell, a professional artist, used to say to me: "Look at the top of that tree, Frank. That is the highest point on the earth at that spot." By this she meant, there are many higher places like the summit of Mt. Everest, but for this place and this time, that is the highest spot. For me, East Africa 1961-64 was a tree top, one summit of my life, certainly then and there, but really as high as any I might achieve later in different ways.

As a young Chicagoan just out of college with a freshly minted bachelor of science in biology from Beloit College and a couple of months' cultural training at Columbia University, which had the USAID contract to administer the US part of the TEA program, I was in a high state of excitement and anticipation to start my three-year overseas altruistic, idealistic adventure. So after a month or to cultural orientation to East Africa at Teachers College, Columbia University it was time to go to East Africa to start teaching secondary school in our subject area.

Lucky for me and the other one-third of the TEA participants, our group was composed of untrained, not to mention inexperienced teachers, folks like me who had no previous plans to become teachers. For us there was to be an initial academic year of teacher training at Makerere University College in Kampala Uganda! What a gorgeous year that was, so much so that some of us nearly forgot why we came to East Africa in the first place.

The swirl of sights, sounds, and smells of Africa set my head spinning like an early NASA orbiting spacecraft spitting out telemetry faster than it was designed for. I could not take it all in, but what I could was a joy. Inevitable inconveniences were the basis for anecdotes to tell in outgoing letters and slide presentations to underline the most apparent differences between there and back home...developing versus developed, but like any liberal pointing out, sometimes rather gratuitously, the underlining goodness and common human qualities I encountered there.

The day of assignment to our schools came. I got Bwiru Boys' Secondary School, a residential school for boys next door to a residential school for girls about four miles east of Mwanza, the second largest city in Tanzania.

On my trip to my posting, Bwiru Boys' Secondary School, in Mwanza Tanganyika (now Tanzania), my "new" used English Ford broke down in the middle of nowhere about halfway between Kampala and Mwanza. As night fell, a young couple with a small child let me stay in their home and fed me.

My hunger was such at that point that I had little trouble eating the sort of mélange of fish or meat sauce on *ugali* or perhaps rice. Whatever it was, I was grateful. It was an early highlight of my of my African experience which was an early highlight of my life. I even appreciated the smoke that filled the single room of the hut to keep out the flying insects.

Although the young couple spoke maybe Swahili, or maybe a tribal language (my 500-word Swahili vocabulary did not match up to what they were saying), we all kept talking, me in English which they knew not, and they in theirs which I knew not.

I left the next morning and some passing South African mining company employees took pity on me and my broken Ford, hauling both of us to their camp and fixing everything, for which I was very grateful. But it was the young couple and their little kid that stick forever in my mind.

On another road occasion at about 2:00 a.m. one morning I found that, to my utter surprise, a young Tanzanian baby boy was born at the moment I hit a big pothole transporting her, her mom, and her aunt on the way to the Mwanza Hospital four miles away. You see, I was marking papers late one night when two local women holding up a slightly bent over younger woman wearing her traditional loose, flowing gown knocked on my door and asked if I could drive her to the hospital. I thought I recognized the Swahili word for sick person.

So this young biology teacher learned some biology in the wee hours of that morning. Did I ever! And the lesson continued, owing to her water breaking in my car and the prevalence of hyenas around the school. We were visited nightly by howling hyenas for a couple of weeks despite my best efforts to clean the car. I still do a very good impression of a hyena howl. Ask me the next time we meet.

I taught biology (which was my major in college) and physics and chemistry (which, despite a few courses, were not my majors). Mr. Ven Mtabi was our first African headmaster at Bwiru, and was a brilliant, fair, and kind man.

There were the Tanzanians and other East Africans whom I met during my three-year stint first in Uganda then Tanzania. Kihago was an artist. He gave me several of his paintings and drawings, which still adorn the walls in my house.

Herman Lupogo, whom I met as a student in the School of Education of Makerere University in 1961, went on to become a general in the Tanzanian army and helped restore order in Uganda during their dark days of Idi Amin.

A.C. Juma, my best friend at Makerere, took me to visit his village in Taveta, Kenya. I remember vividly he was the first African guy who took my hand as we walked across campus. He might have wondered why my hand was sweating. I was initially worried that some American or Brit would see us. It was a marvelous lesson on how many behaviors are culturally based, not naturally as I had earlier thought. I knew some of this stuff intellectually, but not in practice, which was another lesson about the way and the depth of learning.

Sam Kishosha, the former a fellow teacher at Bwiru Boys School and later my guest in the USA when he was assigned some post at the UN Tanzanian delegation.

Rommel Mauma, was one of my many, many excellent, bright, and happy pupils. Rommel later moved to New York and published a book on his formative years. I was lucky to meet him once in New York City. I think he still lives in New Jersey.

Bruce Levin, my wonderful friend and roomie and fellow teacher at Bwiru, possessed a dry wit upon which I thrived from day to day. It sustained me like once when we had to vacate our house for a few days when the safari ants took over. My efforts to fight them were not working. Bruce's more calm approach was the answer.

Finally, I remember John Manuell, a young teacher from England and the kindest, most wonderful, generous man, a better man than I, to be sure. We shared a staff cottage together there at Bwiru for a time. I have visited him and his wife south of London. He is still doing many good works.

I was indeed blest. □

Journey in My Ford Anglia to Visit Maasai Well
Peter Moock

My three years in East Africa were more meaningful and memorable than any comparable period before or since. This is a story from my two years as a teacher of English and mathematics at the Moshi Secondary Technical School (erstwhile known as the Moshi Trade School) at the foot of Mt. Kilimanjaro, 1964 to 1966.

My Tanzania story is about twenty-four hours spent with three other expat teachers: Brad Nystrom, who taught with me at the Technical School, and who succumbed last year to pancreatic cancer; a Brit from Lancashire who taught in Arusha and whose name I cannot remember; and Ted Essebaggers (who was teaching in a different secondary school in Moshi) or Graham Till (a British contract teacher [not TEA] who overlapped with, and then replaced me at "Moshi Tech"). A few years later, Ted and Graham officiated in the New York City wedding of Peter Moock and Joyce Lewinger. I've written to all the principals to find accuracy on this story but they, like me, never wrote back.

The four of us set off early one morning in my second-hand, English Ford Anglia (circa 1958) to look for a Maasai well that we'd heard about that was to the south of, and far off the main road between

Moshi and Arusha. After several false starts, and asking directions in our broken Kiswahili, we arrived finally at the well. A dozen or so Maasai *morani* were using long ropes to haul water up in wooden buckets from the deep, hand-dug well and using it to water their cattle. Magnificent sight!

On our way home, we picked up an "elderly" (she was probably in her forties) Maasai woman, hitch-hiker, carrying a number of liquid-filled gourds. We took her several miles in the direction that she had been walking, until she signaled she wanted to get out. She said little, but she gripped tightly the back of the driver's neck (my neck) with one hand the entire time she was in the car. After that, as the afternoon grew late, we became increasingly lost. The "road" had completely disappeared, and we were driving cross-country in what we hoped was the general direction of the main road.

At one point, we came to a swollen stream. It was too late and the petrol gauge was reading too low for us to think about turning around and retracing the route. I gunned the car to get through the stream which left the floorboards and seats pretty wet, but the old Anglia never gave up! Darkness fell soon afterwards, and we were forced to sleep overnight in the car—four wet guys in a cramped sedan. Pretty uncomfortable digs.

The Brit went out during the night for a pee. It was a dark, moonless night, and he couldn't find his way back to the car. He had to do bigger and bigger circles until he finally bumped into us. This was a bit dicey, as we had been hearing lions grunting all around us earlier in the evening. The other three in the car enjoyed the extra space and slept through it all, never quite noticing that the Brit was missing. We found him in the morning sleeping peacefully behind the car.

In the morning, we drove north until, at last, we could see the main Moshi-Arusha road off in the distance. Unfortunately, between us and the road were the raised tracks of the narrow-gauge railway that used to run between Moshi and Arusha. We drove parallel to this berm for some distance until we finally came to a spot where the engineers had built a tunnel under the tracks. This enabled us to get to the other side of the berm and eventually onto the paved road that we had left the previous morning. We limped back to Moshi Tech. Exhausted and very hungry. But triumphant!

The Anglia's petrol gauge hovered just above empty. ☐

Scenes from a Tropical Hiatus

Eva Murray-Scelzo

Teachers for East Africa associates bonding for the next three years, gathered to view coverage of the March on Washington in 1963 and to speculate on our roles. A watchman greeted us—typical students, loud, and boisterous about some issue—with a scowl and a sarcastic, "Humph, high IQ." That affectionate moniker came in handy for the next overachiever, but off we went to accept the challenge placed before us: "ask not…"

He was gone, the author and anchor of "Ask not…" had been taken. Our hosts were gracious. "We are sorry," they said. Bells tolled, there were memorial services; a distant, hollow, singular drumbeat echoed through the night. Perhaps the messenger would return to admit that he had mistakenly got it all wrong. Scotsman Ian McGregor read Robert Frost's "Out, Out": "And they, since they were not the one dead, turned to their affairs." He played his bagpipe, and the lecture continued.

I was assigned to Gayaza, about twelve miles northeast of Kampala, a girls' boarding school established by Church of England missionaries in 1905, completely self-sufficient with its own dairy farm and agricultural fields, and now in transition toward government directives. Resilient and stalwart, the missionaries had endured air raids and so administered this academic microcosm with precision, economy, and flair. Paper had two sides and a full sheet was not to be distributed toward the end of an exam. To end class sessions, traditional drums replaced a siren, too reminiscent of approaching bombers. Little did I know that my yellow rose bushes would require so much care, like mulch, spray, and trimming. Perhaps they are still in bloom.

Rather than referee five a.m. hockey games, I unpacked and catalogued stacks of volumes in the new library built, stocked, and donated through philanthropic gifts. In keeping with tradition, the library dedication entailed pomp and ceremony, visiting dignitaries, an art exhibition, and spectacular traditional dances from every region of the country.

A resident crested crane, Uganda's protected symbol, had been rescued and nurtured at the school. On opening day, the crane perched itself atop the library building for a prime view and once the drumming and dancing had begun, it suddenly swooped down and gracefully performed its mating ritual amid tiny child dancers who were dressed to resemble its flock. More timely drama could not have been staged. I understood the bird's psyche when the girls robed me in national dress to meet Kimon, one of their elders. I sat at his feet, according to custom, while he outlined my face and was translated to have said, "She looks like one of our children who has come home."

That memory will not go away. □

My Greatest Gift

Jack Paarlberg

Isabel and I brought over ourselves and five children, which according to East African standards is a very large family for an American but not that large for an African. I replaced Neil Albright at Bishop Willis Teacher Training College (TTC) in Iganga, Uganda.

Our son, Bill, attended Nairobi School for boys, a place like a reformatory school. He was fifteen and hated it, transferring to the local secondary school by the second year. Jennifer, age thirteen, picked up Swahili during our eight weeks at Teachers College and had no trouble learning the local vernacular. She loved her two years at the local secondary school. Our twins, Jaan and John, age ten, attended Kaptagat in the "highlands" of Kenya. They often referred to their internment as "a prison overlooking the Riff Valley," but she and he survived with no more than a few run-ins with the headmaster, Mr. Chitty, who was often referred to, not so lovingly, as "Mr. Chitty Chitty Bang Bang."

Our three-year-old, Nicholas, stayed with us in the campus compound. I had thought he would maintain a low profile until the following happened: I was elucidating the quadratic formula when, out of the corner of my eye, I spotted young Nicholas trotting across the campus compound toward the sound of my voice: no windows or doors—after all, it's Africa. He climbed up the entryway into my classroom whereupon the entire twenty-three-male student body stood up and spoke in unison, "Good morning, Master Nicholas."

I stood there dumbfounded while Nicholas found an empty chair and desk in the front row, climbed up on it, and sat. I continued to complete the derivation of the formula, but before I could end it, Nicholas had heard the frantic calls of his mother in the distance and climbed off the chair, and was out the door, running toward his mother's voice, hoping he wouldn't get a not so friendly swat on his behind. Once again they all stood up, said "Good bye," and one astute student wished Nicholas a safe journey. After a short pause, I suggested we break for tea a bit early. All of us exited with small sly smiles on our faces.

Every time my family and I get together to talk about our experiences in East Africa, the children say "Dad, it's the greatest gift you ever gave us." The greatest I ever gave myself too. With a wife and five children, I suspect I had one of the largest families to go over. My daughter attended the local secondary school, one *mzungu* among 700 Africans, and she can still speak Swahili after all these years. ☐

Uganda Voluntary Work Camps

Kate Parry

In my second term at Makerere, one of my fellow TEAs found out about the Uganda Voluntary Work Camps Association. He persuaded me and two of our East African classmates to join, and took us all off to a work camp at a place called Kashongi. President Museveni comes from there, so it has doubtless changed completely by now, but then it was a small village in open cattle country with a single shop that sold sodas and a primary school for which we were to build a latrine. We slept on mattresses in the primary school classrooms, which as yet had no furniture.

The first camp activity was to select camp officials. One of my Makerere friends became camp leader, and for some reason they chose me to be chief cook. It was a mistake—the first thing I did was burn the *matoke*, and all my efforts to keep everyone supplied with boiled water for drinking failed; we were reduced to drinking water from the borehole, which was clean, but salty, and had to be fetched from half a mile away, or else drink Mirinda, which we bought from the shop, and which I've never been able to drink again.

We finished digging our latrine pit and covering it, but didn't have time to put up walls around it; there was much laughter about how anyone using the latrine could be seen by anybody. There was laughter about a lot of other things as well, and everyone enjoyed the music we played on a portable record-player and the dance that always took place after supper. For us *wazungu*, it was a wonderful introduction to rural African life, and for everyone it was a rare bringing together of the worlds of the school and the village.

So when I got to my posting at Kigezi High School in Kabale, I initiated a Work Camps Club there and took a bunch of students to a work camp two or three times a term. The camps were immensely popular, and students kept coming to me with ideas of classrooms that we might build or roads that we might dig. We took our volunteers from the three secondary schools in Kabale, and they always got on well, despite the schools being bitter rivals, and the schools gave us the food that the students would otherwise have eaten in school.

The Kigezi High School lorry took us to our camp site, except when we were working, as we often did, on Bwama Island in Lake Bunyonyi, in which case we used the boat that belonged to the rehabilitation center which was on the island and for which we were working. The rehabilitation center was for disabled people, and a visit of twenty able-bodied school students was always welcome. We built a fishpond for them, and a road, and I've lost count of how many primary school classrooms we built in other places.

I learnt a lot about mud-and-wattle architecture (slapping mud onto a wall is immensely satisfying) and also about the students and the kind of music and dancing that they enjoyed. I believe the students learnt too, about one another, about their several schools, and, I hope, about how they, as educated people, could contribute to their villages' development.

☐

Why Africa is Always on My Mind
George Pollock

Recently in line at the Greendale YMCA in Worcester, Massachusetts, where I play tennis, I noticed a new guy behind the counter. He was black and he had an accent that I immediately recognized. When my turn came, with a big smile on my face, I said, "*Habari.*" His mouth flew open. His eyes looked like they were going to pop out of his head. Then came a huge smile, and I mean *huge*.

"*Mzuri, mzuri sana,*" he replied in Swahili.

"*Asante,*" I said. "*Asante Sana.*"

Since this is America and not Africa, I then reverted to English. "I used to teach in Kisumu, Kenya. Nice to meet you."

"Wow, I was born and raised in Kenya."

I told him that I had taught in Kisumu for two years. I also told him that my oldest son, Gregory, was born in Kenya in 1964, making him a dual citizen of Kenya and the United States.

"I would say we have a lot to talk about, right?"

Mouth open, wide-eyed, he nodded his head. We shook hands, exchanged names, and email addresses, and he agreed to arrange a time for me to hear his story. Here's mine:

Immediately after graduate school, I was accepted into the TEEA. Soon after, Phyllis and I went off to Kenya as newlyweds. Fresh from college and with an intrepid new bride, I was going to save the world. I would do good. I would spread civilization. I would make friends for America. I was young and naive and I didn't know any better.

We spent two years in Kenya. It was the greatest learning experience of my life. First, I saw real poverty. Everywhere I went I saw children naked, walking with bare feet, often with distended bellies, a sign of malnutrition. Just outside of Kenya's capital, Nairobi, were perhaps a million black African souls existing in Africa's largest slum, Kibera. It was a mass of shanties without electricity, running water, sewage, and health care. Life here was short and brutal.

But, newly freed from decades of British colonial rule, Kenyans throughout the country were celebrating independence by singing and dancing in the streets. It was a happy, optimistic time for Kenyans with their own new government under Jomo Kenyatta or the "*Mzee.*" Several times I was at packed Kenyatta rallies where he stood tall in his multicolored beaded cap, fly whisk in hand, and evoked roars of "*Harambee*" and "*Uhuru na Kazi.*"

Sometimes I was one of just a few *mzungus*, but I felt perfectly safe. In Kenya, America and Americans were deeply respected. I felt it everywhere. For example, in 1963 I was in a little village, the only American there, getting my VW serviced when news broke of President Kennedy's assassination. One Kenyan after another came up to me to express their sorrow. Each one extended an open hand, bowed, expressed their sorrow and slowly backed away. Here I was, me, representing the United States of America!

Despite widespread poverty and homelessness, Kenya was rapidly becoming an important regional and transportation hub as its tourist industry began growing in leaps and bounds. Kenya would soon become East Africa's biggest economy and an island of calm, avoiding bloody conflicts that ravished Sudan, Rwanda, Somalia, and Uganda.

And what a teaching experience! I have never seen such eager students. You walk into the classroom and the whole class jumps to its feet. Morning, Sir!" they shout in unison. Then they sit. All eyes are on the *mzungu mwalimu*. With notebooks open and pencils at ready, they are ready and eager to learn. And you had better teach them so they can pass the overseas exam from England, or else.

I'll never forget the time I was telling a story about life in America. A student in the back row, very tall and older than the others, jumped to his feet. "Sir!" he all but shouted. "What you are telling us is not in the syllabus!" He sat down with pencil at ready to take notes.

"Quite right," I said in my best faux British accent. "So sorry. Yes, I'll get on with it. Thank you."

I never again strayed from the syllabus. □

Getting Posted to the Right School

Joel Reuben

When I was selected along with eighteen other TEEA members in 1966, I had six years of classroom experience in the intermediate grades on Long Island. I received my master's in secondary education to go along with my bachelor's degree in elementary education.

I was the youngest of the tutors in that group, and a father of a two-year-old and a three-year-old. My wife Eva was able to work for three semesters on local terms, replacing staff members on leave.

We were one of the two tutors placed in Kenya and the rest of the group split between Uganda and Tanzania. Our posting was to Chadwick TTC in Butere, about thirty miles northwest of Kisumu. Chadwick was a school run by a British ex-patriot couple whom the Kenya Minister of Education, Clement Obare, had been looking to move out to make way for Africanization.

The first TEEA wave in 1964 had brought an African-American tutor to Chadwick. She was a divorced former principal from Chicago who probably was looked at negatively by the ultra-religious Anglican couple who ran the school. I replaced her, a Jewish New Yorker, to their dismay. I made out well with them by working hard, above and beyond the other staff members. They gave us a house with limited electricity and no water heater. My family persevered with the conditions, although I got deathly ill with some kind of dysentery which was quite unpleasant.

Along about late October, a TEEA member from the first group (1964) heard about us and came to visit us from Eregi TTC in Maragoli. He was a Lebanese-American from Michigan who became our great friend. Eregi was the TTC that Minister Obare trained at, and he had great respect for the Xaverian Brothers who ran the school. Whereas Chadwick was to be phased out, Eregi was to be expanded.

Our new friend talked to the principal of Eregi about us, and they agreed to transfer us to Eregi. I was told to write the minister and tell him that my children were living in harsh conditions that aggravated their allergies. It actually was a setup and the head of Chadwick was informed that I was to report to Eregi.

The rest of our two years were spent at Eregi where our living conditions were fine. The Sisters of Notre Dame were added to the staff, and a small convent was built for them. My kids were very popular with the nuns, and my wife wound up going shopping with them for furnishings and clothes. The school doubled in students as we became coed, and I wound up supervising student teachers, helping administer KPE tests, spreading the word on teaching the NPA (New Primary Approach), and running in-service courses for teachers during semester breaks.

It was a fantastic experience for the Reuben family, and we made many dear friends as a result of our tour. We were invited to re-up for 1968 but our kids were now ready for school, and I wanted to begin my doctoral studies. Also, I had a two-year leave of absence from my school district on Long Island and felt I owed it to them to return. Looking back over the fifty years since, it was one of the best experiences in my life. □

Three Hundred TEA Words

Lloyd Sherman

TEA was a God whisper: an unexplained event of goodness, an offering reaching to the ground being, unrequested and totally unexpected, a palette to create a context for being alive. So it was and is that TEA began the composition of a still unfinished symphony.

To this child whose love of adventure ranged from the cowboys of the wild west to the Osa and Johnson adventure in the jungles of New Guinea, to the stories of Bomba the jungle boy and Tarzan, Jane, and Boy, my God whisper came when I glanced across Professor Henssler's desk where I was discussing my final paper for his course on Africa and spotted the New York Times advertisement for Teachers for East Africa.

Following the conference, I asked to see the ad. I took down the particulars. It was March of 1962, two months before I was to graduate from Wagner College. I learned right away that the TEA application period was closed, but they were still looking for science teachers. In that circumstance, in a two-week turnaround, I was interviewed and received a telegram from Ken Toepfer offering me a place in TEA's Wave 2B. The decision to accept the three-year assignment was filled with consternation. Consultation with my valued professors and the love of my life at the time, who was heading to graduate school, all agreed that the assignment was an exceptional opportunity and that things would work out, as they have beyond expectation. Marriage and family would be the fortune of another love.

My journey in East Africa was filled with highlights from a broad spectrum of acquaintances and friendships:

Time with Ted Rice (spending an amazing evening singing with Pete Seeger whose family was staying in his Nairobi apartment for two weeks) and Winfield Niblo, and Bill Wild, all of USAID.

Travels with Lee Smith, Adawale Sengawawa, and Tom Cameron in the Congo, Rwanda, and Burundi.

Trips to Mombasa and Zanzibar with Arden Holland.

Motorcycling to and then climbing Mt. Kilimanjaro in the company of Don Schramm, and climbing Mt. Kenya with Phyllis Reed.

Good times with Don and Maureen Knies and Gray Cowan at Lake Turkana.

Being present at the historic events of Uganda and Kenya's independence; working with teachers at Makerere's Institute of Education, especially with Elsa Meder, who made me drill down to the why I was teaching whatever it was that I was teaching, its meaning and purpose.

Using what I had learned, first, with a host of students from 1963 to 1965 at Narok Secondary School in Kenya's Maasiland, and, later, with the general public, working with Mervin Cowie, founder of the Kenya National Parks, and his successor, Perez Olindo, and Russell E. Train, founder of the African Wildlife Foundation, as the education warden setting up the first Wild Life Education Center in Kenya at the Nairobi National Park.

These experiences were the grist for a life seeking the answers to fundamental questions about the conditions that made a difference in learning which have energized my professional life ever since. My life there was particularly enriched by a deep and lifelong friendship with Gloria and Gordon Hagberg, of the field office of the International Institute of Education.

It was their friendship that exposed me to their acquaintances and many of their personal friends that included Tom Mboya, Mwai

Kibaki, Hilary Ng'weno, and Barak Obama, Senior. A lasting memory was sitting with Mel McCaw, Gordon Hagberg's close assistant, at the Equator Club in Nairobi, on the eve of Kenya's Independence around a small table in a darkened corner having drinks and listening to conversations on the coming event there in the company of Kenneth Kaunda, President of Zambia, Harry Belafonte, and Harris Wafford, Peace Corps Director for Africa, being served by the beautiful Seychelles singer and waitress, Gigi Joseph, with whom I had become acquainted. I was twenty-seven years old, thankful for that God whisper.

> For more about Gordon Hagberg, see "Cold warrior for racial equality" in *The East African*, online at: http://bit.ly/ghagberg. □

TEA Changed My Life
Harold Scheub

It is not an overstatement to say that Teachers for East Africa changed my life, in many, many ways. I had been in the Air Force for four years and had never gotten to travel as much as I would have liked. So, after I got my bachelor's and master's degrees at the University of Michigan, I decided to take a break before working on my PhD.

I had heard about TEA, a two-year teaching project that would involve teaching in a high school in East Africa a year before independence and a year after, and I leapt at the opportunity. I had always been fascinated by the continent of Africa but never thought that it would become such an integral part of my life.

Before we left the US, in June of 1961, at Columbia, a lecture by the Reverend James Robinson, director of Operations Crossroads, told us to do our homework, to know the country we were visiting and its policies. On July 12, 1961, the night before we were to leave New York, I wrote:

> "My last night in New York, and I find myself filled with the inevitable mixed emotions about the flight to Africa which begins tomorrow night at 9:00... This is really what I have wanted to do for a very long time, and it's almost impossible that it should be happening right now, to me! I can't express the feeling of anticipation and excitement I am feeling tonight. It's a new world and a rich new experience, it's the realization of a dream, and I must admit it, it still seems like a dream."

I remember a young Julius Nyerere at the air terminal in New York just before we took off for Africa. On July 12, 1961, I wrote, "Prime Minister Nyerere of Tanganyika told us tonight, we must actually be there to know what it's like."

And there was a telegram from President Kennedy on July 12, 1961:

> "I wish to extend to each of you my congratulations on your selection to participate in this precedent-setting project to supply American secondary teachers for East Africa."

Uganda altered me utterly. I could hear and feel the stereotypes breaking day after day, as I came to know the people of Bunyoro and my students at Masindi Senior Secondary School. The country was magnificent, the people were warm and friendly, the students eager to learn. There were three teachers at Masindi when I arrived there. I taught things I would never have dreamed of teaching, along with English. I was the soccer coach, and the students had to teach me the game.

Along with my love of the classroom, I moved about a lot in Uganda...to Karamoja, to the rain forest, the Ruwenzori Mountains, to Murchison Falls and Lake Albert, to Arua and Soroti.

I loved my teaching experience. The students were splendid, eager learners. With the help of various people and groups in the United States, I was able to build a library at the school. And we engaged in various projects, including drama. I remember directing *Macbeth*, in April, 1963:

> "Macbeth came off very well; we really had a wonderful time with it, and the introduction of Shakespeare into the kingdom of Bunyoro was totally successful. We had quite an audience

of dignitaries the last night of the play, including the Katikiro of Bunyoro (sort of the prime minister of the kingdom) and the district commissioner of Bunyoro. All were mightily impressed and thirty of our boys have become inveterate hams like their teacher!"

I remember going to Mbarara to mark Junior Secondary School Leaving Examinations, accompanying the school soccer and hockey teams to Gulu on April 13, 1962. And I recall seeing the Nile River for the first time, in October, 1961, at Karuma Falls.

It was a busy time, but there were brief reminders from the United States: listening in 1961 to the Michigan–Army game on the Armed Forces network until it was drowned out by static, in late October, 1962; listening to the BBC reports on the Cuban missile crisis; a telegram that I received from a friend in Ann Arbor whose wife just had a baby: "It's a boy. Send impala!"

I remember when independence came to Uganda. On October 9, 1962, I went to Hoima with another teacher and with twenty boys from Masindi Senior SS for independence day celebrations, joining about 5,000 people there. There were traditional dances, soccer matches, the Declaration of Independence was read, and the school girls sang the National Anthem:

> "Oh Uganda, thy people praise thee,
> We lay our future in thy hand,
> United, free
> For liberty,
> Together we'll always stand."

At midnight, the British Union Jack was lowered, and the six red, yellow, and black stripes of Uganda's new flag went up. A bonfire was lit nearby and on the top of a small mountain in the distance, and there were fireworks. I remember the apprehension of Asians in the area as independence came. A mvule tree was planted by Mr. Kaduyu, the new district commissioner. The headmaster gave a speech about the meaning of freedom. Mugisa in S–2 told the boys that they should not go into politics just to become rich, but that greater humanitarian concerns should trigger this decision.

In a letter on March 26, 1963, I wrote:

> "...the time has gone by much too rapidly, and, as wretched as some of the British have been in Masindi, I have no regrets. This has been, in many ways, the most interesting and exciting thing I've done yet. The people of Bunyoro and the boys at school have made themselves so much a part of me that I'll hate to leave."

The students were generous when, after two years, I returned to the United States. In the school paper, "Masindi," Vol. III, No. 4 (1 August 1963), on page three, a student, C. K. Mugisa, wrote,

> "Two years ago we welcomed Mr. Scheub to this school as our first American teacher. It was wonderful to see how quickly he got used to us and we to him... It is not only the fact that Mr. Scheub is a university lecturer and not a secondary school master that has made his teaching at Masindi School so effective, but it is also because he is a born teacher with almost incomparable talents and the energy that he puts in. At the present moment, Masindi School is one of the few schools in Uganda which are well off in both spoken and written English. This fact is true mainly because of Mr. Scheub's valuable work."

This meant much to me.

While in Uganda, I learned how deeply rich the oral tradition was, heard stories and histories, and something began to form, quickly, in my mind. Because my interests as a university student were the oral traditions of the English people, I decided that when I would return to the United States I would change my major to African Languages and Literature. That brought me to the University of Wisconsin-Madison, which had the only degree-granting Department of African Languages and Literature in the United States. While there, I studied with and fell under the influence of one of Africa's greatest writers, Professor A. C. Jordan, author of the Xhosa masterpiece, *Ingqumbo Yeminyanya*. He taught me the Xhosa language, and got me interested in doing research in southern Africa.

I had initially hoped to return to Uganda, but the struggle between Milton Obote and Idi Amin made that impossible. I was not keen to conduct research into the oral traditions of South Africa, because apartheid was then at its zenith. But Professor Jordan, himself a political exile from South Africa, insisted that I do so, arguing that I could never teach courses about apartheid and South African oral traditions if I did not go there.

In the event, it was the best thing I could have done. I crisscrossed the country, collecting some 9,000 pieces of oral story, epic, history, and poetry among the Xhosa, the Zulu, Swati, and, in the southern part of Zimbabwe, among the Ndebele.

I have spent ten years in Africa, two in Uganda, the other eight in southern Africa. During four of those years, a year each time, I walked up and down the southeastern coast of the continent, fifteen hundred miles during each of those wonderful years, never using a car, working without translators and interpreters.

After Xhosa, I mastered Zulu, Swati, and Ndebele languages, and would work in eight South African languages over the years. Among the storytellers I met was the magnificent Xhosa performer, Nongenile Masithathu Zenani, a woman who was to become the closest friend I have ever had. □

Two Remarkable Flights

Harold Scheub

I was a jet mechanic in the United States Air Force from 1951 until 1955. Inevitably, there would be adventure caused by air travel. On July 17, 1961, the Uganda Argus wrote,

> "A super constellation of Capitol Airlines, of New York, started her long flight from New York's La Guardia airfield and flew direct to Santa Maria airfield near Lisbon, a single hop of nearly 4,000 miles. She took off for Kano, where, as the pilot brought the aircraft in to land, one of the port tyres burst."

We arrived in Kano at three in the morning of July 16, 1961: the airline had to fly the tire in from Portugal. We were granted permission to go to the "old city" of Kano where we saw the mosque and were given permission, after some discussion, by "the master," a very old man colorfully dressed who reclined under a tree in front of the big, green-domed structure, to ascend one of the two high towers of the mosque. We went to the *caswa*, the market place, and I remember the dye pits.

And then, there was Cuba. January, 1971, he has a bomb in his briefcase. The young man boards the Northwest Airlines 727 plane in Milwaukee. I am flying to Detroit to visit friends in Ann Arbor. And he sits on the floor just in front of the door leading to the cockpit. The plane is packed, a lot of children, along with business people, tourists, others hurrying to get somewhere. He sits there, staring down the aisle at the rest of us; we are perplexed, nervous. What is he doing there in front of the pilot's door, anyway? He holds the briefcase tightly to his side.

Then, as we near Detroit, the pilot speaks on the intercom: the man is a hijacker, he wants to commandeer the plane and fly to Algeria. The pilot has talked him out of that, telling him that a crowded 727 airplane will not make it to Algeria.

So we are going to Cuba. The plane lands in Detroit, taxies to a remote part of the air terminal where we refuel within a vortex composed of what seem to be hundreds of flashing red lights, police everywhere. No one is allowed to get off the plane. Everyone, including children, are hostages.

At last, we are again airborne, and the interior of the plane is utterly, eerily, silent. The young man stands like a statue with his bomb, the people staring not at him, just staring...quiet. The plane lands at Jose Marti air terminal in Havana, and men dressed in Castro-type army fatigues board the plane and escort the hijacker off. Then the 727 taxies to the air terminal, we deplane, Swiss television is there filming us as we stream into the air terminal to have something to eat, and to learn what is to happen next.

We are there for thirteen agonizing hours, are told that Fidel Castro himself will make the decision as to our fate. Finally, unexpectedly, improbably, we are granted permission to depart, and, after the plane is refueled, we are flown to Miami—where we are met by FBI agents who immediately take from us all the Cuban cigars and rum that we have purchased in Cuba. ☐

Learning from Future Teachers
Reed Stewart

Working at Kenyatta Teacher Training College taught me quite a bit, even after teaching in Liberia for eight years. One of my students very politely rebuked me for not realizing how much knowledge I took for granted on the students' part, leaving them to try to catch up with where I thought I was teaching. Perhaps my own teaching was somewhat improved as a result.

Another benefit of working with those Kenyan students and with the schools and communities where our aspiring teachers were placed for internships was finding the strength of those villages and the many ways in which that strength was similar to village and family life in Liberia. Of course, there were language differences and fascinating variations in the way youngsters were taken through adolescence.

Still, the importance of the extended family and the fundamental guiding role of women, subliminal though they often were, showed up in many ways in the ideas and attitudes of the prospective secondary school teachers:

"How should a particular topic be presented? What's the future of clitoridectomy in Kenya? How should housing be arranged at the practice teaching locales?"

These were advanced students, probably ahead of most other citizens in looking at the future of their country and doing lots of discussion on both serious and trivial topics. It was fun to be working with those students. I learned from them.

Of course, the countryside was wonderful: rift valleys, ranges of hills, near-by giraffe, beautiful storms and clouds, and Mt. Kenya to climb, at least most of the way up. Luckily for me, one of the young men got altitude sickness so that I "had" to stay at a lower camp with him and didn't have to show that I probably couldn't have made it much farther myself.

But what a view over the cloud forest and the plains beyond! □

Kenya Nostalgia

Ron Stockton

When Jane and I get nostalgic for those years in Kenya, these are some things we remember:

Putting our hands on the windscreen as another car approaches to prevent the glass from shattering if it gets hit with a rock.

Sitting in silence as rain pounds onto the tin roof since there is nothing else you can do.

Having students stand at attention when we come into the room. (And they were never late for class). Something I do not miss is the time I glared at a student for failing to stand up, only to realize he had a broken leg and could not rise without help.

The unspoken fear as you drive that you will hit one of the women walking along the road with her basket of food or large stack of kindling on her back.

Using words like *fundi, n'gombe,* and Kikuyu grass and having everyone know what you mean.

Listening to Dick Estelle read books out of East Lansing, my home campus. And listening to Book at Bedtime, from the BBC in London. And hoping you can stay awake until 10:30 p.m. when these book readings end.

Listening to Kujifunza Kiswahili with the ever-encouraging Walter Mbotella (and his ever-so-proper Mombasa version of that language).

Listening to Big Ben ring at noon on BBC News and knowing you were not completely separated from the rest of the world.

Listening (not very often) to Simplified English stories on the Voice of America.

Having all of our American friends over to listen to an early-morning breakfast featuring round-by-round summaries of the Mohammed Ali comeback fight with Joe Frasier.

The smell of sweat and charcoal mixed together.

Listening to singing commercials on Voice of Kenya radio. My favorite was, "Gilby's Gin is good for you, so don't say gin, say Gilby's." This would be prohibited in the US because it was false advertising, but who cares.

British prep school terms such as head boy, old boy, school cert, Cambridge examination, first form, fifth form, prefect, headmaster.

In pineapple season, trying to get an extra pineapple for a shilling from the young boy vendor on the roadside, hoping to unload them before they rotted. (Only later did I read Orwell's short story about an Englishman making a hard bargain with a poor child trying to sell a trinket. Somehow my story of getting an extra pineapple did not seem quite as victorious as it did at the time after reading that.)

Watching the monsoons come right on schedule over the Iveti Hills.

Getting purple sunsets at exactly 6:00 every night. It helped me understand why in Swahili referring to 8:00 as *saa mbili* made sense.

Using local sugar crystals (much cheaper than granulated sugar).

Street vendors selling roasted corn cobs.

Using retread tires, which were so much cheaper than new ones. Also seeing strips of tires on the side of the road and wondering if it was a false economy.

Greeting the "*kuku* man" who came around to sell chickens. He would ask which one I wanted, and I would always take the one that was fighting the most, assuming that it was very healthy. Since I remembered plucking chickens as a boy and what an elaborate process it was, involving boiling water, burned fingers, the intricate removal of feathers, and singing away hair with burning newspaper, I could never figure out how he plucked them to perfection on site in minutes.

The feel and smell of sharp, clear, crisp high-altitude morning air. It's like sex. If someone hasn't experienced it, you can't explain it to them.

Being in Mombasa where a street vendor will take a coconut in his hands and hack an opening with his *panga*. You could then drink the coconut water, which is a unique experience, refreshing beyond words.

Saying to a friend in the US embassy, "Did you hear that the St. Louis Cardinals won the World Series?" and having him reply, "I did. Did you hear that Khrushchev was overthrown?"

Having mulberries delivered to our back door by a traveling salesman. We never figured out where those things were grown, since we never even once saw a mulberry tree.

Discovering decades later what I wrote in my journal at the time: "There is nothing as black as an African night." True, true. □

Memories

George Urch

I split my time in Kenya between acting as a geography tutor at Kenyatta Teacher Training College and acting as coach of Kenya's national basketball team.

At first we fielded a few Peace Corps volunteers and Kenyans learning the game who could run up and down the court better than the Americans, but lamentably couldn't put the ball in the basket as well as the Americans. I think we even played a team from Uganda made up of a few Americans from TEA, including an erratically shooting guard named Goddard.

My wife Dorothy (now deceased) and our two children absolutely loved those years in Kenya. I have a couple of memories that come back once in a while:

> The first day of classes when I realized I had the responsibility to make a difference in the lives of my students.
>
> A quiet morning in Tanzania watching the snowfall on Kilimanjaro.

I miss "Mother Africa" and my colleagues and friends. ☐

Dukas, Dear Dukas

Jim Wallace

When in 1962 I was at Makerere, I recall a small *duka* on campus near one of the main lawn spreads. Quite beautiful then, it seemed. It must have been 1961. I was teaching in town at Old Kampala but spent leisure time on campus, so maybe it was 1962.

In any case, I walked by the *duka* on a sunny mid-afternoon and spied a student in his red undergraduate gown buying one cigarette from the surly proprietor who had two or three in his fist and waited carefully till he had his coin. It was a poignant scene, repeated for me in the classroom when one student would lever ink from his pen to that of a classmate who had just run out.

It was the power of "one," a power that never occurred to me until I went to Uganda. ☐

Culture Shock

Joel Watne

In the first wave of TEA in 1961, I found that with one exception, a guy who had spent six weeks in Ghana, I was the only person who had spent a significant amount of time on the continent. I was born in the portion of French Equatorial Africa that is now the Central African Republic, in a house with mud walls, mud floors and a grass roof. During our training at Teachers College and in London, we were introduced to the concept of "culture shock," warned about it, and given the chance to quit.

As we descended through the clouds on the approach to Entebbe, I could see the tin-roofed houses of farmers among the banana plants. My initial reaction was that Uganda seemed a lot more prosperous than my old stomping grounds in the Central African Republic. What I saw as we rode into and around Kampala, seemed pretty good to me. But one of our colleagues, who name has long been forgotten, was so shocked by his first experience in Uganda, that he quit TEA the next day and took the next available plane home.

Meanwhile, I thought how ironic it was that I, the only TEAer in the first wave to have been raised in Africa, was then assigned to Arusha, the tourist center of East Africa, where hardships were far fewer than many of the more remote places to which my colleagues were posted. There was Malde's camera shop, where one could purchase top-of-the-line Nikon cameras and lenses, and Naranjan Singh's grocery store (scene of the "baby elephant walk" in the John Wayne movie *Hatari*, which provided the name of Henry Mancini's popular tune).

These were but two of an interesting assortment of ex-pats that included a Hungarian, Dr. Saska, whose 160-pound Alsatian would greet me by putting his paws on my shoulders and looking down at me; an entomologist with East African Locust Control, who modestly described his WWII experience as a "Lancaster driver"; a botanist named David Penn, who had been a Spitfire pilot and answered my question as to whether he was related to William Penn by stating that William was the black sheep of the family; a shoemaker who proudly displayed an autographed picture of his customer John Wayne; and an Australian priest at the local Anglican church, whose Northumbrian treasurer kept talking about the "boodget."

Most important for my education assignment were the scores of colleagues and students of Hindu, Sikh, Sunni and Shiite Muslim, Goan, Parsi, and Jain backgrounds, a rich tapestry of humanity that demonstrate that despite all of the cultural and religious differences there may be, we are basically very similar and with similar needs, hopes, and dreams.

However, not all teachers were pleased. When Kenya became independent, quite a few whites of South African origin decided that they could not accept a future under African rule and headed back south. I happened to meet one, who was being assisted in his southern trip by one of our TEAers, whose name I do not recall. His experience teaching at a school in Kenya had resulted in his adopting views similar to that of the exiting Afrikaners. He described how his students liked to change their names periodically. One liked the names of electrical companies, and decided to go by Phillips General Electric Westinghouse one day, then reshuffle the order of the names on another. His solution to the problem of identifying his students was to assign them numbers, and use the numbers as a substitute for a name.

He should have gone south, too. □

II: Teaching and School Life

Not quite ready for retirement, Charlie Guthrie "wanted another in-depth experience in Africa for myself, so in 2011 I put my money where my mouth had been" and went *Back to Africa 50 Years Later* via the Peace Corps. Through the lens of this new experience Charlie re-examines his long-ago TEA days and compares the two organizations and time periods.

Many TEAers witnessed school strikes at their schools but few had heard of them before that untoward phenomenon was commented on at some point during their orientation, either in New York or East Africa. In *Sambaker School Strike*, Jerry Barr details how his attempts to establish an informal classroom style backfire early on in his time at Sir Samuel Baker Senior Secondary School in northern Uganda. What he describes is akin to what initiated a strike at Mzumbe Secondary School in 1963 where Gus Lewis taught.

On a more positive note, Emilee Cantieri's *Students on Strike*, delightful in its telling, records how she disarmed perfunctory attempts to disrupt a Wednesday morning English class at Machakos Teachers College in Kenya. For Bob Stokes, a sense of duty and some logical reasoning carried the day, *When a Student Strike Isn't [or wasn't] Really a Strike*. Emilee's story gives us a glimpse into what goes on in classes and the small and large pleasures that are available there. The same is true of Jim Blair's *Tanganyikan Tales*.

Some of those pleasures came from taking an admiring—or at least sympathetic—stance toward how people may react to some puzzling aspects of science, notably electricity and its invisible bearer, the electron, as we learn in Gene Child's *Duncan Kimamu and Electricity* and Jonne Robinson's *Electricity Too*. Another East Africa electricity story culminates in a BS in EE from Long Beach State some decades later when Gary James finds himself *Supporting a Tanzanian's US Education*.

Moses Howard's *O Levels and Me* is a story of inadvertent audacity, an account of how he, a science master at Ntare High School in Uganda, undermined the derision of students by his British colleagues who mocked student responses to British literature. Dan Callard's *Music Alone Shall Live* reminds us that a stranger in the land also has much to learn and that he may amaze his students in an extracurricular setting.

The fact that the man who worked for him knew no English made it imperative that Ed Schmidt manage a version of the new language: kitchen Swahili is what it was called although the term is not used in Ed's *Dabbling in Swahili*. Ed's account of what the dividends of that dabbling have been is the central delight of his story.

In this section:

Donald Adams	*Wonderful If Random Memories* • 133
Jay Anderson	*Papa, Martha, and Me* • 138
Jerry Barr	*Reporting to Sambaker* • 140 *Sambaker School Strike* • 141 *Hiring a Domestic Servant* • 142
Jim Blair	*Tanganyikan Tales* • 144
Dan Callard	*Music Alone Shall Live* • 145
Paul Cant	*Crossing Cultures* • 147
Emilee Cantieri	*Students on Strike* • 153
Gene Child	*Duncan Kimamu and Electricity* • 154
Pat Colby	*Recipe for Sukuma Wiki (stretch the week)* • 155
David Evans	*Practice Teaching* • 156
Pat Gill	*My English Challenge* • 157
Charles Guthrie	*Back to Africa Fifty Years Later via the Peace Corps* • 158
Henry Hamburger	*Culture Gap in Kakamega* • 168 *Math, Temba, Adongo, and Pedagogy* • 176 *Music at Kakamega* • 177 *The Cook* • 178
Ward Heneveld	*Kiangoma Track Meet* • 179 *Kiangoma and Student Fees* • 180
Sharon Hepburn	*Instant Expert at Twenty Years Old* • 183
Niall Herriott	*Boys and Their Toys* • 184 *A Sense of Proportion* • 185
Moses L. Howard	*About Positive and Negative* • 186 *O Levels and Me* • 187 *Sundowner* • 194 *My African Students* • 198
Jack Humbles	*The Cambridge Overseas Exam* • 200 *Student Teaching Practice* • 201
Dave Hummel	*Snake Story* • 203

David and Carol Imig	*TEA Memories* • *205*
Charles Irby	*Notebooks Have No Accent* • *209*
Gary James	*Supporting a Tanzanian's US Education* • *210*
Bill Jones	*A Kapsabet Gift: A Practical Dictum for Teaching* • *211*
Gus Lewis	*Strike to Study* • *212*
Ben Lindfors	*Boys in the Cast* • *213*
Judy Lindfors	*Owing to Underfeeding* • *214*
Clive Mann	*Athletics in Nandi Country* • *215* *Teaching as a Temporary Measure* • *216*
Dean McHenry	*Personal Reflections on Tanzania over a Period of Forty Years* • *218*
Larry Olds	*Teaching at Teso College* • *221*
Dale Otto	*What a Gift It Was* • *227*
Joel Reuben	*The New Primary Approach* • *228*
Jonne Robinson	*Electricity Too* • *230*
Ed Schmidt	*Dabbling in Swahili* • *231*
Harry Stein	*A Red Pen and Innocence* • *232*
Bob Stokes	*When a Student Strike Isn't Really a Strike* • *233*
Ron Stockton	*Giant Jungle Ants* • *236* *Toad in Stomach, Beetle in River* • *239*
Yvonne Theodore	*The Bees* • *240*
Joel Watne	*Diversity in Arusha* • *241*

Wonderful If Random Memories

Donald Adams

Greetings upon Arrival. After driving by Land Rover nearly 900 hundred miles south from Kampala, Uganda to my assigned school in Malangali, Tanganyika, I anticipated meeting my Headmaster and school faculty. I was to be the first American to arrive at the school from the TEA group. As it turned out, I arrived during school term break.

After parking in front of the main school building, I entered the office and observed three African staff workers working in the room with an elderly Caucasian, wearing white shirt and shorts, in an adjacent office. After I requested a meeting with the headmaster of the school, one of the staff spoke with the Caucasian, then came back to ask me to sit down and wait. Subsequent to a long wait of nearly an hour, the headmaster asked for me to come in and visit with him. At the time, not yet having the experience of managing the office during an overseas leave of the headmaster, I had no idea of how little work he had to do and that the "wait" exercise was to demonstrate to me, that he was not excited to receive an American teacher.

—

Bathroom Shock. Assigned to a house and yard with lovely jacaranda, poinsettia, and hibiscus as well as guava and mango, the aesthetic environment of life on school grounds was very positive. But during the first several days, the hot water which entered the bathroom sink and faucet was a thick rust in coloration. Water was heated in a Tanganyika boiler, a fifty-gallon drum heated by burning wood underneath it. Until all of the rust was cleared out of this drum, the water was unusable for bathing.

—

Creativity. On one occasion while maintaining a local fresh water fish in the biology laboratory, a student was assigned a project to study the fish. With no previous drawing experience, this student created beautiful anatomically correct drawings of the fish, including both external and internal structures.

—

Lights Off. School rules mandated that students be in their beds in the dorms with lights off at a prescribed time. Faculty were required to check the various rooms and locations where students might be studying after "lights off." Students caught breaking this rule were assigned work duties on a subsequent weekend. Although the rationale to ensure adequate sleep for health and for attentiveness in the classroom was valid, it was concerning to punish highly motivated students for studying by candle or flashlight.

—

Nightlife. Every evening during the time period when we could operate electrical lights, a great array of insects would be attracted to the windows of my home. This availability of insects afforded opportunities for study in the biology laboratory. It also provided ample nutrition for the numerous geckos that made their home adjacent to the windows. Also a potto was occasionally to be seen going into or departing from its nest in the attic of my home.

—

Marksmanship. Male villagers frequently carried a short throwing type of spear. Often these spears seemed to be used as walking sticks. During an annual sports day a spear-throwing contest was one of the events. With surprise, upon entering the contest and having no previous experience with throwing a spear, I was awarded second place. My success demonstrated that by 1961, spears were little utilized for hunting or fighting by the local population.

—

Envious. Subsequent to giving my male cook a salary raise, I was told by him that he used the extra money, through agreement with his wife, to acquire a second wife.

Curious. Frequently after a rain, one would see a swarm of termites in flight above their earthen stalagmite home. Individual female and male termites would come together in flight, drop to the ground, lose their wings, and travel away from the area in pairs to begin new colonies. These winged reproductive termites are termed "elates." When removing the male from a pair after they reach the ground, and replacing it with another male elate, the original female elate and transposed male did not again form pairs. But when replacing the new male with the original male, the two again paired and moved away, female in front and male behind.

Apprehension. On one hunting trip in the southern highlands of Tanganyika, villagers offered me their new school house as a place to sleep. Nearly every village during this period of pre-national independence, had constructed a school "house" in readiness for students and teachers (providing that teachers would become available).

These "school houses" were often relatively simple temporary constructions. The one made available to me was a small, one-room structure supported by wooden poles and covered with grass; I could see through its walls.

During the night, I lay awake listening to elephants moving into the area for feeding, followed by an array of night-time noises. Suddenly there were frantic sounds of something being killed close by the "school house," noises that I attributed to lions, followed by sounds of bone snapping. In the morning I discovered the sparse remains of an eland some thirty feet away from where I had tried to sleep. Vegetation was badly beaten down in the vicinity of the kill, and only a few blood stained bones and remnants of skin remained.

Frustration. Coming back to my open-top Land Rover after hunting in the southern highlands of Tanganyika, I found a drunk local man sitting in the driver's seat. Adorned with a Maasai-like fabric (*shuka*), hair colored red with ochre and armed with a long spear, the man refused to get out of the Rover. The hunting location was far south of Maasai country, and this man appeared to be a stranger to the area. Although I carried a loaded rifle, I opted to sit down and wait until my unwanted guest grew weary of the "contest" and departed, which he did in due time.

Lack of Planning. Our geography teacher at Malangali Secondary School arranged a field trip for hiking to the top of the 9,780 foot Mt. Rungwe. The group included four teachers and twenty-nine students. We parked our cars at the Rungwe Secondary School near the base of the forested mountain and began the trek without flashlights, matches, first aid, weapons, or food.

It took most of the remaining daylight hours to reach the top of the mountain. Then by majority vote it was decided to descend into the non-active volcanic crater. Subsequently, we were not able to get out of the crater before darkness, darkness so deep that we each, in single file, needed to hold the shoulder of the preceding person so as to continue the hike.

The lead person was a student wearing a white Arabic cap or "Taqiyah" (white that we could not see), who miraculously could see well enough to lead us down the mountain. By mid-morning of the next day, we arrived at the cars safely after hiking continuously for over sixteen hours.

—

Student Unrest. Subsequent to national independence, a new headmaster of our school on one occasion invited villagers of the nearby town to hold a dance in the school mess hall. Fearing interactions of students in the all-male school with villagers, he mandated that students leave the mess hall after dinner and remain in their dorms for the evening.

It was a Saturday evening and no provision was made for study or recreation. One group of students adopted clothing similar to that of the villagers and tried to co-mingle with them. Other students removed electrical fuses from the mess hall putting it in pitch darkness. After replacement of fuses the dance was held without further incidence.

At First Optimistic, Then Suicidal. Another American teacher and I used a school break to explore Kilwa Kisiwani. We drove to the Indian Ocean and arranged transport on a dugout canoe. Four of us were in the canoe, the two of us plus one man rowing, and another bailing out water with an empty coconut shell.

The water was calm and after a period of time, I became optimistic that we were going to arrive safely. After photographing and sight-seeing it was time to return. But now we found a line of people waiting to get on the same dugout canoe on which we had arrived.

The water in Mso Bay was now rougher than it had been and the distance across the bay exceeded one mile. We hesitated but then got in the canoe and watched with a sinking feeling as person after person also got into the same canoe. The trip back across to the mainland was uneventful except for the man with the coconut shell—he was very, very busy.

—

An Awakening. After teaching biology and health science for nearly two years, I was proud of the status of education in our secondary school. Then I took one of my students as an interpreter on a camping trip to game country southwest of the school. This student confided in me his beliefs relative to superstition. He spoke of how some individuals place curses on others and of how these curses frequently lead to death, how certain individuals in some communities are able to oppose and neutralize these curses, and, he said, that he had actually seen a projectile directed by mind control towards another individual.

While walking down a trail, he demonstrated to me how you walk around an arrangement of small sticks in the trail so as not to be vulnerable to voodoo. By time spent with an educated secondary student away from school influences, I realized that an African student may maintain an understanding derived from formal education while still holding firmly to tribal beliefs.

Close Call. Upon completing my two-year tour at Malangali Secondary School, I left the southern highlands to go to Kampala, Uganda. Upon reaching the Rift Valley in northern Tanganyika during the evening hours, I decided to lay over and take a last look at the Ngorongoro Crater.

Before locating a place to camp, I asked at a small village near the rim of the crater if there might be a place for me to overnight. I was directed to a small isolated guest hut, a one-room facility with dirt floor. During the night I was awakened by the sound of a single shot.

When departing in the morning, I stopped to ask villagers about the shooting. They told me that a traveler from South Africa had stopped for the night near the village. The traveler slept out in the open and was awakened at night by being pulled by the foot from his bed. He managed to reach his gun and fired a shot at a hyena that was at the foot of his bed, scaring it away. □

Papa, Martha, and Me

Jay Anderson

In the spring of 1964, I was student teaching at the Kings College, Budo, the "Eton" of East Africa. Budo's cornerstone was laid by Winston Churchill way back before the First World War. It was an Anglican secondary school, and all the elite of Uganda attended Budo: members of Parliaments, captains of industry, and of course the kings of Uganda's five African kingdoms.

Budo was an all-African school: no Europeans, no Asians, just the "cream" of Ugandan society. The staff was also first rate, all trained at England "public" (private) schools such as Eton, Oxford, and Cambridge, except for a few red-brick sorts, universities like Durham and Manchester, and included, oh my, a Scot, Gordon MacGregor out of Glasgow. And horror of horrors, a Yank. Yes, a Yank, Jay Anderson, Hamilton

College, Teachers for East Africa. Now student teaching here and only because he was first in his class of eighty at Makerere College in Kampala, Uganda. Yes, he was also first in his class at Aberdeen University in 1960–61. Took a First Class Diploma at that Scottish University: not bad for a Yank. But still, he's pretty uncouth.

Now, we were having midmorning staff tea. About 10:30 a.m., all the limeys were grouped together enjoying each other's holier than thous. Gordon and I were blithering with the red bricks. Lowly. A student hanging around the doorway caught Ian Cameron Robinson's, the headmaster's, eye. "Please, sir, you're wanted." Out Ian walked, all pomp and circumstance.

A few minutes later, he came back in and sidled up to me of all the people, the Yank. "You're on call." He explained that it was not me exactly but an American, a youngish teacher that was needed to be interviewed by an American, woman, oldish, so go, we will cover your classes, I think she is some sort of writer person. Be polite, if you can. "Now out!"

So out I went. She was oldish, blond, good-looking, familiar. I introduced myself. She said, "Martha, Martha Gellhorn." I told her I liked her writing and I liked her former husband's writing also. "I don't mind talking about Papa," she said. We both relaxed, and she lit up the first of many fags, and I got out my pipe, and we spent hours and hours talking about World War II, Key West, the Wild West, Africa, and Papa. She did interview me and, yes, I'm in one of her wonderful books, sort of… At staff tea the next day, I got curious looks along the lines of "You Yanks are a funny lot and who was that lady?"

Martha Gellhorn was Ernest Hemingway's third (out of four) wives and the only one who divorced him! ◻

Reporting to Sambaker

Jerry Barr

Oh, was I tired! All day driving in my short-wheel-base Land Rover, going from Kampala to Gulu, Uganda—more than two hundred miles over *murram* gravel roads—took its toll on my rear end. I was driving alone, no GPS or cell phones, no Motel 8, no Race Track, and no Denny's. The miles of washboard taught me that if I got to a special speed, I could jump from peak to peak on the washboard and make the ride at least tolerable, but it was slippery and took a lot of attention to the road conditions.

I was reporting to Sir Samuel Baker Senior Secondary School—Sambaker—located twenty miles from Gulu in the Acholi Province of Northern Uganda. TEA assigned me as a math teacher to Sambaker as my two-year assignment and my first teaching experience. I found out later that British made the word, math, plural and called it mathS! No problem: so now I called it mathS! I just needed to be able to add and subtract or know calculus!

It was dusk, around 7:00 pm and I had a few miles more to go. As I later found out, the locals called 7:00 p.m. *saa moja* (Swahili for the first hour of the evening). Since we were on the equator, the sun rose and set at the same time all year long, so 7:00 p.m. and 7:00 a.m. each were called the first hour of the am and pm. I learned to translate times, adding six hours to the Swahili time. Now I was twenty miles from my destination with dark roads and no traffic.

The sun was setting, but the moon was out and bright. I had built a removable sunroof in my Land Rover and had it opened as I was getting close to my destination. Oh, I was enjoying the end of my drive, looking at the beautiful African moon when suddenly, off the road I went into the side ditch: guess I was looking at the moon too long. My brakes went on, and, luckily, I stopped the Land Rover a couple feet from a serious accident. I was able to back my Land Rover out onto the road and only had a slightly bent frame which I was able to repair later on.

I continued my journey to Sambaker, arriving safely, smartly having stopped looking at that African moon. The folks at Sambaker welcomed me, got me something to eat, and I got settled into my house for a good night's sleep with dreams of the adventures yet to come. ☐

Sambaker School Strike

Jerry Barr

Now I was a maths teacher at Sir Samuel Baker Senior Secondary School located in Acholi province, twenty miles from Gulu in the north of Uganda. My background in education came out of a small high school in Banning, California, and a small liberal arts college called Ripon College, Ripon, Wisconsin. Both had very small classes and plenty of informal interaction between teachers and students. I loved that and brought that innovative teaching method to Sambaker and was going to enjoy practicing my teaching in that manner. Was I in for a surprise!

Setting the ground work: As I walked into my first class on my first day of teaching, all the students stood up, and said together, "Good Morning, sir." I said, "Good Morning. Please sit down." Oh, thought I, not in my classroom: too formal and silly. So I made new rules: standing and greeting me when I entered the room was no longer necessary. Then, raising hands to be recognized for comments or questions, no longer necessary. New rule: Just ask your questions. Soon, my new teaching experience became a nightmare. My classes were chaos.

Uganda was on its way to independence from Mother Great Britain in 1962. The students were very aware of the political situation, and my maths classes were full of questions concerning items other than maths. One question came up often concerning the real reason why we Americans were in Uganda and especially whether we Americans were spying on Uganda.

"Oh," I said finally, "yes, we are here to get information on Uganda's bicycle manufacturing capabilities." This did not go over well. Then, because of the recent behavior problems I was having, students did not fully completed their homework. So my threats came out. "I don't care if you are Milton Obote himself," I said. "You will be punished for not completing homework."

Strike! Strike! Strike!

Mr. first-year-innovative teacher self had now initiated a school strike, and, yes, the Sambaker students went on strike. My inappropriate comments and what the students presumed were insults to the future president of Uganda upset them, and they acted on their feelings. You might well wonder how it was resolved. I formally apologized in front all students at a school meeting, my heart in my hand. The students were forgiving, and I certainly modified my behavior during the rest of my time at Sambaker. ☐

Hiring a Domestic Servant

Jerry Barr

I never thought I would ever have domestic servants working for me in my house, cooking, cleaning, and doing other maintenance work. Starting out as the mathematics teacher at Sir Samuel Baker Senior Secondary School—Sambaker—located in the north of Uganda, I was assigned, and paid rent to the Uganda government, for a house on the school compound that folks called the deer park. It was a ranch-style cement block house, three bedrooms, living room, dining room, kitchen, and bathroom, really nice, except no electricity. Further, the kitchen had a cast-iron wood burning stove, a wood-burning hot water heater, and no fridge. There was indoor plumbing, running water, including the most important appliance in any place called shelter, a European type flush toilet.

However, this all presented a large-scale challenge to this twenty-two-year-old single man; but luckily, the other teachers provided me with plenty of advice on dealing with this situation. They said buy a kerosene fridge and hire someone for house and cooking work, someone called a "house boy" by the Brits. Never did I ever imagine having a servant cooking and cleaning for me, but that's what I did.

Further, the name "house boy" was terribly annoying to me. But as one of the two mathematics teachers for the first year, and the only mathematics teacher for the second year, handling more than two hundred live-in students, teaching math from arithmetic through calculus, doing basketball coaching and boy scouts after teaching, there was no way I could carry that schedule and handle the requirements for living in a house without electricity if I didn't have help. So now, I had to live without even a toaster: What to do?

Not to worry: Francisco Opiga, my newly hired "house boy," took care of that. He had previously worked for Brits, and they fried bread in the bacon fat and out came delicious toast. He hand-washed my clothes, ironed them with a charcoal iron, pumped and lit the pressure lamps, kept the kerosene fridge working, cooked on the wood burning stove, washed the dishes, and made sure I had some hot water for a bath. He got to the local butcher before sunrise because, after sunrise, flies swarmed over the newly butchered steer, and since the meat was sold at two shilling a pound regardless of the cut he got, there early to get the best cuts. If he got there late and got the tough cuts, Francisco put the meat in a papaya fruit in the kerosene fridge, and the next day, he produced mighty tender eating. Thanks, Francisco, because, without you, I would have been a lost soul. ☐

Tanganyikan Tales
Jim Blair

I was TEA 3C, married with a ten-month old son when we departed New York for Moshi. I had two transfers: a move to Lindi while in Dar and later a transferred to Magamba Secondary School, my assignment outside Lushoto. And I have lots of memories of travel throughout Uganda, Kenya, Tanganyika, and Zanzibar. I climbed Kilimanjaro, crossed the Serengeti plains during migration time. My wife had twin boys at a mission school with very natural childbirth, taking just one aspirin.

Magamba, with an elevation over 4,000 feet, was a new boarding school. There was no heat in the dormitory, and the boys were always cold. Each boy was allowed just one blanket. Many were issued sweaters by the missionary teachers, but some were not. A few boys learned to knit their own.

They faced larger challenges than the weather. Nearly all the boys were small and suffered from one malady or the other—hookworms, malaria, bilharzia, dietary deficiencies. One of the boys, Simion, had an enlarged heart which killed him before he could graduate. Andrew had only one leg, his right leg completely gone from the hip down. He walked with a large stick in his huge right arm and could walk/hop five miles to Lushoto and back with no noticeable discomfort. John had walked from Sudan and went on to be the leader of the southern Sudan revolution. Gadi went to California Polytechnic Institute and majored in electrical engineering.

All the boys had to take turns cooking meals which were invariably ground corn, red beans, and, sometimes, bananas. They had a full day of classes and then had an enforced study time each night, either two or three hours. They worked so hard to learn. All from small, subsistence villages, they were learning in English, which was their third language after a local language and Swahili.

Textbooks were British, and I wondered at the rationale for teaching British history. Science, math, English, Swahili, geography—okay, but British history? But it had to be done because that was what was on the Cambridge exams, and the boys had to pass those exams or their education would be over. For most of them, there was no opportunity to move on, pass or not. And there was no real infrastructure in Tanganyika to absorb hundreds and eventually thousands of high school graduates. But once they had learned about the world, none of them wanted to go back to the villages. I used to wonder whether it was right to teach them about a world that they could never be a part of, but I now believe that it was the right thing to do. ☐

Music Alone Shall Live

Dan Callard

TEAers, after returning from their service in East Africa, often acknowledge that they have come away from their experience richer for it than their African students. Sometimes we are not even sure we have enriched anyone's life at all, though it takes at least four beers to arrive at that sorry conclusion!

Like many other TEAs who needed a teaching diploma and went to the Faculty of Education at Makerere to obtain one, I spent some time at the Makerere Demonstration School. I taught clarinet there that year, and during this time I tried to learn to play some local instruments—the harp, the lyre, the flute, pan pipes, the one string fiddle, the long drum, and above all, the xylophone—the glorious *madinda*.

More important, I tried to figure out Kiganda music, which is mostly very fast and full of counterpoint. A typical tune I remember, Ssematimba, has eighteen notes. The countermelody also has eighteen notes, but they fall exactly between the notes of the melody, creating a thirty-six-note tune. Out of all this rapid fire musical line played on a *madinda*, a third player sits on one side of the instrument and picks out the actual tune of Ssematimba, a song about a famous man. *Madinda* composers write the first two parts in such a way that the tune emerges from some of those thirty-six notes, and then a singer sings along with this third *madinda* player. It takes a little while to get to this point! Then, one by one, other instruments find their cues from this bouillabaisse of rampaging melody: two pan pipes, the fiddle, the bass drum, the long drum, and finally the rattle. This corps of about ten musicians is actually a setting for a dance, and so the final musical element glues it all together.

The only European I knew who knew how to do all of these things was the music master at Makerere Demonstration School, Peter Cooke. I learned how to play all of these instruments from him a bit, and I learned to take the counterpoint and orchestration seriously, and I learned how to make harps, lyres, and *madindas*.

Once I was posted to western Kenya to teach, I found similar instruments, though they were played singly or in very small groups. The court of the Kabaka could afford to pay many musicians, as well as the lesser officials in the countryside, but most of the people in East Africa didn't know about this amazing Ugandan sound. Also the missionaries had warned the locals to give up their pagan sounds, and many of my students at Kamusinga were ashamed of their musical culture.

The Baganda and the Basoga have managed to maintain their music. They often sing of bicycles, banana lorries, and nylon, but the instruments are vintage. My point is that their music, along with other elements in their culture, stayed put and evolved on their own terms. The British government saw that the Kabaka and the ubiquitous Ggombolola structure would save the Crown a lot of bother, and perhaps the missions didn't hammer the locals to give up their pagan habits as relentlessly as they did in Kenya.

I'm afraid I was tarred by the brush of colonialism as well. All choirs in Kenya had to sing "Pretty Little Polly Perkins of Paddington Green" in order to enter the annual contest; biology students likewise studied English frogs, not the local species. The Cambridge Overseas Exam had yet to be relevant to the African student, and the weight and dominance of western culture was felt throughout the land. We all tried so hard to distance ourselves from colonialism. I hope we succeeded. I was so crazy about *madindas* that I built a *madinda* shelter in the garden Dennis Huckabay and I looked after in Kenya. Actually the man I bought the materials from built it, the local Sikh hardware store owner, who said he wanted "to do something for the school." I forget his name.

I didn't have to make the music club members play it—they were as amazed at the speed and complexity of Kiganda music as I was. My wife-to-be Judith, who taught at a nearby girls' school, also learned how to play this instrument. When we were married in Welwyn Garden City, we hauled out the logs that the school carpenter back in Kenya had shaped out of lusambya wood, laid it out in the Friends Meeting garden, and entertained all the guests. For years after we settled in Cincinnati and then Philadelphia, we took all of our instruments around to schools and summer camps and libraries.

The son of the Makerere Demonstration School's music master has become proficient in all music Ugandan and is spreading the word in Britain. In my home state of West Virginia, the university has a music department that studies the *madinda*. I have nothing against Polly Perkins, but it is nice to see the tables turn, if only a little bit. □

Crossing Cultures
Paul Cant

My arrival in Mpwapwa to take up my teaching post was not auspicious. Three days before, I had been on the staff of a large government secondary school in Tanzania's second city, Mwanza, set on the beautiful, bouldered southern shore of Lake Victoria. That afternoon, taking tea on the balcony of my staff villa and watching the pied kingfishers diving for food in the shallows near the lake shore, I was disturbed by the school messenger. He handed me a telegram, and his expression as he did so augured nothing good.

"This came for you, Bwana. It is urgent," he warned me. I thanked him and tore open the envelope and read the terse, telegraphic message:

> "You are transferred with immediate effect to Mpwapwa Government Secondary School. Your ticket for tomorrow's train from Mwanza Station to Gulwe Station in the Central Region awaits you at the station's office."

My heart beat in a small panic—I had never heard of Mpwapwa, or Gulwe, and I had only been at my post in Mwanza for two weeks. The question, "Why me?'" erupted in my brain in protest, closely followed by another: "And where the hell is Mpwapwa?" I took out an atlas and searched for it, in vain.

That evening, I received commiserating visits from friends and colleagues, but none of them had any answers to my two questions. One, who had an East African colonial background, did, however, throw out a suggestion: "Maybe it's somewhere near the capital of the Central Region, a town called Dodoma." That name rang ominously in my ears; it sounded far too close to "doom."

Next evening, I boarded a splendid Tanzanian State Railway steam-powered train. The locomotive, made in Austria, probably when Tanganyika was a German colony, was massive and in beautiful condition. When its deafening whistles blew for departure, I heaved my luggage aboard and felt the thrill of anticipation that train journeys always gave me. Minutes later, great blasts of steam set the train in motion. I was on my way. Into the unknown.

But the thrill of departure soon died. Night closed in as we headed south from Lake Victoria and the landscape was lost in darkness. I had a respectable dinner in the restaurant car, and settling back into my compartment, I fell into an existential reverie, about why I was where I was. What obscure motivation had made me answer the advertisement for a course at the University of East Africa followed by a two-year teaching contract in one of the federation's three countries, Uganda, Kenya, and Tanzania? Why on earth had I committed myself to this? Why on earth was I on my way to—what was it called?—Dodooma?

All through the following day, my spirits fell further. The train rolled remorselessly on across the vast expanse of the country's interior, and the views out of the compartment window were bleak. This was the "*nyika*" that had given the country its old name—a featureless plateau of thorn scrub, without people, without towns, without even animals. An endless emptiness.

Night closed in again before we reached Dodoma, and I asked the ticket inspector when we would arrive at Gulwe Station. "About twelve o'clock tonight," he informed me. How then would I get to Mpwapwa? A spurt of adrenalin burned into my stomach.

"Oh my God," I whispered.

That night, at the end of the dry season, was starry. The heavens blazed—the Milky Way splashed across the sky overhead, and the Southern Cross lurking on the horizon. And then, adding excitement to my apprehension, mountains rose up on each side of the train. I scanned their black profiles and stared ahead at the pool of light from the great lamp on the locomotive that bored into the darkness. Now, we must be close, it was near midnight. Leaning out of the window, I heard the gigantic chuffing of the engine fade, and then the brakes squeal. We came to a stop. I saw a water tower looming on one side, a dark, corrugated iron building on the other. No light, *no one*. But from the back of the train, I heard a shout: "Gulwe for Mpwapwa." I had arrived.

As the train pulled away for another night's travelling, on to Morogoro and on to Dar es Salaam, I stood with my suitcase and trunk in the dust at the side of the track, resisting the impulse to clamber back on board. But no, in a minute, the train was gone. I was alone, in the darkness, in the shadow of Gulwe Mountain, under the star-strewn sky.

I cannot say how long I waited there, but at last I saw in the distance a faint light making its bobbing way towards me. A light, a torch in a man's hand. Eventually it reached me.

"Hi, you must be John Archer. Follow me, I've got the school truck parked back there. Welcome, I'm Pete Dean."

My tongue, liberated from the silence of the journey, bombarded Pete. "Am I glad to see you, Pete. I had visions of being eaten alive here by hyenas. How far is it to the school, and this Mpwapwa, what is it, a hill station? Does it have a club? Fill me in."

As we drove along the deserted *murram* road to town in the Bedford truck, Pete assured me that Mpwapwa was a nice place, that I'd like it. "Of course, it's not Toronto," he warned, "and our big town, Dodoma, isn't much to write home about."

I detected the unusual lip-rounding in Pete's pronunciation of "about," and he explained to me that he was a Canadian volunteer. He was in his second and last year in Mpwapwa.

I stayed in Pete's house on the school campus that night, and next day moved into my own. It was an old, one-story structure, built, I estimated, in the thirties. The roof was of corrugated iron, painted a deep red, the front balcony had been enclosed in wire netting against mosquitoes, and the bath water was heated in an old oil barrel over a wooden fire. All in all, the house possessed a certain colonial charm, and its large garden was full of flame trees, japani shrubs, and bougainvillea.

The first thing I unpacked was my new Philips record player and my classical LPs. I was at that time possessed by the great works of the classical repertoire. They transported me, each in turn as I acquired the records and came to know them from beginning to end, into an ecstasy that lifted my soul, into an abstract delirium. This music I valued the most of all art. It became my daily aesthetic substance, a constant source of pleasure and pride. It was, I felt, the greatest artistic achievement of Western civilization.

As I played my classical records at night in Mpwapwa, there was other music in the air—the relentless, distant drumming of the Wagogo in their scattered villages. Well, I thought, music is inherent in the human species, and as I turned over a record to listen to the final movements of a Handel organ concerto or a Shostakovich symphony, I could not help but compare the magnificent musical complexity of the classical work with the monotonous beating of the African drums.

I spent two years teaching in Mpwapwa. My students were boys and young men from all over the country. They were intelligent, friendly, and keen to learn. My work was enjoyable and fulfilling. When I "taught" them George Orwell's *Animal Farm*, I was rewarded by their passionate engagement in the story, and by their appreciation of the parallels between the inexorable erosion of the farm animals' dream of freedom and the development of the one-party state in their own country.

My social life in Mpwapwa was almost entirely expatriate. My colleagues were mostly British or American, and three individuals among them were exceptionally stimulating company. One was a sophisticated New Yorker who had the largest private collection of Bach records that I had ever seen and, night after night, listened to. Another was from Pittsburg, a left-wing loner who liked to lecture me on everything from the Einsteinian dimensions to *L'Annee dernière à Marienbad,* or to the coded existential angst in Mann's *Magic Mountain*. A third was Indian, beset by religious yearning, and struggling to choose between Catholicism, Judaism, and the polytheistic faith of her Brahmin parents. Friends such as these made my two years in Mpwapwa rich.

Relations with my African colleagues were more limited. They were agreeable, completely free of any racism on either side, and mostly maintained at dances in the town community center or at the bar in the club, where we downed the local lager beer, sold under names like Tusker, Whitecap, and Kilimanjaro.

With our students, relations were more strictly demarcated. In the classroom, there was intense contact and exchange, but once classes were over, they went their way down to the dormitory complex, and we went ours to our villas, to the club, and in the holidays, on safari all over East Africa. It was true that one or two colleagues became personally attached to particularly brilliant students.

The New Yorker used to talk of "my Boniface" and tell us that he would surely rise to the top of Tanzanian society. Another would read the essays of his favorite to us over dinner and conclude with: "Brilliant, don't you think...worthy of Sartre!" I, probably because I had been through the English boarding school system, never cultivated such "special" pupils. I knew that some enjoyed my teaching more than others, but I treated all with the strictest impartiality. I was, I suppose, still influenced by a naive faith in British imperial justice. No favoritism.

My time in Mpwapwa came to an end with surprising speed. The two years had passed without heed, and now I was packing up my things ready for departure, on the same train that had brought me to Gulwe two years before. The last thing I packed was my record player, and on the nights before departure, I began an intense reconnection with European culture by playing my classical records at high volume, Beethoven, Brahms, Stravinsky, Handel, Mozart, and the rest, over and over. On one of the last nights, there was a knock on the front door. I opened it, and was astonished to find John Mtwaro standing there.

"Sir," he said, "I have come to say goodbye to you."

"Really, John? Well, come in, come in."

As he sat down, I lowered the volume of the record drowning the sitting room in music.

"Sir," John began, "it is hard for me to express my feelings. Your teaching has been very important to me. I would like you to stay here with us, not go back to England."

"That's very kind of you, John, but you know, I feel it's time to go back to where I come from, my family, my part of the world."

"Well, Sir, I shall miss your teaching very much."

He stood up abruptly and came to shake my hand. I was afflicted as he did so by a rush of emotion, a disabling sense of separation and loss. To control my voice, I had to say my goodbye in hard, constrained tones.

As I led John to the front door, he suddenly stopped and said to me: "Sir, you should not listen too much to that music."

"Why not?"

"It is very sad."

"Sad?"

"Yes, it has no singing. It has no human voices." ☐

Students on Strike

Emilee Cantieri

About halfway through my time at Machakos Teachers College, I had an example of how one person's behavior can affect others. I was assigned to teach various subjects, as most of us were: British and African history, education, domestic science and English composition and grammar. A British teacher took my classes every Friday for speech lessons, to make sure—God forbid—that my students did not develop an American accent and a Southern one at that.

The day of the strike was a Wednesday, and my lesson plan was to read and discuss a play, with the students taking parts. As usual, they were in the classroom when I entered. They stood and said as one, "Good afternoon, Miss Hines," though without their usual smiles.

I said, "Good afternoon, students. Please be seated." I distributed the playbooks and went down the line, asking who wanted to read each part. Not a hand went up. "Very well," I said. "Please answer the following questions, allowing about a paragraph for each answer."

I hastily made up questions and wrote them on the board. The students wrote for perhaps fifteen minutes. I collected the papers and again suggested that we might read the play. I ran through the names of the characters, asking for volunteers, with the same results.

"All right, since you don't want to read the play, please answer the following questions on the story we read Monday."

I started writing again, when a voice came from the back of the classroom, "Please, Miss, I will read."

Others quickly volunteered, glad to avoid any further test. We read the play and discussed it, and afterward, I asked, "Why did you refuse to read today?"

"It is not you, Miss. We were angry at another teacher," one explained.

"It's wrong to take out your anger on me for what someone else has done," I said, and they agreed.

"We will not do it again," someone said. The group nodded agreement.

Ultimately, the students were eager to learn new words and phrases, and kept a small notebook of them, noting various ways the word or phrase could be used. It was very satisfying as a teacher. They would then make a special effort to use the word in my presence. I had some difficulty explaining "Freudian slip." One day, close to the end of term, we were setting up chairs for assembly when I referred to a teacher by another's name. Chairs were stilled as my girls said in unison, "Freudian slip, Miss Hines."

The morning I left Kenya this form of girls came out in their night clothes to see me off in the pre-dawn darkness. I had seen them off on buses and lorries at the end of other terms, but it was now my time to go. They had handmade gifts for me, and I went down the line, hugging each one. They were special, and said they'd write to me, but they didn't. I only saw one of them again, when TEEA visited Kenya in 2003. □

Duncan Kimamu and Electricity
Gene Child

Teaching physics at Kenyatta College just outside Nairobi from 1969 to 1971 was often an adventure because of the lack of experience of my students. They were the most intelligent group of students I ever taught in my thirteen-year teaching career, but they lacked practical experience with what we might consider everyday things. Since they had come through the Kenya-British educational system, they all had taken a secondary school leaving exam after finishing their four year O-level secondary school years. Their test scores placed them in the eightieth-to-ninetieth percentile of students nationally. The top ten percent were offered positions in the University of Kenya.

Each year the students went back to their home villages during our Christmas break. Duncan Kimamu, a third-year student, was from the Gala district in far northeastern Kenya, not far from Somalia. In order to go home, he had to ride the train to Mombasa on the east coast, an overnight trip, then get on a bus for an all-day ride north to Wajir. His family were nomadic herders so moved from camp to camp, following their cattle to wherever the infrequent rains had produced enough grass on which they might forage. After arriving at the nearest village, Kimamu visited with the locals to find where his family was at the moment. He then walked several hours through the bush to find them.

When he returned to Kenyatta College after the vacation, he related a story about visiting with his grandfather while at home. His grandfather wanted to know what he was learning in college. Duncan replied that they were learning about electricity. His grandfather wanted to know what this thing called electricity was. Duncan explained that using electricity you could listen to people talking on things called radios. The grandfather had listened to a transistor radio so he accepted that. Duncan then said using electricity you could use light bulbs to light your *shamba* at night. Finally, he said that you could use things called electric motors to do work for you on your *shamba*. The grandfather exclaimed, "That is not possible!" □

Recipe for Sukuma Wiki (stretch the week)

Pat Colby

500g (1 lb) kale or some other greens such as spinach
2 Tablespoons oil
1–2 onion, chopped
1–4 tomatoes, peeled, and chopped
1 green pepper, chopped
Leftover meat
salt and pepper to taste

Heat oil in a large frying pan. Fry onions until soft. Add tomatoes, green pepper, and leftover meats, if you have any. Cook together until well heated. Add spinach and cook over low heat for 20-30 minutes until mixture is well blended. Season to taste. Serves 4. □

Practice Teaching

David Evans

As a member of the very first B group, I spent a year in the post-graduate diploma course at Makerere before being posted. I did my practice teaching at Nyakasura, the prestigious Scottish missionary school in Fort Portal, where the boys wore kilts complete with sporrans and red knee socks.

The school was located in the foothills of the Mountains of the Moon where it was often cold, especially in the mornings when the students lined up in a field for inspection before going to chapel. The teachers were mostly from Scotland and were used to cooler weather. The school uniform included a red sweater, but the boys were not allowed to wear their sweaters unless the "sweater flag" was raised—yes, there really was a sweater flag. The duty officer of the day decided whether it was cold enough to justify wearing the sweater! As a result, the students often stood shivering in their short-sleeved white shirts during morning inspection and in dark classrooms, because the duty officer used to Scottish weather was not cold.

Among the many memories of my practice teaching days, several stand out. When I arrived, the headmaster welcomed me. He then said something to the effect of, "You are an American. All Americans can swim, so I want you to coach the swimming team." While I could swim, what I did not know at the time was that the "pool" was a smallish, open concrete tank fed solely by very cold water coming down off the Mountains of the Moon! Swimming lessons were short.

Another time, I found myself summoned to the headmaster's office because he had received complaints from some of the prefects that the students were upset. It turned out that my refusal to write complete notes on the blackboard so students could copy them was the problem. I felt that students should learn how to take notes without just copying them.

After some discussion with the headmaster, we reached a compromise. I would write partial sentences on the board and ask the students to finish the sentences, and then gradually reduce what I wrote and increase what they wrote. This was one of many lessons I learned about how to introduce change in a constructive way. ☐

My English Challenge
Pat Gill

Research shows that if we educate the women in a county we raise the educational level of the entire county. My job was in Uganda in a girls' school that went from our traditional ninth grade to two years of community college. When I arrived, they had just put in a science laboratory with water and electricity. There were no supplies or equipment. I began to put together what we needed for the facility and did get some microscopes from the local university.

My main subject to teach was science. The students were involved, and we used many of the local trees and plants to teach what was needed. However, as time went on and there were faculty that had to go home for family reasons, I taught geography and some math.

My biggest challenge was the time that one class did not have an English teacher. I was the only one available to take this class and the only American on the faculty. The problem was that they thought I didn't speak English, so how could I teach it? I went to the small book room we had and found we had enough copies of *Oliver Twist* for the class to use it. We read and discussed it and I taught them the songs from the play on Broadway that I had just seen before I went to Africa.

I feel that singing improves speaking and they are so talented in singing. Two years later when I left Uganda they had an assembly to say good bye to me. The class sang the songs I had taught them. I almost cry when I tell this story. ☐

Back to Africa Fifty Years Later via the Peace Corps

Charles Guthrie

Why I Went. In 2010 I retired. Retirement suggests that you now have more time to spend on being than doing, but I wasn't quite ready for that. After my 1960s' TEA experience, a stint in the Army, and some necessary years of further education I became a teacher. During the thirty plus years of teaching that followed I had encouraged a number of young students to go into the Peace Corps after graduation.

Now I wanted another in-depth experience in Africa for myself, so in 2011 I put my money where my mouth had been and joined the Peace Corps. I was posted to Rwanda to teach English, just as I had done in neighboring Tanzania almost half a century earlier. I entered with all of the excitement I had experienced joining TEA in 1964, but now with a lifetime of experience behind me and some nagging uncertainty about my age and capacity.

The Peace Corps initially tried to send me to Jordan. I refused this assignment since all of my professional experience had been in Sub-Saharan Africa and Latin America. Typical bureaucracy! Rwanda was actually not one of my choices. I really wanted to return to Tanzania. Even though I knew better, deep down I was hoping that two years in the Peace Corps would give me a kind of closure on Africa that resembled my earliest experiences with TEA, what today we reflect back on as a gentler perhaps less complicated version of Africa. It was not to be. What follows is a comment on my experience in Rwanda. While I felt like I learned much about Rwanda and its peoples while I was there, I have to remind you that most of it was filtered through my rather narrow perspective as a secondary school teacher.

—

Training. Initially there were thirty-seven in my Peace Corps wave, all there to teach English. (That number had dropped to twenty before our tour was completed!) As in all Peace Corps experiences, volunteers lived with a local family for three months while studying the language and history, adapting to the culture, and submitting to a daunting range of Peace Corps classes required by Washington.

My family were small farmers, up at dawn, to bed early. Husband, wife, and two children of secondary age (another three were already grown and gone). Electricity had just recently come into the village and usually worked, so we had light. Water was available behind the house in a stone rain collection tank (except during the driest months) together with the latrine, a kitchen with fireplace for cooking, a few chickens, three pigs and two cows in stalls, all crowded into a very small fenced-in back yard. Living with my host family was the easy part. Familiar to me, and enjoyable.

The fact that I was older than my host parents wasn't a problem, and my previous experience in Africa made fitting in easy. The classes were the difficult part. A few were necessary and helpful, others…not. It made for some long days. The language, Kinyarwanda, was the first of my major challenges. In these classes, surrounded by eager millennials, I was dragged out of denial that I was indeed beginning my eighth decade! Not only could I not hear some of the sounds of the language, I couldn't remember the vocabulary that I stayed up late every night trying to memorize.

All of the challenge and uncertainty of full-time student status returned, without the sharpness of youth. After four decades of making life difficult for my students, I now received frequent visits from the amused and mocking ghosts of students past. My younger colleagues had the reverse experience—easy being a student, but challenged by the culture.

—

My Teaching Site. After completing training, I was posted to a private secondary boarding school of about 600 students several miles east of Kigali where I spent the next two years. I taught several sections of Forms 4, 5, and 6, twenty-eight hours and nine preps a week. By far the most difficult aspect of those two years for me was coping with the extremely low level of student motivation. There is a good reason for this situation. Because of its colonial past, the dominant foreign language was French.

In 2008 President Kagame with little preparation mandated the switch to English at all levels of education, to begin in 2009. It was a policy imposed upon a very unenthusiastic population. The result has been chaos. At that time the US seemed to still suffer from the delusion that Rwanda was a promising experiment in democracy and that Kagame was a hero leading the charge.

The truth was unavoidable for any who cared to look beyond the social and economic life of elites in the larger cities and the showy projects funded by foreign aid. Peace Corps agreed to come in to help make that shift and found themselves caught between a forced policy and an extremely ill-prepared and reluctant population, including teachers, headmasters, politicians, and a host of other officials. Spoken opposition to policies from the center routinely met a bad end, so resistance to the change went quiet, joining other undercurrents to create a negative atmosphere in many schools where we were teaching. My Peace Corps group was the third wave, arriving in 2011.

Teaching English in Tanzania didn't confront such challenges. By the time students reached our secondary schools most already spoke English and had their sights on the Cambridge exams. In my school, Malangali Secondary School, motivation to improve English was high among most students and it made my job much easier. At the least they accepted the fact that success would require it. Not so in Rwanda, except in a very few superior schools where top students already had a background of experience with English. I spent two years in Rwanda daily confronting classes of forty or fifty students with literally no foundation in English and no real desire to learn. When Peace Corps volunteers got together, a frequent topic of discussion was the problem of student motivation. It might have helped if we had had some kind of resources for teaching English, but we did not. The year that I arrived in Rwanda the government produced a very basic English textbook, but it was supplied only to the government secondary schools. Private schools (comprising over fifty percent of all schools in the country) had to pay for them, not possible for most. So, no textbooks, no dictionaries, no library. In vain I found myself searching for resources that were relevant and could spark interest.

Like the students, teachers and headmasters were also struggling to make the shift and neither had the time nor the enthusiasm to learn a new language, and yet the school curricula and examinations required it. A few of the younger teachers had attended the university and were a bit better prepared, but the response of most was to simply continue in Kinyarwanda and endure the threatened consequences and mounting pressures from above. And desperately look for another job. Teachers poured in from Uganda to teach English (and to work in the public sector). They were resented. The arrival of enthusiastic Americans to save the day was also understandably met with resentment.

—

Looking Back to Compare. In most ways, my experience in Rwanda was so very different in both time and circumstance from my TEA years in Africa that any attempts at comparison seem a bit silly, and mostly just produce nostalgia. After years of following Africa's troubled course since my first sojourn to East Africa, nostalgia is perhaps an earned as well as a preferred form of remembering.

A half century ago, both Peace Corps and TEA volunteers confronted a very different context. We had stepped innocently into a new and very optimistic post-independence situation that colored our perspective, and we reaped the benefits in ways that we scarcely recognized at the time. We believed all things were possible, a naiveté that combined happily with ignorance. The first real East African histories were only just being written. We worked hard at teaching, but we tended to plan from one vacation period to the next, producing some of our most memorable experiences (and photos). We applauded ourselves that we were different from Peace Corps (who had no vehicles, nor were they allowed to drive—still true), because we actually worked for our respective African governments instead of the US, innocently claiming a kind of legitimacy.

Some would argue that we in TEA/TEEA were more committed and professional than Peace Corps, then or now, because we either had teaching degrees and experience or had spent a year together at Makerere adapting to the area while earning teaching certification. Possibly, though I would not want to press that too seriously. I would argue that today's Peace Corps volunteers, most of them recently graduated from college, are just as adventuresome, just as ornery and full of themselves, and just as bright and committed as our TEA group back in the day. In some ways perhaps more so. The difference might be that they grew up in a world profoundly altered by technology. All Peace Corps volunteers had laptops and were connected to each other and the world through Facebook and email and texting, with some variation depending upon the availability of power and cell towers (very widespread in Rwanda, a presidential priority).

Being plugged in was not even a matter of choice. The first thing that the Peace Corps did with volunteers when they landed in Kigali, literally the first thing, was to haul the group to a store to buy cell phones. Some got smart phones! We couldn't opt out. Showing my age, I was the only one who even considered it. My mild protests were met with incredulity, or gentle smiles in the way that young folk patronize the elderly.

Throughout our tour, although the Peace Corps application had declared laptops optional, email and cell phone were the regular means of communication between the Peace Corps office and volunteers. Minutes could be purchased in most villages.

Most Peace Corps volunteers also had blogs to share their experiences with friends and family back home, stimulating questions that could then be so easily answered by email. Blogs were encouraged by Peace Corps as a way of helping to inform and educate folk back home. All blogs had to be approved by the Peace Corps! So, volunteers always knew they would be able to remain "in touch" with what they left behind. That tends to alter the way you think about where you are. Peace Corps, as with the international education community generally, continues to talk about the importance of "cultural immersion experiences."

Even popular culture has taken up the cry with the pithy "Wherever you are, be there," without quite owning the meaning, I might add. Volunteers in my group kept in touch more or less constantly, when and wherever power was available, which was most of the time. My experience leads me to question whether you can really "be there" when the pervasive plugged-in culture draws you elsewhere. At best it sets the bar for immersion extremely low. And it is certainly a very different way of being there compared with our 1960s experience. After two years experiencing it, I have concluded that it definitely changes the way that you reflect on your experience and how you spend your spare moments or even longer periods of free time.

In my two plus years with the Peace Corps, I often recalled how radically different was TEA's communication with us. The only official contact of any kind I had with TEA administrators in my two years in Tanzania was one overnight pass through visit from Don Knies that as I recall consisted of a brief perfunctory question—"How are things?"—an equally perfunctory answer, and several beers before he headed back north. I think I was the southernmost TEAer in our group.

My recent Peace Corps experience, on the other hand, was full of continuous contact with Peace Corps—regular site reports, reports of how we were doing or not doing or intending to do, safety warnings, updates/reminders of some program or another, surveys (related to how we were doing!), surveys of daily expenditures to determine appropriate living expenses, special project reports. And during our second year came the dreaded newly introduced sophisticated computerized bi-annual reporting system that no one understood and was never free of glitches, Peace Corps Washington's attempt to put the Peace Corps throughout the world on the same digitized reporting system so that gathering statistics about performance would be more effective and meaningful, in line with the country's rage for accountability. Technology has so transformed the volunteer experience as to make it almost unrecognizable compared with "back in the day." Were TEA to be launched today, they would require levels of accountability similar to Peace Corps now.

—

Rwanda's Current Situation. I want to mention a few aspects of Rwanda's current situation since it has a very direct impact, I believe, on the attitudes of students and teachers, and thus on the Peace Corps volunteers' teaching environment. It has been twenty years since the genocide. Given that length of time, I was surprised by how raw the memories remain of the 1994 genocide, especially, of course, with those in their early twenties or older (some of the teachers, and even a few of my students).

Memories are even stronger though not openly talked about because it's against the law in the countryside away from the cities, where memorial sites are plentiful and victims' families still live in daily contact with the perpetrators. Even among my students, a number of whom were orphaned by the calamity, twenty years has not erased a strong sense of something not quite right. It is true that the young are growing up in a vitally different setting. Their focus is much more on their own problems, media projections of the good life (via the urban rich) and the pop culture icons than on what happened in the "distant past."

But it is very difficult to avoid the realities, such as the few who control the wealth and access to jobs and the few who benefit. And it matters who those controlling elites are. Everyone is keenly aware of the gross inequalities of both wealth and opportunity, but no one talks openly about it since it tends to reflect the shadows of ethnic conflict.

Every year in the month of April (when the genocide began) there are countrywide government memorials of the "Genocide Against the Tutsi" that fail to acknowledge the great losses among the Hutu, so many of whom fought against the extremists and were themselves victims. Colorful banners are everywhere. Officials at every level of government are responsible for organizing or participating in public displays, including marches or gatherings where programs filled with speeches remind all of what happened, who was responsible, who halted the genocide, and what the government is doing now to ensure "never again." All schools similarly organize required gatherings of students and parents or villagers. Attendance is "voluntary."

Every family has lost members. But much more effective as historical reminders are the stories that are quietly handed down in families to the post-genocide generation, effectively reinforced by existing social and economic patterns of discrimination. They conclude a different interpretation from the party line. Especially important to the impact of this interpretation is the joblessness. When failure to find any kind of work after so many years of schooling combines with the recognition that so many opportunities depend upon who you are and who you know rather than what you have accomplished, the consequence is a very deep resentment.

Since returning I have read a number of articles on Rwanda, assessments of the state of affairs under Kagame's leadership that often praise the rapid growth. Mostly I see them as cherry picked descriptors of conditions in the country that do not accurately reflect the Rwanda I experienced. Until fairly recently it seems the popular press (as well as various business, Christian, and other non-profit organizations) in the west has had a seriously misplaced love fest with Rwanda. Perhaps still.

Although the number of rosy political assessments of post-genocide Rwanda is definitely declining, it is disturbing how many still continue to confuse the possible with the reality. Clearly visible are the health care initiatives, and transportation and other infrastructure projects, especially in and around the larger towns and cities, or wherever the well-to-do decide to settle. In these areas there is no denying some positive change.

More importantly, however, is who benefits from this change. Development initiatives are not so visible in the rural areas out of the global spotlight, where most Rwandans live. But modern communications project these images of rapid improvement (implying opportunity and the good life) into areas that are not likely to experience it for some time to come, if ever, raising expectations and undermining commitment to rural life.

The Rwandan government takes great pride in its public security, and in its claim to be free of corruption. That is definitely true for public security. As for corruption, that may also be true at the highest most public levels and in the area of foreign business activity. But, if you pay attention to the workings of local government, or to how loyalty to the government is rewarded, you might conclude differently. And if you repeat that government claim to folk that trust you enough to talk openly, it produces a range of responses from laughter to anger, and the stories begin to come out.

Everyone knows how things actually get done in Rwanda and who benefits! It would be naïve to think that this knowledge does not negatively affect students' response to government policies or to the official preaching that they will benefit for their hard work in the classroom.

—

Concluding remarks. And finally a few shorts to conclude my Peace Corps story.

Age: Although I confess to some fleeting worries before leaving, my septuagenarian brain did not really impair my full participation in the experience. In fact, years of life experience more than compensated.

Potential Ageism: My relationship with the young volunteers was refreshing and supportive. Once they got past the initial visual shock in our first meetings (I was told they asked: "What's that old dude doing here?"), I was completely accepted. My similar initial concerns about them quickly turned to respect.

Gender Equality: Although Peace Corps Rwanda and the volunteers made very serious and worthwhile efforts to support Rwanda's official much touted policy of "gender equality," the reality in daily life makes a joke of the claim.

Technology: As with other places in the world, technology (especially the media and cell phones) is completely transforming life and expectations in Rwanda.

The Physical: Climbing Rwanda's volcanoes was more of a physical challenge than I had, but almost as much fun as Elgon and Kilimanjaro were fifty years ago.

Freedom of Movement: There is no trace of the freedom we had back in the 1960s to hitchhike, or go just about anywhere we wanted when we wanted. Peace Corps' zero tolerance for driving any kind of vehicle, or even riding on the most common public transport while in the cities (motorcycle), significantly changes the kind of experience available to volunteers. Certainly safer, but different.

Freedom of Speech: Not.

Vacations: In TEA we were free, with money saved and vehicles available, to be as carefree as we wished. Peace Corps volunteers are urged very strongly to use vacation time to focus on community projects. Mine was building and supplying a community library. I was impressed with some of the volunteers' projects.

Foreign Influences: The Chinese are everywhere!

Prevailing Attitudes: Absent among most Rwandans that I encountered is the feeling of hope that I remember from the sixties, a sense that there would be opportunity, that things would get better. For the well-to-do at the top, yes, but not for the rest.

—

A Personal Reflection. I have been back for almost seven months now [this writing from 2014]. I did not have any kind of "re-entry crisis" that sometimes follows for the young who are experiencing this for the first time and confronting a totally different set of questions about their near futures. I had minimal preconceptions and expectations of this experience, and the few that I did have were quickly blown away by the totally different context of Rwanda.

Returning from the Peace Corps I find myself at the end of a long journey reflecting on all that has happened in the past half century, as I am sure all of you do these days. I also reflect back on my recent two years in Peace Corps and find that I seem to be asking some of the same questions I have asked for years, the same questions that my very young Peace Corps volunteer friends are now asking: Does service make a meaningful difference? How can you do service effectively?

Now you and I are old, with decades of experience that has prepared us to answer questions no one is asking, with more time for existential ponderings than perhaps is healthy, but with a blanket of warm memories from our first years in Africa to counter the faded dreams and resulting cynicism that too often seem to characterize our views of the continent in more recent years. I have no regrets about joining Peace Corps. Quite the contrary. But for my family, I would do it again. It was a rich experience, even if not quite the one I had envisioned. It offered new challenges, new friendships, and optimism about the young folk who will be taking over from us. □

Culture Gap in Kakamega

Henry Hamburger

The superficial environment of many Kenya high schools is surprisingly similar to what one finds in the States. Behind the modern concrete buildings, collared shirts, and painstakingly enunciated English sentences, however, stands a very confused schoolboy stranded between two cultures, as out of place at a circumcision ceremony as at a performance of *My Fair Lady*. This dilemma is in large part a natural outgrowth of a very difficult transition period.

—

The Cambridge Exams. Educational ideas in the wind in Kenya are much like other things which leave the ground. If they are hurled skyward with too little thrust they fall to earth—in Kenya they fall on the hard rocks of the University of Cambridge Examination Syndicate. And just as man-made projectiles have broken free of the earth, so will Kenyan education some day break away from its foreign examination board. Meanwhile, the principal objective of the secondary student here is still not to understand himself, his society, his past, or the world at large, but to pass "the Cambridge," a battery of tests which conclude his high school career.

These examinations set an internationally recognized standard and success in them is the passport to good jobs and higher education at home and abroad. While it is possible, by careful appraisal of past exams, to discover the topics and types of questions favored by the examiners and to learn techniques for answering them, a high grade is indicative of at least fairly good understanding and the ability to apply the material examined.

Some of the arguments for and against this particular examination system are applicable to any system of student evaluation, but one criticism is unique: The Cambridge exams are written in England, by Englishmen, for English-speaking people. The secondary students of Kenya speak English, but they *are not* English, so that while a sequence of ideas may be logically connected in their minds, the whole sequence sometimes has no connection with reality for them.

A classic example is the way the Kenyan student learns about ice. Long before he reaches high school a geography teacher tells him about the seasons—not so much about his own dry and rainy seasons as about summer and winter. He learns that in winter the sun's rays strike Europe at an angle so that it is cold and lakes are covered with ice. In high school he learns that this ice on European lakes can be mixed with water in a metal cup and he is taught to compute the resulting temperature of such a system.

If at this stage the teacher is resourceful enough to obtain some ice and bring it to school, the class has an exciting new experience. As the ice is brought in, the student watches expectantly from his seat. Then he comes forward, reaches out, and for the first time in his life holds ice in his hand. "Eh-h-h," he exclaims, "it is cold!" Why certainly it is cold. Why does he seem so surprised? Surely he has been told it would be cold. How cold? Why, exactly 32°F. And how cold is that? Colder than *anything in his previous experience*, and thus outside his true understanding until the first touch.

In English literature the student has more difficulty; he is continually faced by such a welter of new words, expressions, manners of speech, ideas, experiences, and patterns of behavior that he hardly knows where to begin. Here he comes up against the reinforced barrier of foreign language under laid with foreign culture.

A rough idea of the nature of the problem, though not its magnitude, can be gained by considering the American high school student reading his first Victorian novel. The origins and significance of wealth and social class are a bit strange at first, but they can be related with some effort to personal experience. The facial expressions, activities, and material objects which are described are more or less familiar.

Now assume that an African and an American schoolboy are confronted with a description of an English gentleman who is "rather inclined to an excess of billiards." The American may not understand whether billiards is generally the pastime of the knave or the noble, but he knows pretty well what the game is about. The African, on the other hand, may skip that sentence and have a try at figuring out the next one, consult a dictionary, or make a tentative guess as to whether a "billiard" is a game, a food, or a loose lady. Any of these procedures will do occasionally, but none is satisfactory if every third sentence presents a similar problem.

Understanding the simple meaning, however, is only the beginning. Of the many facets of a novel which may transcend its value as a narrative, the most interesting to the young student is often its humor. When Mark Twain's *Celebrated Jumping Frog of Calaveras County* was translated into French, he complained about the evident injustice of trying to render, "I don't see no p'ints about that frog that's better'n any other," in the Gallic idiom. But while humor may lose something in *language* translation, it is likely to lose everything in culture translation.

This is painfully evident to one who, like myself, has taught in his own country. One of the fastest and most effective ways to establish a sympathetic understanding is with a good laugh which teacher and student can enjoy together. In my American classroom, I could tell with reasonable accuracy what would get a response and what would not. Here, not only did my early attempts at wry comments fall flat, but certain incidents, which had previously meant nothing to me, appeared to be sources of great merriment.

In the early years of high school the difficulty of imparting humor can be ludicrous. After about a month of discussing simple machines with first-year students, I had convinced most of them that even though a machine enables a small force to move a large load, the work accomplished by the machine is no greater than the work put into it. "Work," I summarized with a grin, "is not obtained for nothing." I wrote the statement on the blackboard and jotted beneath it, "and life is not easy." A hand went up in the back of the room. "But sir," came the earnest, knowledge-seeking voice, "what does 'life is not easy' mean?"

For the young Kenyan studying for his Cambridge exam life is, *indeed,* not easy, and it may well be asked whether every secondary student must be subjected to the difficult process of absorbing a foreign culture. If he has difficulty enjoying the English literature to which he directs much of his attention, can we assume that he is compensated by being bi-cultural? Perhaps. But a maturity based on an understanding of the common features of two diverse cultures will not emerge in a boy who is unable to participate fully in *either* culture. Bi-culturality must not be confused with "bi-alienation."

—

Two Homes, Two Languages. Several incidents suggest that secondary school not only produces confusion about Western culture but also creates ambivalent attitudes toward home and community. One of the boys told me that his maternal uncle—a very close relative who has financed his entire education—had asked him to take over the circumcision duties for his community upon completion of high school. The boy has refused and is now unwelcome in his uncle's home.

I witnessed another example of this alienation during a community baptism ceremony a few miles from the school. The participants were mostly children, but all their parents, friends, and relatives were there. While we were waiting for the preacher to arrive, there was a good deal of religious singing and dancing. The baptism itself was a total immersion ceremony among the reeds of a shallow pond. After the service all the younger children, who were not old enough to be baptized and had been sitting patiently in the hot sun, engaged in some total immersion for non-religious purposes. The entire morning was very colorful to an outsider.

One of the other guests, a freelance journalist, lost no time in setting up his camera. Some of the rest of us, however, were not sure how polite this would be—until we saw our schoolboy host take out his own camera, and, in the best tourist tradition, start taking pictures of these curious unenlightened folk, who just happened to be his neighbors.

This emotional detachment from home life caused by exposure to different ideas is intensified by actual physical separation. Almost all high schools are boarding schools. It is imperative that they be so, since lack of electric lights and the presence of many small children and other distractions make home study virtually impossible. The appalling record in Cambridge exams of some day schools bears this out. Thus at the age of 14, 15, or 16 a boy leaves home physically as well as mentally.

The separation is not complete, since the student goes home for vacations. Then, however, he may find a minor language barrier developing there too. The vernacular language is used in elementary schools in rural areas, but children who live near towns where there are two or more tribes may learn in a foreign language medium (Swahili, the *lingua franca*) starting in first grade. All students switch to English in fifth grade. One young man told me that when speaking about his father's farm and the objects of his childhood, he would be most comfortable in his native language, but the ideas he learned in school could be best expressed in English. If he wants to discuss his future education, his thought processes are in English, but if he is to tell his family about his plans he must mentally translate imperfect English into imperfect vernacular—a procedure which is not very conducive to a relaxed family relationship.

Is this situation unavoidable? Can we perhaps help the boys to bridge the gap between home and school by finding those aspects of the traditional culture which can be introduced and developed within the modern framework of the school? An obvious potential area for such a project is traditional music.

When I arrived at Kakamega, there was an English violinist on the staff, and his music appreciation society invariably packed his living room for classical music. To complement this group, I organized a "music-making" club to encourage members both to make and play indigenous instruments. The Baluhya tribe to which two-thirds of these young men belong is one of the most musical in East Africa. A seven-stringed plucked instrument called the *litungu*, a kind of one-stringed violin, and a variety of drums are widespread, while maracas, reed flutes, and several other instruments are in more localized use.

—

The Old Music. My wife Judith and I discovered our first *litungu*-player strolling along the road near our school, entertaining himself and a few friends. After a short concert, he agreed to be the first guest-performer and guest-lecturer to the music-making club. A week before he arrived, I mentioned to the members that I had seen a musician, described the instrument, and asked if any of them had seen anything like it or perhaps knew how to play it. At first there was no answer. Then there came a ripple of laughter, a good deal of whispering and a bit of foot-shuffling, but still no verbal response.

Only after putting the question to some of the older individuals rather than to the whole group was I informed that, yes, they had seen such things but, no, they did not know how to make or play them. This reluctant, somewhat amused response to the mention of their traditional culture was puzzling and a bit disturbing.

At first, I feared I had said something which bespoke ignorance or disrespect. Over the next few months, however, similar experiences convinced me that the laughter was largely a cover for embarrassment. To the extent that there was real laughter, the source of humor was that a Westerner should be interested in such an uncivilized profession as *litungu* playing.

Without presuming to condemn or praise the entire colonial and missionary operations, one can safely say that neither of these influences was, on the whole, helpful in maintaining the African's respect for his traditional music. Some missionaries went so far as to try to eliminate indigenous instruments altogether. Most colonists were a bit more subtle, merely sowing a general contempt for the African tradition. Perhaps, then, it is natural for the new generation to turn its back on the old music and all that goes with it. As far back as they can remember, these students have seen the educated Westerner looking down on the traditionalist African. Now they are the educated and to gain security in their new superior position, they look for something to be superior to, and the handiest, most familiar object of derision is their own tradition. They cannot deride it strongly, of course, for it is a part of them—it is what their parents are made of—and thus it gives rise to very discomforting ambivalent feelings.

Our *litungu*-player arrived in due course, and there was better-than-average attendance at the club that day. The uneducated old school custodian stopped by and danced to the music—to the mixed delight and embarrassment of the group. The first song—with improvised Swahili lyrics—claimed that white men eat eggs and that one particular white man hires *litungu*-players for a small fraction of their proper worth. The performance was quite a success and his explanation of the simple but ingenious construction of the instrument even elicited a couple of questions. But in the weeks that followed no one wanted to try to make a *litungu* and the boys seldom touched the one which the musician made and sold to me.

The music-making club flourished on the guitar. The group made three playable guitars and also used a couple of factory-made instruments. It is ironic that, although the guitar-picking in the current African popular recordings which they emulate is quite accomplished, the songs are repetitious, harmonically over-simple, and quite inferior to those sung with the *litungu*, which is often tuned in a minor key.

Shall we conclude then that a rich tradition is being lost, spurned by those whom we might have hoped would be its proponents? I think the explanation is not that the students have rejected the traditional music and the rest of their cultural heritage but that they feel uncomfortable with it within the school environment.

This feeling seems to diminish after the student has become a little more secure in his knowledge of the outside world and his need to exalt himself by degrading his people decreases. This observation is supported particularly by the behavior of the brightest and most adaptable students, many of whom go overseas to universities. When they return to their native country, they usually are anxious to develop it into something quite different from what it has been, but they are not hostile to the past and can be counted on to preserve what is of interest and value in the modern world. Even the less successful boys are laying the groundwork for the future—their children who will be born into more modern homes, will have a much easier adjustment.

> I was guided in these thoughts and words by my wife, Judith Hamburger (now deceased). This story appeared in *Technology Review*, Volume 67, Number 8, June 1965, at http://bit.ly/culture-1. □

Math, Temba, Adongo, and Pedagogy

Henry Hamburger

I know that even in 1963 what meant most to me, and probably to many of us Americans, was genuine understanding of the concepts. Along with understanding comes—in math certainly—the ability to see that there is more than one right way to solve a problem and that there are ways to check yourself, not just hope you're right and move on, but know when you know. Math has known knowns.

With that kind of knowledge comes confidence, independence of mind, satisfaction, even pleasure, nay excitement that can pull students in, keep them open for more, draw them along, and give them a life resource of both skill and intellectuality. I like to think that is happening with some of my College Bound tutees and that it happened with some of my Kakamega students. Among the latter I think of two.

Young Joseph Temba was a mediocre student that I had in Form 1 before I was assigned all A-level classes. He once marveled to me that it seemed like I actually really liked math. Later, he would come to me with puzzles. A year after I got home, he wrote that he had a new baby brother named (one shudders to think) Henry Hamburger Temba.

Doing math has something to do with the structure of human brains in general and particular ones too. It also has to do with coming to the realization, the conviction, that it is all going to make sense. I was firmly convinced that Adongo had the brain, the understanding, and the motivation to succeed at a great university and said as much in an impassioned plea to the MIT admissions office. (They wanted to know if he could prove that he had $6,000 for the first year's tuition, room, board, and so on. Now "that" was culture shock.)

Some of this may sound particular to math, but some of it surely transcends it. We found ways either to bridge the culture gap or to make it not matter.

Music at Kakamega

Henry Hamburger

Among the many musical instruments I have learned to play poorly, the *sukuti*, a west-Kenyan drum, holds a special place in memory, along with the guy who, for a price, had taught me three different ways to strike the lizard-skin drumhead, when he stopped showing up.

You can derive your own *sukuti* lessons from the demo at http://bit.ly/sukuti. You can see another instrument from the same region, the lyre-like *litungu*, at http://bit.ly/litungu.

From the latter video I have learned that the *litungu* is no longer confined to a mere seven notes but now has eight strings, an ordinary scaleful so to speak, tuned compatibly with our keyboards, possibly an asset, depending on your viewpoint.

These instruments were played in the vicinity of Kakamega Secondary School in 1963–65 when I was there teaching "advanced level" pure and applied mathematics, aka "maths," and I still have one of each. As part of a righteous respect for host country and culture, I founded a music club, enticed a *litungu* player to perform at the inaugural meeting, and urged students to make their own local instruments. Gently but firmly, they let me know that they had no interest in such things but that if I would purchase the hardware, some of them would build a guitar, a project that actually succeeded. We shared an interest in music, but my students and I had passed by each other on a cultural bridge.

Straddling that bridge with a kind of Anglo-African musical sensibility was the school's choir leader, one Arthur Kemoli, whose musical genius and hard work made him a national figure (his obituary is at http://bit.ly/kemoli).

In time, Kemoli graduated and was replaced by my student Caleb Oyuke, later to become the pioneer dean of sciences at Kenyatta University, who invited me to be faculty sponsor of the choir. I did little in that role, but when my tour was up, Caleb graciously awarded me a framed photo of the choir, mouths open with song, with him leading. I have it still, but now, forty-seven years later, I am soon to return it to the school in response to a request from current principal Oliver Minishi via John Basinger, another American and Kakamega teacher of the 1960s. □

The Cook

Henry Hamburger

TEA had told us that hiring cooks would be expected of us: not to go local, not to shrink the job market, to put our energies into teaching. And so our alarm clock became the scraping of overdone toast, butane-broiled by loyal Josiah. Josiah was a cook or *mpishi*, though of course he did keep house without ever being asked. Had his own lamb's-wool bottomed sandals to skate around in to polish floors and must have done some repairs because he once asked me for a *sapana*, which I never did find in my Swahili dictionary, but ultimately decoded as the Bantuized form of the British word for monkey wrench, long after he had borrowed one somewhere and done the necessary.

Oh yes, and he was a great cook, replete with secrets from the previous *memsaab*. We thought of him as a friend, though to the extent that he realized it, it embarrassed him. Well, it is what it is, and even the despised word "boy" arose when he informed us that we should not bring him stew meat (Level 2 in the meat hierarchy, below fileti), but boy meat, chewier, presumably more satisfying, and a step up from cat meat. Poor Falstaff the dog got Level 5; maybe that's why we could never teach him to stop barking at students who came by.

Our gardener ("shambaboy"—how did they think these things up, and why?) was younger, more assertive, the new generation. I wish them both well and, as I write, feel a pang of regret that we never kept in touch after parting. □

Kiangoma Track Meet

Ward Heneveld

My last year was 1967 at the new Kiangoma Boys Secondary School in the foothills of the Aberdares west of Karatina in central province, Kenya, and we finally had the school's first Form 4.

One of the Fourth Formers, Kariuki, ran the mile in less than 4.5 minutes and was training for the provincial meet. I don't remember if that was the sole impetus, but as headmaster I scheduled the school's first full track meet in the middle of the year. In the mile run, Kariuki of course came in first, but Mwangi, a Form 1 day student, was only about fifty yards behind him; and both were close to one-quarter mile ahead of the rest of the runners.

I was surprised, as were others, because Mwangi had not distinguished himself at all since joining the school at the beginning of the year. So, when a half hour later Mwangi lapped everyone in the three-mile run, I was convinced there was something going on with this young man that I had not appreciated.

When I called Mwangi aside later, I found out that he was an orphan who lived with his sister, her husband, and their children about six miles from our school. Mwangi admitted that he was running that distance to and from school every day! Closer observation of him in class revealed that he spent a good part of each day sleeping. Duh!

So, I asked him how much he'd need to be able to find a place to rent near the school. When he told me something like about twenty dollars a month, I hired him at that rate as my gardener. The next day when games started, including training for the provincial track meet, I found Mwangi digging weeds in our garden next to the games field. I chased him onto the field and told him to do his work for us outside of the school day.

The teachers and I also noticed that Mwangi had chosen to sit in the back of the classroom, obviously in order to doze less ostentatiously. However, now that he was not sleeping anymore, my wife Cheryl, his English teacher, realized that he was squinting at the board all the time.

We moved him to the front of the class, sent him to the eye doctor, and funded the prescription glasses he needed. At the end of the next term he had moved from being in the last three or four students in academic standing in a class of thirty-five students to being one of the top fifteen students. And he was still running regularly after school.

Cheryl and I left at the end of that year, and I have often wondered what Mwangi's life after Kiangoma has been. ☐

Kiangoma and Student Fees
Ward Heneveld

In the late 1960s the new Kiangoma Secondary School for boys was not easy to get to. On the main road from Nairobi to Nyeri, one turned left onto a dirt track about half a mile past Karatina. Twelve miles of ups and downs led to Murkurweini village center where there was a grocer, a butcher, a couple shops, and a bar. Another half mile past the village, a right turn onto a one-lane track led to the school where my bride Cheryl and I taught.

The quarter-mile-long track ran along the underside of a ridge with deserted huts from the days of Mau Mau laid out in rows below the road, and it ended in a circle in front of the four-classroom stone block that had been a missionary primary school. To the right of the school building was a shed, and behind it the football field with two small stone-block houses next to the field's end close to the school.

If one arrived during school time, there would be boys in shorts lounging around the grounds or in the classrooms. Their makeshift (and unofficial) hostel for what was supposed to be a day school was about one hundred yards down the promontory that the school rested upon.

About 120 of the 140 boys stayed in the hostel, which an annual "development fee" funded and which had dirt floors, walls made of offcuts from the outside of logs (flat on the inside, rounded with bark on the outsides), and steel cots for which each student had to provide his own mattress. The schoolboys helped a local villager prepare their meals in a couple large black pots into which one of them could fit on a wood fire that used the wood from the nearby abandoned huts as we purchased them and dismantled them one by one.

There was no electricity in the area, including at the school, and running water came out of a couple taps that had recently been connected to the water supply in Mukurweini. The views in all directions were rich in distance, color, and the sounds of life, particularly cattle. The hillsides were dotted with *shambas*, small farms of under an acre, and on a clear day Mt. Kenya loomed in the distance. It was a spectacular setting to live in.

During the school terms, the days were very full. Classes started near eight in the morning and continued until mid-afternoon after which there were games, mostly soccer on the football field. In the evening, the allowed thirty-five students in each form gathered in their respective classrooms from the hostel to study under the light of one petromax pressure lamp hung in the middle of the classroom.

The day started again early the next morning. This simple infrastructure and the daily rhythm focused on learning were to the students the most sophisticated environment they had ever been in. They mostly came from the kind of small *shambas* and mud and wattle huts with grass roofs that we could see from the school, though many came from as far as twenty miles away.

Whenever they went anywhere, it was on foot and often without shoes. Cheryl and I were rich because we had a car, two or three of our own petromax lamps, a kerosene refrigerator, and natural gas for a water heater and the stove.

One of my tasks as the headmaster was to collect fees in cash from these students whose background had been mostly outside a cash economy. The school was funded by the Government of Kenya, but each year we had to subtract from the approved budget something like Ksh.350 (about US $50) multiplied by the total allowed number of students. I was required to collect this 350-shilling government-imposed fee and the Ksh.150 development fee (about US $20) from each student during the year. This meant setting a portion of the fees for each of the three terms and then making sure that each student paid what he owed when the term came around.

For most students, Ksh.350 was a lot of money, and they usually couldn't obtain all of what they owed for a term by the first day of the term. In order to be responsive to this very real cash flow problem while being sure that the school received the fees due, we insisted that at the start of each term each student must show up with some cash and be ready to commit to an exact date by which he promised to provide the balance due that term.

It took a while to get this rule established. For example, early on the son of a local shopkeeper who lived nearby showed up with no money and said he'd bring it the next day. When I sent him away even though I knew his family could pay, he was back in an hour with the full amount due that term.

On the other hand, I remember one boy who came with some cash on the first day of the term, left when I looked directly at him from the doorway of his classroom on his due date three to four weeks later, and came back only after two weeks. When I asked him why he was gone so long, he said he had to go home (a day's walk or so), raise money for a taxi trip to Nairobi, travel to Nairobi (two hours in the daily local taxi out of the hills to Nairobi), and move around among relatives in Nairobi's low-income areas until he had accumulated the cash for the school and the taxi fare home.

Once this rule of some cash plus a committed date for the balance being provided on the first day of each term was established, all I had to do was walk into a classroom during class on the agreed date, look directly at the student whose payment was due, and he'd gather up his books and leave. He'd come back as quickly as he could obtain the money to pay the balance of his fees.

For each of them, time away from school was an extreme punishment, because they would miss material in all subjects that they might need to answer questions on the school-leaving examination, and in those days, it was this exam that determined their future opportunities for education, employment, and a career. For these privileged young men receiving a secondary education all further education and training for jobs after secondary school was free. ☐

Instant Expert at Twenty Years Old
Sharon Hepburn

Bwiru Girls School is a boarding school in Mwanza, Tanzania. Teaching was only one of the many assignments that were expected of TEA teachers. Before I even started teaching classes, I was assigned to the dispensary when Mrs. Nemeskaal left. My only qualification was the science subjects I had taken in college. I became an instant expert.

Soon, I and other new teachers learned about duty days which included overseeing breakfast, lunch, and supper and monitoring evening preps and lights out. Then too, having the responsibility of field hockey coach meant getting the girls to use the *pangas* on the tall grasses that covered our hockey field so that we could actually try to play. And I managed the vote book. That duty involved accounting, but money management has never been my strength. However, since teaching maths was actually a teaching assignment that I was happy to handle, the handling the vote book, in someone's eyes, seemed a fitting job for me. Among the less tedious extras were playing the piano for morning assembly, making refreshments for 10:00 a.m. break for tea, advising the science club and invigilating Cambridge exams.

Being in charge of the dispensary was the scariest job. Mama Susannah was very knowledgeable, and using her bits of English and my broken Swahili, we worked out a system. Any cuts or skin problems went directly to her and I attempted all else. Of course, the first week there was a line out the door, students waiting to see what the new teacher could do with *dawa*.

Very soon, however, the novelty wore off and tasks became routine: Usually, the first step was to take the temperature of the student. Regularly, we dealt with malaria, the most prevalent ailment affecting students. It responded well, however, to the quinine drugs. Victims of bilharzia, on the other hand, had to be taken in the lorry to the hospital in town.

The worst situation developed when a girl fell on the rocks. My limited knowledge did not clue me in that she had broken her femur, because she was able to walk. The medical staff chastised me for not bringing her to the hospital sooner. Of course, their X-rays and training didn't help me feel better about my mistake. How happy I was when Judith took over the dispensary! □

Boys and Their Toys

Niall Herriott

A newly arrived VSO (Voluntary Service Overseas) recruit for the school had a very puzzled expression in the staffroom. He asked me was it usual to have a long gap six inches high in the bottom of the wooden wall of the rooms of the line of accommodation chalets.

The mystery unfolded further that night. The VSO had returned to his room for an early night, exhausted after the long flight from London and had fallen asleep. He was awakened by the hooting and clackety-clack of a model train, instantly recognizable from his childhood. He had jumped out of bed to see the train emerging from the gap in the wall on a curving track and disappearing back into the next apartment.

Naturally he went next door to ask what the hell was going on. An elderly Englishman opened the door and explained that it was only now and then that he needed to extend the track in through the gap to give his train a good run and he hoped it was not a problem. He also explained patiently that he had cut out the gap in the wall with an inefficient electric saw and that it really was quite a hard job to do.

The VSO thought better of having such a dingbat for a neighbor and immediately sought and was given alternative accommodation. Never a dull moment at that school. ☐

A Sense of Proportion
Niall Herriott

In Uganda bizarre things happened all the time but we quickly learned to take them in our stride. One day I was preparing to leave the school to go on holidays when I heard the sound of windows being smashed and some whooping and hollering going on. Nearly all the other teachers and most of the students had gone.

I quickly realized that some of the students still there were staging a "strike" despite classes having finished for the holidays. There had been some annoyance over the recent suspension of a student who was found to have a substantial stash of the local home-made hooch called *enguli*.

What to do? I went to the headmaster's house, Father Ben, an old Dutch missionary priest. He was trying to use a screwdriver to fix a lock on his back door and seemed unaware of the situation. I assumed he was hard of hearing. I started to fill him in on the details.

Ben looked at me exasperatedly and then went back to fiddling with the lock. "Ach, can you not see that I am busy?" he said.

Oh well, nothing for it then but to head off for one of my favorite haunts, the City Bar, in nearby Kampala for a couple of cold beers. ☐

About Positive and Negative

Moses L. Howard

"Excuse me, sir, I'm asking."

"Yes, Sendagire, go on."

It was our ten-minute session at the end of a chemistry class at Ntare School in Mbarara, Uganda in 1961, a time set aside for students to ask questions on any part of the lesson they didn't understand.

"It's about positive and negative, sir."

"Yes, go on. What is it about positive and negative?"

"It is confusing, sir. You have taught us that in an electric circuit electrons flow from the negative to the positive. Isn't that right, sir?"

"Yes, that is correct."

"But, sir, if negative flows to the positive, it must be moving, acting, sir. We have been led to believe if something is moving and active it is positive. And now in chemistry, if it is acting, doing, why isn't it called positive?"

"Oh, I see, and you are absolutely right. A long time ago, researchers discovered that there were two opposite types of electric charges, and they could have been called just as you say, one black, the other white, but they were designated positive and negative. Had those scientists been as analytical as you are now, they would have been named as you suggest, but they agreed to call them as we are calling them now, and it would be too confusing to change them."

"You said *agreed*. Is that the way much knowledge is based, on agreements made long ago?"

"What do you mean?"

"I am thinking about electrons. We can't see them, sir, but *they* agreed long ago that electrons exist."

"But there is evidence that they exist. We can test that evidence."

"But, sir, I am thinking about math also, sir. There are rules about which we have no proof, but they are accepted. We use them consistently to solve problems, sir."

"Such as what?"

"I think one word is axiom, a self-evident truth. I can't think of the other."

But here another boy, Mugisha, stepped in to help. "We talked about postulates, which I think are like axioms…and theorem, which is an idea or belief, or method generally accepted as true, but it needs a proof."

They chorused: "We cannot. How can we, as students, accept that, sir?" A spirited discussion followed. "Proof, where was the proof?"

This conversation occurred in a high school chemistry class in which one student was to become the president of Uganda. I am sure I learned as much in that class as did the students, and yet I have in front of me a book written by the president, entitled *Sowing the Mustard Seed*, in which he has inscribed the following:

> 30/12/2009
> To: Mzee Moses Howard
> Of the USA (formerly of Ntare 1961-62)
> From: President Museveni of Uganda
>
> "You were a great chemistry teacher.
> You solved the problem of valence for me."

President Museveni's book is a history of Uganda during and soon after the coup of Idi Amin. It covers years following the coup. It describes the country during the revolution in which the president and his fellow students fought a bush war, deposed Amin, and are now serving as rulers of their country. □

O Levels and Me

Moses L. Howard

In our staff room at Ntare High School, following examinations, British teaching masters pulled long, dissatisfied faces. The O-level English examination results never reached a desired level. It never failed, no matter how many passes students achieved in other subjects or even how well scores rose in Language, the students never reached the sought-after level of their counterparts in England. Therefore, the teachers of English and writing thought scores were abysmal in English and writing. In African schools, according to their voiced complaints, scores had always fallen low in language usage and writing.

As usual, a lot of discussion was generated about how to raise these scores for the next exams, a year away. One morning, the conversation centered on how students had not understood the classic English text, *Tom Brown's Schooldays* by Thomas Hughes. Members of staff read aloud, with picky laughs of derision, how students had responded to the behavior of Tom and the school bully Flashman. The students' written responses criticized Tom and Flashman, saying they would not be tolerated in an African school. The Prefect would "shut them down." The students did not take into consideration cultural differences or class background, or elements they misunderstood in the language nuance of the English author.

Although teachers had provided students with cultural information about English public schools and detailed the physical surroundings of those schools, the students evidenced no clear understanding of that information or how to use it accurately in critical written commentary about that classic novel. They clearly were not English boys who had imbibed this knowledge in row-house front parlors or by breathing English air. They were not English boys who had listened daily, from birth, to the conversations of parents and neighbors across backyard fences. They had not read English prose in unison with other British boys in schools from primary levels upward.

Still, the masters, for the most part, were unsympathetic. They did not take into consideration what was before them: boys who came from villages where there were not centuries of knowledge about the evolution of English literature, boys who had scant knowledge of the history of those people or of their language. In front of them were African boys from villages who had never set foot on English soil. They had rarely heard the language spoken accurately and had never listened to their parents and neighbors speak English. "They nor their parents," one master noted, "are allowed at our clubs, where they'd see our crude attempts at rugby. And who among us even have witnessed, out here, anyone bowl a perfect score at cricket?"

I listened to all of this with interest until old Robson, one of the elder lecturers, stated the whole thing more clearly. "These chaps are rather good, actually. I doubt that any of us, in their stead, could do better."

"How do you say that?" Other masters quickly challenged him.

"These blokes are actually expected to do the impossible," he went on. "They are born in African villages where only Bantu languages are spoken, not written. They live there, listening to uneducated vernacular all their formative lives, and then, they are asked to become English boys by the time they are thirteen, speaking and writing polished English as if they were in a Rugby school, with the background of a Tom Brown and a Flashman."

"Hear, hear! We know that. It's been said often enough before, but what's the answer, Robby?" they queried him.

"It's plain enough what's needed. But how to supply it is a major drawback."

"Well, well, a solution to our annual worries is imminent. Tell us, Robby, tell us what's needed."

By now, Robson was laughing that everyone was turning his attempt at levity into a referendum on his ability to solve the insolvable problems of low O-level English scores. "I don't think it bloody fair for you chaps to mark me as the Oracle at Delphi because I point to what is commonly known by all of us."

"Just tell it. What is the creaking bloody answer? I warrant you we all stand to be indebted to you for it."

"Well, now I need to shorten this." He looked all around at them. "What is needed is an examination set on a book written about them and their environment. I am sure that would go a long way toward improving English and writing scores."

"The catch is there is no such book in existence."

"Then someone should write one."

"Who, by all means?" Eyes darted around the staff room. "Who knows the intimate relations of the lives of these chaps? You would have to sleep in their huts, eat cassava, *ntulas*, cabbages, their plantain and groundnut soup. You'd have to see them born, see them married, go to funerals. None of us have done this."

Someone else looking around seized on a lecturer who to this point had been uninvolved. "The nearest description to that is Bottram." All eyes fell on the geography master, who taught bare-chested in class, wore colored togas, and behaved much as if he was Lawrence of Arabia in town and on safari.

Bottram declined, saying with emphasis, "I write factual geography books. I have long been of the opinion that exams should be written on scholarly investigations and information of nonfiction rather than on fabricated tracts. What I write can be shown, measured, and verified. Half of *Tom Brown's Schooldays* is sentimental haberdashery. It's propaganda, preachments on manners and morals, written to influence rather than to educate and inform."

While the whole staff looked at him, smiling, he added, "That's your field, fiction," he pointed an open geography book at Robson and waved it at the other English masters. "That's your department. If Jim Hilton were here, you could possibly get him to write a *Goodbye, Mr. Mulumu* instead of *Goodbye, Mr. Chips*, and you would have your local novel. But, frankly, it will have to be someone closer, someone among them someone who lives in an African village.

"How about Ngugi's *Weep Not, Child*?"

"I am afraid not. It's too cerebral and psychological for the purpose. It has to be simple, everyday, down to earth," Old Robson put in. He was a respected old don from Oxford who had himself been prepped at Eton and knew English schools.

Then, Robin Dawes, who was always kidding me about how I spent every moment in the village, even spending nights with friends and student families there, now spoke up. "Moses should be the one for that task. He knows the village better than any of us."

"Can't you deliver us from this dilemma, Moses?" they shouted with laughter.

I thought it was a great joke and said so, since I taught chemistry and biology. The other English masters thought so, too.

"But that would be even worse." They pursued that old American joke. "He's an American, and you know they don't speak English over there, not even as well as any of the other colonies." There was quiet in the staff room, with all of the English masters looking at me and the three other American teachers to see if we regarded the comment an insult. After a pause, we all laughed and the subject was dropped.

While the staff room conversation had taken an unusual turn, it had been an ordinary day. I went back to preparing chemistry lessons and going to sports in the evening with the boys. I was helping them learn basketball, which had been recently introduced to Uganda, and they tolerated me in their soccer games.

Every free moment, as was my habit, I escaped to a nearby village called Ruti, another name for trees. A family had adopted me on my first visit. They had made me welcome, and I joined the family of four boys and five girls, two of whom were already primary schoolteachers. I worked on their farm, cutting pineapples, gathering papaya, digging drainage ditches in the banana plantations, and milking goats.

Time with the family was always enjoyable. However, the father, a Gombola chief, was experiencing a problem with his son at secondary school who was having difficulty deciding between being a British boy or an African one. He had adopted the habits of his British masters, copying their speech and trying to be a dandy at home in the village, neglecting to care for the goats or to pick coffee berries. It was a problem similar to one experienced by my brother back in America with his teenaged son who neglected his studies, trying for a career in music instead of keeping up his grades.

Back in the staff room at school, they kept up their ribbing, not letting go threads of the conversation about my writing a book, suitable for evaluating African students in English. "Moses," they would say, "how is the African school-days book progressing?" They often asked that question instead of greeting me or engaging in an exchange about the chemistry and biology classes I was teaching. I knew I was not a writer with skills approaching those of Thomas Hughes, and I knew I didn't know enough about Africa to write such a book, even if I had possessed the skills. But they kept asking as if they intended to goad me into doing it. I had told myself that I couldn't do it, but I was offended by their constant inference that I could.

So one evening, instead of going to Ruti, I began a narrative about the place. I wrote about what I knew. I based my story on what was happening there, knowing I could never reach a level anywhere near the almost perfect scenes and themes in *Tom Brown's School Days*. Nevertheless, I went on.

Over the holidays, I wrote every chance I got, and I produced a text of more than a hundred pages and thirty thousand words. It was a story about a boy in an African village who wanted to be British. He mimicked his school masters and lost his father's confidence and his father's goats to marauding dingoes, to wild dogs roaming the countryside. The boy feared the vicious dogs and thus feared becoming a man. I called the story *Dogs of Fear*. In Ruti, the people called me Musa (for Moses), and because I was always on the go, they called me Nagenda, which means going. So I put a fly leaf on my book, entitling it *Dogs of Fear* by Musa Nagenda. I dumped the manuscript on Old Robson's desk when he was at prep one evening.

Two days later, with his usual good humor, he said, "It doesn't measure up, old chap. It's not anywhere near Tom Hughes's *Tom Brown*, but it has a quest." It was two days before school holidays, and so nothing else was said until we came back six weeks later. During that time, I had come down with a swollen toe, so painful I couldn't walk to class. I called the headmaster and said I would be absent. That evening Denis Wills, one of the English masters, came to see me and diagnosed my condition as gout. He brought me medicine from the apothecary and a list of foods to avoid. Among those forbidden were beef and liver, two of my favorites.

As Denis was leaving, he called me Musa Nagenda and said James Currey, an editor from Heinemann's educational books, had been looking for me the previous day. The chap had a manuscript that he wanted to publish, but no one seemed to know the author. The book was *Dogs of Fear*. Robson had been away, and no one else besides Denis knew that I was the author. Denis, in fact, was a writer himself. I had discussed writing with him a few times in the midst of writing the book. He knew I was the author, but didn't know if he should tell that to Currey. When Robson returned, he confessed to sending the manuscript to Heinemann without my knowledge.

The book was published in a new junior series by Heinemann, and Gene Ashby brought the first copies to me where I was living in the holidays with my Tutsi wife and two children on my *shamba* in Ankole. That book was followed by two more: *The Ostrich Chase* and *The Human Mandolin*. Heinemann showed these books at a book fair in Frankfurt, Germany, where an American publisher, Holt, Rinehart and Winston saw them and brought out American-published copies.

Perhaps needless to say, *Dogs of Fear* was never up to a standard where it could be set as a book for a national examination, but it was sold over the world, was translated into Norwegian, and garnered the author fan mail from young readers in Australia and New Zealand. It was used as practice books for local exams, and in America, it was selected for a section in a sixth-grade reader called *Bright and Beautiful*. That was in the 1970s. The first two books are out of print now, but anyone still interested can Google them. They are in libraries and knocking around on Amazon.com. □

Sundowner

Moses L. Howard

Sometimes personal items left in odd places can lead to humor, romance, or mayhem. When I first arrived in Kampala at Kyambogo Teacher Training College, I was assigned a house in the usual way that teaching masters are housed when they arrive on school compounds.

The house assigned me had recently been vacated by a newly married couple. The groom had taken a new job in Malaya and left his bride with neighbors. She would live for a few months at Kyambogo in a house with friends on the school compound, until he settled in the new post and came back for her. He was due back any day now. Together, they would move to their new post.

In the headmaster's office, before I took possession of the house, I was greeted with an invitation to attend a sundowner at the home of one of the college's history masters. The headmaster ushered me into a nearby office and introduced me to my host, the young history professor named Brian Walton. Kathryn, Brian's wife, sat with him in the company of their house guest, Erin, a young woman of about twenty-three years. Dressed in a green blouse and pink culottes, Erin smiled beautifully. I noticed the yellow hair and freckles on her nose.

Brian said, "I say, the sundowner is soon. Come promptly at six o'clock, so you won't miss any of the antics."

Since I had not worked among the British in the tropics before and had no idea, I asked, "Sundowner, what's that?"

Brian and Kathryn, who had spent a honeymooning summer in Canada and America, exchanged smiling glances. Kathryn said, jokingly, "It's like an American cocktail party, held on the lawn at sundown, except it's more fun."

"Everyone comes," Brian added, "has drinks and toasts all around, while meeting everyone else."

I left them and walked up hill a short distance past school buildings and science labs, thinking of meeting my first students in just three days.

I found the two-bedroom house assigned to me empty. It had been recently cleaned, scrubbed from top to bottom. African servants moved my jumble of chemistry and biology books and bags in and made the beds, and all was ready for my occupancy. But as I walked through the house, my footsteps echoed softly. Although it was empty of former tenants, there lingered throughout the rooms, over most of the house, the smell of perfume. The house was empty except for the bed and bedding, and my unpacked trunks and suitcases still rested in the hallway, awaiting my choice of a room for them.

I went through each room with the doors standing open, finding the rooms empty, mute, and receptive. The servant opened windows, bringing in wind that fretted and billowed the white curtains about. And yet, still lingered the odor of that perfume. It was a haunting essence that spoke of a feminine presence. The scent was strongest in the large master bedroom. So I put my things in the small bedroom and got dressed in casual shorts and sports shirt, hoping I was appropriately dressed for the sundowner.

Inhabitants had apparently forgotten that *sundowner,* the word itself, referred to a single drink taken at the end of a hard day, usually a mixture of Malibu rum and pineapple juice and Angostura bitters. On the several tables set up on the manicured terraced lawn were numerous bottles of vodka, gin, bourbon, Irish whiskeys, Johnny Walker, Harvey's Bristol Cream, and various wines that had slipped through customs and made their way to the several tables. And now jibes of joy and "cheers" rang out as glasses clinked, then were raised over and over again among jokes and bright laughter, saluting everyone and everything.

A lot of liquor, beer, and wine, local and imported, flowed to and from glasses held in tanned hands and tipped to happily creased faces. Gaiety prevailed and goodwill rose in animated voices and wafted over the school compound. I was toasted several times by Elliot, the geography master, and again by Brian, and I was introduced to the occupants of the spacious lawn again by those who did not know we had met in the headmaster's office.

After an hour—those sitting at tables now gladdened with the musical clink of empty bottles and glasses—the headmaster called for glasses to be filled for the sundowner. He made an impromptu announcement that there was an American on the staff and said, jokingly, that they should just remember that, in spite of our different views on education, America and England are still allies. Brendan, who was Irish, said something about the Irish Republic and if I met him in the staff room he'd teach me how to make a cup of real Irish tea. With that, someone corrected him: "Coffee, Brendan, Irish coffee."

Allan, the staff Rugby coach, said he needed another bloke for the Rugby side and wondered whether I could join up. Responding to his vernacular, I said I was keen for it. The wives, led by Kathryn and Erin, were friendly and met me, a bachelor, with sparkling eyes.

Toward seven o'clock, the sun sparkled through trees. The headmaster saluted everyone, downed a stiff drink, said Cheer-io, and ambled off down the graveled road to his house. I was not clear-headed, having drunk a proffered glass of *waraga*, the local African drink—comparable to American gin or moonshine—and the shandies that Brendan had urged on me.

By the time Elliot and his wife Susan raised their beer steins, making excuses to leave early for a trip to Kampala the next day, the party had thinned as couples drifted away, the sunlight fading, dusk replacing it. When I signaled the distracted, alcohol-bemused few still remaining that I too was leaving, it was to no one's notice. As I started uphill toward my house, out of the shadows of a mimosa tree stepped Erin. She stumbled against me as if she had drunk over her limit.

When I put up my hand to prevent her fall, I caught a whiff of the same perfume from my new house.

"I say, Moses, do you mind if I walk up to yours with you?"

"With me?" I was surprised.

"Yes, I left a few personal items in your house. This is a good time to retrieve them since Martin is coming back any day now."

"Are you...did you live here? Are you the couple who just left this house?"

"Martin and I jolly well loved it. I hope you won't mind terribly if I nip in and get my things." She was unsteady on her feet and almost missed the bottom step. My arm guided her up.

She wobbled directly to the master bedroom and, looking behind the door among noisy hangers, she soon held up her lacy night gowns and other garments, and the perfume odor engulfed us. It struck me then why her things had not been seen by the servants or me. The doors were all the way open, and no one looked behind them.

But still holding her night clothes, Erin swayed, suddenly seemed weak, and sank tumbling to the floor among her personal items.

"Erin! Erin!" I called her several times, then knelt beside her, got my arms under her and lifted her to the bed. I looked out of the window down to the sundowner, thinking, *What do I do now? Should I go for one of the women to help? Should I go down there for help?*

But all the lights were out and it was dark. I didn't want to leave her alone that time of night. Besides, what Erin needed right then was to sleep. I shook Erin a couple of times, but she was snoring. *Better to let her sleep in the bed that she was used to sharing with Martin.* I covered her with a sheet, put a pillow under her head and then went to my room, where I unpacked and went to bed.

The next morning, I was awakened by the crunch of gravel under Land Rover tires and the blaring of a horn. I open the door, then quickly Brian was in the living room with another red-faced chap whose eyes were angry and his mouth couldn't stay still.

Brian said, "I say, Moses, we have searched the whole blasted compound. Have you seen Erin? She didn't sleep at ours last night, and here is Martin just returned, looking for her."

Before I answered them, my eyes glanced toward the master bedroom, and Brian and Martin rushed in there and found Erin still asleep, with her lacy night gowns, still on hangers, lying on the bed beside her. Martin took Erin into his arms. She was fully dressed in the clothes she'd worn the previous evening. His frowns changed to satisfied smiles when he saw my wrinkled bed and me still in night clothes.

He took his bride away, over his shoulder. She was finally awake, and embarrassed and apologetic. "Gee, Moses, after all the trouble I caused, I suppose you'll never speak to me again." Martin's face relaxed, and I could see Erin and I had provided an amusing story that would be told over and over at future sundowners. ☐

My African Students

Moses L. Howard

In Africa, my students often came to tea at my house. They asked me to explain lessons, but they were more interested in personal relationships.

"What is this dating?"

"Do most boys have cars to drive around with girls as we see in the movies?"

When they discovered I was approachable, the questions got more personal. They were always respectful and seemed convinced they could ask me anything and get a civil answer. I tried to give honest answers. I felt every exchange was a moment of teaching and learning. I was learning and teaching, and so were they. I am sure they asked me questions they would never ask their British or even African teaching masters. There is usually a stilted reserve between teacher and student in Africa. With me somehow it was different; I was an African American, they were curious, they lifted the barrier and connected with me.

Their queries mirrored both curiosity and concern about me and my adjustment to living in Africa. They took a special effort to educate me. So when they learned from Sandeg, my friend the surveyor for the road builders in whom I had confided that I had found a girl I wished to marry, a student from my sixth form, named Kajubi, came to talk with me about it. He began in a formal manner as he would if he were asking questions on a lesson we had in chemistry.

"Sir, we know you are an accomplished science teacher, sir."

I said, "Yes," looking into his anxious eyes. I wondered where this was going. "Yes?"

"Your parents were farmers in Mississippi."

"That's right," I said

"Were they successful, sir?"

"Moderately so," I admitted.

"Please explain 'moderate' as it applies."

"Well, sometimes they succeeded and sometimes they failed. It depended upon factors such as seeds, weather, seasons, planting, rainfall, soil, errors."

Here he shifted abruptly… "You were married in America before coming to Africa, sir?"

"Yes," I hesitated, then added, "The marriage didn't work."

"So you are divorced now, sir?"

"That's correct."

"Does that mean your marriage failed, sir?"

"Yes, a divorced marriage means that marriage failed."

"Is marriage like farming, sir, sometimes succeeding and sometimes failing?"

"No. A marriage should succeed so that a couple remains married for life."

"But you said your marriage failed, sir. Does it means you did not know how to marry?"

"To an extent I think that's correct."

"Have you studied marriage sir, so now you know how to marry?"

"Yes."

"You failed before, sir," he reminded me.

I nodded my head. "Yes."

"Do you now know all about success in marriage?"

"No, I don't. I don't know everything about marriage."

"You admit this, and yet you intend to do it again."

"Not everything."

"I am still asking, sir" which meant he had questions on a related topic.

"All right, go on."

"When is your uncle or some other close relative coming to help you?"

"No one is coming."

"Sir, how will you get the girl's parent to agree for her to marry you? Who will speak for you?"

"I have no one to speak for me."

"Where are your cows, sir?"

"Why do I need cows?"

"Sir, don't you know about the bride's price? You must give a number of cows in order to marry a girl." I stood before him puzzled. I had heard about bride's price, but I had not yet reached the point of proposing.

"Sir, do you already have a plot of land?"

Before I had a chance to answer, he said, "Sir, have you built your house, yet?" When I paused, he then offered, "These are questions my father would expect me to answer promptly, sir."

Kajubi shook his head. □

The Cambridge Overseas Exam

Jack Humbles

In a letter home in 1964, Jack wrote the following:

I am giving the Cambridge Exam this year down at Old Moshi Secondary School. I have been asked to be the main invigilator. During the exam today, I had only seventeen students in chemistry to observe. One student splashed acid in his eyes but we quickly washed his face and eyes and he was okay. That was Monday.

On Tuesday during the physics exam, we found out that their physics teacher had not put out the correct equipment and that made the experiment impossible to do. He noticed this after the exam. The students were so upset during the test because things didn't work for them. We will have to write a report to the headquarters of the Cambridge and explain what happened.

Wednesday was the chemistry practical in the lab and the students were to do a quantitative analysis. The students were to analyze an unknown substance, but the teacher had not stirred it completely, so some students got a weak solution and others a strong one. Another chemistry exam with terrible results for the students. □

Student Teaching Practice

Jack Humbles

At our college, all the students leave for about one month to do practice teaching in surrounding primary schools. I was to report to the Bukoba area across Lake Victoria from the college. I left Mwanza late evening on the boat Usoga with my VW. We arrived in Bukoba after having breakfast on the boat. Bukoba is a lovely little town pinned in between Lake Victoria and large hills on all sides. Many of the hills are sandstone. A little tea is grown here with coffee and banana trees. We stayed at the Lake Hotel. In front of the hotel was a white sandy beach with palm trees and hippos.

It was really interesting going to the little primary schools observing our student teachers. All the little children wearing colorful uniforms. John Bend, British, and I enjoyed a large and complicated dinner: first soup, next is fish, third is meat with potatoes and vegetables, then pudding followed by a fruit tray, then cheese, and finally coffee served on the patio.

Another student teaching practice took me to Mwadui [south of Mwanza], where there is a world famous Williamson's diamond mine (see http://bit.ly/mwadui). There are many small villages around the mine, but none with a hotel for Europeans, so we teachers got to stay right at the diamond mine.

It was fenced in with barbed wire, guards all around, passes needed, and so on. It was like a small town of about five hundred people with a very good restaurant, post office, shopping center, a club with swimming pool, electric lights in all the homes plus running cold and hot water. In the shopping center were special shops for shoes, dresses, pastries, a meat shop, a men's shop, radio and record store. All the yards were beautiful with very green grass and many colorful flowers and trees. Every Wednesday night a movie. There is also a gas station and a Catholic church, an Anglican church, and a mosque. Who knew?

There are three of us here from Butimba. We have been given guest quarters with three bedrooms, two sitting rooms, and a small service area. The service area is used by the caretaker. He fixes morning tea for us at 6:30 a.m. and washes our clothes every day, and our cars, and cleans our rooms! We eat all our meals at the restaurant. There is no choice of food, but it is all good and too much. Every morning we had hot cereal, eggs, bacon, coffee, and a full quart of milk with cream on top. For lunch we started with soup, then meat and at least two vegetables, cold milk again, dessert, coffee, and cheese. Supper is also a very large meal.

The days kept us really busy. We had forty-four students to supervise, spread over fifteen schools. The schools were spread apart with the farthest being almost sixty miles away. I spent most of the day just driving. One day we were able to take a tour of the mine. It was an open pit that looks like a strip mine in southern Indiana. They sift and search through about ten tons of dirt and rock in order to find one diamond. The mine was located in an almost semi-desert area.

But with all the wealth here, it was much more modern than Dar es Salaam. All the streets were paved, all the water was safe for drinking, and there was electricity full time. Also they had their own city buses and school buses for the kids. There are rumors that the mine might not last more than three more years, but the UN says twenty years.

What will happen then? However, I checked the internet, and the mine was still operating as of 2015.

In August we had another practice teaching month for our students, and about sixty-six of them were assigned to small primary schools around Mwanza. They slept at the schools and four of us teachers drove around to observe them. We had to visit each student at least four times.

These schools were very poor, some with dirt floors, and the children sat on big tin cans as chairs. There were no desks for them. In one school, the "blackboard" was a torn chunk of ceiling board painted black and attached to a tripod of limbs. Much of the school work was done outdoors so the children could write in the dirt with sticks. Most of the schools I visited were better with desks and cement floors. But even there, books were scarce, sometimes one textbook for the whole class. Teaching aids usually could not be found. ☐

Snake Story

Dave Hummel

I was a member of Wave 6 of TEEA 1969-71. This was the last group of TEA/TEEA to be sent to East Africa. I was posted to Kenyatta Teacher Training College to the Biology Department. The college was at Kahawa, near Nairobi. Along with my wife Jeanette and four children I spent two years in an adventure of a lifetime. There are many experiences that I could share about these two years but I will concentrate on two snake adventures that relate to my students of that time.

The staff and students had built a "Snake Pit" in the biology department area. It was made out of concrete and was about eight feet square and five feet deep. We landscaped it so there were rocks, plants, and a water source at the bottom. The students provided the upkeep and feeding. The snake and lizard inhabitants were nonpoisonous examples of reptiles of the nearby area. The purpose of the pit was to help our students overcome their fear of reptiles and teach them the benefits they can provide for the natural environment. The approach seemed to be successful. Many of the students both male and female became very comfortable handling and caring for the snakes.

Sometimes an objective lesson can have unforeseen circumstances. One day as I was teaching, a student from another section came into the room. What was unusual about his appearance was that he was holding a snake of about two feet in length just in back of the head as he had been taught for safe handling. He was very proud of his accomplishment and asked if I knew what kind of snake it was. One look and I realized he had captured, by hand, a young black African spitting cobra. I asked him to keep a very tight grip on the snake while I went to get a secure cage. We deposited the cobra into the cage, and then I, the student, and the class started to breathe again. The snake ended up at the Nairobi Snake Park and not in our pit.

Another snake experience concerned a student of mine during his student teaching at a girls' secondary school about twelve miles north of the college. The school was in an agricultural area with many small *shambas* and apparently some snakes in the area. One part of the biology department's goals was emphasizing the teaching of lab experiences by our students when they did their student teaching. The department tried to help our students develop labs that could be done with a minimum of lab equipment and using local resources. My student had planned a laboratory lesson and had to take his students to the lab. The lab was a building a few steps from the main buildings and very little used.

The student teacher got his forty girls seated and started to introduce the lab activity. He was interrupted when a spitting cobra crawled out from under the teacher's desk. There was some confusion among the girls, as forty of them tried to exit through the doors and open windows all at the same time.

The student teacher managed to dispatch the snake but only after the cobra ejected some venom, a little of which did get into the student teacher's eyes. He was able to flush out the poison with abundant water and was treated at the local hospital. Luckily no damage was done and the lab proved to be very successful the next day.

The student teacher, being a dedicated blossoming biology teacher, preserved the snake in a jar of formaldehyde and proudly showed it to me when I came on my observation the next week. It just goes to show that trying to introduce good biological teaching practices in the African teaching environment of those days could have some very interesting and unexpected outcomes. □

TEA Memories

David and Carol Imig

A collection of more than one-hundred blue fold-over airmail letters, written from June 1961–December 1963 to parents and siblings, provide infrequent opportunities to review the great adventure in our lives. They convey the excitement and the challenges of living at a rural boarding school in Kagera Province, Tanganyika.

Newly married, we recorded our experiences on the Kleenex-thin letterforms that served as our bridge to home and family—typewritten on Sunday afternoons on an old portable Royal, carried seven miles to town by the school messenger, and posted at the single post office. They were our form of Instagram. We kept up with world news through squeaky BBC broadcasts and the *East African Standard*, which arrived weeks after publication.

We were part of the first-wave C, recent graduates who were schooled in teaching but had never taught. Our training began with lectures in steamy Manhattan at Teachers College, followed by time at London's Institute of Education and then two months at Makerere in Kampala. Lectures on British Empire history and English literature, with instruction in Swahili, and lots of readings on American educational foundations were intended to prepare us for our teaching assignments. An eager young tutor at Makerere, named Senteza Kajubi, and time spent reviewing school syllabi and prior Commonwealth Examination questions would prove to have been the most helpful parts of the orientation.

While in Kampala, we would live on Kololo Hill with another couple and go daily to the Makerere campus to have tutorial sessions with other team C members. We made mock lessons and talked about teaching, while Carol would teach at the Aga Khan Primary School, but there was also lots of time for tennis and basketball and board games and adventures around Kampala.

Somehow we were deemed ready to begin the next phase of the adventure. Assigned to the boy's secondary school at Nyakato, we travelled by steamer from Port Bell to Bukoba on a very bright December day in 1961. We had passage on the old SS Usogo that circumnavigated Lake Victoria weekly and remember it being over-loaded with peddlers and merchants returning to an uncertain but newly independent Tanganyika. We were assigned a cabin and took our meals with the few English passengers on board and had pangs of guilt that we somehow weren't living up to the expectations set for us.

We arrived at nightfall with an abundance of goats and chickens and staggering loads of baggage that soon disappeared down the gangplank. We arrived on Independence night and to the celebrations that were underway as we docked. We were met by Bill Streets, another TEAer who had arrived as part of Wave A the previous August. He hustled us off the pier and into a taxi that carried us and our baggage to the former British agricultural station that would be our home for the ensuing two years.

Bill lent us kerosene lamps to see by, electricity wouldn't arrive until the following spring, and deposited us on our doorstep. The students had gone home for Independence Day celebrations, and most of the faculty were gone for winter break so it was a quiet beginning. Later we would be told that the house had been vacant ever since a previous teacher had murdered his wife in the bedroom.

Miraculously, Robert arrived the following morning, fluent in English, Swahili, and Haya (and knowing some German handed down by his grandfather who had fought the British in WWI). He would take over our lives and make "things" happen. On that first day, he helped prepare a long shopping list of things we would need and directed us toward town.

We opened a bank account and received the first book of checks (we still have them), and retrieved our VW Bug from customs and then visited the two Indian stores that sold groceries and the Lebanese shops that sold lamps and other essentials, visited the market to haggle for potatoes, carrots and oranges and cartons of milk. We saw the sights, the old Anglican church, the wharf, the Catholic school, the hospital, and the constant stream of women in brightly colored wraps with babies bundled on their backs and baskets piled high on their heads. We took lunch at the Lake Hotel and sat by the shore of the lake with hippos far too close.

The new term didn't begin for a month so we explored the region and met lots of people. We would soon be part of a vibrant American community that emerged from the several schools in the Bukoba region and the influx of missionaries from the strife torn Katanga Region. The few African teachers at the school greeted us, and we were introduced to school officials for the region (their wives were a constant source of information about local habits and customs and where one got eggs and scrawny chickens, fillets and loaves of bread). We spent long hours preparing lessons for lower form courses in English, history, and geography (the remaining British expatriates taught the Forms 3 and 4 lessons while we became accustomed to the school and teaching).

We often reflect on our naivety and innocence and speculate on what difference there would be were we to return today to those same assignments. We decided to forego membership in the local European club and didn't attend service at the Anglican church, instead attending church services at the local car garage with a transient minister preaching the Sunday sermon.

At a time when British education policy promoted multi-tribal school enrollments (and a dozen tribal affiliations were represented in our school population), there were virtually no local tribal students and little contact with Haya peoples. A half century later, we regret the opportunities foregone in not engaging the leaders of the half dozen villages that surrounded our school. We admired their magnificent traditional houses of woven bamboo and grass and banana frond.

We regret that we didn't explore the bringing together of the young men we taught in the boarding school to understand the dynamics of their engagement with one another. We regret that we didn't become more informed of the "laughing sickness" that possessed young female students (and captured front page coverage in the *Chicago Tribune*) at neighboring upper-primary schools. We were in the midst of the transformation of Tanganyika from colonial rule to independent status to democratic socialist state, and we lacked resources and the maturity to fully engage students in discussions regarding Julius Nyerere's rule.

What we do remember with great fondness are the Sunday evenings when TEA teachers, coping without their household help, gathered for potluck suppers, when there were real conversations about race and politics with fellow-volunteers—often across race and class as first time experiences. We remember when our tutor and our mentor would visit and observe our teaching, the TEAers from Mwanza or Kisumu arriving off lake steamers for a meal or overnight stay, the "culture shock" experienced when we traveled to the cities of Kampala or Nairobi, the army ants parading up one-side of our house and down the other, the fruit bats at sunset, the monkeys in the overhead trees, and the majestic crested cranes in our yard.

We remember the smell of marigolds and the swaying of a hanging light over our dining table with repeated quakes in the Great Rift. We remember the care to be shown on walks across the football "pitch" to teach and the wildlife at night on inspections of the dormitories to ensure that "lights were out."

We remember absent textbooks for several courses writing copy on chalk boards and making due with limited copy books. We remember the history text that did begin with "our ancestors, the Angles and Saxons" for a classroom of thirty-seven very African young men (all older than their twenty-two year-old teacher). We remember the drumming of rain on the metal classroom roofs and how dark it could become without electricity and lighting.

We remember trying to convince US groups to send library books and the difficulties of shipment and customs. We remember the nights when students would showcase their dancing and drumming talents and mimic their teachers' "best" teaching habits. We remember celebrating football victories over neighboring schools despite how awful was our coaching. We felt the enormous responsibility that we had assumed and came to wonder if we really could make a difference.

We returned to an America in the aftermath of the Kennedy assassination and to one soon to be consumed by the Vietnam War. We pursued more degrees, grew a family, returned to West Africa to work for USAID for five years, were successful in our careers (and subsequent teaching), and constantly were reminded of the opportunities that TEA provided. Hopefully, our students (and the African teachers we replaced to take university degrees) succeeded as well. This holiday season we will again open our collection of those airmail letters and reminisce about those good times. □

Notebooks Have No Accent

Charles Irby

Upon my arrival at Machakos Boys' Secondary School in August, 1963, I started teaching biology to Forms 1, 2, and 3 and reviewed the subject matter to Form 4 students, who were awaiting the Cambridge exam in the November.

When the term ended, I had a delegation of Form 3 students stating that they could not understand me due to my lingering New York accent and that I talked too fast. So we held Form 3 biology instruction on Saturday and Sunday and three nights after classes for about a month. This time all went well, and the students told me that they appreciated all that I did for them and now they had the information in their notebooks.

Oh, those notebooks! ☐

Supporting a Tanzanian's US Education

Gary James

In early September of 1982, I received a letter from a young man I had known from my TEA teaching experience at Mzumbe Secondary School in Tanzania. I was part of the TEA 1A group that went to Tanganyika as it was known in 1961. The person who had written to me was the son of one of my African colleagues at Mzumbe. When I first met the young man, he was only five years old, but I had remained in touch with his family since returning to the US in 1964.

He asked me about coming to the US to continue his studies as he had not been successful in finding a place in Form 5 in Tanzania. After consultation with his father, I agreed to sponsor him and he would attend the community college where I was working in California. His original plan was to complete a two-year occupational course, then return to Tanzania.

Eight years later he completed his education with a bachelor of science degree in electrical engineering from the state university at Long Beach, California. While I supported him with room, board, and tuition, he also helped out by working various jobs at the colleges where he was studying. He was very good at fixing things and made a lot of money by purchasing old MG sports cars, towing them to the house, tearing them apart and, once he had them running again, selling them at a nice profit.

Reluctantly he eventually left the US and returned to Tanzania in 1990. One of his first jobs upon returning was to travel around the country with Pope John Paul II and organize the public address systems for his various stops. Although not a Catholic he became quite friendly with the pope and was given a rosary by him when he returned to Rome.

Since then, he has set up his own computer business and is currently working as the computer specialist for the EU in Tanzania. He is married and has two children. His precocious daughter has her own television show for children Saturday mornings on the national television station. ☐

A Kapsabet Gift: A Practical Dictum for Teaching
Bill Jones

I waited until the class was over before I spoke to Harrison Mwangi. I was teaching a Form 3 class, focusing on explicating narrative elements in stories, mentioning in the course of the lesson Chekhov's observation that a skilled writer could manage a number of narrative threads and bring them to satisfactory resolution just as a skilled archer might shoot a series of arrows in the air, each on different trajectories, but control the shooting with such skill that all the arrows hit the target at the same time. Harrison had nodded as if in agreement with what I had said. When I asked him whether he knew Chekhov, he said he did.

"I love the Russians," he said. "They remind me so much of Africans."

What was I to make of this comment by a baby-faced boy no older than sixteen? No one in the world, I am certain, had linked Africans and Russians in this way before Harrison had. And when he told me that he liked to write and had written a novel but had thrown it down a latrine because he didn't like it, I knew I was in the presence of an unusual intelligence.

Here was evidence of headmaster Alan Flay's contention that all the Kapsabet boys were intelligent, had IQs of at least 116, and could do anything masters wanted them to do. Flay's assertion, I came to see, was, in fact, a fabulous fabrication: intelligence testing for African students didn't exist. He knew nothing official about their IQs, but the effect of his assertion was that teacher expectations were high.

Over time, Flay's assertion and the day-to-day functioning of students like Harrison came together for me as a powerful, practical dictum for teaching: High academic achievement is inexorably tied to teacher expectations and to honoring the intelligence of students. □

Strike to Study

Gus Lewis

One day about the beginning of November, our headmaster at Mzumbe Secondary School announced that all the seniors had decided to leave their classes and study on their own for the coming school certificate exams. All day for several weeks they studied in the dining hall, out of contact with teachers. I let my students know that I was available, but only one student came to see me.

This was a big letdown for many of us who thought (of course) that we could be a big help in the preparation and that the seniors were probably sacrificing good scores for feelings of the moment. Review of four years of material, and the taking of practice exams, was well under way. But the students had a particular point of view: most of their teachers were American. Many had not taught seniors before that year.

What did these teachers know about British exams taken by African boys? And at least in science, the teaching methods were different from the past. They had previously spent most of each class copying a great deal of material from the blackboard—material to memorize and to use in answering exam questions. In fact, the Cambridge questions did often invite memorized answers. Now the Americans were working, through discussion, for a deeper understanding of the subject, and were not providing the answers to memorize. Who wouldn't be tempted to think that he could organize his own study time, free from the class schedule?

We science teachers were needed to help administer the exams. After the exams, the seniors just went home. I don't remember any graduation ceremony. For me, also, it was time to leave for home. I never heard the results of those exams, but one student did acknowledge to me that I had predicted the exam contents pretty well. ☐

Boys in the Cast

Ben Lindfors

Upon my arrival at Kisii School I was crowned "Master in Charge of Dramatics," a position which had been left unfilled for many years. I taught English, thus I could direct plays. Here was my plight.

The boys in the cast of *The Merchant of Venice* came back to school from vacation full of enthusiasm, but certain key players, Bassanio, the Prince of Morocco, and the Duke of Venice had been unable to learn their parts because they had spent every day of their vacation, sunrise to sunset, helping their families to bring in the peanut crop. Word came that Portia hadn't been able to raise enough money to pay all of his tuition so wouldn't be returning to school until the third week of the term.

I reorganized the schedule of rehearsals, set the tentative performance back a week, and hoped there would be no further delays. But more delays there were, some unavoidable, others avoidable. For example, a rehearsal of Act Two might happen this way:

MASTER IN CHARGE OF DRAMATICS:
(stalks into dining hall, glowers at the assembled cast, growls)
"Where is Shylock?"

CHORUS:
"In bed, sir. He's got malaria again."

MCD:
"Well, where is the Prince of Arragon?"

VOICE OFF STAGE:
"He's not here, sir."

MCD: *(forte)*
"*I know that!*"
(piano)
"Where, pray tell, is he?"

BASSANIO:
"He's captain of the volleyball team, sir.
They are practicing for the match on Saturday." ☐

Owing to Underfeeding

Judy Lindfors

While Ben and I were teaching English at Kisii School, one of my responsibilities was to edit the school newspaper: articles the students wrote that I would post on the bulletin board in the school dining hall. My favorite article was one in which the student was bemoaning the fact that, during announcements at lunch, some students engaged in lengthy complaints about the state of the school latrines. He was very unhappy about this practice for, as he wrote:

> "When someone starts wondering how dirty the latrines are, one's taste for eating is lessened considerably."

He went on to describe the dire consequences this could have, concluding with this magnificent sentence:

> "If this continues to happen, many people's normality will be impeded, owing to underfeeding." ☐

Athletics in Nandi Country
Clive Mann

Before living in western Kenya, in Kalenjin country, I had had little interest in athletics. At my grammar school the third term was "athletics," the other two rugby and cricket. I could perform without letting myself down in the last two, but I was a bit of a joke in athletics, except for javelin and long jump, but even in those I was probably average or a bit below for my age. Running I hated. I was always last but one in the class cross-country; the kid I beat had the excuse of being overweight, whereas I was rather scrawny.

Whilst in Uganda I began to hear of Kenyan athletes, especially mid- to long-distance runners, who mostly seemed to come from what was then Rift Valley Province. Having a dilettante's interest in linguistics and social anthropology (anthropology was my ancillary subject for my B.Sc.), I investigated and discovered that most of these names were Kalenjin, more specifically Nandi. On a visit to Eldoret, someone pointed out the legendary Kipchoge "Kip" Keino.

When I was posted to Kabarnet, I would pass St Patrick's Boys' High School at Iten on my way to Eldoret, and on a few occasions I dropped in to discuss matters with the head of biology. The school had been run by Irish Catholic Missionaries, the Patrician Brothers, since 1961. I met the headmaster, and other brothers, and quickly discovered that they were absolutely fanatical about sport. In 1969 they were about to introduce cricket, having purchased "the whites."

In 1976, a year after I left Kenya, Brother Colm O'Connell joined the staff, and seemed to work miracles with boys as regards their prowess in athletics. He is known as the "Godfather of Kenyan Running," having established many training camps. A list of the Olympic medalists, world champions and other great runners he has coached includes many women, and he is credited with getting women more interested in the sport. You would also notice that almost all names are Kalenjin, with one notable exception, David Rudisha, who is Maasai, but his father was an athlete, and he trained under Brother Colm. I regret I left too early to meet him. ☐

Teaching as a Temporary Measure
Clive Mann

I have to confess that I was not a committed pedagogue initially. It was pretty much assured in those days that if you had a degree you would get a job of some kind. In the last term of my last year as an undergraduate at University College London I was passing through the corridors of the college on the way home from the student union bar. Affixed to a column was a poster titled, "Why not teach for a time in East Africa?"

My original plan was to do a PhD in vertebrate paleontology, but I had not been a very diligent student, and my final grading would not have been sufficient to gain a grant for this work. Moreover, I had fallen out with my would-be supervisor. A couple of years before I had been part of a four-man undergraduate expedition to study seabirds on the Dahlac Archipelago in the Red Sea off the Ethiopian, now Eritrean, coast. We had reached our destination by land and sea, including an off-season pilgrim ship from Saudi Arabia.

It was an amazing, adventure-packed mission, from which we returned unscathed, with one of my companions (now late) becoming an eminent ornithologist in Tanzania and Zambia, and another the Dean of Liverpool Cathedral. This was a life-changer for me, and caused me to fall in love with, and to have a deep interest in, sub-Saharan Africa. If my feelings have been altered over the years, it is that they have intensified.

The deal was that we would take a Dip.Ed. course at Makerere University and then teach for at least one contract (21–27 months; 31 in my case) in either Kenya, Tanzania, or Uganda. Food, lodging, transport, and the course were paid for, and we even got some pocket money. A dream come true.

I was quite nervous of standing in front of a class of school pupils. I missed giving my first demonstration lesson in front of Prof. Lucas because of malaria. A substitute lesson was arranged to be observed by Tony Seddon, but he was indisposed, so I took the class unobserved.

Unofficially, a group of us went once or twice a week to a Sudanese refugee camp at Bombo, not far from Kampala. The buildings had been erected to house Emin Pasha's Sudanese *askaris*, the Muslim descendants of whom lived nearby. The refugees were mostly not Muslim, and were fleeing from the tyranny of the northern Sudanese. This was where I began to feel that I liked teaching. The pupils were grateful for everything we did for them.

The facilities were as basic as they can get. An agreement between the governments of Sudan and Uganda stipulated that they were not to receive education or be given employment. If government officials appeared, we made ourselves scarce. We did manage to get a few of them jobs as *askaris*, but the firms employing them insisted they had shoes. Some of these lads, particularly Dinka, had extraordinary long feet, and our cast-off Bata Safari Boots didn't fill the bill. However, it was discovered that some cobblers could work wonders and cannibalize two pairs to make one. Problem solved.

My next teaching practice at Tororo Boy's High School I thought went well. I received no criticism. Brother Howard, a Canadian, was my mentor and seemed very casual to the point that he smoked while teaching. Moira Harbottle suggested I did not follow his example. Teaching was beginning to grow on me.

For my final teaching practice I was sent to Soroti Senior Secondary School, which was also to be my posting. Although I was only supposed to teach half a timetable during practice, I was given a full one, and also taught extra lessons after school. Later I was to take on the school choir, Boy Scouts, photography club, film club, cricket, and probably other chores that I've forgotten. I was also a housemaster and head of biology. I managed to shed cricket—little interest in school, and Boy Scouts—by getting them amalgamated with the Teso College troop.

I really enjoyed being in the classroom/laboratory with the pupils, and they seemed to like me. I have recently re-established contact with over fifty of my ex-pupils, and become good friends with a number.

Moira Harbottle commented that I was now teaching well, unlike when I was at Tororo. Early on I got a visit from my girlfriend in Kampala. She arrived without warning to stay a few days. I had no transport so I borrowed a bicycle from a pupil and took her around town side-saddle on the carrier. One ex-pupil, now in Canada, remembers this and said it caused quite a stir in a predominantly Asian town, an Asian girl on the back of a bike ridden by an *mzungu*!

I extended my contract as far as I could, went back to UK, and then went on to teach for two contracts in western Kenya. Later I spent eleven years teaching in Borneo. Teaching as a "temporary measure" was not to be. Abortive attempts to work at a publishing firm and to sell *Encyclopedia Britannica* were very short-lived, and I remained at the "chalk face" until I retired in 2002. □

Personal Reflections on Tanzania over a Period of Forty Years

Dean McHenry

Morning had broken when the up-train on Tanzania's central line reached the Gulwe (Mpwapwa) station last May. It had been forty years since I first had arrived at that station and the rush of memories from my increasingly forgetful mind was intense.

The whole first TEA group had met at Columbia Teachers College in New York so long ago. Julius Nyerere, who had been at the UN, came one evening to talk with us and inspire us; that long flight, including the flat tire in Kano and the chance to go up a minaret in the great mosque there; the classes at Makerere; the vacation trip by car up to Karamoja, through West Nile, into the Congo and back to Kampala;

practice teaching at Kapsabet Secondary School in Kenya; and then the boat and train down to Mpwapwa.

Those of us in B-Group were not the TEA pioneers at Mpwapwa Secondary School. Joe Brady and Alex Cutrules were already there. Joe put us up for quite a while until other houses became available. Like many others, the experience molded much of what was to follow in my own life.

It was partly the historical period. When Tanganyika became independent, our group was at Makerere watching the fireworks and riding through Kampala in lorries with great hopes. No, it was more than hope, it was an assurance that the good life was going to come to our East African friends. So fascinating was the political change that I decided to shift from an undergraduate major in geology to do graduate work in political science with a focus on Africa.

But, when my term at Mpwapwa was over at the end of 1963, I took nine months getting home before starting graduate work at Indiana University. Most of those months were spent hitchhiking down to South Africa, catching a freighter from what is now Maputo to Dakar and traveling by local transport across West Africa, back to East Africa and down the Nile before heading east across the Middle East. It all intensified my sense of appreciation for the immensity of Africa and my sense of humility about what I knew of that continent.

I went back to Tanzania to do my dissertation research on development in Kigoma Region and taught a year at the University of Dar es Salaam before taking up a position at the University of Illinois. In a course I co-taught with Seth Singleton, an American Fulbrighter, was the head of the Revolutionary Front on campus, Yoweri Museveni, Uganda's current president. Unlike my TEA days, the vision of a socialist society had been developed, and radical voices echoed across the university. A couple of years later I was back for more research and spent two years in the mid-1970s at the University of Dar es Salaam. My research was on Ujamaa Villages and I had a little Honda CT-90 *pikipiki* that got me to villages all over the country.

After finally getting married in 1981, I immediately dragged my wife to Nigeria, where I taught for a year at the University of Calibar. When my wife got pregnant, she left three or four months before I was able to do so. Three years later, I got a Fulbright to teach at the University of Dar es Salaam again. This time it was luxury, as the university put us up, along with many Tanzanian faculty members, in the Africana Hotel. Our three-year old son was a wonderful companion, and my wife loved Tanzania.

Then there was a long period during which I studied Tanzania from a distance. I published a book in 1994 titled *Limited Choices, The Political Struggle for Socialism in Tanzania*. Not many copies were sold, but I felt an obligation to my Tanzanian friends to complete it. By the mid-90s the socialist era of Tanzania's history had passed and a multi-party system was being born. Reviewing the effort to build socialism was thought by many people to be a waste of time as a new era was beginning. Shortly afterwards, the Tanzania Studies Association was formed as an affiliate of the African Studies Association, and I happened to be elected its first President, an undeserved honor but one that would not have occurred had there been no TEA.

Two years before he died, we brought Julius Nyerere to Claremont Graduate University (CGU) and gave him an honorary degree. The story is a TEA story, in a sense. One of my pupils at Mpwapwa Secondary School was a boy named Mustafa Nyanganyi. I recalled taking a picture of him in his white shorts and shirt standing on a poached elephant during a geography club field trip. To make a long story short, he became Tanzania's ambassador to the US, a post he held until early this year. We met and he graciously said he would get Nyerere to come to CGU, which he did. Nyerere was as sharp and as charismatic as he had been that night at Columbia Teachers College.

As the train moved west from the Gulwe (Mpwapwa) station, the rail line and countryside looked much as they were years ago. But, so much else had changed. Dar es Salaam is a huge city; there are supermarkets and Western-owned hotels; the confidence we had on December 9, 1961, that Tanzania would build the good society in our lifetimes has gone; the great *ujamaa* vision is now a target of bitterness; there are some very rich people, but also many, many very poor. Still, there is a spirit and beauty that remains. I'm not sure whether this is wholly real or whether my eyes are distorted by the memories as well as by my age. ☐

Teaching at Teso College
Larry Olds

I arrived in late January, 1962, at Teso College Aloet (TCA) a few days before the first term of the new year. I had already spent a term as a teacher at Makerere College School and learned I was a "maths teacher," as the British say, not a "math teacher" as we would say in the US.

When I arrived, I moved in the teacher's house farthest from the classrooms with one of my Teachers for East Africa colleagues, Doyle Knirk, who had already spent his first term in Uganda teaching science at TCA. My recollection is that all the teachers at that time were expatriates. We did have two student teachers from Makerere, James Bukosi, who was from Kenya and a British classmate whose name I don't recall, who also lived with us during that first term. Before I left Uganda the next year, Frank Pakose (he later became headmaster), a maths teacher from South Africa joined us. In 1963 when the West Campus was added to the school, several of the teachers from the former technical school also joined us and improved the ratio of expatriates to Africa teachers.

Although all European when I arrived, the teaching staff was a diverse lot. The headmaster, Johnny Jones, and the football/athletics master, David Jones, were Welsh. The Anglican/Protestant religion teacher, Graham Hutchison, was from Northern Ireland—Ulster, he would say. The Catholic religion and French teacher, Louie Albers, was a Dutch Mill Hill priest. The head of English, Barry Bleach, appropriately was English and also the cricket and tennis master. All were old timers compared to the four Americans on the staff. In addition to myself and Doyle Knirk, who I mention above, the other two Americans were Anne Womeldorf, who taught English, and Dr. Stout, a Fulbright scholar whose year at TCA as a science teacher ended shortly after I arrived. Doyle and Anne were also part of the TEA program that had taken me to Uganda.

When I arrived at TCA, all of the teachers belonged to the Soroti Club in town six miles away, which still had a whites-only policy. I wasn't interested in joining since I both objected to that policy and didn't drink alcohol nor played golf or tennis at all which seemed to be the main reasons for the clubs existence. It was also the case that no one invited me to join, a fact that served me well a few weeks later.

I was interested in starting basketball at the school and set out to get some backboards and rims, as well as supports for them. The school carpenter was set the task of making the four-foot by six-foot backboards. I found a welding shop in town that made the rims as I instructed them to do. What remained was finding the supports for the backboards.

When I heard that the Soroti town waterworks had old pipe available, I went to see the manager who at that time, still months before independence for Uganda, was still a British civil servant. He had heard that I wouldn't join the Club and asked angrily why should he help me with the backboard supports. I was able to say honestly that no one had invited me to join and besides, I didn't drink. I avoided having to add that I would not have joined as long as they discriminated. The manager mellowed and relaxed, and I drew him the design we needed to have a portable system that could be put onto the ends of the tarmac tennis court for basketball and removed for tennis matches.

Those same basketball backboard supports were being used when I returned for a visit to TCA thirty-eight years later, but then they were buried a foot or so under the *murram* of the new court rather than sitting on top of the tarmac. The rims were moved high on the backboards so they would still be ten feet off the ground.)

By the way, later that year the Soroti Club abandoned its whites-only policy and elected a local Asian businessman president. I did join for the latter part of my stay, played some squash, and attended a few of the weekend curry dinners with the changing and now diverse membership.

I taught maths to all forms but mostly to the A-stream classes. Form 1A was my favorite class, a group I taught both years and from which many of the basketball players emerged. I also taught calculus for one term to the first A-level class when it began in 1963. The Form 4A class my first year did fairly well on the Cambridge Overseas Mathematics Examinations, not as well as I would have liked, or as well as other classes would have in the future had I stayed and mastered better what it was the examiners wanted in the answers to their exam questions.

One major issue I didn't resolve in that first year stemmed from the difference in style in the American and British approaches to geometry. I introduced an American approach instead of myself mastering the British approach which might have given the students better examination results.

On the other hand, I had a remarkable encounter with a former TCA student in Kampala five years later. We met by chance on Kampala Road by the post office. I don't recall his name, but he was then studying to be a maths teacher, by then involved in learning about the "New Maths." During that 1967 stay, I was myself teaching the new maths, which emphasized understanding the meaning rather than rote learning. I asked him how he was doing with new maths. He replied, "It was easy because of the way you taught us"—one of the most memorable compliments I ever got for my work.

When one of the senior teachers and his family left Uganda, in January, 1963, I moved from the teacher's house furthest from the classrooms to the one closest, a slightly bigger house with large well-tended gardens. There I was joined by a new American teacher, Keith O'Dell, also a maths teacher, and a young British Volunteer, Andrew Jarvis, who was spending a year teaching physics and maths before he began his studies at Oxford. The house was large enough, so we also put up two American student teachers from Makerere for the first term of that year.

Because I was also a trained physical education teacher and myself active in sports, I also taught those classes on the school timetable. In addition to starting both basketball and softball teams I also became the athletics master my second year at TCA. I did have personal experience in school putting the shot and had fooled around throwing the discus a few times, but no experience with running or training runners. It was with this assignment that my one main conflict during my TCA experience developed.

Without personal experience in training for running events (but with considerable experience with intense level of training for other sports I had played at the college level, American football, basketball, and baseball), I consulted several training manuals and developed a stretching and fitness routine.

A large group of students came for the first training sessions for the new athletics season. TCA after all had some of the finest runners among students in the country. That year was no exception. After that first day, however, when I led the students through the stretching and fitness routines, most did not come back for the second or third day of practice. I then did not allow them to travel with the team for a weekend competition. This caused a big conflict with head prefect, Omaria, who was also the athletics captain and one of the country's best in the half mile.

Only eight boys who had come to practices made the trip to the meet. Later I learned that the boys did not come back to practice because they were "sick" which really meant sore from the stretching and fitness routine. They were not used to the movements they were asked to make during training and didn't understand that the way to deal with the soreness was to continue to stretch and exercise.

And in the sports culture of the school practice wasn't a requirement to compete. The team captain and the sport master just picked the competitors they thought were best. In retrospect I came to think my approach to sports discipline was wrong for the circumstance: right if the goal was to be "as good as you can be," but not if it was to encourage participation and enjoyment.

There were two outstanding members of the team. Omaria whom I mentioned above. He finished second in the half mile in the national championships that year. The other was Edward Esegu, who clocked a 9.4 second 100-yard dash at a meet at Busoga College Mwiri. The world record at that time was 9.2 seconds.

For the first part of my time at TCA, I left on many of the weekends to continue my involvement with basketball and other activities in Kampala, by making the 220-mile Friday afternoon drive in four hours in my Volkswagen bug. After the first half-year or so, I greatly reduced the number of trips except for going to Kampala to attend the Independence Celebration on Kololo Hill in October.

The rest of my stay I confined my trips to the school breaks, except for one or two in conjunction with my role in selecting and coaching the National basketball team. We had a training camp for the players during the school break. Two players from TCA, Andrew Aliat and Paul Nyangan, were on that national team, making the trip to Nairobi in April, 1963, for the first games by a Uganda team.

Students from TCA participated in the American Friends Service Committee (AFSC) exchange programs, which allowed a few selected students to attend high schools in the US for one year. In 1962, we sent three students on the program. One of them was known then as Atigo. During the second school break in August, I collected him from his home—my first trip to a student's home in a rural area—and took him to the bus to begin the journey. He didn't come back like he was supposed to. He was an outstanding distance runner and received a scholarship to the University of Wisconsin where he stayed to finish a degree. He later became a politician, Latigo Lal, becoming a leader in Museveni's party. I saw him on a trip to Uganda in 1996. One of the students to go to the US in 1963 was Edward, whom I visited in Illinois after returning from my two years in Uganda.

I have other memories of the time such as teaching the boys waltz, foxtrot, and polka at dance club; starting school basketball and softball teams which played matches against Lango College; playing cricket for the first time in the student-teacher cricket match; supervising the Junior Secondary Exams at a remote rural school; being uncomfortable with the formality of the classroom and being called Sir.

The personal side had many rich experiences: time to read, listening to music tapes, dinner parties, rugby in Mbale, occasional outings for dinner and a movie in Mbale sixty miles away, visiting the orange plantation near Lake Kyoga, hippo hunting with Fr. Louie Albers on Lake Kyoga, excursion to Moroto, camping in Murchison Park with Shuters, hitch hiking from Kampala where I had gone for a Ford Foundation fellowship interview to Gulu to join TCA teams in an athletics and basketball meet, hosting other teachers from our TEA program, and social life with my teaching colleagues.

However, because I was at Teso College at the end of the colonial era and my teaching colleagues were expatriates rather than Ugandans, I missed developing the friendships I now wish I had with Ugandans of my age. I would have liked to have more conversations with local people like the wide-ranging ones we had when for the one-term James Bukosi lived with us. To some degree, I developed a relationship Frank Pakose after he joined our maths department, but we never had exchanges of the quality of those meal table discussions with Bukosi.

But beyond that, when in looking back at that time, I see I was very young, only twenty-one, when I arrived. My first two years in Uganda, nineteen months of it at TCA, were full of wonderful, rich experiences that helped form who I would become. I hope I taught, at least in some small part, as much as I learned. □

What a Gift It Was
Dale Otto

What a phenomenal gift to witness the people's joy, pride and anticipation as each country achieved independence—Tanzania just as we arrived, Uganda in our first year of teaching and learning, Kenya near the end of my group's classroom time. This has been a continuous lift to me, a source of what should be when I chafe about what is.

My teaching experiences were quite a ride, ranging from panic (when just before the first teaching term I fully realized how little I knew) to more clearly seeing how irrelevant our required curricula and exams were to students' lives, needs and potentials, and finally after two years how little I still knew about organized learning and responsive teaching. A layer above these were deep delight in meeting my students each day, sharing a duplex with Bob Maxon and two Kenyan colleagues, and East Africa travels during each term holiday.

—

Volkswagens. A drive into Ngorongoro Crater in a well-used camper van required two of us to get out and push on the van's front because reverse was the only way back out. How nice it was to find out that a Beetle would float across flooded streams. And how extra nice it was for Ed Schmidt to let me drive his Beetle in a road rally. We did pretty well, because Ed was such a good (but white-knuckled) navigator.

—

Mountains. Mt. Elgon, where I met Flora, a gifted local woman who had learned to sculpt in clay from Italian prisoners of war. Mt. Kenya with Ed Schmidt and Joe Gores, a very cold slog up and a magnificent gift to the eye both up and down. Mt. Kilimanjaro with Dick Ramsdell, a phenomenal experience at a time when the snow pack and glaciers were still intact at the summit and the vista nearly limitless.

My lament is always that I didn't clearly know what a gift it was to be living and working among people so different from and yet so very like ourselves. My gratitude rests on the foundation given to me by TEA for continually dealing with the question, "What are the consequences of how I spend my time and energy?" □

The New Primary Approach

Joel Reuben

In 1966-67 the New Primary Approach (NPA) was instituted in teacher training colleges in Kenya. It was a philosophy of teaching based on children learning by doing rather than the Colonial method of teaching by lecturing. The students at Eregi Teacher Training College consisted of prospective P-3 teachers who had seven years of primary schooling and two years of teacher training. We also had P-2 students who had seven years of primary and two years of secondary school, and one class of P-1 students who finished secondary school but did not choose to attend university.

Regardless of their own educational background they had all been taught under the lecture-type education modeled by the British. Their introduction to NPA was quite different than how they had been taught. Part of my tutoring them was to introduce them to making and using visual materials and creative lesson plans that would involve their students' active participation, rather than sitting and listening and hopefully memorizing material from the teacher. Then, we would send out our students to observe in the local schools in Maragoli, and in their second year we evaluated them as student-teachers.

Each morning during the student-teaching period I would meet my fellow African tutors and we would pile into our VW bus, and I would drop them off at different schools and I would go the furthest school. After a full day of assessing our students' performance, I would reverse the process and pick up the other tutors and we would discuss the lessons we observed...the good the bad and the ugly!

Another part of my duties was to supervise the administration of the KPE exams. Unfortunately for me, the Kenyan teachers were threatening to strike by disrupting the usually chaotic period of testing so vital to the measurement of student achievement. The results of the tests showed which students would go on to secondary school and which students would go on to teacher training colleges, and which students would end their schooling with a seventh grade education.

With threats coming from the dissatisfaction of the local teachers, the decision was made to use tutors to help run the testing and ensure its integrity. At 7:00 a.m. a gun-toting policeman arrived at my house to accompany me to a testing center some miles away where I distributed the test packets and supervised the exams. The *askari* and I had no problems, and the gun proved not be needed.

During the three semester breaks when our students went home in December, April, and August, Eregi TTC was chosen by the ministry to offer in-service courses to local teachers who wanted to learn about the NPA methods. They came for one week of intensive training and our goal was to send them back with new strategies for teaching.

When I returned to the South Huntington, New York, schools in 1968, in addition to my return to the classroom, I became a resource for the district in terms of being asked to speak at each district school about my experiences in East Africa. I showed slides, brought artifacts and carvings for the students to examine, and hopefully added to their knowledge. It was my way of giving back to the district which had given me a two-year leave of absence after only being in the district for two years. I did not have tenure, and the leave the board gave me was unprecedented.

I continued teaching there until I retired in 1992. In the 1970s, I wrote two books for the Sterling Publishing Company's Visual Geography Series: *Kenya in Pictures*, written by myself, and *Tanzania in Pictures*, written by fellow TEEA, the late Howard Carstens and myself. □

Electricity Too

Jonne Robinson

"Madam, are you believing in electricity?"

I had found myself in rural central Tanzania teaching English at a school for African young men, not exactly what I had been expecting, but the situation required that nearly every native speaker of English among the teaching staff, aside from those who taught science and math, was put to work as an English teacher.

This was the part of the class devoted to oral English when the students were encouraged to speak English, not just read and write it. Oral English was quite freeform, not like the rest of the class, where despite my best efforts, the students liked the certainties of Grieve, the standard textbook inherited from the old regime. Grieve by name, grief by nature was how it seemed to me.

I liked oral English. One never knew what was coming next. I sensed this was going to be even more a case of "strap yourself in and see what develops" than usual. We had somehow got onto the subject of African medicine, which some called witchcraft. I tried to convey in a way that was not dismissive of their beliefs that I was inclined not to believe in it. This comment was one student's reply.

"Yes, of course," I replied.

"Are you seeing it?"

"No, but I can see the effects. When the electricity generator goes on at 6:00 p.m., the lights come on. That's how I know it exists."

It is similar with African medicine. We see certain things. People become ill, they die, and other bad things, or people may want certain things. People consult the African doctor, and we cannot see the power, but we see what happens. For example, this one has become ill, and his son sees the African doctor and the father gets well. Or it may be that a man's wife turns against him, and he sees the African doctor and things become well between them again. Thus I learned that "seeing" and "believing" are really different things. □

Dabbling in Swahili

Ed Schmidt

Swahili was introduced to Wave I TEAs by British-East Africa educator Arthur Bull at Teachers College in the summer of 1961. Lessons continued during our ongoing orientation at Makerere, but use of the language began only when I arrived at my posting to Kakamega High School in western Kenya, where I shared a house with John Basinger, who had come to East Africa a few months earlier.

Michael, John's cook and "house boy," knew no English. And very little about cooking. The daily list he took to the *duka* regularly included *chungwa na ndizi na papai* (oranges, bananas, and papaya) for the mixed fruit that was his standard dessert. Once, when he was too inebriated to get a fire going, he reported to us, "*Kuni ni choka*" (The firewood is tired). Nevertheless, Michael was the victim of my earliest attempts to use Swahili.

There were a few places to go for a beer in the evening. Among them, the Kakamega Hostel, which had a bar in a corner of a large hall, and Mohammed's *duka*, a mud-and-wattle structure plus several small rooms off a central courtyard for private groups. At either place, I often tried to come away with a couple new words that I would bookmark in my dictionary before I went to bed. The next day, I made flash cards for the new words on little cards measuring 3/8 inches by 1-1/4 inches, which I stored in match boxes and went through a couple times a day. I still have them.

I eventually reached a level that was serviceable, but I never got proficient or studied the language in a consistent, organized way. In 1983, and again in 1985, I spent six weeks in Kenya conducting stove building workshops with groups of church women on a project organized by my good friend Peter Indalo. I always had a multilingual assistant, but my Swahili improved, too.

I did a lot of brushing up in preparation for the 2003 TEA-Alumni trip. I used my old edition of *Teach Yourself Swahili*, which included sentences to translate like, "Sir, there is no charcoal for the iron."

In Arusha, when we were asked to do an interview in Swahili for Tanzanian television, I was the only one in the group to volunteer. I had trouble understanding some of the questions, so asked that they be repeated in English. I hope my answers in Swahili were comprehensible. ☐

A Red Pen and Innocence

Harry Stein

TEA Group III-A assembled at Teachers College on the last Monday in June, 1963. Dave Scanlon spoke to us and the words that I so vividly and lastingly remember were about how we both should and must pay particular attention to the practices of the departing and remaining British headmasters and traditions we would encounter. Kenya was a crown colony although a few weeks earlier internal administrative control had passed to a Kenyan government.

Although he did not say so, I sensed that what Dave meant was that we should not to be deferential but rather vigilantly follow the protocols and procedures at our new schools. We were there to accomplish school and student goals. We could experiment with ways and means but never with outcomes: we were education technicians and not innovative dreamers. Dave's words were useful and made me effective. But this is getting ahead of the red pen and my innocence story.

On a Friday at about 4:00 p.m., I arrived at Kapsabet, the first O-level school in the Rift, located in highland, Nandi District. The 190-mile trip upcountry from Nairobi was uneventful. The school's lorry met me in Eldoret and took me over a 30-mile *murram* road journey to the school where I all too briefly met Bill Jones, who was departing that day for Nairobi and home. Then, I met George Ayton, the H.M. George was a pleasant and helpful head who gave me a form to complete asking for it by the end of the day.

I took the form over to my new home and after perfunctorily interviewing and meeting Ndombie, my cook, and Michael, my *shamba* man, I realized that I needed them much more than they needed me. Remembering George's request, I sat down at the dining room table and completed the form, placing it in an envelope. Michael delivered it to the office, and I started organizing my work, the start of three years at Kapsabet.

The next morning following assembly and student work assignments, George called me into his office. He had the completed form in front of him and in a playful but also gently mindful voice said that I would have to complete the form again. I had used a *red* pen and only the governor general used a *red* pen for official business. George was not scolding. His tone was not harsh. But I was not Malcolm McDonald.

I had not followed Scanlon's admonitions. "Do as they do." There was no way that I could have known, and functioning like a practical, innocent American, I had picked up the nearest pen. I took the incident seriously because not all people or circumstances might have yielded George's genial but direct guidance. The message I gave myself was to be more alert and fit in. I went back to the house and redid the form, this time in green. Why I picked green I don't know. Maybe, this was the nearest pen on the table. Why not the more conventional blue or black? I returned the form personally to George. He looked at it and smiled. He was soon to leave and I remember his saying, "You will like it here and fit in." He was right.

I returned to Kapsabet in 2002, and have been back four times to visit and work with teachers trying to fit in. ☐

When a Student Strike Isn't Really a Strike
Bob Stokes

It all started with a classified ad in the November 1967, *Atlantic Monthly*: "Train Teachers in East Africa! Teachers College, Columbia University."

Eight months later, the family was in Kenya, raring to go for the greatest two years of our lives. It was a wonderful life being a rich American in Kenya ("rich" is relative) at a time when the moon landing was made, working in a college right next to the golf course, and having friends in three countries in the same program.

What with the rewards of working with the students, and of house servants, game parks, Malindi, and visiting friends, it seemed hard to believe that I was getting paid for all of this! But wait: everything TEEA tutors did was not always rock and roll, and I still remember one day near the end of the two-year tour when I earned my pay.

Back in 1970 the quickest way for a Kenyan principal to make a name with the government was to put down a student strike and make the Nairobi papers. Striking students were considered traitors, not only to Kenya but also to their families and clan. After all, they were the lucky ones who were fortunate enough to have been selected for training that would free them from the life sentence of working on the *shamba*, and they had better show their appreciation, by God!

All student discipline at our college was handled by the Kenyan principal and his assistant which was the way it should have been what with the language and cultural limitations of expatriate tutors. During month long teaching practice, students would be taken by college bus out to the rural elementary schools early in the morning and then collected at the end of a long school day. The conditions at these schools were difficult to say the least with no water and the very minimum of school supplies. I remember observing one kid trying to teach sixty-five children in standard three while the regular teacher was off working on his *shamba*.

One evening when all the students were back at the college, they refused to enter the dining hall for their evening meal. The Irish expatriate tutor who had the duty tried to find out why they weren't eating and was told that the principal had refused to send any lunch out to them that day because they hadn't been washing the *debes* (large containers) which contained their maize and bean lunch, and the college cooks had been complaining. Very soon the principal and his assistant took over, and no expats were involved any further in the matter that night.

The next morning, the messenger came around to all the tutors' houses with the notice that a staff meeting was to be held at 8:00. As I approached the office, all the student teachers who were due to go out that day were sitting on the grass with the buses waiting and uniformed police in attendance. I got a sick feeling in my stomach, and all I could think was, "Student strike!"

The principal confirmed this as soon as we got inside. The provincial education officer (PEO) was in attendance, and the principal announced that the striking students were to be expelled for the defiance of authority. He went on to tell us about the unwashed debes, and how the students had refused to wash them after being warned, and then wouldn't eat their evening meal on the previous day.

The staff was thunderstruck to say the least, as here were 125 of our graduating students being kicked out forever. Questions started, and the PEO told us that the entire staff was expected to support the principal in the expulsion. I felt the need to speak: "Did the students," I asked, "refuse to board the buses this morning?" The principal responded that they had not, but that he had ordered them not to go, but to wait outside the office.

So I said that then there was really no strike as they had not refused to go out to their schools. And I went on to say that we had been hired by the Kenyan government to train teachers for the nation, and if we expelled our entire graduating class, we had failed in our duties. I said that the fault seemed to be ours, and rather than expelling them, we should be looking for some way to do the job for which we had been hired.

Then the stuff hit the fan!

The PEO said he was shocked by the lack of loyalty on the part of the staff, but the tutors were now aroused and were unanimous against expulsion. A compromise was reached, and all the students were suspended until they could get either their father or chief to come back and plead their case with the principal.

Every student complied, teaching practice went on, and the class graduated. I graduated myself the next month, much to the relief of the principal, who had lost the best chance he ever had to make his reputation nationally. ☐

Giant Jungle Ants

Ron Stockton

When I was twelve, I read a boy-adventure book called *Tom Stetson and the Giant Jungle Ants*. Tom, a high school junior, went into the jungles of Brazil to visit his uncle, a medical missionary. According to the flyleaf:

> "Tom and his uncle strive to rescue a friend from the primitive customs of the savage tribe, and at the same time fight fierce animals, poisonous plants, and stinging insects."

Among the most traumatic of Tom's experiences was the attack of giant jungle ants. Tom described the attack:

> "On they came in perfect military formation, a column of gigantic black ants. There was a battalion of warrior ants in front, followed by an orderly procession of worker ants, twice as small as the inch-long warriors. As they advanced in a column ten yards wide and two miles long the animals of the jungle frantically hurried out of the path of their invasion. From the swaying limb of a tree 300 feet tall and 50 feet in circumference Tom watched, frozen with horror, as the black army slowly advanced toward the tree. On and on they came, in strict military formation, their tiny black eyes glinting savagely in the sunlight. Then to his horror, the whole column stopped, as if the leader had given a command. The advance column wheeled toward the base of the tree. They began to crawl slowly up the bark toward him on every side."

What I learned from this book was that places far away were not only strange but scary. And some had giant jungle ants. But a decade later when Jane and I went to Kenya, what we found was different from that book. To start with, there was no jungle. Machakos School, forty miles east of Nairobi, got thirty inches of rain per year but was on the edge of a dry plateau that got under ten. With thirty inches, you can grow crops. With ten, you herd cattle. That was Maasai territory.

Of course, we heard stories about ants. These stories usually involved an army of marching ants that suddenly appeared in someone's front yard, heading for the house. They were not ten yards wide, but they were a threat. If you didn't divert them, they would march through your house as if they owned it. One person told me about a farm couple who heard their baby crying in the night. When they went into the nursery, they saw the baby covered with ants, biting his face. These were the stories of nightmares. The white farmers had an emergency plan for dealing with marching ants. They would have cans of gasoline sitting in wait. When someone saw the ants they would lay out a burning V formation, hoping to deflect them away from the house.

I was never sure these stories were true, but when you are in that situation, you tend to believe what you are told. Anyway, the anthills that we saw, some reaching ten feet into the air, made us think that whatever fantastic stories we heard were probably not exaggerated. But I had never actually seen an army of ants.

One day, that changed. We lived on the school compound which had three classroom buildings, four dormitories, a kitchen, and dining room for five hundred boys, and a dozen or so teachers' houses. Our house was the last one on the road. In front of the house was our cement veranda, flat on the ground, with a tin canopy over it. When it rained, you could stand there for a minute, shake off the water, and wipe your feet before you went in.

When school ended at 3:00 p.m., it would take Jane and me just a few minutes to get home. One day, as we came strolling in, we saw the veranda covered with ants.

These were not just the neighborhood ants that wander around and eat whatever they find, but instead a real, honest-to-goodness army of marching ants. The ones on my veranda were probably exploring for food. The "army" was a few feet away, fortunately marching across the driveway rather than through our house. The middle rank was two or so inches wide, and was so compressed that it looked like a solid black ribbon with branches coming from it. On the periphery, five inches out on each side, were the warrior ants. These were big suckers with pincers that you wanted to avoid.

The Maasai, pastoralists, who lived on that vast expanse of land that got ten inches of rain, would reportedly use warrior ants as sutures when they got a cut. They would pick up an ant, press the two pieces of torn flesh together, hold the ant up to the cut, and when the ant bit into the cut, they would twist off the ant's head, leaving the pincers in place. It sounds primitive, but you didn't have to walk twenty miles to the nearest clinic. The formic acid emitted by the ant, which stung like the blazes, would also purify the wound.

But if you were an inexperienced American, it was easy to let curiosity get the best of you. You might decide to inspect that two-inch-wide line without realizing there were warrior ants on the periphery. While you were standing there like a dolt looking at the parade, the warrior ants could be up your leg in a trice, as the British would say, and do damage to the delicate parts. There were stories of men tearing off their pants and performing an inelegant dance for whomever was around for the show.

I was smart enough to avoid that scenario. Since the ants were in possession of our entryway but not marching through our house, we decided to bend to reality and go in through the back door until they departed. The next morning, they were still there, marching faithfully in step. That afternoon they were there, and the next morning, and the next afternoon, and the next morning. It took them three days to disappear into the distance.

Once I ventured close enough to the center of the parade to get a photograph. I put my house key down on the ground to give some perspective. I was very careful to make sure those warrior ants did not grab onto my shoes and get up me, in a trice.

> For a longer version of this story, with photos, see http://bit.ly/JungleAnts. ☐

Toad in Stomach, Beetle in River

Ron Stockton

Jane and I were at Machakos Boys' School in 1965 when the Ministry of Education asked secondary teachers to monitor Standard 8 school-leaving examinations. I was assigned to Kitui, well off the main roads. Kitui had a reputation among our students as a center of witchcraft.

When I mentioned my assignment to a class, three students took me aside with great concern. They suggested that I not expel students caught cheating or they might put a toad in my stomach. Since I did not want a toad in my stomach, I was very cautious about my behavior while in Kitui.

I drove up with my colleague Ed Christensen in his VW Beetle. Beetles were the perfect car for Kenya. They had an advertising campaign that showed a sedan beside a Land Rover. The slogan was, "You need two cars, or a Volkswagen." Beetles were amazing. They could go over mountains or ford streams or cross the bush (as long as you did not run over a thorn). If they got stuck in the ditch, two men could push them out. What they could not do was cross a river. I know because Ed and I tried. The streams had become rivers because of the rains so our road was blocked. When this happened, you had three options: go back, sit there until the rains ended, or swim across and trade cars with someone on the other side. We decided to try option four, to carry on.

That Beetle was as determined as it could be and did great until it got stuck in the mud mid-stream. Ed and I pushed on that sucker for several minutes, but it would not budge. We could see the bubbles coming out of the exhaust pipe as the faithful engine kept chugging away, but finally it choked and gave up the ghost. Alas, we had no Plan B for being stuck in the middle of a raging stream.

Meanwhile, a crowd of curious people had gathered, watching our futile efforts. Ed went over and asked if they could help. They were not inclined to push but one offered his cow. We "rented" the cow and tied it to the VW and pulled it out. Ed paid a reasonable fee, and we were off to Kitui. Fortunately, there were no toads. ☐

The Bees
Yvonne Theodore

This is my saga about one of my unusual "extra, extra curricular" activities at Mt. St. Mary Namagunga, Uganda, the school to which I was assigned in 1961.

Soon after my arrival at the school, my students had many questions about "Americana" to which I responded that, no, I was not Chinese. Yes, I could actually learn to distinguish, as well as properly pronounce, Ds and Ts. And, as an American, I enjoyed eating cooked pineapple. Apparently, I neither looked nor sounded like anything they'd ever seen before. And, I must say, my Baltimore accent didn't help the situation one bit.

To me, their questions and my responses were important in our bonding process. However, they were nowhere near as important as an event that occurred during my walk home one day in the company of some students during a lunch break.

It was a peaceful, sunny day, but, curiously, as we were happily walking along, the sun disappeared; the sky turned jet black. The normally quiet campus began to hum with the sound of millions of bees on everything, everywhere. They weighed down tree branches and every leaf in sight. Immediately, the lot of us went on autopilot.

My students cowered, cringed, and cried. I myself became almost catatonic but managed to gather them together, ran with them to the house, opened the door, pushed them to floor in the back room, and covered them with one of my bed sheets. They were great: they followed my directions and stayed put while I surveyed the outside, through the window, of course. Every inch of every banana tree was weighted down with black bees, for whatever reason they do such things. I joined the students. The bees just "hung out" on the banana leaves, ostensibly until it was time for them to move on. We stayed put too and emerged safe and sound.

That event proved to the students and me that we shared a very important quality: the sheer will to work together to survive. We had the "right stuff." We emerged with not a broken bone among us, not a hair out of place, could still walk and talk, and none was found to be allergic to bee stings. So, heh, we returned for afternoon classes.

Me? I later baked them a pineapple upside down cake, which didn't even begin to change their minds that Americans had some weird eating habits. But, we could bond, though. ☐

Diversity in Arusha

Joel Watne

When I was assigned to a school in Arusha, it was the Arusha Indian School, which served the Asian population of Hindus, Sikhs, Sunni Muslims, three sects of Shia Muslims, Goans, Jains, Parsis, plus one Tanzanian African, one Somali, and one Greek, the son of a Greek Orthodox priest. After Tanganyika's independence, it was renamed Arusha Secondary School, and the African component of the student body greatly increased.

The first year, the headmaster was a Pakistani Sunni who disliked Brits, and by extension Americans, but was fond of Scotch. He was eventually replaced by an African Catholic. I went from being rated the worst teacher in the school to the best by the simple change in who wrote the evaluations.

Meanwhile, the Pakistani headmaster made me coach the soccer team despite my lack of familiarity with the sport, and also coach of the field hockey team, about which I knew even less. I pretty much let the team members decide who should be captain and decide who would play what positions since they obviously knew more about the subject than I.

A problem arose on the soccer team when some players complained that the captain (the headmaster's son and a very good student) was favoring Muslims in selecting starters. He responded by resigning, and I let the team choose their captain, which the headmaster felt was a decision I should dictate. I told the team that I did not care which religious community a player came from and that we should be fielding the eleven best players we had, even if it mean eleven Hindus, eleven Sikhs, eleven Sunnis, eleven Shiites, or eleven Goans, although it would be highly unlikely for any of those possibilities to be the case. There was no more visible religion-based friction on either the soccer or field hockey teams, and working with them was a very enjoyable experience.

My Goan contacts at Makerere College led to meeting members of the Arusha Goan Association, and they let me play club field hockey with them to learn the game. This led to my becoming the only non-Goan member of the Arusha Goan Association, a Norwegian-American Lutheran sticking out among all of those Asian Catholics.

But there were some limitations on inter-communal action. When we had a school program for the parents, part of the talent show included an Indian stick dance in which the dancers hold a stick in each hand and clack them together. We had two versions of the same dance, the first by Hindu girls in red saris, and the second by Ismaili Muslim girls in pastel blue and pink saris. ☐

III: Trips and Travel

Perhaps the quintessential travel tale here is *Travel during Heavy Rains, 1962*, the detailing of Sharon Hartmann's determined efforts to get to the wedding of Marty Lemke (nee McCall) in Bukoba in northwest Tanzania on the western shore of Lake Victoria from Morogoro in the south during East Africa's rainy season.

Would it have been entirely possible for Americans to disregard the romantic masculine associations Hemingway evoked while they were in East Africa? They also present opportunities for the storytellers to tie the trips to some consequence to themselves personally or to themselves as educators.

Ted Hoss makes a big gesture in *Family of Travelers*, crediting the traveling his young family undertook from 1968 to 1970 in East Africa for giving his five children and thirteen grandchildren "an itch to explore."

—

In this section:

Jerry Barr	*Nile Perch Fishing in Lake Rudolf* • 245
	Sambaker and Spare Time in Northern Uganda • 248
	A Multi-use Souvenir Found in Northern Uganda and Kenya • 250
John Beyerle	*Long Break in Southern Africa* • 252
Bill Cahill	*Turbans and Windscreens* • 253
Betty Castor	*Scaling Kilimanjaro with Schoolgirls, April 1964* • 254
Ted Essebaggers	*School Outing to Lake Manyara* • 255
Anita Hayden	*East African Safari Rally* • 259
Brooks Goddard	*My First Christmas in East Africa* • 260
Sharon Lybeck Hartmann	*Travel during Heavy Rains, 1962* • 269

Niall Herriott	*Feeding the Crocodiles* • 271
Ted Hoss	*Family of Travelers* • 272
Moses L. Howard	*Field Trip: Kampala to Mombasa* • 273
Don Knies	*Our First Date* • 279
Charles Kozoll	*Africa, 1962* • 281
Lucy Larom	*Adventure on the Narok Road* • 283
Clive Mann	*The Driving Test* • 284 *Travelers' Rest* • 285 *Gorillas at Last* • 287 *Total Eclipse of the Sun 30 June 1973* • 290 *The Kerio Valley* • 292
Dagmar Telfer Muthamia	*Christmas, 1965* • 294
Larry Olds	*Walking on Kilimanjaro* • 296
Joan (Hoffman) Schieber	*Christmas on Kilimanjaro* • 299
Ed Schmidt	*I Learned as Much as I Taught* • 300
Jane Stockton	*To Kilimanjaro and Back* • 301
William Stoever	*Hitchhiking the Congo* • 302 *Kilimanjaro Catharsis* • 306 *Murchison Hippos* • 307
Julie Richardson Sulman	*Screams in the Night* • 308
Mary Ryan Taras	*Adventures along the Nairobi Road* • 310
Beverly Templin	*Road Trip* • 311
Brenda Tillberg	*The First Flight to East Africa* • 312
Joel Watne	*Mount Meru* • 314 *The Crazy Dutchman* • 316 *East African Railways Curry* • 317
Jim Weikart	*Death Is Just an Option* • 317

Nile Perch Fishing in Lake Rudolf

Jerry Barr

When I first arrived in Uganda to attend teacher training at Makerere College in Kampala in October 1961 as a member of the first TEA group 1C, I heard about some great perch fishing in the Nile River. These fish could get to three hundred pounds. As I fished in numerous lakes and streams in California, Wisconsin, Minnesota, and Ontario, Canada for bass, walleye, northern pike and trout, I thought why not try to fish for some perch and do it in the Nile River—hubba hubba! So I bought some heavy duty fishing gear in Kampala and got ready to try my luck at landing some of those Nile perch.

As part of the teacher training at Makerere College, I was assigned to practice teach at a school in Jinja, Uganda, which was about one hour east of Kampala. I was assigned to a two-week practice teaching session at a girls' school on bluffs overlooking Lake Victoria. It turned out to be very informative experience and also gave me an unbelievable view of this great lake.

The source of the White Nile is located in the city of Jinja. In 1961, Nile perch were found only in the Nile River and not in Lake Victoria. The Owen Falls Dam and formally Ripon Falls kept the Nile perch from going into Lake Victoria as it had done for millennia. So, on my time off practice teaching, I fished from the banks of the Nile, right below Owen Dam. I pulled out some nice perch there, nothing big, but keepers and a nice meal. This set my appetite for more Nile perch fishing in Uganda.

While attending courses at Makerere College before getting my two-year teaching assignment, I met another TEA 1C teacher, Tom Kehler. Tom loved to fish also, so we planned some fishing trips in the future. Tom was assigned to a school in Kampala while I was assigned to teach mathematics at Sir Samuel Baker Senior Secondary School (Sambaker) located in Acholi Province, twenty miles from Gulu in the north of Uganda. After the Makerere College teacher training was finished, I went up to my assignment at Sambaker, and Tom went to teaching in Kampala. I fished and camped in northern Uganda, fishing below Murchison Falls and in the Aswan River, which was a tributary of the Nile River. I caught a lot of perch, including a thirty-pounder from the Aswan River.

Tom got in touch with me, asking if I was interested in going with him in buying the actual boat that was used in the filming of the movie *The African Queen* with Humphrey Bogart and Katherine Hepburn. Since the boat was located on Lake Albert, and too difficult for me to use it often enough, I declined. Tom did buy it, and we fished on it in Lake Albert a couple times. Tom's story concerning this boat is another great story.

During the second teaching year, Tom and I decided to take a two-week fishing trip to the great remote rift Lake Rudolf that was located in northern Kenya. We heard that the lake had great Nile perch fishing. After great effort—remember in those days and in northern Uganda, I only had a manual Royal typewriter and carbon paper to type the letters, and one phone that was available in the headmaster's office at Sambaker, to go through the process of getting the required special entry permit to enter that area of Kenya. I succeeded in getting the permit.

The big day came for this exciting journey, Tom driving up to Sambaker from Kampala, a long eight-hour drive! We equipped my short-wheeled Land Rover with food, water, gas, spare parts, and camping equipment. Remember, in 1963, there were *absolutely no* services available for travelers in northern Uganda, so driving across northern Uganda over the so-called gravel *murram* roads was a real adventure. We needed to be prepared for everything.

We set off to Moroto, the district headquarters located in the Karamoja sub-region of Uganda, on our way to the shores of Lake Rudolf. Moroto was located on the eastern border with Kenya and on the way to Lake Rudolf. We set up a camp on the outskirts of Moroto: no hotels or motels there.

The next morning, we proceeded to Lodwar, Kenya, which was a very small village twenty miles west from the shores of Lake Rudolf. This small and very isolated location in Northern Kenya was where the

"Flaming Spear," Jomo Kenyatta, was imprisoned during the Mau Mau revolution in Kenya. While we were in Lodwar, we found no evidence that Kenyatta ever was there.

We set off later that day from Lodwar. We went east on a one-lane trail using our compass, knowing that we could not miss Lake Rudolf. After a couple hours of cross desert traveling, we arrived on the shores of Lake Rudolf. There was a village of small grass huts located on the shores of this great rift lake. There were absolutely no tourists' amenities. So we set up our camp and cooked an evening meal looking forward to the adventure fishing on the great lake in the morning. As we did not have a boat, we planned to fish from the shore, hoping to land some Nile perch.

What a surprise we found! In this small village on Lake Rudolf, a local fellow named Okello had a modest open wooden boat with a small inboard motor but no gas. It turned out that he worked for a Brit who was harvesting crocodiles from Lake Rudolf. The Brit had a small grass hut on the shores of Lake Rudolf and this boat and motor. As we found out, he had been arrested a few weeks earlier since what he was doing was illegal. He left his stuff at his camp site on the shores of Lake Rudolf including this very modest wooden boat. As Okello had not been paid and was in charge of the boat, he told us we could use it if we supplied the gas and paid him a daily fee. We had the gas and the shillings! What luck: here's our boat!

So we set up camp on the shores of the sand dunes of Lake Rudolf. There was an open grass hut used by the illegal crocodile hunter on the sand dunes which we used to store our equipment and to cook in. The dunes were beautiful, clear soft sand stretching for miles. We shed our shoes and walked barefoot through these sands during our entire trip. The Turkanas, the local folks, were very cordial to us.

We went out fishing on the next day, and what a day of fishing! We trolled using wooden artificial baits and caught many Nile perch. It was a good thing because we needed to catch fish to eat, as we had brought limited food. Of course, we had no ice, no GPS, no Wal-Mart food markets, no nothin'. Each day we went fishing, we caught far more fish then we needed, but Okello told us that the local villagers would be very happy for any fish we could provide them. So, we kept all the Nile perch we caught and had plenty for ourselves and the local folks.

During the ten days we were fishing, we caught over 1500 pounds of perch. The largest Nile perch Tom caught was ninety pounds, plus I had a fish on the line for three hours before it broke free. Of course that fish now must have weighed a gazillion pounds, or at least that's my story.

As the final lucky ending to this story, we were told that a Kenya game warden had been living on these sandy shores of Lake Rudolf and shortly before we arrived, his wife had been bitten on her foot by a snake—a venomous sand viper. She had been taken to a Nairobi hospital and later died. As we found out later to our astonishment, those snakes lived hiding just under the sand and were prevalent throughout the dunes. For ten days, we had walked all over the dunes, bare footing it, and were lucky not to have been bitten by those venomous snakes.

After our great fishing adventure on Lake Rudolf, we headed back to Sambaker, and Tom returned to Kampala to his teaching assignment. What an adventure! □

Sambaker and Spare Time in Northern Uganda

Jerry Barr

My assignment made by the TEA staff in Uganda, was to teach mathematics at the Sir Samuel Baker Senior Secondary School (Sambaker) near Gulu, Uganda, twenty miles north on the Kitgum Road and more than 200 miles north of Kampala in the Northern Province of Uganda for the next two years.

There was no electric service, no local restaurants serving food I would be interested in eating or shopping centers, no movie theaters, no TV or other recreational activities I was accustomed to, and not even a radio station playing music. So arriving at Sambaker for this two-year teaching assignment, in an area far from what I was accustomed to, provided me with an infliction of what some called "cultural shock." It was serious at the beginning, but I worked it out.

Sambaker was a boarding school, so the students lived and studied on the campus. Because there were no living facilities in the area for the staff, housing was available on the Sambaker property, and that's where I lived for two years. Most of the staff were married couples, British and American and one Uganda math teacher—so there I was, a twenty-two year-old heterosexual man in this very different environment, and needed to find some activities to keep me happy and occupied during the off duty time.

As a kid, I was very active in the Boy Scouting movement ending up being an Eagle Scout, I loved camping, fishing, and some hunting. So, looking around where I was to be living for the next two years, and knowing it was the most magnificent and beautiful wild area in the world, I decided I was going to see as much as I could during the weekends and vacations. And that was going to involve camping in the bush.

I needed to get some camping equipment necessary to get into the bush. There were no motels or restaurants or commercial camp grounds where I was going. I already owned a used short-wheel-base 4x4 Land Rover, which was absolutely necessary. I fixed it up to sleep two, and outfitted it with extra jerrycans and water containers—I had to carry plenty of petro as there were no service stations around either, and I needed pure drinking water. I installed a front winch and carried plenty of cable with a Tanganyika jack to get me unstuck if I got bogged down in sand or mud—again no AAA around to help.

I bought a nice small light weight tent that slept two. It had a rubberized floor and netted door and window. I wanted to keep the bugs and snakes out! Since it did not come with a rain fly, I was able to find a Gulu sewing business to make the dining fly and connected a rain fly for the tent. Then, with a couple small camp beds, pressure light and cooking equipment, and other items needed to make safaris into the bush, I was ready.

But there was a problem—camping in the wild bush in northern Uganda could be dangerous as there were genuine threats to safety from large aggressive animals. I needed a fire arm for protection. A large-caliber hand gun would probably be enough, but in British Uganda, a hand gun was not allowed, so that meant getting a rifle. Still, getting a rifle was another matter. In British East Africa (in 1962, Uganda was still under British rule), fire arms control was extensive, but after several letters and applications, I got the permit and purchased a used 9-mm express bolt-action Husqvarna big game rifle (without a scope) for a reasonable price. I also got some fishing gear and a .22-caliber rifle. So, I was ready for some camping, hunting, and fishing adventures in the bush.

The assumption by the Uganda government, was that if you had a rifle in the bush, you were going to hunt. So, once I had a rifle, I was required to purchase a hunting license. Since I was considered a resident, I got a "resident hunting license."

I had all the necessary equipment and was ready to realize a dream—camping, fishing, and hunting in the wild African bush. My weekends and vacation time were now going to be full of African wild bush adventure.

> For a longer version of this story, with many delightful pictures, see http://bit.ly/sambaker. □

A Multi-use Souvenir Found in Northern Uganda and Kenya

Jerry Barr

A few months before graduating from Ripon College in 1961, I applied and was accepted to be included in the first wave of Teachers for East Africa (TEA). I had traveled around the USA extensively but never overseas, so this was a great upcoming adventure. My family, and especially my f, were very apprehensive on this undertaking. My dad even produced a National Geographic map of Africa and, pointing to East Africa, he said, "Jerry, look, there are not even any roads there! How are you going to get around?" Of course, he needed a Shell road map of Uganda, but where would you get that in Chicago?

During my US travels, as a young fellow, I always was on the lookout for souvenirs and that desire continued during my East African teaching assignment with TEA. Probably all persons in this program did the same. As a maths teacher (TEA-1C) working at the governmental senior secondary school called Sir Samuel Baker (Sambaker), located in Uganda's northern province, I got out in the bush many times in my Land Rover during the two years I worked there.

As there was virtually no commercial accommodation or restaurants available in northern Uganda, I had to have all the necessary equipment for sleeping, cooking and eating packed in my Land Rover during these outings. It seemed everyone I met on the various outings always had something interesting to sell. People had homemade musical instruments, self-protection items, wood carvings, fresh fruits, skins, food items, and so on.

Of course, wanting some souvenirs, I was always ready to buy or trade for interesting items, and I still have them. Most of my souvenirs were made for commercial sales, but I was able to find some real handmade locally interesting items. Probably the most interesting item was a stool that many people carried around. Since these stools were all handmade by their owners, they came in many different shapes and sizes. I bought several during the two years I camped, fished and hunted in northern Uganda's Karamoja District and northern Kenya's Turkana District. Now here's the kicker. These stools had a dual purpose. Can you guess what the second purpose was? They were used as a pillow—that's right, a pillow. Of course, they were not soft, but thinking about it, when sleeping on one's side, something is required to keep your head up and even with your body. And these stools did the trick. ☐

Long Break in Southern Africa

John Beyerle

During the long break at Christmas in 1963, I got a ride to Bukoba, Tanzania, to hook up with Tom for a trip with Jerry Schieber to South Africa. We took a boat to the railroad at Mwanza on Lake Victoria. We crossed Tanzania by rail to the town where Jerry was teaching. We fixed Jerry's Land Rover up to sleep three.

We went into Dar es Salaam and took a boat to Zanzibar. Tom had to get vaccinated as he had forgotten his yellow card. We returned via boat. Leaving there, we came back and joined the Great North Road.

We entered the Rhodesian and Nyasaland Federation, our goal being Southern Rhodesia (Zimbabwe). When we got there we toured the old Zimbabwe castle, then went to a political meeting where they were discussing what to do about the native peoples. Apparently an election was imminent. We visited Rhodes's grave. On to Victoria Falls for the full moon rainbow circle. Standing on the bridge over the gorge, we saw a perfect circle instead of a bow.

After that it was on to South Africa. We went to Basutoland via a switchback road that took your breath away. Then to Swaziland, through Zululand to get to Natal, midnight mass in the cathedral, the only integrated place in the country. Down the east coast towards the Cape. Stopped and went to see some cave drawings by aboriginal people. The men in the drawings all had erect penises.

Down to Cape Town, we saw beautiful scenery with the mountains on the right and the sea on the left. We stayed in a hostel, went to the Cape of Good Hope then swung up to Johannesburg, visited De Beers and the gold mine. I came away with the feeling that the whites had a deep distrust and fear of the various tribes. This distrust kept whites in a constant state of siege. There was no night life.

Once we left South Africa, we hauled out for Tanzania.

I took the train back to the lake, got a boat to Kampala and a bus back to Mbarara. I arrived completely broke and had to call the Ntare

School to get a ride home. Who knew that the future president of Uganda was in our classes at the time? □

Turbans and Windscreens
Bill Cahill

We learned upon arriving in Chewoyet in 1963 that every male Sikh who lived in the area thought that he was Jaswant or Joginder Singh, the brothers who finished the East African Safari year after year and won it in 1965 in a Volvo.

We were visiting Frank and Elsie Harris on the slopes of Kilimanjaro and followed the radio bulletins at the end of that race. The Singhs had a lot of fans. Joginder Singh also won in 1974 and 1976.

Anyway the *murram* and gravel road between Kitale and Makutano usually took me a half an hour to drive at speeds of up to sixty miles per hour. I think every Sikh could do it in fifteen minutes while simultaneously producing a great wave of tumbling rocks and stones cascading high into the air as they zoomed along. We were advised by other drivers at Chewoyet to press our hands against the inside of the windscreen immediately if we ever saw a car coming rapidly toward us driven by a turbaned figure. So whenever we saw a turban coming, Fran and I would shout "Sikh, Sikh!" and try to protect the windscreen. Sometimes it worked, sometimes it didn't. We lost three windscreens in two years. It was a strange experience to hear the loud "crack!" and suddenly find oneself sitting in a pile of glass pebbles, the windscreen having shattered in an instant. I hasten to add that we had several Sikh friends while in Kenya, and they always nodded knowingly when I repeated this story.

One strange aspect of the experience was that one could still drive a VW Bug at speed without having wind blow in one's face by closing the side windows. The driver didn't feel anything in his face, just a gentle zephyr. It had something to do with the shape of that particular car. □

Scaling Kilimanjaro with Schoolgirls, April 1964
Betty Castor (Elizabeth Bowe)

Although there are several Kilimanjaro climbing successes among our TEAers, my own experience was unique for several reasons. Number one, I participated with a group of students. Second, those who organized the first ever ascent for schoolgirls at the Outward Bound Program in 1964 knew they were making history.

When my headmaster at Kibuli Secondary School, Kampala, Uganda asked me to participate as an instructor in this inaugural program, it was certainly not because of my climbing expertise! I had none. It had much more to do with drafting a teacher to assist in a pioneering climbing curriculum for forty-one secondary girls—and also enable three of our own students to participate. Who knew that this would be such a groundbreaking experience? The Outward Bound climbing school had previously achieved renown for working with young men. Now, in the middle of East Africa at the foot of Kilimanjaro, the school at Loitokitok, altitude 6000 feet, was going to translate its male success to a first time group of young secondary schoolgirls!

The girls selected to participate were a diverse group, drawn from throughout East Africa and were made up evenly of African, Asian, and European students. The purpose was to build support and encourage cooperation among the girls. During three weeks of training, the girls learned the rudiments of climbing and independence on the mountain (along with this novice instructor). They also participated in challenging physical contests and academic topics as well. Preparation for the final climb was intense. The girls carried backpacks of thirty and forty pounds. In terms of today's climbs, these girls were superwomen! No oxygen tanks; no porters.

On the final day's struggle to reach Gilman Point, girls encouraged one another. Amazingly, everyone made it to the summit! The *East African Standard* subsequently described the expedition as an "almost unheard of feat, setting out from the foot of the mountain together and all reaching the top—a rare 100 per cent record." The newspaper also indicated that it was the first recorded expedition of African women to scale the mountain.

When I discuss this expedition with friends and colleagues today, they all share my own awe at what we accomplished together. It was a memory I shall never forget. ☐

School Outing to Lake Manyara

Ted Essebaggers

We had arrived at the park entrance in two vehicles on Friday evening from Moshi for the Mawenzi Secondary School weekend outing. We found the visitor dormitory just outside Mto-wa-Mbu close by the park entrance.

The boys and I prepared a light meal and were spending the night in one large room on metal-framed bunk beds, while our English headmaster and his eighteen-year old-son R were staying elsewhere, presumably in more comfortable quarters. It was hot, there were lots of mosquitos, and it proved a most uncomfortable and restless night sleeping directly on the creaky springs without mattresses. We had light bedding along, but no nets!

Early next morning after a school breakfast of sweet tea, bread, and jam, we entered Lake Manyara National Park: our headmaster in his 1962 two-door blue-and-white Triumph Herald, and I in my 1953 Land Rover, both fully loaded with students. We may have been exempted from paying park entrance fees as we were with the Ministry of Education and had booked beforehand; otherwise we had to pay 5/- a day per person, 10/- for each car, 3/- per student, 5/- for a guide. (These are amounts in Tanzanian shilingi [TSh].)

In any case, we had a most interesting and exciting time almost straight away viewing elephants and lions in the thick forest near the entrance. The guide explained those animals liked to get away from tormenting flies outside the forest. Outside, nearer the lake it was flat and marshy, then rocky and steep up towards the Rift Wall to the west. As we drove along very slowly, we saw all sorts of wildlife.

For our Form 4 boys, this was an experience of a lifetime seeing wildlife up close; they were excited and had difficulty keeping their voices down when we saw something. And we did see a lot: buffalo, hippo in the pools, various types of antelope, gazelle, monkeys, baboon, giraffe, zebra, and wart hog—though no rhino or leopard. We drove slowly down to the hot springs at Maji Moto at the south end of the park. There was much laughter and making of funny faces at the strong, unpleasant sulphur smells!

The main purpose of the trip was to give our students that first-hand experience of seeing animals in the wild before they completed their final exams and left secondary school, and before our headmaster retired and returned to England; as the day progressed, it was obvious how much the boys were getting out of it judging by their enthusiasm.

We had taken sandwiches and drinking water along into the park that Saturday, and had stopped for a picnic; but by the time we left the park at closing time, we were all tired and famished. R and his father drove on to their overnight quarters after agreeing to meet three senior boys and me next morning for a short two-to-three-hour trip north to have a look round the ruins at Engaruka.

That evening, the boys prepared a fire and cooked up a hearty meal of maize meal porridge for us at the dorm. As we ate, everyone enthusiastically shared the experiences of the day. When we turned in for the night there was some banter about mosquitos and no mattresses. Much was in Swahili between the boys, and though English was what our students were expected to speak in and around school, this was an outing. Anything they thought I might like to hear or I asked about, they happily explained to me in English. Not knowing enough Swahili, I would otherwise have been left out of much of the conversation.

Everyone was worn out from exposure to the sun, fresh outdoor air and all the excitement of seeing so much wildlife; so we soon got ourselves to bed. After a period of tossing and trying to make myself comfortable in bed, I suddenly started having cramps and terribly sharp abdominal pains. I waited as long as I could, but then had to get out of bed, wake the boys, and explain to them that I needed urgent help. Something was seriously wrong with me.

Two boys went off to wake our headmaster and inform him of the situation. It must have been around midnight. After a short time Mr B came, spoke with me briefly, and decided it was an emergency. So out we went to his little Triumph and drove to the local clinic, with me feeling every little bump of the road and asking him to drive very slowly.

Once there, it was I who had to get out. I knocked loudly on the door trying to rouse the nurse-in-charge. Someone came to an adjacent door to inform us that the nurse was not home but at a bar down the way.

Off we drove to the first bar, stopped and asked for him. Luckily Mto-wa-Mbu was not big and soon we located 'our man' at the adjoining bar where Congo beat and highlife was blaring loudly. People were drinking heavily and everyone apparently having a good time or arguing about something very loudly. 'Our man' soon came found us, loudly identifying himself, but in a most friendly way. He too had been drinking, but said he clearly understood our situation and immediately offered his help.

Without delay he was in the car and we were on the way to the clinic in pitch darkness, he showing us the way and saying that all would be well and not to worry. It was not far. Upon arrival, he got out of the car, still talking quite loudly, helped me out and up the steps, found his keys and unlocked the little clinic, lit an oil lamp, then helped me up onto the treatment bench, asked me to lie down, to relax and not to worry. Everything would be all right!

By now I was feeling just a bit worse and not too sure about him. He went to a big *almirah* full of instruments, bandages, and medicines. In a couple moments he was back with a large syringe filled and ready, asked me to turn on my side and pull down my trousers. He then skillfully jabbed me in my buttock without hesitation! He had injected me full of a pain killer (most likely morphine), which knocked me almost completely out. I was feeling very giddy, but the pain quickly subsided. I was reeling and wobbly!

With support I was soon down the clinic steps and back into the car and on our way back to the dorm with me in the front and more comfortable seat this time. He and the students helped me to my bed, wished me a good night and in a flash I was asleep, only waking the next morning, which was Sunday. I must have been covered in bites!

Midmorning Sunday my headmaster came to the dorm to check on me and decided to drive me up the winding escarpment road to the Lake Manyara Hotel where we could enquire after a doctor. It was a very bumpy ride on that rutty road and quite painful. Luckily there was an Asian doctor staying there. The good doctor was soon examining me on a hotel bed. Within a short time, he had his diagnosis. In a most professional manner he informed me I had a badly inflamed appendix and that I should have it removed in a few weeks' time when the inflammation had subsided and I was feeling better. So that was what it was, and I could carry on with my activities! After all that pain, I wasn't fully convinced. We were far from any hospital, and I was not satisfied I was at no risk at all.

Fast forward. After returning to Moshi and many weeks later, I had an appendectomy in the Moshi Government Hospital. My doctor was the surgeon Dr. Amin, another Asian. Everything went extremely well, and after a day or two in recovery in the Grade B hospital, I was back to work. Dr. Amin had personally given me a spinal anesthetic, a first time for me, and I was awake during the operation. European friends could not believe that I had had the procedure done in Moshi in the grade B hospital instead of going over to the grade A hospital in Arusha. But I was fine. After just two or three days, I was discharged and have never had any problems since. I was most grateful to Dr. Amin and went to his house to thank him personally.

But back to Mto-wa-Mbu. My headmaster was clearly counting on me to take him to the ruins at Engaruka. After visiting the doctor at the hotel and having a bit to eat, he was ready. This was his last chance before retirement. I knew the way (and in my Land Rover). It was not an order, but obviously something he seriously wanted doing. There was room for five or six of us crammed in, a full load for my little canvas-covered Land Rover and on a very rough track.

I realized how risky driving out into the bush like that was for me because of my condition; but I was feeling a bit better, was agreeable, and so we set off. After an hour or so, we had a serious mechanical problem which I managed to fix. The drive shaft had loosened and had to be refastened and tightened. Fortunately I had heard this happening and felt it, and as we were not driving fast, I immediately stopped the vehicle, got out, and went back along the track and found the loose nuts and bolts that had fallen off. I also had a few extra in my tool kit under the front seats. So I got down under the vehicle with my wrenches knowing what to do, refastened the loose drive shaft, tightened up the nuts, everyone got back in, and we proceeded northward.

I do not remember reaching the ruins at Engaruka that day. Unfortunate for my headmaster. It was now getting to be afternoon, we had had the mechanical delay, I was somewhat nervous, and still had some cramps and pain. I realized we had to return to the dorm to pick up the rest of the students, and then make the long drive via Makuyuni and Arusha back to Moshi that night, some 175 miles, a four- to five-hour drive in the dark. So we gave up Engaruka, turned round, and returned to Mto-wa-Mbu to pick up the Triumph Herald and the rest of the group, and made our way back to Moshi.

Monday there was school, and the Form 4 students would have much to tell. □

East African Safari Rally

Anita Hayden

In the UK, before I left the country, there was a car race that went through all three countries in East Africa. It was very popular TV viewing in England. Soon after I arrived in Tanganyika as it was at the time, the rally passed by the Arusha area so a bunch of us drove out to see the cars pass by in a cloud of dust.

Years later when I was in Korogwe, Tanzania, a missionary called Peter Garland somehow managed to volunteer the teachers at Korogwe to man a rest station and timing area for the rally. It was at the top of an escarpment in the Lushoto area.

We had to work at night as that was when the drivers were expected. They never stopped on this race, just drove nonstop. It took us over an hour to drive to our post at the top of the escarpment. There we had to provide water, snacks and give the racers whatever they needed. We had to do time checks on them.

When they drove down the mountain, it only took them about ten minutes. We got to meet all the best rally and track racers of the time. I remember meeting Stirling Moss, who was at the peak of his fame around that time. The racers were spaced well apart, and it was daylight before the last ones went through. We were all exhausted but thrilled at having played an important role in an important race.

Unfortunately, the race was discontinued soon after due to politics among the three countries. It had always been a lot of fun to watch them make their way through the terrible mud holes after a rain. We all kind of knew what that was like, didn't we? □

My First Christmas in East Africa

Brooks Goddard

I shall start this letter early (December 14, 1964 in Kampala, Uganda) before I have to line up for the opening of the University Games and before I must return this typewriter to its owner. In preparation for leaving, I have put mine in my trunk and locked it up.

As I may have already said, the University of East Africa becomes a reality next year with campuses at Kampala, Nairobi, and Dar es Salaam. The Games will be contested between the three schools. Makerere is by far the most established school, Nairobi next, and Dar relatively new. For university standards Nairobi and Dar cannot compare with Makerere although I assume they are rapidly improving.

At 9:30 a.m. the Games will be officially opened I gather in a somewhat formal manner of the Olympics. The Africans do not lack for officiousness which they probably get from the British. At 10:30 a.m. in the volleyball game followed at 4:30 p.m. by basketball and 5:30 p.m. by squash. It will be a busy day, and although I am playing only one day, it will, at least permit me to partially fulfill any obligations I or the Makerere students think I have to the college.

Tomorrow we leave for Nairobi on our start to Ethiopia. As you can see on the map, Nairobi is out of the way, but we need to get visas and travel permits. The road from Lodwar in Kenya north for 250 miles to Maji in Ethiopia may be quite a strain, and we have to get permits to go north of Lodwar in Kenya. In Nairobi we shall also get drivers licenses to pick up when our international ones expire. We hope to come by some travel and gas information about our trip also.

—

My Christmas account continues on December 27 from Kampala.

I had hoped that this first letter to you while I was on vacation would come from Addis Ababa in Ethiopia, but as you can see, I am writing this in dear old Kampala. Tuesday morning we set off for Nairobi—five of us in a short-wheel-base (88-inch) Land Rover, just barely comfortable. We arrived around 11:00 p.m. and found room at University College. For the next two days we ravaged Nairobi for information concerning our trip and awaited the Ethiopian visas.

We left Nairobi before noon and drove northwest to Kitale where we slept in the auditorium of a vacationing primary school. The following morning we obtained the necessary travel permit and food provisions and set out for Lodwar. In Kitale we left paved roads for what turned out to be ten days. Fifty miles or so north of Kitale begins what they call the Northern Frontier District (NFD).

Toward nightfall and twenty-five miles south of Lodwar we encountered much water in the road, and when we stopped to help another party, the water in our engine prevented the motor from starting up again. Fortunately the party previously stuck had sent an *askari* (policeman) on ahead on foot to Lodwar, and an hour later, a Land Rover arrived to pull the stuck party out of the mud who then had to pull us into Lodwar. Both of us in the two cars had had longs days on the road and when the pull rope broke several times, so did our patience. When we finally pulled into Lodwar, we were all ready for some food and sleep.

Lodwar is the farthest point north that the police like people to go which we found out the next day when we asked the Assistant Regional Government Agent/ARGA for permission to continue north to Lokitaung and the border. Disappointed we took a side excursion to ninety miles round trip over to Ferguson's Gulf on Lake Rudolf where we didn't see much except a Turkana famine relief camp which had been there since 1934 (somebody told us later that the Turkana—the local native tribe—knew a good thing when they saw one). The next morning Dave Newbury and Dennis Huckabay had a talk with the ARGA who said he wouldn't make any decision on our travel but that we could telegraph Lokitaung again; which we did. Four hours later we were told that we could indeed come north. Around 1:00 p.m. on December 20 we left for the 130-mile trip to Lokitaung.

To complete the irony of this effort to get to Lokitaung, twenty-five miles south of Lokit we met the ARGA stuck in the mud, who had the day before denied our permission to come. But since he had been stuck in the mud all day, he had not been in Lokit to deny us this time! So we took the Lokit ARGA and his friend back to Lokit where we had a few beers and slept on the ARGA's back porch. Of course, now that we had gotten this far, the Kenya police wanted nothing else than to keep us going and get out of their jurisdiction so on December 21 we got a truck escort to the Ethiopian border at Namuruputh. After checking with the border guard there, we were given a guide to make sure we didn't get lost in going to the next town which was Kalam.

We arrived in Kalam about 3:00 p.m. As are many of these "towns," Kalam is only a police/army post surrounded by many native huts; settlements are all they are, and the most you can ever hope to find in these spots is drinking water (or any kind of water). We sat in the heat in Kalam while somebody and somebody else looked at our visas and passports, and finally a good hour later, we were told we could leave. We headed north hoping to reach a station called Bume which we have never seen, on a map or in person.

An hour and a quarter north of Kalam we got stuck in a mudbank. To our good fortune a truck soon appeared and promised to free us but insisted that we turn back to Kalam as the road north was impassable due to mud and water. We argued with the officer in broken English, Swahili, and Italian for almost an hour, but to no avail. So back we drove to Kalam where we could stay, said the officer, for two days, and if it didn't rain any more, then we could attempt the passage.

We returned to Kalam in the dark; almost every night on the road we ended up driving after dark. We ate and hit the hay only to be woken around 4:30 a.m. by rain. Well, it rained and it rained forcing us to seek higher and drier ground which we all eventually did but not before all of our things were wet. The rain ceased at about 11 a.m., and we set the things out to dry knowing, of course, that we were here for the day and maybe longer. The Ethiopians were very nice to us, and we made as good a time of our stay there as possible.

The next day we drove back to Lokit and then to Lodwar. All along the road we noticed the damage that this one day of rain had done to the road. The ten miles into Lokit were on a river bed, and we almost got lost. From Lodwar we drove to Kapenguria, twenty-five miles north of Kitale, where Dennis and Dan Callard had practice taught back in October–November.

We arrived there on Christmas Eve, and when Dennis and Dan inquired as to where we could stay, one of the staff invited us to a lamb dinner which we gratefully accepted, it being our first good meal in over a week. Kapenguria is where Kenyatta was tried for Mau Mau, and Lodwar is where he was "detained—what a place to be imprisoned!

Christmas Day we were treated to a delicious breakfast of eggs, bacon, fresh pineapple, toast, and tea—probably the best tasting and most appreciated breakfast I have ever had. We loafed around during the day recuperating and thanking our stars that we had reached a decent spot for this day.

At 5:00 p.m. we drove twenty-five miles into Kitale for a seven course dinner at the K Hotel which tasted like heaven and complete even with plum pudding; with drinks the cost was sh.25/= or about $3.60. We then drove back to Kapenguria and sat around a fire sucking candy canes that Dave produced from his duffle bag.

The following morning we were half of us awake when we hear singing, and around the corner came about fifteen Turkana women singing and dancing (Kapenguria is principally a Pokot reserve; Turkana are mainly west and southwest of Lake Rudolf—we saw plenty of them in the Lodwar-Lokit area). I thought they would simply pass down the road, but, no, they came right up to the front door, waking the others with their singing.

We really did not know who to handle the situation, but we finally made out that they wanted something. We offered them cigarettes, which they rejected, but accept some chewing gum and a tin of meat. We were told the singing was of the Christmas celebrations and perhaps part of Boxing Day, which in England is the day after Christmas and the day when the servants are given presents. At any rate, after four minutes, they left to visit the next house which was the home of the staff member who had been so nice to us—a couple from Fergus Falls, Minnesota. They went through the routine for them as well, and we rounded up 10/= to pay them so we could take some pictures. This done, they left. We then packed up and drove the rest of the way to Kampala arriving about 9:00 p.m.

Although we did not reach our destination, the trip was a success. The car was really packed down as we traveled in the Northern Frontier District (NFD) carrying forty gallons of gas, ten gallons of water plus our packs and sleeping bags. The short-wheel-base Land Rover is just fine for two or perhaps three, but not five. Our meals while camping were sparse indeed being a cup or two of tea for breakfast, nibbling for lunch, and soup and a little meat for dinner. Traveling on *murram* (a clay-like dirt) was, of course, very dusty, and the heat of the days contributed to our general disheveled appearance.

Most of the time we were in Turkana-land. The Turkana are a Nilo-Hamitic tribe as are the Karamojong of Uganda and the Maasai of Kenya-Tanzania, which form the group of tribes in East Africa which have most resisted westernization. The men are quite scantily clad with a piece of cloth that they throw over one shoulder and drapes around most of their trunk. They usually carry a small miniature-sized stool on which they either sit on or rest their head and a stick or two, occasionally a spear.

The women wear many, many strings of beads around their neck and in their hair, which is matted into string-like strands with a mixture of grease, mud, and dung (and/or maybe, I don't know) and are generally bare-breasted with pierced ears and large arm bracelets; cow skins form a skirt that hangs from the waist as well. Generally they seemed quite friendly, except in Lodwar where the begging got a little too much to take. Mainly though, they crowd around the car strictly out of curiosity. Now and then one of them knows Swahili so you can attempt a broken conversation. Out of the entire tribe, I think there are three or four in secondary school.

As we traveled we would see them tending their herds of goat, cattle, donkey, or camel—many of these animals are used for bleeding for a liquid and protein drink (the Maasai have a famous drink of goat's milk, cow's blood, wood ash, and urine). Donkeys are used as beasts of burden by the smart people. We did not see many wild animals (they don't even want to live there!) except a stray hyena, gazelles, and a few birds of prey. In other places, we did see some monkeys and baboon.

The Turkana live in what they call *manyattas*, which are arrangements of maybe five huts in a circle. As they are made of hides and leaves and sticks, they are not easily seen by a casual glance.

We have a little over two weeks, and I don't know what we'll do with it; probably hang around here until after New Years and then maybe to Queen Elizabeth Park in southwestern Uganda.

—

I continued on January 18, 1965:

We left Kampala on January 6 after I had been in the infirmary for a day with stomach pains and intestinal problems. About 8:30 p.m. we arrived in Mbarara, about 180 miles southwest of Kampala. We stayed there in a secondary school which was on vacation. The next night we spent in a small primary school about ten miles north of Kanungu. The short distance traveled that day was due to poor roads and to going down a mountain only to find the necessary bridge over the stream washed out. The headmaster and the people at this little school were very happy to have us, and, I gathered, considered our visit somewhat of an honor.

The next day was wonderful as we traveled on the western-most road in Uganda in this region which takes you close to the Congo and through the Impenetrable Forest. We seemed to climb in the Land Rover for hours and figured that we got as high as 8,000 feet—all twisting road, of course. Traveling through the Kigezi district you can't help but notice the beautiful, rolling, yet almost entirely cultivated hills—practically no valleys. Despite all the cultivation in this area (and this type of contour cultivation, rolling hills topography continues into northern Rwanda and eastern Congo), the people are rather poor due to poor crops last year and the fact that the area is densely populated (the Belgians moved 35,000 people from Rwanda to Congo within the last ten years).

That next night was spent in Kisoro, the western customs station. There is a quaint Travelers Rest with accommodations for six to eight people, bar, and dinner along with an older German man who prides himself on living forty years in Africa, being more African than most white people, and ordering his employees around.

Coming into Kisoro we saw for the first of five volcanoes of this area—huge things that majestically rise out of this soft, hilly area. The one near Kisoro is called Muhavura. Leaving Uganda and entering Rwanda, we now began to drive on the right and pull out our too-long-forgotten French—fortunately one of the lads knew it quite well.

We reached Kisenyi on the northeastern shore of Lake Kivu early in the afternoon. What a water front! Kivu is one of the few lakes in this part of Africa that is not diseased with bilharzias, a parasitic something-or-other that is carried by a certain kind of snail and, as I understand it, attacks only humans. Apparently it is not very pernicious but is difficult to get rid of and painful in the process. The water-front road is beautifully landscaped with palms and scrubs, the road divided by landscaping, just simply marvelous.

We located the rest house only to find Congolese (American) missionaries occupying the whole thing. However, one of the families was on a field trip back to their Congo station, so we had a place to stay. These were Baptist missionaries whose stations were mostly along the road that goes from Goma-Sake-Lubero; Rutshuru is also in their district. Their work is now confined because, obviously, of the war (although there were no rebels in the immediate area; 300 men guarded the Goma airport) and the official US government policy which said no US citizens in eastern Congo. However, most of the men were going in for two or three days stretches to their stations (and in most cases these stations were their homes as well) to keep the work moving.

A Rev. Elvin Peters volunteered to take us in for two days, and we gladly accepted. We inquired into any risks and considered everything; we came out feeling that this was an excellent opportunity to see a small part of the Congo with somebody who knew the area, the people, and the language well.

On Sunday, January 10, after a delicious dinner, we drove up to his station at Burungu. We had dinner and chatted, and the next day were shown around the station which consisted on a large school room for five grades, a dispensary, a ward building, a church, and living quarters for two European families and two single people. The land was about twenty acres with water supply. Peters had built two of the houses by himself. As a matter of fact, he seemed to like the tinkering aspect of isolated missionary life so much and yet complained about the conditions that it seemed as though his tinkering with machines, electricity, and plumbing had somehow trickled over into tinkering with people's spiritual beliefs.

I would have believed him to be more sincere if he'd repeated, "If I didn't think God wanted me here, I'd leave tomorrow," a lot less. After seeing his station, we visited a tea factory and noticed several tea plantations and farms going along as if there never was a war [this war became known as The Congo Crisis and lasted from 1960 to 1965: the Lumumba-Katanga-Mobutu mess].

We returned to Rwanda that night; we had been 110 km, or about seventy miles into the Congo. The next day we went into Congo again, only into the city of Goma to buy curios and stamps (and African stamps can be beautiful!). We managed to waste the whole day there, but left Kisenyi the next day for Gabiro and the national park.

Kagera is not a big attraction, but we stayed at the lodge for next to nothing and had two exotic dinners—one of Cape buffalo and one of topi steaks (topi is a largish antelope with small horns). We saw some good game, a lot of graceful impala. Saw a total of five lions from a combined distance of 900 yards—they were just dots against grass or dirt. And then home—yes, a week late, for which, I guess, we shall be dipping into a bit of hot water. But we don't know what just yet.

About last Wednesday, I began to develop headaches during the day, which aspirin controlled until the last several days. Saturday after returning was just too much, and I entered the infirmary getting out this morning.

I think that these two trips have lowered my resistance through little sleep, poor and irregular meals, and the continual jumping around of the Land Rover, which is by far the most uncomfortable vehicle I have ever traveled in. You do not really notice the ebbing away of your physical strength in the heat of the exciting daily fare, but I'm sure it catches up with you in the end. So, I expect that I'll soon be fit;

I hope to start up with tennis again Wednesday or Saturday—the Uganda Open is the next big tourney in April. ☐

Travel during Heavy Rains, 1962

Sharon Lybeck Hartmann

We had a romance in TEA Wave I. Marty McCall (1C) and Dick Lemke (1B), met in September, 1961, and were engaged by December. Marty asked me to be her maid of honor in a wedding scheduled for June 1962.

However, by February, staffing pressures at their Bukoba schools had forced an advance of the wedding date to March. Because of this change, none of their family members could come, and three of Marty's TEA bridesmaids could not get away from their Ugandan and Kenyan schools. However, the wedding weekend was a three-day holiday in Tanganyika, and checking the various train, boat, and plane schedules, I thought that I could attend and make it back to Morogoro in time to meet my classes the following week. I said that I would be there.

The day before the wedding, I was supposed to take the train from Morogoro to Dar es Salaam. But my train was cancelled by record flooding caused by heavy rains. So my headmaster drove me the 120 miles to Dar in time to catch my day-long East African Airways DC-3 flight to Mwanza. The route was very indirect. Half the passenger area was filled with cargo including crates of live chickens. Although I was headed north, we first flew south to Iringa where we had a long layover. I was ticketed on a connecting EAA flight from Mwanza to Bukoba, that evening putting me in Bukoba on the night before the wedding.

Despite the delays, we landed in Mwanza about an hour before my next scheduled flight. I was waiting for it to be announced when I realized that the man at the EAA desk was getting ready to close down the airport. I asked him about my flight.

"Oh," he said casually, "that's been cancelled. Flooding at Bukoba. Last flight went today at 9:00 a.m." I expressed surprise and showed him my ticket. He said "We must have called you this morning."

I pointed out that I was already airborne at that time on a connecting flight of his airline. He did not care. With rising panic I said, "But my friend is getting married tomorrow in Bukoba, and I am her maid of honor."

He continued to shut down the facility. He was so uninterested in anything I said and so gruff and dismissive in his occasional responses that I began to cry. I have never seen such change in a human being in my life. "No! No!" he said. "Don't do that! We'll figure out some way to get you there!"

He took me into town, stopping at the home of one bush pilot on the way to see whether he would make the flight. He refused, saying that not only was Bukoba flooded, Mwanza airport was closed the next day for repairs. From the hotel the EAA guy checked me into, I called Marty to explain the situation. Throughout the evening I received call after call from him as he tried Land Rovers (lake too high, roads flooded), boats (same problem with docking facilities), and more pilots. Finally, he called at nearly 11:00 p.m. and told me that a pilot who worked for the UN on a rural mapping mission would take me.

The next morning, I called Marty just before the pilot arrived and told her I was on my way. He took me to the airport, where I climbed into the seat next to his in his two seater plane, while he walked out to a big Caterpillar tractor actually on the runway and asked the operator if he would just move it over a little so that his plane could take off. The plane's wheels cleared the driver's head by less than ten feet, and we were on our way.

Once we got out over Lake Victoria, the pilot put the plane on auto-pilot. He then handed me a very fine hand-drawn map of the lake. He pointed out exactly where we were by showing me various islands below us, and told me to tell him when we had reached a point on the map near Bukoba. Then he began to read a movie magazine. When we reached that spot, about an hour later, I told him so.

Meanwhile, Marty had gone down to the Bukoba airport and told an official that a plane was coming in from Mwanza. He told her it was not—hat Mwanza was closed for repairs and Bukoba was flooded and could not land planes. She was still arguing with him, when they heard our plane. He said, "Son of a bitch" and ran for the control tower.

Back in the plane, as we approached, it was clear that the runway was under several feet of water. We landed with sheets of water shooting up on both sides of the plane. As we taxied to a stop on dry land, I said to the pilot, "So how are you going to get out of here?"

He said, "I don't know." But I got to the wedding! ☐

Feeding the Crocodiles
Niall Herriott

It was the first, and nearly the last, outing of the Wildlife Society I had recently initiated in the school. Fifteen students and I were being ferried towards Murchison Falls, as it was then called, on a wide flat-bottomed open boat. And there it was, an amazing sight, with the mighty Nile funneling through a gap in the rocks about twenty feet wide in a powerful foaming white jet as tall as a two-storied building. But what really impressed the students were the scores of huge crocodiles basking on the mud-banks below the waterfall.

"Eee! Eee! Look! *Kubwa sana!* So big!"

The boatman cut the engine to let the boat glide in towards the mud-banks for a closer look at the crocs or just to scare the students, maybe. But he misjudged and the boat came to rest beside the bank. The huge reptiles slithered off into the water. All except one, a particularly large and vicious-looking character, which was now half on the boat and half on the bank.

Panic and pandemonium erupted. Everyone rushed to the other side of the boat. Female students were hugging male students and vice versa, with everyone yelling and squealing. The boat dipped to one side dangerously. The croc was trying to reverse off the boat rather than attack anyone, but they were all reluctant to move back from the side a little and avoid swamping the boat or even capsizing.

A newspaper headline jumped into my mind: "Seventeen people devoured by crocodiles at Murchison Falls." I was propelled into action. I grabbed a pole and jammed it into the croc's open jaws. The boatman grabbed another pole and we managed to lever the beast into the water as the boat gradually separated from the mud-bank. Through the sweat pouring down my face, I could see a ring of gnarled snouts in the water around the boat.

Another fiasco narrowly averted in the checkered annals of Namilyango College. And what a bloody fiasco this one would have been! □

Family of Travelers

Ted Hoss

I was part of the 1968-70 TEEA group. My wife, who was pregnant, and our four children embarked on the great adventure in June of 1968 that would take us to New York City, Columbia University, and to Kagumo Teacher College in Nyeri, Kenya.

Columbia was under siege by students. One night two buses loaded with armed police parked in front of our apartment at 116th Street. They were going to meet the students who were standing their ground on Broadway in front of the University. From the start, we felt we were on the ground swell of history. The friends we met, the teachers we had, the experiences provided by Columbia will always be with us. Our life in Kenya, our experience there, the knowledge gained of divergent cultures have shaped our beings. Our youngest son was born in Nyeri.

On returning from Kenya, we traveled to Egypt, Europe, and the UK. We have since visited all fifty states. My last big adventure was a ten-day stay on the Amazon River deep in the Peruvian jungle.

I returned to the school district from whence I came. I continued to teach English to eighth graders for forty-one years. I taught in a bilingual college in the evening for twenty-five years as an adjunct professor, teaching English as a second language. I used the skills taught me at Columbia in the TESL program.

I am retired now. My wife and I are empty nesters. One daughter returned to Africa and Niger as part of the Peace Corps. Our other children have traveled extensively. We have thirteen grandchildren who now travel the world. It's in their blood. One just returned from studies in Rome. A grandson is headed to Madrid, Spain.

Like Ewart Grogan, we had an itch to explore. We did it. We are richer for it. Thank you, TEEA. □

Field Trip: Kampala to Mombasa

Moses L. Howard

At the city bar in Kampala, Gene Ashby and I made our radical decision over drinks. It was better to teach marine biology on the beach in Mombasa amid the remnants of East African colonialism across the road from Lord Delaware's Plantation outside of Nairobi than to teach those subjects from books and pictures in our classrooms.

We thought it such a great idea that we petitioned old Porskitt, our headmaster at Kyambogo Teacher Training College, to allow us to go on a field trip by bus to Mombasa with forty students, males and females.

We thought he would "freak out." But as he gazed at us through those thick eyeglasses; his eyes became gleeful and young. Instead of rejecting us, he said, "That's the spirit we need around here." He helped us plan the trip by calling headmasters at other schools to feed our students and put us up for the night when we passed through their area.

We secured a bus and two drivers. For further security, one of us drove my old beat-up Datsun in case we had bus trouble and needed to go to the nearest town for a mechanic. At the end of term, our field trip began—with disciplined, self-controlled teacher trainees who were twenty to twenty-five years old. Some were married; most had never before traveled this far outside their communities.

Our first stop was at the Owen Falls Dam at Jinja, where we toured the sugar and cement factories. From there, we hastened over a smooth tarmac road to Tororo Girls School near the Kenyan border where we spent our first night's lodging.

We crossed into Kenya in the early morning. The bus droned on, passing white and black rhinoceroses. Among the flat-topped mimosa we caught glimpses of reticulated giraffes. We made good time; soon we passed Eldoret and by late afternoon we were approaching Nakuru.

This was a talented group of trainees. With this leisure of travel, they showed many sides of creativity. Some were phenomenal musicians on drums or stringed lyres. Others drew or painted pictures and hung them throughout the bus. Several took on the task of writing a journal of our field trip. At intervals, they read portions of their compositions to the rapt attention of the whole group. Our women students decorated their half of the bus with silks and colorful scarves. Odors of perfumes and powders drifted from it through the rest of the bus.

We arrived early evening near the alkaline Lake Nakuru, and we saw white birds sitting as if on tables in the foliage of green, flat-topped trees. Birds flew up in droves—grebes, cranes, nightjars, noisy yellow weaver birds, many kinds of starlings—whirling and wheeling around in the blue sky above the trees and hills; very eye-catching and interesting.

But nothing rivaled the myriad masses of pink and red flamingoes feeding and ruffling up and down on the shores and even in the middle of the lake. The flamingoes flew up, marched along the lake ends, fed in the shallows, standing erect, their beaks on their long necks upside down, siphoning and filtering food into their bodies. All the while their feathers ruffled displaying the fuchsia and red plumage fueled by the algae and shrimp they ate from this alkaline lake water.

We spent the night at a secondary school near Lake Nakuru. Then quickly, in the morning, packed and boarded our bus with sleep still in our eyes. We passed a hill overlooking the lake. The moaning drone of our bus motor disturbed the nesting flamingoes. Frightened, they rose up in flocks. Soft, whispering waves of flamingoes, flaring wings floating upward from Lake Nakuru, through sparse green tree tresses in the early morning mist, looking like a sparkling pink veil floating in the sky over our yellow bus.

The scenery captured our eyes. Books, magazines and newspapers, lay about, but not many were opened. I remember many titles:

> *Weep Not, Child*
> *Living in the Village of Ghosts*
> *Things Fall Apart*
> *Gone with the Wind*

More books lay on a poster that read "When Elephants Fight it is the Grass that Suffers":

> *Cry the Beloved Country*
> *Great Expectations*
> *The American Constitution*
> *Tom Brown's School Days*

From here, the bus raced around curve after curve and up and down hill. Relaxing students slept or swayed up and down the aisles with the moving, droning bus, visiting with each other in their seats, laughing, exchanging jokes. The drivers, good humored and cooperative, knew the road and good naturedly coaxed us to stop at outdoor cafes that had food, beer, soft drinks, and latrines.

When we passed one town by, there was soon another, with roads always crowded with people headed to the next nearest town, loaded with baskets of maize, cassava, bananas, pineapples, sorghum, gourds of honey; there were bicycles loaded with sacks of beans or a person, a woman or child perched on the back carriage seat or riding in the handlebars of the bicycle or a motor scooter. No matter where we passed in the afternoon, there were these crowds headed back in the opposite direction.

Then five miles before we reached Nairobi, our luck changed; we had punctures in two rear tires. Latria Semakula (the women students' matron), Gene Ashby, and I held a brief staff meeting in the Datsun.

I was in charge of discipline, so in the end I was stuck with the bus. Gene loved to drink, so it was best he went with the drivers for mechanics and supervised some of the trainees who wanted to hike or hitch rides into Nairobi. He drove some students in our Datsun; others hiked or caught local buses and taxis to town to see the sights of Nairobi, promising to meet up with Gene at the post office. I stayed with Latria and most of the girls until the drivers and the garage repairmen came. They slowly, but expertly, in about six hours, repaired our bus tires.

When Gene and the last of the students finally dribbled back, we went to our host school in the hills above Nairobi. We were up in the hills in a school, a good distance from town where people were dancing in the bright lighted bars of Nairobi where our students really wanted to be. However, when we arrived at the host school, the young students there were having a dance and no one wanted to go to bed. After a while, our trainees all began dancing, having fun right there.

Early the next morning we went through Nairobi without stopping after Gene promised the students he would bring them back. It was early afternoon when our bus reached the outskirts of Mombasa. The drivers pulled to the side, out of traffic, to give the trainees a view of the entry. Cameras clicked amid students' shouts expressing excitement and joy when they saw the four big tusks that marked the entrance to Mombasa.

Students became impatient as our drivers searched for our school quarters along the length of spacious beaches. After being attracted by the many tourist hotels and camps along the beautiful white sandy beach, we finally located our school and unloaded our bags. Wearing skimpy shorts and barefooted, we headed for the beach. We all gathered there, happily dipping our toes into warm ocean water.

I expected the students to don bathing suits and head for the water. But only Mudede and Geld Patel and several others dove in and swam a ways out, shouting and throwing handfuls of water toward those on the beach who were not enticed to join them. Others walked along the sandy beach, sat under palm trees, joked about the many crabs, especially the hermit crabs which they collected, observed, and called "homeless" ones because they were always searching for a new home.

Only four students were keen to learn goggling and snorkeling, so we found the beach rental kiosk and rented equipment. All we could do that first evening was get used to the process of putting on the equipment. The students spat out the salt water. We could not collect any specimens, because we had neither container nor preservative.

The next morning, four students who wanted to snorkel came with me in the Datsun into Mombasa town to find a chemical warehouse where we bought formaldehyde and a large 100-gallon garbage can-type plastic container to hold our specimens. I ordered ready-made preservative in gallon jugs. That was easy, because I'd learned there were "collectors" operating along the beach, securing specimens for biological supply houses in England and Germany.

On our first day of collecting, a young German university student on holiday collecting specimens popped out of the water near us, in goggles and a snorkeling outfit, with a plastic collecting bag slung over his shoulder. He soon made friends with my crew, pointing out a small fish with spines he told us to take care not to touch or step on, because it was poisonous. He told us that he worked with his father during holidays collecting specimens for sale to a laboratory back home in Frankfurt, Germany.

Every low tide I combed the beach for specimens and shells, and made notes about them. While collecting with students, I taught them and made notes about their questions that I planned to include in my lessons back at the college.

Our German university student joined us frequently and was very useful in sharing information about collecting. He informed us that there was no danger of sharks because the coral reef came up too high.

As long as we did not venture out beyond the barrier, there was no danger. That information relieved the fears of other students who soon joined us in swimming out to look or collecting and writing in notebooks. Our artists drew pictures daily.

Our group established a routine. I goggled and snorkeled with four and sometimes as many as eight of the teacher trainees and the collector from Germany. Meanwhile Gene took field trips with a large cadre of teacher trainees as far as Nairobi, to parliament to see Jomo Kenyatta and to see the big colonial plantations of Lord Delaware, the horse farms, and the air field. He told any listener that he was a social studies teacher back at the college and had finally thought how he could enrich and enliven his courses. The students wanted to make sure they learned something of the colonial experience of Kenyans. Uganda was never a colony and was spared that colonial past; it was a protectorate during colonial times, when England ruled through the chiefs and kings they found already in Uganda.

With these established routines, we had meals in the school and on the beach, and we spent quiet evenings reading, writing, reflecting, cataloging, and preserving our specimens. We met every evening to sightsee, visiting the forts and historical sites along the beach.

Gradually students filled our plastic collection container. More and more of our number cultivated visits to the beach. Mrs. Semakula had most of the girls in bathing suits, where they often frolicked in the water during the siesta period; a time when the beach was free of fishermen and collectors.

Our week slipped away day by fast-moving day. Then it was gone, and we left Mombasa with our collection utensil full and headed over the long road through Kenya.

Leaving Mombasa behind us, the teacher-trainees slept, recounted their adventures, or quietly wrote in their journals. We quickly passed Nairobi, stopping at our host schools on the way, but now hurrying back to Kyambogo University in Kampala. We arrived on a quiet, seemingly deserted campus late one night; school was still on holiday. It would be several weeks before staff and students would savor our adventure when we reported at a special assembly or taught our newly acquired knowledge to newly arrived students.

Now, still, years after, in a protected corner of the Science Laboratory at Kyambogo University, which was formerly Kyambogo Teacher Training College, is a one-hundred-gallon reinforced hard plastic container of marine animals and plants preserved in formaldehyde and alcohol: starfishes, octopus, crabs, oysters, clams, seaweeds, puffer fish, hermit crabs, limpets, sand fleas, and algae-kelp, varied and sundry of marine specimens we collected on that field trip taken with forty teacher-trainees from Kyambogo to Mombasa.

This collection forms the physical lab parts of an introductory course in marine biology that the present science staff offers to the teacher trainees in landlocked Uganda. Teaching social studies is not much changed. The teachers still use maps and pictures, but videos make lessons more interesting and up to date. ☐

Our First Date

Don Knies

I had met my future wife Maureen, a British nurse, at a friend's house at Makerere, but our first real date was a safari to Lake Turkana in northern Kenya. With my buddy, Jim Warford, a TEA teacher at Bungoma, Kenya, and Maureen and her friend, Daphne Micklethwaite, we traveled north in my old Land Rover.

All went well until we reached Lodwar, the place where Jomo Kenyatta had been imprisoned. Maureen was driving, her first experience with a four wheel drive vehicle I later learned, and she put us into a ditch. I stupidly and boorishly shouted at her, and she responded by silently ignoring me. We proceeded on to the southern end of the lake where luckily a tax collector was being taken over to a fishery camp by Turkana warriors, and we were able to hitch a ride in their canoes.

These Turkana were quite spectacular—tall, powerful black men with headdresses of mud and cow dung festooned with ostrich feathers, naked except for capes tied at the throat, carrying their little stools and long spears, propelling their canoes with wooden paddles like a well-drilled boat racing team. Slipping through tall reed beds swarming with birds, we crossed the open water of the lake to the camp. There the young British fisheries officer, somewhat surprised by our visit (he told us he never had visitors), let us set up camp under a thatched shelter. He also took an interest in Maureen, who obviously had no time for her uncouth American escort. Despite my ostracism causing a somewhat strained atmosphere, we spent an interesting couple of days swimming in the lake (we were assured that fish were so plentiful that the huge crocodiles didn't bother people), watching the Turkana fishing with nets, broiling tilapia filets on the campfire and sharing our Tusker beer with the fisheries man. It was an unforgettable glimpse into a stark and ancient way of life.

Unfortunately, on the way home to Kampala, Maureen suffered an infected mosquito bite on her leg which immobilized her and was serious enough to put her in hospital for a week. While she was there, the fisheries officer came down from Lake Turkana and tried to see her. Luckily for me, he arrived at the hospital out of visiting hours and the tough old matron, bless her heart, wouldn't let him in. Presumably, he went back to his lonely station on the lake and was never seen again in Kampala.

At the same time, I was suffering remorse for my behavior and visited Maureen every day—being sure to go at the correct time—bringing flowers and apologies and words of good cheer. Evidently, Maureen changed her mind about this contrite penitent, because when she got out of hospital, we began conventional dating, and the rest is history: we have been married for forty-six years. ☐

Africa, 1962

Charles Kozoll

In December of 1962, three of us decided to travel to South Africa using a variety of methods: boat, train, bus, and hitchhiking. On the way back, one of the others, Dave, and I decided we would spend a few days on the beach in Beira. It was easy enough to hitch a ride to the Mozambique border. But we waited for a couple of hours before an English-speaking Portuguese man offered us a ride in his truck. On the way, Dave kept asking questions and making remarks about buildings and fields enclosed with barbed wire.

The driver took us to the beach that was crowded with Brits stationed in Rhodesia and Malawi. It was mid-afternoon. We rented a one-room beach house and had fun on the beach. After three hours in the water, we went back to our room to rest and then had an excellent shrimp dinner. We had one more day and were scheduled to take a diesel rail car to Blantyre in Malawi.

The next day was uneventful until late. There was a knock on our door. It was the man that had driven us to Beira. He said we were to come with him to the police station to talk to his boss. His boss, a senior police officer, who wondered why we were in Beira asked many us questions. Our explanation seemed to satisfy him, and he began to talk about how blacks had little or no intelligence and they were doing God's work to protect him. Then he took us to dinner and drove us back to the beach.

The next morning we left for Malawi, the only Americans in a car that was full of Brits returning home. I had the habit of writing down the names of places we had visited in my journal. This time I wrote down the distance between towns. At the border with Malawi, the train stopped. That border was in the Limpopo river basin that is below sea level and very hot. Two men in police uniform came on the train and went directly to Dave and me. They took us off the train and started checking our baggage. They found my journal with the names of different towns and began talking among themselves. The temperature must have been 100 degrees, and the Brits were telling them to leave us. One of the police officers was on the phone with Beira for what seemed forever. After an hour we were cleared to go but they took our film. Three months later our developed film was returned.

About a month later, I was posted to western Uganda on the border with the Congo for two months at a boys' school operated by the Brothers of the Holy Cross. There was a mixture of brothers and others on the faculty. One of them was a young man from Canada who had a motorcycle. We started talking about a trip to see how far we could get into the Congo during a four-day break in the term.

All was well for the first two or three hours and then the bike blew a tire. We left it with a local store and started to hitchhike. A Rolls Royce stopped for us and in it were the governor general of Uganda, the Queen's representative, and his wife. We rode with them to the last town before the border.

In that town, we were able to go further in a truck with a Greek driver going into a major town in the eastern Congo. We got to the border as it was getting dark. The Congolese border guard with a submachine gun wouldn't let us in: we must have a *"laissez passer"* and told us to leave.

It was now dark and very quiet. We were able to see a sign for a mission about eight miles away. We began to walk and it remained quiet. Usually on a Saturday night, you could hear drums in the villages we passed. It must have been close to midnight when we found the road to the mission. We knocked on the door, were asked who we were, and finally let in.

"Don't you boys know this is a 'disturbed area' and if the police found you, you would have been shot," our host told us. Because we were exhausted, what he said didn't register and we quickly fell asleep on the floor. During the next two days, we toured a national park in western Uganda with a *Newsweek* correspondent and his family and slept at a student hostel surrounded by elephants. ☐

Adventure on the Narok Road

Lucy Larom

I remember our first year in Nakuru, 1963. It was rainy season, and we wanted to go to Narok. We were advised only Land Rovers could get through but, young and stupid, we intrepidly embarked on the trip. Hank and I and David, who was about three years old, were in our Morris station wagon and another couple (also from TEA as I remember) in a VW Bug.

I drove so Hank could drink his Tusker beer and smoke and navigate, which was standard procedure in our family. It was a lark. We would descend into increasingly deep and deceptive puddles or lakes in the road and slewing out mud would emerge on the other side. Sometimes the car would go sideways. We'd just hold our breath and gun it.

Somewhere, about half way in, the Morris got stuck in the mud so we left it behind and piled in to the VW. In the Morris were my shoes. About three miles out of Narok, the VW got stuck. We spent the night in the forest in the VW, four adults upright in the seats, and little Dave in the back. He slept after eating the only morsel of food we had. I don't think any of the adults slept. I remember hearing strange sounds coming out of the forest at night: a funny loud door creaking noise that I later learned was the rock hyrax, and a strange plaintive haunting cry between that of a baby and some strange clawed night beast. We afterwards thought it might have been a leopard.

When it was light, we walked the three miles into Narok. I was barefoot but quickly built up a red mud pack on the bottom of my feet that acted like the sole of a shoe. Hours later, we dragged into the house of the TEA couple teaching there. I remember a tomato vine that climbed all over the side of their house that was as big as a tree.

The men gathered some Maasai *morani* and went back and dragged the two cars out of the mud. That's all I remember except seeing red-ochred *morani* for the first time up in the forest and a group of three girls who had recently been circumcised and, as I remember, wore dark leather skins and white triangular masks over their faces. ☐

The Driving Test

Clive Mann

When I arrived in East Africa, I did not have a driving license. For a few weeks at Soroti I mostly walked, cadged lifts, or borrowed a bicycle from one of school boys to whom I gave my servants' quarters. Soon I bought an old BSA 500cc motorbike that I shared unofficially with a Peace Corps volunteer who was not allowed transport. Then I bought a 600cc Fiat painted red, white, and blue. It couldn't go more than thirty miles without boiling until I took it apart and removed the woman's underwear from an important pipe in the cooling system. Then I could attempt fifty miles.

These vehicles were cheap enough for me to buy with my salary, but I wanted real wheels to go exploring. I had my mind set on a two-stroke, three-cylinder Saab owned by a Turkish diplomat friend in Kampala. This only had a few thousand miles on the clock and looked brand new. Moreover, Ata Ahmet was being posted to Washington and had to sell. Even at "mates' rates" I still needed a government loan, and the only thing that stood in the way was my lack of a valid driving license. I had to pass a bribe through Saira's Driving School in Soroti to get a license. All Saira did was to give me one lesson as I was a perfectly competent driver, loan me a car for the test, and relieve me of a lot of money.

The driving inspector, grossly overweight, came once a month from Mbale. If you didn't pass a bribe he would do things like getting you to park on a hill and put a matchbox behind a rear wheel and tell you to move off. If you rolled back a couple of millimeters, it was sufficient to crush the box and you failed. Roger Wigglesworth refused to give a bribe at first and having failed three times, he eventually succumbed.

When I took the test, there were two Asian lads also in the car. Each drove for about three minutes. One couldn't master three pedals, and the other didn't get out of second gear. We all passed. The inspector was eventually given fourteen years for corruption.

When I wanted to get an International Driving Permit on leaving Uganda, I took all the paperwork plus two photos to the appropriate office in Kampala. I was asked if they were "passport photos." When I replied "yes," the guy said they were not suitable because the form said "passport type photos." I went off to the City Bar for a couple of beers, returned an hour later and found, as I expected, the guy had gone off duty and there was someone else in his place. I presented the same documents and photos again. On being asked what sort of photos they were I said "passport type."

"Fine," he said, and I got my license.

Getting a UK license is another story, and my final (third) test was in Hemel Hempstead where there is an amazingly complicated roundabout. Convinced that I could never pass in the borrowed Mini Cooper that thought it was on a racetrack, with new Czechoslovak nylon tires that slipped all over the place on the wet tarmac, and an explosive clutch, I went into a pub and downed three pints of weak lager. I came out whistling. The inspector had previously done the same job in Eldoret. He started whistling. I passed! □

Travelers' Rest

Clive Mann

Near Kisoro in southwest Uganda there was, and perhaps still is, a charming inn called Travelers' Rest. At the time of my visits in 1966 and 1967, it was run by a very interesting character called Walter Baumgartel, a German by origin. It was situated close to the Virunga Volcanoes where Uganda, Rwanda, and Congo meet.

Walter had early on discovered that there were mountain gorillas in the nearby mountain forests and had become quite knowledgeable about them. Their presence was known before, and in the 1920s a "Gorilla Sanctuary" had been established, but not many outsiders had seen them. Having stayed overnight with friends in Kabale, I set out very early for Kisoro and arrived mid-morning.

After checking in with Walter, I had coffee with him and told him I was keen to get to the gorillas. He said that up the side of Muhavura towards the saddle would be most productive and, eyeing my two-stroke, three-cylinder Saab, opined that I would get much of the way on four wheels as it was now quite dry. The way he spoke I assumed he had sighted them recently. Too impatient to wait for the cook to make sandwiches, I took a loaf of bread and some fruit and a flask of coffee and set off.

I did in fact get quite someway in the car. The track was rarely used and not very eroded, and it was dry. Memory fails me now, but at some point I did come across a very steep stretch which I thought a Land Rover might baulk at, and chickened out. I found a spot where I could do a multiple-point turn, locked up the vehicle and set out with my rucksack and binoculars.

I was not particularly fit at the time, and it seemed that living a few years at 1500 to 2000 meters wasn't helping too much on the slope that was actually not often very steep. I was getting pretty hot, and stopped at times to rest and listen for sounds. A few small antelopes, including a reedbuck, and some monkeys whose identities I seem not to have noted made up the mammalian fauna. I confess that I was worried about encounters with Cape buffalo and elephant, and I listened for them as much as for gorillas. I guess I was still some way from the saddle when I decided to return.

Back at Traveler's Rest the few other guests had eaten and one was sitting at the bar. Walter was not around, but good food soon made an appearance for me. After eating I chatted to the man at the bar, an Englishman from the High Commission, and told him that I had followed Walter's instructions to find gorillas.

"But Walter hasn't been up there for eleven years!" he replied.

Later that night I was on my way along the verandah to the *choo* with a candle that blew out. I muttered an expletive as I stubbed by toe on a chair, and the twin barrels of a twelve-bore were suddenly thrust through a window in my direction. I uttered something pathetic like "It's only me," and the gun was withdrawn, I later discovered, by the man from the BHC.

I was having a drink or two with Walter on my last evening. I was then the sole guest. In pouring rain a rather beaten-up open-back LWB Land Rover turned up. It was driven by a middle-aged bearded Belgian man who seemed to be wearing nothing except for a ragged trilby, a long translucent woman's mac and a pair of Bata safari boots. With him were two African ladies and four or five mixed-race *watoto*. Walter organized them with a room, and I thought no more of them. The next morning I left early. Seeing gorillas had to wait a few more years.

About a year later, I returned to Travelers' Rest, but for the forest birds, without any real hope of gorillas. Walter hadn't forgotten that I was there the previous year when this odd group turned up in the rain. He told me they stayed a couple of days and then disappeared without paying.

"Let me show you what I found under one of their beds," he said. Taking me to an out building he pulled a tarpaulin off two metal trunks. He opened them to show me a veritable armory of shotguns, rifles, handguns, and scattered among them various ammunition, some in boxes, some loose. □

Gorillas at Last

Clive Mann

Having spent a week at Walter Baumgartel's Travelers' Rest in Kisoro on two occasions and failing to find gorillas, I decided to try the Impenetrable Forest, also in Kigezi, Uganda. I knew of the rest house at Ruhizha in the forest at about 2800 meters, but I couldn't discover if there were any booking arrangements. Anyway, as well as water, camping equipment and basic foods my Land Rover had a folding sleeping platform which could be used inside or on the roof rack, so I was entirely self-sufficient.

I arrived about two hours before sunset and found other people already there. There was a middle-aged MuKiga man organizing charcoal fires and a motley bevy of guests: Patrick, an English teacher from Makerere School with a pupil, Benjamin; Aiden, a math's lecturer from Bristol; Jo-El, an undergraduate New Yorker, and Vivien her friend. There was plenty of room for all of us.

That evening we sat around the fire inside and drank beer. We arranged for two guides to take us to look for gorillas the next morning. We had bizarre conversations about what to do if we came across our quarry, and we warned each other that we must not carry through the charge: beer and altitude were having an effect. At some point Jo-El went outside.

On return she beckoned me to join her to watch a partial eclipse of the moon. Although her company was beyond pleasant, after about twenty minutes, the bitter cold drove us inside. We joined the merry throng laughing and hooting about "charges" and so on. The cold had had a sobering effect on Jo-El and me, and as we were to muster at five a.m. we decided sleep was called for.

Well before five we were huddled around mugs of steaming tea, and our two guides were introduced to us. They were pygmies but not as small as some that Tom Heaton and I had come across in the Bwamba Forest a few years earlier. Whatever we do, they said, we must not run from a charging gorilla. Only then will he carry through his charge and perhaps injure you or worse. Someone bitten by a gorilla is deemed a coward because it means he ran away.

For hours we went up and down through the forest. The only tracks were those made by elephants. The guides had to cut swathes of vegetation for us to pass. We found gorilla nests from the night before, and nearby their curious dung, which resembled beads of horse faeces on a string like pearls. This was much more exhausting than I had expected, and our guides began to wonder if they would produce the goods before some of us were too exhausted to go on.

In mid-afternoon we were climbing a very steep hill where it was predominantly grassland with large bushes, some of them giant celery, a favorite of gorillas. We were virtually at the top of the incline, the two guides first, next Aiden, me, and the rest in some order I cannot remember. Very close there were a couple of sharp barks, and this immense male appeared in front of us on hind legs and doing a drum roll on his chest. There was a blinding flash in my eye and I lost consciousness. I couldn't have been out for long because the next thing I remember was looking downhill and seen a couple of dozen oranges from the string bag on Benjamin's rucksack rolling down the hill.

The guides helped me piece together what had happened. Aiden had lost his nerve, swung round wildly and his elbow connected with my eye. No harm done, but the gorillas of course were long gone. Aiden was ribbed over beer that night because of "not carrying through the charge." Next day the guides had sighted our gorillas across a valley where they could be observed peacefully feeding but at a considerable distance.

The others returned to Kampala, and I stayed on for about a week doing some bird ringing and exploring lower areas of the forest such as Kitahulira towards the Congo border and telling the guides that I was only interested in pursuing gorillas again if they were no more than two hours from the rest house. I had arranged to meet Jo-El at Makerere. She had been invited to a party given by the eminent field biologist, the late Lancelot Tickell, and she took me. We did not have a late night as the next day we were setting out for Kapsabet to get more supplies, and the day after we started a two-week safari through the NFD, calling on Mike and Judy Rainy at Maralal for a night en route.

I never saw gorillas again. Now it is so much easier (they have been known to come to you!), but frighteningly expensive. I did it on a shoestring, but it was hard work. □

Total Eclipse of the Sun
30 June 1973

Clive Mann

I learnt that in 1973 there was to be a total eclipse of the sun on June 30, and the area of totality would include northern Kenya. It was a Saturday afternoon in a long weekend; could hardly be better.

There were others in Kapsabet who were also keen to see the phenomenon, so I organized a convoy of four vehicles to drive up to the area of totality, three normal cars and my Land Rover. According to the press, it seemed that the more serious astronomers, international tourists and many others were planning to go to the east side of Lake Rudolf (now Lake Turkana), probably around Koobi Fora. We decided to go to southern Turkana to the west of the lake as it was not such a long journey, and more likely to be passable to ordinary cars. The settlement of Lokichar seemed to be well within the area of totality, and we made that our target.

If memory serves we set off early on Friday morning, travelling via Eldoret, Iten, Tot, Lomut and Kaputir. As I had a Land Rover I elected to be "tail-end Charlie." We made good time, with few problems due the other vehicles grounding, or needing to be pulled through sand, and found a very good spot to camp a few miles north of Lokichar. Drivers were excused the usual camp duties, and I erected a few mist nets to catch birds for ringing before breaking out the "Tusker."

Just before nightfall a Turkana lad wandered into the camp. We gave him tea and food and he seemed reluctant to travel on. He had been to Lokichar to buy a padlock and was on his way back to his *manyatta*. Since he seemed to have miscalculated and still had a few miles to go in the dark. We suggested he sleep under the verandah of one of the larger tents.

Next morning, the day of the eclipse, I spent some time tending my mist nets. One car decided to continue to Lodwar or beyond with the hope of some extra seconds of totality. The rest of us decided we were happy where we were and that we would get at least four or five minutes anyway.

We speculated on how the Turkana boy would react to the eclipse. He was about fifteen, and had had no schooling; the last total eclipse of the sun affecting that area was in 1926. Had information about this been passed on orally? We quizzed him, but he didn't show much interest. There was much speculation in the press that a big gathering of people at Koobi Fora pointing telescopes and long lenses at the sun, only for it to disappear, and the land plunged into darkness, may perhaps lead to violence by local people against these intruders.

The exact time I cannot remember, but probably sometime after about 1:00 p.m., the shadow began to creep over the sun. It got progressively dimmer, some birds began to sing, and others flew in parties to communal roosts. But it was not really becoming dark, until the point when totality started. Then it was rather like a switch being thrown. The difference between 99.9 percent coverage of the Sun, and 100 percent was immense. I think we had well over five minutes of totality, but I am no longer in contact with any of my companions to check.

We marveled at the phenomenon until it started to get light again, and then realized the boy was nowhere to be seen. Had he panicked and run off into the bush? We called him, and soon he ambled nonchalantly into the camp, totally unfazed. He had merely gone to relieve himself. We tried to discuss the eclipse with him, but he showed no more interest than if it was an unseasonal shower.

The others who had gone further returned. They had also had perfect views. The next morning we broke camp and headed homewards. North of Tot, a group of very drunk villagers had set up a road block and said we could not pass. It was essential that we did, because even if I had managed to find an alternative route, the ordinary cars would not have made it. Tim remonstrated with the ring leader using "settler Swahili," which then developed into a shouting match with Tim losing his temper. I asked his wife Judy to bring him back to the car and calm him down.

I went forward to talk to the man who was really quite het-up by now, as were some of his companions. I rummaged in my wallet and found an old collecting permit from Nairobi Museum, which was badly frayed, and stained with blood, mud, and sweat. I buttered the guy up and said I realized he was doing important work, but I had special permission from Mzee himself to take people along this road, and showed him this permit. I assumed he would not be able to read the English, but perhaps he could read KiSwahili.

I heaved a great sigh of relief when I saw that he held it upside down, and pretended to read it to his companions. Smiles broke out. Hands were shaken. The barrier was removed and we were invited to join the drinking, which we declined. The partial eclipse in Kapsabet was not noticed because of complete cloud cover. We discovered later that all the folk who had gathered at Koobi Fora saw little, as they also had clouds obscuring the sun at the crucial time.

Reflecting on some of the most wonderful experiences I have had, I think I put this at Number Two. Number One goes to a few hours at the feet of Ravi Shankar as he played, amongst other things, a superb morning raga, five years later in London, even if I had to be helped up from the floor where I had been sitting cross-legged for so long. □

The Kerio Valley

Clive Mann

When I lived in Kabarnet, Rift Valley Province, Kenya, it was necessary to cross the Kerio Valley to reach Eldoret via Tambach and the Elgeyo-Marakwet Escarpment. The roads were steep, rocky, and at times very muddy. Tarmac did not begin until some way past Iten.

Occasionally I would go down from the Tugen Hills where Kabarnet was sited to the valley to explore and look for birds. The area seemed pretty underpopulated, but things changed within a few years when the huge fluorspar mine was developed and a new road was developed to give easier access to Eldoret.

At about 700–1000 meters lower than the Tugen Hills, the vegetation was quite different with much acacia reminiscent of Karamoja. In the past Afrikaner farmers from Uasin Gishu district had hunted the area thoroughly, not just for skins and trophies, but for all parts of the animals. They "harvested" them like crops, with no regard to protection ordinances.

Game was thin on the ground. I was told by an ex-game warden that elephants were no longer, although some disputed this. Apparently there were still black rhinos, and I once came across a freshly-used blood-stained rubbing rock. I never heard of lion there, but I'm sure there must have been leopards. Buffalo and large antelopes had been hunted out. Medium-sized crocodiles were often close to the road. But I went mostly for the birds.

In February 1971 Peter and Hazel Britton accompanied me on a more ambitious investigation along the west side of the valley, following the bottom of the Elgeyo-Marakwet escarpment to Tot and beyond. We took both Land Rovers, and decided to spend four nights in the valley. We camped in a beautiful glade somewhere north of Tot. It was dry and hot. One morning we set off in my SWB Land Rover to do a circuit from the camp back to the main road, up the Elgeyo-Marakwet escarpment and then along it, returning to the camp via Tot.

Even if the road was bad, we reckoned we could do this before nightfall. It was plain sailing until on the road down to Tot we found it blocked by a huge bulldozer that had thrown one of its tracks. There was insufficient space to pass between the machine and the vertical mud wall to the right, and only about a meter between it and the edge of the road on the left. A quick mental calculation told us that if we retraced our steps, we would get back to the camp well after nightfall, and it would probably be impossible to find in the dark. The edge of the road fell away at about a thirty-five-degree slope, plunging hundreds of meters to the valley below.

I'm not exactly a brave person, and what I suggested terrified me at the time. I would shift all gear in the Land Rover to the driver's side, and tie open the driver's door, and also the rear door as an alternative escape route if it rolled. Then I would drive off the road onto the slope with as much of my body hanging out of the door as possible.

The Brittons sensibly did not want to encourage me, but finally accepted it was the best solution. They would stay on the road and watch, or not, in the case of Peter. I drove at a snail's pace parallel to the road hanging out of the door, ready to jump. When I was safely back on the road. Hazel swore that the upper wheels had left the ground briefly on two occasions. I praise the Land Rover and not my skill.

We got back to the camp in good time, and I made short work of a couple of "Rex" cigarettes, was excused camp duties, and allowed to drink a couple of Tuskers in peace. ☐

Christmas, 1965

Dagmar Telfer Muthamia

One of my most memorable trips was during the Christmas break 1965. My duties at Kaaga Girls School in Meru kept me from traveling with my friends so I decided to go by myself to Lamu on the coast of Kenya close to the Somali border. Fortunately there were two Peace Corps volunteers who were also headed to the coast so they joined me in my VW bug.

We spent the first night in Nairobi and the second in Mombasa sleeping on the floor at a house shared by local Peace Corps volunteers. The next day we drove north along the coast. I parted with my companions at Kalifi and continued on to Malindi. After a few days in Malindi, I took a six-seater Cessna to Lamu. It was possible to drive but not advisable, as the road was often washed out and travelers were subject to attack by the Shifta, who were Somalis fighting for their independence from Kenya in a desire to re-create Greater Somalia. You could also take a *dhow*, the traditional boat of the Indian Ocean trade, but that took several days and was also risky.

The flight of a mere half hour landed on Manda Island, across from Lamu from which a small motor boat carried us to Lamu Island and town. Sitting in the boat, watching as the town neared, I was drawn into the beauty of this remote, exotic place that had existed for almost one thousand years and was a result of ancient trade along the east African coast to Arabia, Persia, and India and a testament to the Swahili people and their culture created by that trade.

During my stay I took many walks through the maze of narrow streets closed in by two or three story buildings of coral and mangrove with wooden shutters and doors carved in intricate patterns. There was still a town crier. It was a Muslim town with most of the women wearing the black *buibui*, which left only faces and hands visible. A few of the women wore a costume with an interior tent-like structure so that even the general shape of the woman was not discernable. Walking along these streets was like having traveled back in time. There were no cars, but here and there I saw donkeys.

The pilot who took me to Petley's Hotel on the water front introduced me to other guests and to a retired couple who lived nearby. They invited me for afternoon tea and regaled me with stories of colonial life in Kenya, which included their acquaintance with Joy Adamson, who had been the only other foreign woman in Isiolo, my host's first veterinarian assignment in the 1930s. They said Joy's attitude was one of absolute distain for other women. She refused to ever talk directly to my hostess, but rather only to her husband or other men.

There were only about twelve non-Muslims on the island that year, so I assumed I would have no Christmas. As it turned out, I did. On Christmas day I was invited to join a few others for lunch and drinks by Bunny Allen and his wife, Kenya settlers vacationing there in a hut with concrete floors and walls and a grass roof. They owned two farms and ran a safari business catering to rich Texans. Bunny was a stereotype of the great white hunter.

Other guests included his brother Bar Allen an eccentric who sported a monocle. Bub Miller was a sweet old man with a hearty appetite who had retired to Lamu on a limited income. Darky, a Cockney, wore an Arab cap and a Somali man's skirt or *kikoi* and ran the only bar in Lamu on the ground floor of Petley's. Jim Allen, no relation to the other Allens, was a history professor at Makerere and had much to tell me about Lamu and the characters who are the "white settlers" or *wazungu*. Jim later founded a museum on Lamu, which I saw when I returned in 1988.

We all gathered again at night for Christmas dinner at Petley's. There was one addition to our group, Mr. Ngugi, the district commissioner. It was nice to see him again as I had met him when he was the D.C. in Meru. Lamu seemed so different and far away that we all felt like old friends.

The next day Jim Allen and I did some exploring of the town and some shopping. After our morning excursion, we had lunch. Then it was time to leave on a three-seater plane and return to Malindi. In the ancient, exotic, romantic, isolated Swahili town, I had a sense of the very old coastal culture and the recently old colonial Kenya.

Bunny Allen died in 2002. See http://bit.ly/b-allen. □

Walking on Kilimanjaro

Larry Olds

My teaching colleague from England, Malcolm Maries, and I had driven like crazy to get across the Serengeti Plain from Mwanza at the southern tip of Lake Victoria in time to meet my college friend, John, arriving at the Arusha airport. John was set on climbing the mountain. I was lukewarm about the idea at best; Malcolm just didn't want to do it at all. A friend of John from the summer program that had brought them to East Africa became the fourth in our party. John's friend, Michael, was eager to try the mountain but he was not, like John, an extremely fit long distance runner, or like Malcolm and I, an active athlete.

Getting to the peak of Mt. Kilimanjaro is just a long uphill walk. It doesn't require climbing gear like ropes and special shoes. It just requires walking. The easy way to do it was to go through one of the hotels that would provide a guide, porters, food, sleeping bags and everything else needed for the trip.

There were three camps with huts for sleeping on the journey, the last, Kibo Hut, at the base of the snow near the top. The usual journey was to take three days to get to Kibo, then get up way before dawn the fourth day to get to the top at daybreak. The afternoon of the fourth day and the fifth would be spent returning to the bottom. We didn't do that. We were the same people who had driven like crazy in a single day through the Serengeti, one of the most extraordinary national parks in the world. Why would we treat this marvelous walk on the mountain any differently?

Sally Fechtmeyer, a TEA colleague of Malcolm, and I taught near the mountain. She was an outdoors woman. She had enough camping gear to outfit us all with what we needed. After we spent the night at her house, and she helped us round up the gear and the food we needed, she drove us to where our walk would begin. We had decided not to start at the usual starting place near the tourist hotels, but to drive as far up the mountain as we could. There was a road and then a trail to the first hut that a four-wheel drive vehicle might have managed.

Pretty late in the morning, Sally took the four of us crammed into my VW Beetle as high as we could go, to a point from where we set off walking with the intent to get to the second hut the first night. One of the reasons that there were two huts and that people spent two days, not just one, was that people need time to adjust to the altitude. We ignored that and successfully made it to the second hut.

We were on our own without a guide. The path was clear, however; there never was a question about where to go. We didn't have porters either, or a cook. Porters would have run on ahead with the gear and would have had a hot meal waiting for us when we struggled into the camp carrying our cameras. That was the usual scene. For us, we carried our own stuff in backpacks. Ours were primitive. And it was the first time I ever carried a backpack.

After our first night on the mountain at that approximately 11,000-foot mark, we were in pretty good spirits when we set off for Kibo Hut, the last of the huts nestled at the base of the snowline. We made a mistake, however. Without a guide, or anyone else experienced with the mountain, we didn't know if there would be wood for a fire at Kibo Hut. Since there was plenty around at the second hut, we loaded up our backpacks with wood to be sure we would have it that night.

The second day went well too, considering. But for the burden of the extra weight from the wood, we might not have been so exhausted when we arrived. It is a truly glorious walk. We walked on the winding path upwards toward the base of the lower peak of the twin peaked mountain in the brilliant, clear increasingly rare air.

Then we turned down across the long saddle between the two peaks. The views were spectacular. The walking got tough as we began the rise back up the side of the higher peak. The views never wavered in their magnificence. We had made pretty good time too, considering it was the first time any of us had walked on a mountain. John's friend was the only one who was beginning to feel altitude sickness.

As we bedded down early for the night, three of us had had enough. John was the only one who still cared about going to the top. It didn't seem like we had slept very long, but my watch said two a.m. when John said, "Does anyone want to go up the mountain?"

His question was met with silence though the next day's conversation confirmed that all of us were awake. John cursed as he rolled over, but still no one else spoke. I couldn't go back to sleep. About fifteen minutes later, I got up and said, "Let's go." John, his friend, and I set off for the peak in the moonlit night. Getting out on top of the world in that moonlit night should have been enough of a reward to get going.

Now thirty-five years later, I find myself thinking that walking up the stairs is tough: I should remember walking that day. Without a backpack, it was still tough. It was fifteen or twenty steps, then stop and rest; later it would be ten steps, then stop and rest. I learned later that we suffered from not having the experience of a guide who would have slowed us down. I was following John, who set a pace way faster than the ordinary. John's friend only lasted about twenty minutes, felt the altitude sickness, and went back. I lasted about two hours before giving up, going back to the hut, and back to bed. John went on alone, reached the top, and rejoined us at the hut about ten a.m. He looked terrible, exhausted, except for the glow he now carried.

We let John rest awhile before we headed down. We passed the hut where we had spent our first night, and made it back to the first hut to spend the night. The final leg we easily accomplished in the morning, and telephoned Sally to pick us up at one of the hotels. We had been barely seventy-two hours on the mountain. The next time I thought I would take the full five days, walk, and carry only my camera. I probably would enjoy the walk more. □

Christmas on Kilimanjaro

Joan (Hoffman) Schieber

One of the incredible benefits of teaching with a group of people in East Africa was that we were able to travel on school holidays, visiting other teachers and exploring other parts of East Africa. During the end of year holidays in 1962, a friend and I visited another teacher who lived on the slopes of Kilimanjaro.

The mountain was held in high esteem and was kind of a magical place—a snow-capped, glacially covered mountain on the Equator rising up out of the flat plains. On Christmas Eve night I attempted to attend midnight mass at a village church on the mountain. I was given careful directions about how to find the church. But the night was dark and the way was unknown to me and I missed a turn or made a wrong turn somewhere. I drove on and on until it was clear I was lost, near midnight, alone, on the slopes of Kilimanjaro!

Even though I was bit frightened, looking out at the sky filled me with amazement. It was a clear night and millions of stars filled the heavens. I could only think of that first Christmas night—the night I was on my way to celebrate—a night also filled with amazing stars.

I managed to retrace my path back to my friend's house without incident and tried the journey again early the next morning in early daylight. That time I was successful. But every Christmas since then, especially when I attend mass at midnight, I remember that Christmas night on Kilimanjaro and the glorious sky full of stars. □

I Learned as Much as I Taught
Ed Schmidt

TEA let me continue to morph from a math education student into a physics teacher. I organized the lab to enable the students to proceed pretty much on their own which they were delighted to do. That experience probably helped get me into grad school. Later I learned I'd been part of an experiment by the Berkeley physics department in which they ignored their usual requirements. Together, we failed.

But TEA taught me resilience, so in June 1966 I followed my Swedish girlfriend to her home country after my draft board decided I was too old to be drafted for Vietnam and allowed me to leave the US. The relationship soon fell apart, but I had found a job working on an archeological dig near Stockholm. The Swedish government had a law at the time that if you wanted to develop land which contained a Viking site, you had to pay the government to come in and excavate the site before construction.

TEA had also emboldened me about travel, so when the ground froze and the job shut down in December, I headed south—mostly hitchhiking, but partly by public transport—through Denmark, Germany (including

West Berlin, surrounded by East Germany), Austria, Switzerland, Italy, Greece, Turkey, Syria, Lebanon, Jordan, and finally Israel.

In Israel at that time, tourists, including gentiles, could work as laborers on a kibbutz. I did agricultural work like picking bananas, oranges, avocados, and so on, for a couple months, departing in late April and missing the Six-Day War by several weeks.

Then it was on to Greece by air, followed by Yugoslavia and Austria. As I recall, I hitched straight through from Salzburg to Copenhagen in twenty-four hours. From there, I used most of my dwindling resources on a passenger ship to Iceland where I got a job, first packing up an Eastern bloc trade exhibit, then on construction, and earned enough money to get back to the States. ☐

To Kilimanjaro and Back

Jane Stockton

We had arrived in Machakos in August, 2004. Ron and Iris Berger, the other American couple on the compound, were our mentors. They showed us how to live and shop and travel in East Africa. So when Ron B. suggested a Kilimanjaro climb for the Christmas break, we said, "Sure, why not?"

Neither Stockton was particularly athletic. I had fumbled my way through a series of physical education classes in high school and college. Ron S. had taken "adapted phys. ed." his whole life after rheumatic fever left him with a heart murmur. Ron B. started us on a conditioning program, run a hundred/walk a hundred, and Iris took me to have a pair of sturdy walking shoes made.

The hotel's introduction to the climb was deceptively luxurious. Spacious grounds, good view of the mountain, orientation to the climb, equipment rental, and off we went, four of us with eleven porters and guides. The views were spectacular. The sight of the moorland as we emerged from the rain forest was magical. The food was good, as was the company. We were led by the legendary Fernandez. Even the ten-mile walk to top hut across the saddle and up 3,000 feet was bearable.

At 1:00 a.m. the following morning, we were awakened for the climb up Kibo. Iris would not attempt it. The 16,000-foot altitude at top hut had already gotten to her: and she was the athlete and dancer in the group. Taking two steps forward and sliding one step back in the scree, we struggled up the peak. As we got higher, it was also "take ten steps and then fall asleep standing up."

Somehow we kept going; we reached the crater's rim and looked down and realized we'd made it to the top of the world's highest freestanding mountain.

What do you do after that? We started down, digging our heels into the scree to keep from pitching forward. I was desperately afraid of falling onto that gravel and landing on my sunburned nose.

We've learned a lot about hiking since 1964. We use sunscreen; we always have a giant supply of bandaids for covering (or preventing) blisters. And we'd never wear a newly-made pair of shoes, especially for a final-day twenty-three-mile walk down a mountain. Somehow, we made it down, bleeding feet, aching knees, and all.

The memories were worth every ache and pain. So was the feeling of accomplishment. Ron's beard, begun on the day we started the climb, is now forty-seven years old. □

Hitchhiking the Congo

William Stoever

I took an overnight steamer up Lake Tanganyika to the town of Uvira, on the eastern edge of the Congo Kinshasa, now the Democratic Republic of Congo. The map showed a road heading north towards Bukavu and then veering northwestward toward Stanleyville, a dotted line indicating a dirt road passable only during the dry season. It appeared to pass through a vast undeveloped sparsely-populated jungle area.

This was the road I set out to hitch on. I lugged my suitcase to the edge of Uvira and stood there...and stood there...and stood there, seeing nary a vehicle passing.

Finally, after a couple hours, a truck came along and stopped. It was a beat-up dusty old thing that had doubtless plied the jungle roads for many years, a Dodge with running boards and rounded fenders, two worn tires on each rear wheel, faded from whatever original color to a nondescript gray, with a cab in front and a freight pen in the rear. Three men were crowded into the cab, rapidly dashing any hopes I might have had for a comfortable seat. One of the men gestured to the rear pen, where twenty or thirty people were standing, mostly men but interspersed with a few women and children.

I handed my suitcase up to some fellow and clambered up into the rear. The other standees shifted around a bit to make room for me, but we were still wedged in almost shoulder-to-shoulder. I was the only white person on the whole vehicle, but my fellow passengers didn't register any surprise at seeing me.

We started down the road, and red dust billowed out behind us. The road was rutted and bumpy, and the truck's shock absorbers were long since broken, so the freight pen's steel floor communicated every bump and pothole straight up my legs. Fortunately, I managed to get a position standing beside the metal fence enclosing the pen, so I could at least hold onto something as we rattled along; pity the poor standees in the middle of the pen who tried to stabilize themselves against the bumps and lurches without any support. The muffler was obviously rusted out, and the roar of the engine added to our discomfort.

We passed almost no vehicles and very few pedestrians and only a very occasional thatched-roof hut alongside the road. Jungle trees and vines and undergrowth crowded around us, right up to the edge of the road, creating the impression of lurching down a narrow winding corridor. The sun beat down through the opening overhead, making me and

I'm sure all the others hot, sweaty, and miserable. I was probably the only one to get sunburned, though.

After an hour, my legs began to ache. I tried shifting my weight back and forth between my right and left legs, but that brought hardly any relief. It got worse and worse as the hours wore on. No room to sit, even if I'd wanted to sit on the hard metal floor. There was nothing I could do about it...unless I wanted to get out and stand by the road surrounded by jungle; I could envision myself standing through the night, plagued by malaria-carrying mosquitoes, fighting off jungle predators and getting miserably hungry and tired.

The dust gradually penetrated into my nose and lungs, making me feel like I was dying of thirst. Nagging feelings of hunger began to gnaw at my stomach. My fellow passengers seemed hospitable enough, but we could hardly communicate, and I'm sure they were as uncomfortable as I was, and nobody felt like talking. A child vomited on floor. Her mother tried to comfort her but couldn't really do anything to alleviate her misery.

Once we stopped in front of a tiny thatched-roof mud shack, a 'shop' in a small clearing. The women immediately headed to one side of the clearing and squatted down to urinate, while the men headed to the other side and peed into the jungle. I did too, of course.

The "shop" sold bottles of orange pop and packages of cookies and almost nothing else. I had become uncomfortably thirsty and hungry, and figured I'd better take advantage of whatever nourishment the situation offered. I drank three bottles of orange soda, at room temperature of course; I figured—I hoped—it was safe to drink. It was sickeningly sweet and hardly quenched any thirst and made me feel bloated, but at least I figured it would help keep my body hydrated. And the cookies: dry sugary flavorless things, repulsively bland, zero nutritional value, a highly unsatisfactory "meal." But if you're desperate enough, at least it was cheap.

One of the privileged riders from the cab approached me while we were stopped by the clearing and spoke in English: "The fare is two dollars."

I didn't see any other riders making any such payments; maybe that was a 'special fare, just for me.' I suspect the driver spotted me as a way to make some quick cash. Well, he had me over a barrel: if I refused to pay it, they might have abandoned me in the clearing until another vehicle came along, which might have meant waiting for who knows how long, judging from the almost total lack of traffic on the road. I reluctantly handed over the money.

Eventually, after five or six hours, we reached some small market town at a junction with another red-dirt road. The driver said something in a local language, and all the other passengers scrambled down, and so I got off too. My body ached, my back hurt, my legs were excruciating, my muscles were stabbing with pain, my eyes and nose hurt from the dryness, my skin and hair and clothes were caked with red dust, and I was agonizingly thirsty and hungry. All-in-all, it was one of the most miserably uncomfortable rides I've ever had.

I had no map and no idea where I was in the jungle vastness, except presumably somewhere on the road to Stanleyville. Fortunately, I found an old woman cooking some kind of pancakes-with-a-bit-of-chicken on a charcoal stove under a tree. There were flies buzzing around, but the woman kept brushing them away from the dough. I watched as she poured some batter out of a metal bowl and spread it on the surface of a flattened piece of metal that served as a griddle. She pried a few scraps of meat off the carcass of a chicken with her fingernails and flicked them into the batter, making five pancakes. I hoped her fingers were clean and the batter wasn't rancid and the chicken wasn't contaminated.

After a couple minutes, she flipped the pancakes, and soon after that put them on a piece of brown paper and handed them to me: fifteen cents. Well, at least they'd been cooked, so I had hopes they'd be safe to eat. You take risks when you're desperate. Actually, surprisingly, they were rather tasty.

> For more of this and other adventures, see *Hitchhike the World* by William A. Stoever. https://amzn.com/B00AZNWZYQ. ◻

Kilimanjaro Catharsis

William Stoever

"You want to climb all the whole way up Kilimanjaro?" the hotel proprietress exclaimed. "And with your own pack!"

"Well, yes, I guess so," Julia Davis replied. She was having her doubts, now that she was actually in sight of the mountain. She was in the lobby of the Marangu Hotel, which stands on the slopes of Kilimanjaro in northern Tanzania, East Africa. She looked questioningly at her fiancé. His smile radiated confidence and pride. "Reuben says he'll help me do it."

"But, madam, Kilimanjaro is the highest mountain in Africa. Most climbers become ill before they reach half-way to the top," the proprietress protested.

"Yes, I understand that," Julia replied. "But Reuben has wanted to climb Mt. Kilimanjaro ever since he was young. And I can go with him. I really can. I'll try very hard." She was only twenty-one, just out of college, and Reuben was her source of strength, just as he had been for the past four years.

"The gentleman is like a mountain himself, so big and strong. But you, madam, are petite." The proprietress looked doubtfully at Julia's five-feet-four-inches and one hundred twenty pounds. "Perhaps you can succeed if you hire some porters."

"Aw, now, ma'am, we don't have the need of any porters on this hike," Reuben protested. "Me and the other men will carry most of the load. We'll only give Julie a small pack."

"It's the altitude that makes the climb so difficult. Kilimanjaro is over 19,000 feet. The porters are accustomed to the thin air. But the lady …?" The proprietress shook her head.

"I don't know, Reuben," Julia said doubtfully.

"Aw, honey, now don't you worry. We'll make that old mountain look like an Iowa ant-hill," Reuben declared. He was twenty-seven, six-feet-four, and two hundred twenty-five pounds.

"For you, sir, I have less doubt," the proprietress replied. "But the lady is too pretty. She is not a pack-burro."

Julia knew she wasn't as pretty as she might be, in her Bermuda shorts and short brown hair. People had told her that she would be a knock-out with longer, blonder hair and a sheath dress. But near Reuben, she felt more at ease in her present style. It suited the times like this when he treated her more like a younger sister than a fiancée. She said, "Thank you, Ma'am, but I think I can make it. I'll try very hard."

"That's my Julie. She's got what it takes," Reuben beamed. It was times like this that he was proudest of her.

"Madam, I cannot forbid you. I can only warn you." The proprietress shrugged her shoulders.

For more of this story, see http://bit.ly/stoever. ☐

Murchison Hippos

William Stoever

Doug Smith and I hitched to Murchison Falls National Park, Nile River, Uganda, one weekend. Somebody at the lodge told us there was a youth hostel nearby, so after supper we started walking down the gravel road.

It happened to be a dark, moonless night, and we could barely see the road ahead of us. We heard grunting and snuffling sounds all around us, but it was too dark to see who was making them. We'd gone a few yards down the road when a Land Rover came along. We stuck out our thumbs, and the driver stopped for us. When he turned on the headlights, we saw a mother hippo and her baby crossing the road not thirty feet ahead.

Thank heaven we hadn't walked close enough to alarm her! Mama hippos are ferocious in defending their calves. Despite their size and blimp-like appearance, hippos can run twice as fast as most humans, and their jaws are strong enough to bite a ten-foot crocodile in two. If we'd walked much closer, this one might have attacked us and severely injured us. Fortunately she ignored the Land Rover.

The driver dropped us at the 'youth hostel,' which turned out to be a dilapidated oval-shaped adobe structure with a tin roof held up by mud-brick pillars. It was open-air, with large 'windows' all around, except they had no glass; we were sheltered from rain but not from wind. It was on a mud platform about three feet higher than the surrounding swampy ground, with a couple dozen decrepit metal cots but absolutely no other facilities. Well, it would do for our needs. We each selected one of the less-dilapidated cots and spread out our sleeping bags.

Sometime in the middle of the night I awoke and had to urinate. No problem: I could simply step outside the structure and pee off the raised platform. By that time the moon had risen, and I could hear lots of grunting and shnuffling, and see lots of huge dark shapes moving around: mama hippos and their babies! They came up from the river to feed on land at night. They ignored me as long as I stayed on the platform, but I suspected they might have attacked if I'd ventured to walk among them. We were marooned on an island in a sea of hippos!

In the morning they were all gone, leaving no trace except for eight-inch piles of smelly dung. □

Screams in the Night

Julie Richardson Sulman

We were at Bungoma Secondary School in western Kenya. Over our half-term break, Ron and I, Jill and Roger Jones from Wales, Brit Les Hooper, Peace Corps volunteer Bill, and thirteen Form 4 students went up Mt. Elgon. Ron, Jill, I, and two students rode to the hut eighteen miles up in a trailer pulled by a tractor. We picked up the rest of the group about two-thirds of the way up. What a ride! We were lucky we didn't have internal injuries.

That afternoon, some Elgon Maasai youth came down to our campfire to talk. One of them mentioned that hyenas had been seen in the area. They also said that hyenas had a tendency to grab vulnerable animals by their heads and that their breath was foul from eating dead or injured animals.

That evening, Lodrick, one of the students with a rather vivid imagination, insisted that we barricade the door to the hut from the inside to keep out hyenas. Another student, Edward, was feeling sick from the 14,000-foot altitude. Thus, the stage was set, and everyone unconsciously had hyenas on the brain.

We slept on the floor in two rows: one the students and across, the adults. About 1:30 a.m., we were awakened by the most bloodcurdling, horrified screams I've ever heard and a frenzied scrambling about. Suddenly something flung itself over my face and I yelled. Bedlam prevailed for several seconds until all the flashlights were turned on, and we could see that nothing was amiss.

This is what had happened. Jill was awake and heard all of this:

Edward woke up sick and leaned over Lodrick, making retching, animal-like noises and breathed into his face. Lodrick reached up, felt Edward's head, thought it was a hyena, and screamed. God, what screams!

Edward then thought that a hyena was trying to drag Lodrick out of the hut and grabbed his feet. Lodrick, of course, thought that he was being attacked at his feet and drummed his heels on the floor. More screams.

At this point, Ron flung himself over my face to protect me from the hyena and—the original screams coming from the other end of the hut—I screamed, thinking "God, that hyena moves fast."

This unnerved Jill, next to me, who had until that time thought it was just someone dreaming.

Roger laid back and played dead, hoping that whatever it was would leave him alone.

Needless to say no one got much more sleep that night. □

Adventures along the Nairobi Road

Mary Ryan Taras

Sometime in 1964, I received a message from Fred Malkemes (3A), "Come quickly, I have the *Casta Diva* sung by both Callas and Sutherland!"

So I set off from Kakamega to Nyeri, Kenya where we could sit at the foothills of Mt. Kenya and enjoy the gorgeous music that Fred had borrowed from the various embassies in Nairobi. At the end of the weekend, I left a bit later than I had planned for the seven-hour trip back. We had all been warned about driving after dark, but I had enough time to get home if I did not dawdle, and I had beautiful music playing in my head.

Just east of Kisumu, I saw three sheep, standing in the road with their heads underneath one another, too late and I hit them. Three Asian men driving by stopped and pulled my bumper out so I could drive, and then jumped back into their car, yelling, "Drive away now!" and sped off. Immediately my car was surrounded by a small but angry crowd pounding on my car and trying to grab my car keys.

The only fluent Swahili I ever spoke was at that moment. I kept hold of my car keys and closed my windows. At that moment, a man approached, saying that he was a policeman, and that that I should follow him to the police station. This was the conversation:

> Me: Can you guarantee my safety if I come with you?
>
> He: No, Madam. These people surely wish to beat you to death.
>
> Me: Then I will drive to the police station in Kisumu and report the accident.
>
> He: Very well, Madam. I will send them a message. Please drive on.
>
> Me: But there are all these people surrounding my car. I don't want to hit them.
>
> He: Begin to drive, Madam. They will get out of your way.

So I continued on to Kisumu, stopping to pick up Mary Hines to join me at the police station. There, the officer informed me that there were no charges, and I was free to go. I wanted to pay for the sheep, but they refused, saying the sheep owner was responsible. By now it was very dark, and I drove the remaining way very slowly so as to avoid hitting a parked lorry on the way.

First class next morning, I was writing on the board and a student came up behind me. I was startled and jumped back. The girls said, "Wa Miss! What is wrong?"

So I told them my story. Their response was, "Wa Miss! What do you expect? They are Luo. They are not even circumcised!"

And we continued on with the lesson, and the *Casta Diva* has always had a special place in my heart.

> Note: The soprano prayer *Casta Diva* in Act I of *Norma* is justly famous. See http://bit.ly/Norma-1. ☐

Road Trip

Beverly Templin

I was in my Fiat 500 driving from Nairobi to Mombasa about 9:00 p.m. in the summer moonlight. I was traveling at an ordinary speed with car lights on. It was a warm eighty-degree evening.

I was just passing through when suddenly two herds of animals appeared. There were about twenty huge gray elephants on one side of the road. A herd of about twenty beautiful giraffes stood in the moonlight on the other side. Their bodies reached about eight feet with necks reaching at least fifteen feet. The spots were variegated in the moonlight. The new babies were moving with the herd. All were minding their own business without making a noise. Both herds had various-sized animals, large, small, young, and elderly.

I didn't feel alone. I felt like they were my "close" friends. In the moonlight, they looked smaller in the distance. I felt safe after passing the herd, even though my Fiat 500 was small in the crowd and had almost stalled in the loose sand.

The animals were in the Tsavo Game Park, which is a designated game refuge. Grass is available and plentiful. The park is a vast area covering many miles of grassy savannah for the animals to roam freely. During the monsoons, rains come at mid-day, followed by sunshine the rest of the day. Visitors come to the park on safaris, carrying cameras, riding in zebra-striped vans, their cameras focused on any and all animals in the park. It would have been my greatest delight to share this special moment with others, and observe these "wild" animals in their natural habitats.

This was a casual evening in the moonlight for the lovely elephants, giraffes, and me, and I shall always remember "being close" to these majestic creatures. ☐

The First Flight to East Africa
Brenda Tillberg

As I remember it a half-century later, the Adventure began the way so many Adventures start, with everyone standing around waiting. Someone was being interviewed; photographs were taken; I was getting tired of waiting. Finally the formalities were finished, and we were allowed to clamber up the steps and board the plane that would take the first group of TEA teachers to Africa.

As often happens in Adventures, I was disappointed with the transportation. I had been picturing the planes in National Geographic ads, but what we actually got was a long tube of a rented plane with seats so closely packed that my knees were in someone's back, and their seat pinned me down if they reclined. Still, the report was that the pilots were experienced and competent, and the stewardesses were very nice, even if this really was their first fight beyond Cincinnati.

We all fit onto the plane, about one hundred each of Group A and Group B, plus assorted organizers and administrators and a whole lot of luggage. We headed out over the Atlantic Ocean, to refueling stops at the Azores and Nigeria, then on to Uganda.

It seemed to me then that the plane was not really designed for the task that it had been given. The TV dinners, followed by TV breakfasts and TV lunches, heated a few at a time in the tiny kitchen area took hours to distribute. The glowing yellow Sahara desert overwhelmed the air-conditioning system. We were informed that the drinking water was running low as the Sahara passed beneath us. When a group gathered to sing, "All day I faced the burning waste without a taste of water," they were told they must sit down, because they were making the plane unbalanced.

Night brought welcome coolness as we headed toward Kano, Nigeria. There was a slight bump as we landed there, but nothing noteworthy. However, we were told that a tire had burst, and that we should leave the plane.

As we headed along the path to the passenger terminal, I realized that the Adventure had improved. We passed multicolored lizards under the lights in the warm darkness. We were led to chairs where we could stretch out and nap. As the day progressed, a true English breakfast was served. For the first time, I had baked beans and fried tomatoes along with the scrambled eggs and toast. And we had a tour of Kano town, dry and brown, with square mud houses and children playing in the streets.

As the day progressed, Portugal provided a tire and we took off into the evening darkness. We were served another breakfast, the only meal still on the plane, and landed at the tiny airport at Entebbe Uganda at about 3:00 a.m. The airport staff was overjoyed to see us as now they could finish up and go home to sleep. I was impressed by the green grass and multitudes of plants. I hadn't really believed that the whole of Africa was Kano brown, but I really had had no actual proof.

As we were taken to Makerere by bus, I could see outlines of banana plants along the roadside. I had never seen a banana plant before, but somehow I knew that was what they had to be. At Mary Stuart Hall, a.k.a. The Box, the women were led along the open corridors to their rooms.

I was exhausted. I spread my blanket on the mattress and lay on top of it, planning to sleep at least until lunch. Little did I know that my own African Adventure included a family of casqued hornbills that would greet the African predawn from the tree next to my window, and that I would be wide awake in plenty of time for breakfast. ☐

Mount Meru

Joel Watne

Arusha is on the south side of Mt. Meru, at about 5,000 feet above sea level. The mountain reaches 14,968 feet above sea level, rising from a surrounding plain at about 3,000 feet. A dormant volcano, it probably was much taller before an explosive eruption thousands of years ago blew out the northeast part of it, leaving a crater that is open towards Kilimanjaro, about thirty miles away, and about a mile taller.

I led a group of my students to the top of Mt. Meru which took about a day. We rode in a truck to the end of a road up the western side of the mountain, and hiked up to a hut at the tree line, about 12,000 feet. We got a few hours rest there before starting for the top at 3:00 a.m. Each of us packed his own lunch. One of my Sikh students amazed us all with the super-hot green peppers he ate like popcorn. His eyes watered; his nose dripped—and he kept on popping them into his mouth. All the other students were also Asian and used to far spicier food than Americans, but they watched him in open-mouthed astonishment.

Before dawn, we started the hike to the top. No technical rock climbing was involved. The surface was loose scree that made the task similar to climbing a gravel pile. We would take three steps forward and pause to catch our breath, sliding backwards about two steps. It took until noon to make that last 3,000 feet.

Once at the top, we sat on a rock protruding over the crater, dangling our feet over the edge, and looking down at the ash cone in the crater several thousand feet below. Ahead of us, across the intervening plain, stood Kilimanjaro, the tallest free standing mountain in the world, and a truly magnificent sight.

After about a half hour of enjoying the view, I noticed that thunder clouds were forming nearby and thought that an exposed mountain top did not seem to be a particularly enticing place to be during a thunderstorm. The descent along the same route we came up was very quick. We would take two steps, then plant our feet and slide down about twenty feet or so, and repeat the process. It took only twenty minutes to get back down to the tree line. However, the sharp scree shredded the sides out of the sneakers I was wearing, but they were the only casualty of the trip.

On a subsequent day I decided to drive all around Mt. Meru on my Vespa. I started northwest on the paved highway to Nairobi, then turned east on the gravel road north of the mountain which connected with the paved highway from Arusha to Moshi. About two-thirds of the way along that road, I came upon a herd of giraffes standing on and next to the road. I knew that if I came up behind a giraffe and startled it, those powerful hind legs could probably kick me halfway to Nairobi.

But dusk was approaching. I knew that it would take a lot longer to turn around to get back to Arusha, and there was a possibility of becoming lion lunch going in that direction. And the giraffe is not an aggressive animal. The giraffes happened to be facing me, so I knew my presence was not going to be a surprise. So I decided to drive towards them slowly and hope for the best. As I approached, the giraffes stepped back, two on the right side of the road and two on the left, and watched as I drove under their heads, arched over me like swords at a military wedding. I felt that I was being honored.

The rest of the trip was uneventful, and I was soon back home in Arusha with a very pleasant memory of that close encounter. □

The Crazy Dutchman

Joel Watne

While in Arusha, I decided to ride my Vespa motor scooter to Dodoma to visit a colleague teaching there. The distance was about 250 miles, but I figured I could make it in a day. The first seventy miles or so was paved and an easy ride. Part of it included a climb up one side of the Rift Valley.

I came upon a herd of impala standing on the road, looking the other way. The wind was blowing toward me, so they did not hear me approaching until I got within a few yards. Once they became aware of their presence, their drummed their hooves on the pavement as if unable to move forward. Then they started running, and soon I was riding about fifteen feet behind them, beeping my horn, and watching them take periodic leaps over imaginary objects, until they came to a spot where the slope to the right made it easier for them to escape up the valley wall. I kept going, and the pavement ended. There followed miles of good gravel road, followed by miles of so-so gravel road, until I got to miles of loose sand with furrowed tracks made by passing trucks and buses.

About half way to Dodoma, I came upon another motor scooter, a large blue German Messerschmidt scooter driven by a Dutchman. It turned out he was riding from Holland through the length of Africa, headed for Cape Town to catch a ship headed for Australia. He was taking two days to make the run from Arusha to Dodoma, and thought I was plumb nuts trying to do so in one day. I thought he was plumb nuts driving from Holland to Cape Town on a scooter.

Whether I was wrong or not is unclear, but he probably was correct: by the time I reached Dodoma, I was very saddle sore. After spending the weekend with my colleagues, I felt that my posterior had sufficiently recuperated to make the run back to Arusha. Within an hour, my posterior made it clear that I had not fully recuperated, and the rest of the trip was uneventful but a very painful reminder that the crazy Dutchman might not have been so crazy after all. □

East African Railways Curry
Joel Watne

While at Makerere College in late 1961, I ate at a table with a number of Goans, including some from Arusha, Tanganyika, where I was being posted to the Arusha Indian School. Once a week, the meal included curry, with which I was entirely unfamiliar. I liked it and assumed that I now knew what curry was.

Then came the train ride from Kampala to Nairobi and Moshi. The Sikh waiter brought me the menu, and I confidently selected a curry dinner. He soon presented me with the meal, and I took one bite. It was instantly obvious that this fiery stuff was not at all similar to the Makerere cuisine. I started gulping all the cold water within reach to put out the flames, and the waiter did a pretty good job of suppressing his laughter. □

Death Is Just an Option
Jim Weikart

"I stay in Angola, above the ground or under it." The Benguela Railway station master, a Portuguese, described his determination. With the words his right hand moved showing what "above" and "below" meant. He smiled, a pleasant and disarming showing of teeth.

Jack and I sat across the desk from him, taking in his stoicism. It was June of 1965 and we were on vacation from teaching in Bukoba, Tanzania, and this town, Lobito, was in the orbit of the MPLA (People's Movement for the Liberation of Angola), one of the three liberation fronts. An uneasy truce existed between them before the proposed November election. My support for the Mozambique Liberation Front in New York led to an invitation to Lorenzo Marques for the independence celebration.

To get there, I decided on a transcontinental odyssey by train from Lobito on the Atlantic coast of Angola to Lorenzo Marques on the Indian

Ocean for the June 25th independence day. Jack Tuttlebee, a friend, spoke fluent Brazilian Portuguese, so I convinced him to travel with me.

In Tanzania whites still had a residual if unearned respect from the years of colonial indoctrination, respect I'd always used to travel advantage. In Angola I could sense the times were changing. But, in Angola, this was still the honeymoon period after the Captains' Coup in Portugal had overthrown the Salazar dictatorship and granted the colonies an immediate road to independence. And, supposedly, the three liberation movements would kiss and make-up and abide by the proposed procedure leading to the November Angolan independence day.

Jack and I had the day in Lobito before our train left the next morning for Zaire (also known as the Congo). And the "above the ground or below it" station master offered us a ride on a survey engine for the morning if we wanted. We did. And spent most of the day on the rails near Lobito. After the fact, I wonder if the station master didn't think that two Americans in their mid-thirties headed out across Angola when most everyone else white was trying to get to the coast were probably American agents and he wanted to cooperate.

My room at the Hotel Terminus looked out the back. In the morning I got another reminder we were in a country near chaos. A ragged Portuguese man was wandering, looking into garbage, talking crazily to himself. Sure, I could have been anywhere in the world, but I saw him as representing a transitional Angola. A man with no way out—here, "above the ground or below…"

We boarded the first-class wagons of the train, assigned to a cabin still glowing with polished cherry wood panels and sparkling brass fixtures adorned with crystal lighting, everything made larger by mirrors. I volunteered to take the upper bunk. Jack, overweight by fifty pounds, didn't resist. We settled in and after some wait the train began to move on its 750-mile two-day journey. Our cabin opened onto a corridor, where we could stand and watch the countryside go by if we didn't wish to stay in the cabin. We shared first class with a unit of the Portuguese Army of eight men. Under the truce, a similar unit of FNLA (National

Front for the Liberation of Angola), UNITA (National Union for the Total Independence of Angola), and MPLA were also assigned to the train.

The train stopped frequently at small towns as it proceeded up into central Angola. Jack and I went to sleep on the early side and awoke with daybreak. When we got to the dining car, four Portuguese soldiers sat at one table. The dining car, like the cabins, was polished cherry, sparkling brass, crystal, and mirrors. I didn't see any other passengers and I thought again that the trains going out of Angola were packed with both Portuguese settlers and native Angolans fleeing the war zone during the truce.

Jack and I had no assurance we would find a train on the Zaire side once we reached Luau. We might be two of those fleeing a war zone. The train passed through small town after small town. At each stop women would gather along the train selling things to eat to the Angola passengers going up-country in second and third class. At noon, after the Portuguese soldiers and Jack and I finished lunch there was a skirmish alongside the dining car when the steward tossed out empty bottles and a group of pre-teen boys fought over them. My junk was another peoples' gold.

Around 5:00 p.m. of that second day, the train pulled into a large station at Huambo. Word came down that it was a lengthy stop and we were free to leave the train. Jack and I wandered across the tracks and found a restaurant on the other side of the road. We sat and ordered food, comfortably placed at an outside table looking across at the train. There were fresh strawberries for desert, but I misunderstood the Portuguese and thought they were canned. I had to endure watching Jack eat his strawberries. At the end, he was sitting with a plate of leftovers.

"I'm giving this to the beggar by my chair," he said.

The beggar wasn't visible to me from the other side of the table, and I was outraged when Jack dumped his plate onto the ground beside him. Jack laughed at my discomfort—which evaporated when I saw the "beggar" was a small dog. We ordered coffee, but as the waiter set it on the table, we heard the long whistle of the engine.

"You think that's telling us to get back?" I said.

Right then there was a clanking of railroad carriages as their couplings were yanked by a moving engine. The train began to move!

I jumped up as did Jack. I threw money on the table and ran toward the train. It was slow but picking up speed. Jack, still overweight, couldn't keep up with me. So I ran on and caught the train in the second-class section, swinging, grabbed by helping, laughing Angolans. I turned around, but could not spot Jack. The train continued to pick up speed.

Solutions for recovering Jack ran though my head. I'd have the train stop at the next crossroad and wait for Jack to arrive by taxi... But that was my only plan. The next train was three days away. But Jack had made it. He swung aboard way back in third class along the last carriages of the train. A friendly Angolan had seen him and let me know before I even reached the first-class cabins. One crisis averted.

We were now traveling through UNITA territory, having started in MPLA land. The commander of the eight-man FNLA, whose territory was not along the train route, was friendly and took a great liking to my camera. I felt in other circumstances he might very well have requisitioned it. Jack and I must have been very foolish, but the presence of the armed units of potential and soon-to-be-real enemies on the train didn't bother us.

Then a surprising thing happened when we arrived at the border town, Luau, across from Zaire: suddenly there was a loud UNITA demonstration to welcome the train. Perhaps one hundred men, women, and children, singing and dancing, waving UNITA banners clustered along the train as it came to a stop. A contingent of twenty to thirty UNITA soldiers in uniform, including a local leader, appeared like magic off of the train. The MPLA and FNLA units were nowhere in sight.

Luckily, Jack, with his Portuguese, got to talking to one of the UNITA soldiers. He asked how we could connect to the train in Dilolo across in Zaire. The man invited us to follow him and we joined the dancing, singing uniformed group walking away from the train to the UNITA headquarters nearby.

Once there, while we waited for information, the soldier showed us bullet pockmarks in the walls of the headquarters from the pre-truce fighting. Not reassuring. After about an hour—and another hour before tropical darkness would set in—somebody showed up and said he thought a train was leaving from Dilolo that evening, time unknown. In a historical sense, that made sense, since the Benguela Railway schedule had been set to hook up with the Congolese. Jack asked how we could get there. The UNITA leader told him UNITA would take us across.

We stood around making conversation, or rather Jack did since he was the Portuguese speaker, and Jack passed out his business card, New York University professor. Our UNITA host wistfully wished that he could one day attend New York University. At last, after dark, a Land Rover arrived. Jack and I sat in alongside the driver; several others including the leader got in back. It was very dark now, the sudden complete dark of the equator, as we drove toward Dilolo.

While we were still in Angola, the road suddenly had medium-size rocks like softballs tossed across one side of the road, and the driver was going straight into them. I flinched, suddenly having a vision of land mines. I knew then that this trip was ill-conceived. Thus far we had safely traversed Angola, a country on the verge of civil war, and now we were entering another country, Zaire, famed for chaotic anarchy, not the kind by choice but informed by the collapse of civilized conventions. The leader said something from the back seat to the driver, and he steered over the good side of the road. "Road work markers," Jack told me. Road work, not mines. Maybe things weren't so bad.

In Dilolo, the Land Rover came up on the train station. There was a train on the tracks. We got out of the Land Rover and, lucky for us, our UNITA host and his men came with us. The station was an example of the worst nightmare of anarchism. A few hundred people were milling about without lines or direction. I could see no opening to even get to the ticket window. And I had never had an answer to my letter to the Congolese Rail Line about space and reservations. This looked like the end of the trip for Jack and me. A woman cried out in grief in the crowd to our right.

"What happened?" I asked our host through Jack.

"Somebody has stolen all her things," the leader explained. He shrugged as if to say, "That's Zaire."

Me, I wondered how we could get back across Angola to Luanda and how could we get out of there.

> Note: Discerning readers will realize that liberties were taken with the date of this story, which occurred in 1975 not 1965, but it is otherwise accurate. ☐

IV: Surprise

Africa is famous for wildlife so it's no surprise that most of these surprise stories involve dangerous animals.

Camping in Uganda is Gene Child's account of encountering elephants in Murchison Falls that were agile enough to negotiate moving between closely pitched tents without disturbing the crisscrossed ropes that anchored them. What was the curious draw that called up that display of skill?

And why does Brooks Goddard's story of a school trip to Kenya's Aberdare National Park have the provocative title *The Head of a Leopard*, and what does that trip have to do with the establishment of the Wildlife Clubs of Kenya?

Yet not all surprises involved animals.

In this section:

Gene Child	*Camping in Uganda* • *325*
Elaine Durham	*Manone's Mercedes: Joe, Joshi, and the East African Safari Race* • *326*
Brooks Goddard	*A Prank Gone Wrong* • *327*
	The Head of a Leopard • *328*
Bob Gurney	*Things That Fly, Three Versions* • *329*
Moses L. Howard	*Place of the Lions* • *331*
	A TEEAer Becomes an African Farmer • *332*
Jack Humbles	*Wildlife but No Elephants* • *335*
Clive Mann	*The Snake in the Toilet* • *336*
Mary Jo McMillin	*Indian Friends, Indian Cooking, in Four Parts* • *338*
Miles Paul	*Bessie and the Cobra* • *343*
Jerry Schieber	*A Lunchtime Experience* • *344*
Joan (Hoffman) Schieber	*A Eureka Moment* • *345*
	The Mikado in Morogoro • *346*
Joel Watne	*Celebrity Contacts* • *347*

Camping in Uganda
Gene Child

In 1969 my family and I were participating in the USAID-sponsored TEEA project in Nairobi, Kenya. I was assigned at Kenyatta College, attempting to prepare Kenya-born students to teach physics in secondary schools. Prior to that time, most of the secondary school teaching positions had been staffed by British expatriates. During the Christmas break, we attended a TEEA workshop in Kampala, Uganda.

After the workshop, we decided to tour some of the game parks in Uganda with our friends, the Bierstekers and the Cutlers. We drove north out of Kampala toward Murchison Falls in the north of Uganda. The first night, we camped in a campground along the banks of the Victoria Nile River. Our rather large two-room tent was pitched next to that of our friends, Alex and Ruth Cutler. The tents were spaced only about five feet apart with the tent ropes crisscrossed.

That evening, we popped some popcorn on the open fire in our newly purchased wire basket popper. I burned the first batch because the flames were too high so discarded it next to the fire pit. The second popper-full was done to perfection. We finished off that popcorn quickly before we retired for the night with our son Dee and daughter Colene, who were eight and six years old at the time. As we were preparing for bed, we watched the hippopotamuses emerge from the river to browse on the lush vegetation.

In the middle of the night, my wife, Arlone, nudged me awake and asked, "Do you hear something strange?"

In my groggy state, I sat up to the sound "snuffle, grunt, snuffle!" I picked up the flashlight at my side, got out of my sleeping bag, and shined it out the front window of the tent. All I could see was an apparent wall of grey. An elephant had found the discarded popcorn and was snuffling it up as fast as he could. Arlone asked what we might do. I replied, "There is not much we can do. Relax and go back to sleep."

We cowered tensely in our bags for what seemed an eternity, but eventually the snuffling stopped and we were able to get some sleep.

In the morning, when we tentatively emerged from our tent, we found all the burnt popcorn was gone, but the most amazing thing was that there were elephant tracks in the soft earth between our neighbor's tent and ours. The elephant had stepped gently across the ropes and not disturbed a single one. The Cutlers were surprised to hear of our visitor during the night. They had slept through it all. □

Manone's Mercedes:
Joe, Joshi, and the East African Safari Race

Elaine Durham

In the spring of 1970 Carl Manone, head of TEEA, went back to the States on leave. Before boarding the plane at Entebbe he handed the keys of his beloved Mercedes to the most trustworthy and dependable person in the TEEA office, D. T. Joshi. After seeing Carl off, Joshi drove the car to Carl's house, parked it safely in the locked garage behind the locked gate, and came to work in his good old Cortina. Joe Durham, who once had a Mercedes back in the 1950s, began discussing Manone's car with his office mate, Joshi.

The first ever Uganda start of the East African Safari was only days away. The road rally was the talk of the city. Joshi knew everyone in Kampala, so of course he knew Shekhar Mehta, the Uganda driver participating in the race. Pre-race excitement spiraled in Kampala and in the TEEA office. Would Mehta have a chance? Would Joginder Singh win again? Would the winning car be a Peugeot or one of the newer Japanese cars? Believe it or not, a Mercedes had won three times in the past. At about this point it dawned on Joe and Joshi: they had Manone's car. He was in Pennsylvania. What if they could convince Carl that they had entered the East African Safari, driving his Mercedes?

Can you see that twinkle in Joshi's eyes? And the smoke drifting up from Joe's forgotten cigarette as they begin to plan?

Soon the whole TEEA office was involved in making "official" race car signs, symbols, and numbers. Joshi produced helmets and a pair of goggles. The Mercedes was strategically positioned in the Apollo Hotel carpark so the news vans would appear discreetly in the background of any photos. Signs were taped in place on the car. The two drivers, in helmets, short sleeve shirts and ties, posed with car #99. Photos were taken. (And race officials wanted to know just what the two men thought they were doing.)

Pictures were quickly printed by another of Joshi's friends. Back at the office, Joe wrote a press release, which was mimeographed for authenticity, about the late entry of the TEEA sponsored rally car. Photos and press release were bundled together, the envelope addressed to Carl's Pennsylvania home and airmailed off. A little over a week later, just after the start of the race, a frantic cable arrived:

What have you done with my car?

For an idea of what was causing Carl's panic, see the VOK video on the 1969 Safari Rally at http://bit.ly/69rally. Now imagine a very anxious Carl Manone getting off the plane to find Joshi waiting in Carl's spotless Mercedes and hear his hearty laughter once he realized he had been the victim of a slightly early April Fool's prank! □

A Prank Gone Wrong

Brooks Goddard

We were young and stupid, but one of our number on the teaching staff (which included several TEAers) of Kagumo School in Central Province, Kenya, had just completed his master's thesis and wanted to celebrate. There we were, sitting around and feeling rambunctious. Why not set off some fireworks—someone had roman candles, another had a few cherry bombs, and others had the odd firecracker. We thought the array of things would scare the students studying in the classrooms only a bit and gave consequences no further thought. Watches were synchronized and the fireworks went off.

We retreated to the house of one of the perpetrators for some beer and the telling of tales. Then the headmaster knocked on the door, and we expected doom to descend. In an unexpected gesture of magnanimity, however, the old goat told us that he realized what had been done but that we needed to go out immediately to the grounds to calm the students who thought that their world had come to an end. That *shiftas* had come down from the Northern Frontier District (NFD) to attack the school, that djinns had come out of the forest, and worst of all that many had flashed back to the Emergency when there were nighttime curfews and folks might be shot at without warning. Students had dived under desks, had jumped out of windows, had run away for the night. To say that we all felt foolish would be an understatement.

This experience was sobering, but has stood as an excellent example of unintended consequences for me ever since, and I have used it in various conversations over the years. ☐

The Head of a Leopard

Brooks Goddard

Having started a wild life club at Kagumo School in central Kenya, I asked the warden of Aberdare National Park to guide us around some game areas in the park. We would be in the school lorry, eager for any possible sightings. He agreed, but when we showed up on the appointed day, he said that he had to excuse himself to shoot a leopard which was raiding nearby *shambas*.

We went off with some rangers and had a lovely afternoon. Upon returning to the office to drop off the rangers, I spied the carcass of the leopard (pronounced, of course, *lay-o-pard*) and asked what was to become of the head. It was wrapped up in newspaper and given to me on the spot. Realizing that I was beyond squeamish and had no taxidermy skills, I approached Tony, the biology teacher, for assistance. Turns out Tony did have taxidermy experience, and, yes, he would be glad to clean the skull for me if I would let him have the eyes. Such a deal, and I readily accepted. I got the cleaned skull and a great story.

Tony's classes were studying eyes the following week. He decided that he would tell his students certain cautions about rubbing their eyes. With the leopard's eyes in a dish under the demonstration table, Tony starting rubbing his eyes vigorously, screamed and shouted, and held up a leopard's eye as his own. His students burst into their own screams ("pissed themselves," in the vernacular), only to be calmed when Tony revealed the truth.

I still have the skull sitting on my desk, and the Kagumo School Wild Life Club morphed into the Wildlife Clubs of Kenya, whose founding father was this young *mzungu* from Boston. (See wildlifeclubsofkenya.org.) ☐

Things That Fly, Three Versions

Bob Gurney

Mosquitoes. My room, on top of Nakasero Hill, far above the malarial area in the valley below, had a fine metal mesh covering the windows, but still the mosquitoes came in. The trick was to fling a pillow as hard as you could at the space in front of the spot where the insect was perched. Each night I killed between six and ten, leaving blood stains on the walls. After a year, the wall was turning red with my blood and with that of others whom I didn't know who lived down the hill.

—

Spiders. I had arrived late one night in Gulu, in the north of Uganda. I had misjudged the distance, I didn't get there till late. It was dark, I was shattered from the driving. I arrived at his house which was in the middle of nowhere. I was too exhausted to eat, too tired for a pint. My friend showed me to my room. When he opened the door, I felt it had not been used. The air was warm and stale. He pointed to my bed and wished me a goodnight's rest. I approached the bed, which looked well made up, only to be greeted by an astonishing sight.

As I sat on the edge to remove my shoes and socks, I found myself surrounded by an incredible performance. The room was the home of an extended family of large jumping spiders. Up and down they went, as if on strings, reaching four or five feet. It was like a ballet. From where I was sitting, on the edge of the bed, some seemed to rise even higher. I began to have the feeling that they were protesting at being disturbed. Or was it that they were just pleased to see someone from Kampala? I was too tired to bother about them, fell back on the bed and went out like a light.

—

> The **butterfly** counts not months but moments and has time enough. —RabindranathTagore

They want to cut more of the forest down in Uganda. I once rode my Vespa through a great cloud of butterflies in Mabira Forest. They were all yellow. A friend told me recently that he, too, had passed that way, a long time ago. He had driven through the same spot on his motorbike. He had sunscreen on his face. A huge number of butterflies stuck to his face. They made him look like a brave in war paint.

I asked him the other day, fifty years later, if he could remember the colors. They were, he said, all different: black, yellow, red, green, and white.

They say that the butterflies are in danger of disappearing on that road to Kenya. On a good day, a lepidopterist could once catch up to fifty in his bait traps. Now he would be lucky if he caught more than five. They want to cut the forest down in Uganda. They want to grow sugar cane in its place. Like the fruit bats on Kampala Road the butterflies are living on borrowed time. □

Place of the Lions
Moses L. Howard

Africa is an exotic and beautiful place and, because of its natural beauty, the traveler is often forgetful of the imminent and constant dangers.

I served in Uganda about nine of the ten years that I was in Africa, and I married and bought a *shamba* in Ankole, on which I helped to build a three-room mud house with cement floors. It was fortified with strong doors. My wife and two children lived there, close by a county chief's family. At night all kinds of creatures visited us. Lions roared, big cats ate our goats. Along with a farm worker, I once clubbed and captured a civet foraging in our chicken shack.

One day, with the sun blaring down on our yard, my four-year-old son Ngoma wandered outside into the yard carrying his lunch sandwich. A large hawk-like bird swooped quickly and furiously from the sky down, and before my eyes took the sandwich out of Ngoma's hands. I was frightened: the fast-moving, windy whisk and beating rush of the wings, the quick violent swoop must have injured the boy. But Ngoma stood before me, holding his undamaged arms up, hands out into the air, gazing in awe into the sky after the retreating bird. The encounter had not bruised or scratched the skin of his arms.

Over the hills, a short distance from our house in Ankole, long lines of villagers of all ages gathered at a borehole, pumping and filling their pots with water. I think we had all attached almost no meaning to the place name, Wonchunchu, which in Runyankore means "place of the lions," a name given in olden times. Apparently, the lions had not forgotten, for villagers often lost lambs and goats to lions.

One day, not knowing the meaning of the name, I went for a walk in those *murram* hills. The hills were steep, speckled with caves, stunted bush, and isolated mesas. Before I knew it, I was no longer meeting people. I was alone; no goat boys chasing their goats or playing flutes met me. I stopped in the shadows of a clump of trees to wipe sweat from my hot face. A soft wind blew toward me, and I looked under a copse of trees in a *murram* half-cave and saw this tawny figure reclining. At first I was not sure, but then I became aware of the rising and falling of its body...breathing. The large head and flowing mane shocked me. I stood momentarily disoriented. Frozen for an instant, I was unable to move. Yes, it was a lion!

I am surprised now that I did not panic and run away, which might have fatally drawn the lion's attention to me, a rushing, moving prey. Quietly but hurriedly I slipped away in the direction from which I had come, and soon I was panting but meeting goat herders and hiking villagers again. I shivered in fear and wonder of what would have happened had the wind from me been blowing toward the lion instead of the wind blowing from the lion to me. It could have revealed to the lion my scent, and things might have been far different in the "Place of the Lions." □

A TEEAer Becomes an African Farmer

Moses L. Howard

In 1965, I had been in Uganda four years. I was married to a Tutsi woman and had one child, with a second child on the way. One evening after tea, one of my science students brought to me an African woman whose father was a county chief in Ankole. She offered to sell me twelve acres of her land. It was too much land for me. Besides, I was not a citizen and the law stated that only Ugandan citizens could own land.

This land-owning woman encouraged me in every way to purchase it. She was, I now think, an early-era African feminist. She said, "Since you're married to an African woman and have children, then why not buy the land for your wife and children?" At her urging, I investigated land ownership law at the land office and found that it was legal for me to purchase land in my wife's name.

I bought the land. It was surveyed and put in my wife's name along with the child's name. I put on a caveat that restricted the sale of it until the child reached the age of twenty-one. This pleased the seller very much.

It was my intention to make sure the land offered a safeguard of care for the mother and child. I was looking ahead, thinking of the welfare of the child and mother in case something unforeseen happened to me, or in case she decided to divorce me and marry another man. There was the possibility that I might not be around and without the caveat, the land could be sold, and without that land, the child could be left with no means of care.

My students heard I had bought land, and they came to visit me with large eyes of expectancy. They said, "Sir, what will you do now?" It was a question that said I was in some kind of trouble.

I heard one student say, "...but he is the son of farmers in Mississippi."

The other's retort followed: "But this is Africa. Can he farm *matoke*? Can he grow cassava?"

That was more like a dare. It rattled my thinking just a bit.

That is the beginning of how I acquired land in Uganda and slowly became an African farmer. I thought I could at least grow beans and tomatoes in Ankole.

In preparation for planting, I hired a local farmer's helper to make a potting shed, roofed it with grass roofing, and made benches for the wooden trays in which I had about four inches of soil. I planted beans, corn, squash, tomatoes, and peppers. My students asked, "What is that for, sir?" None of the nearby farmers had a potting shed. And I was just doing what I had seen done back in Mississippi.

Other African farmers in our village of Kaberere, which was about eight miles from the town of Mbarara and Nymatangia Catholic Mission, came to visit often and offered advice. "Pay attention to the rainy season," one warned me.

Further, I made use of the British government's Experimental Stock Farm near Mbarara, which was still in operation just three years after Uganda became independent. At the stock farm, African farmers got farms started by purchasing baby chickens and pigs and by hiring, at a nominal fee, heavy farm-machines for tilling and plowing. I hired the plowing of two acres and immediately planted beans, yams, and peanuts.

I tried to solve the water problem by buying a large five-hundred-gallon metal tank. I placed it beside the house to collect the roof runoff during rains. At first I thought to use it as drinking water. I found lizards skittering over the corrugated roof and birds dropping their feces on the roof, and all this drained into the tank, contaminating the water. The water could be safely used only for washing work clothes or for scrubbing our cement floors. But the tank was now almost full of rain water.

I went back to teaching at Kyambogo in Kampala, and in my absence I forgot to transplant my tomato and pepper plants from the potting shed where they were still growing, cared for by my wife and my farm-helper.

Upon my return to my farm, the neighboring farmers warned me that the rainy season was over and I could not transplant my tomatoes. The searing sun would shrivel and kill them. It was now the dry season, and we were harvesting beans and corn. I was disappointed, but still I went ahead and transplanted two long rows of tomato plants from the potting shed.

In three days, they lay shriveled and parched, and then died. Nearby farmers came, looked at them sadly, and shook their heads in pity. My schoolboy students said, "Sir, this is Africa!" as though they reminded me that I must not act like I was still in Mississippi.

But then I thought there should be a way to grow these tomato plants. So at night, I thought of a possible way to protect my plants from the searing rays of the sun. I dug a deeper hole for each plant, and at night I transplanted more and covered all around the stems at the top of their roots with grass and banana fibers. My farmer friends watched, smiled, and shrugged their shoulders as if they expected failure. Then each night I took a bucket filled with water and poured water from my big tank into each hill around the roots and covered around the base of each plant with more grass.

The next days, I watched the plants carefully. They did not wilt, and after a week of pouring water from my big corrugated tank the tomato plants were green and still healthy in the hot sun. They were growing taller and taller.

My neighbor farmers came to look, and they raised their eyes in surprise, clearly mystified that my tomato plants were healthy. They saw my family visiting the bore hole for drinking and cooking water. I finally told my farmer friends the secret of my mulching and watering the plants at night from water in my tank.

From then on, they visited me often and soon the tomato plants bloomed, and there were small tomatoes that kept on enlarging and all during the dry season they grew, and we had plants loaded with tomatoes as large as tea cups. My neighbors became more interested. We talked about mulching as a way of having plants grow during the dry season. They visited and went home with several huge tomatoes. We all knew then that we could plant during dry season if we solved the water problem. ☐

Wildlife but No Elephants

Jack Humbles

Sunday down by the lake, I saw three monitor lizards, the largest about three feet long! That night termites starting swarming about my house. I turned off all the lights except the front porch one, stood by the glass doors, and watched.

About ten bats began to catch them in midair. When the termites tried to rest on the walls, the geckos captured them. Then a white-tailed mongoose walked right onto my porch and ate all the termites that fell to the cement floor. I was about two feet from the mongoose.

After my sea-freight wooden crates arrived, I left them on my front porch for several days and finally decided to move them to my storage area. Under the first one moved, I found a small cobra! It was beautiful: shiny jet black, black collar, yellowish chin and throat. It raised its body, spread its hood, and slowly moved towards me. A stick was near, so I was able to capture it. It then became part of the school zoo.

Two weeks later as I was driving to town, prison guards stopped me and said that a snake had been found in an open field by some prisoners. All the guards knew that I was interested in snakes for our biology lab at the college. I got out a large burlap sack from the back of my VW and told them to drive the snake towards me. I walked out into the field near the prisoners and soon a snake about four to five feet long crawled right into the burlap sack. I put it in a large glass cage back at the college and only later discovered that it was a spitting cobra.

The Snake in the Toilet

Clive Mann

I'll call him "S" for the purpose of this account; he was also in group 4B. We both did our second teaching practice at Soroti, which was to be our posting, he at Teso College, me at Soroti Senior Secondary School. We had a luxurious drive to Soroti after being collected at Makerere by a large smart black saloon with a cheerful and cooperative chauffeur. As this was also to be our final posting, we had to take all possessions with us. After bundling as much gear as we could in the boot, and other bags in the front passenger space, we set off lounging on the back seat like young lords going to a shoot.

As we passed through Kampala, S asked the driver to stop at a large Goan shop, I guess a kind of "mini-mart," on the main road. I assumed he'd gone for cigarettes, but returned with wooden crate of White Cap that he placed between us on the back seat. We stopped for food and more beer at the Crested Crane in Jinja and again at the Rock Hotel in Tororo. It was dark by the time we got to the Soroti Rest House where I should have been dropped. It seemed to be shut up, but I found another resident who suggested that I came back tomorrow, and allowed me to dump my gear in his room. S suggested I go on with him to Teso College and get a lift back the next day.

Little seemed to be happening at the college—they may have been on holiday. We drove around the compound and found a group of prefects who were expecting S. They apologized for his house not being ready and showed him to another one to use until it was. There was one problem; the *choo* didn't work. But that was not really a problem, because nearby was a disused dormitory with a number of lavatories, some of which had been checked and found working. We decided to finish off the few beers left, and then were surprised by a couple other English teachers who had heard that S had arrived. They came bearing gifts—bottles of beer—and we settled in for a good yarn.

After a while S picked up a torch and went in search of a *choo*. Soon we heard loud shout followed by S rushing into the house holding his shorts around his knees. "I've been bitten on the backside by a bloody snake," he said revealing his wound to us. Bright red marks were obvious on his right buttock.

"Quick, slash open the wound and suck out the venom," he shouted.

"No chance!" we chorused, noticing that the skin had not been broken.

The noise alerted our helpful prefects who came rushing, and on hearing "snake!" shot off to get *pangas*. I insisted I go with them to ensure that the snake should not be sacrificed unnecessarily. We went to cubicle he had used, the furthest. We carefully shone our torches into the bowl. There sat a rather puzzled broody hen on her nest.

I did not relate this story until after the death of S more than twelve years ago. ☐

Indian Friends, Indian Cooking, in Four Parts

Mary Jo McMillin

Tonight our Indian teacher friend, Pillay, stops by for pizza. It's exotic and new for him, as he insists I allow him to help roll the dough and scatter on the toppings. He works with the deft hands of a seasoned cook. A few days later he invites us over for dal soup and curried chicken. I arrive while he's still in the kitchen and get a first-hand view of how to pop the mustard seeds and slowly brown the onions to finish the soup, adding tamarind and coriander leaves. Now that's exotic.

Pillay's Dal, serves 4-6

7 oz. (1 cup) Toor Dal, Channa Dal, or other Indian yellow or pink lentils

1 whole green chili
2 whole peeled garlic cloves
1 teaspoon turmeric

4 Tablespoons vegetable oil (or pure olive oil)

1/2 teaspoon brown mustard seeds
1/4 teaspoon cumin seeds
1/8 teaspoon ajwain seeds (optional)

6 oz. (1 medium) onion peeled, quartered and thinly sliced (1-1/2 cups)

1 oz. (large walnut-sized piece) dry tamarind

1 cup diced fresh or canned tomato
salt, cayenne (chili powder), lime juice to taste yogurt and coriander (cilantro) leaves for garnish

    1. Rinse lentils and place in deep pot or pressure cooker with one quart of cool water, chili, garlic, and turmeric. Pressure-cook ten minutes or simmer covered until mushy tender. (Soak lentils in water for one hour to hasten cooking time.)

    2. Heat oil in medium frying pan and sizzle mustard, cumin, and optional ajwain seeds until they begin to make a popping sound. Add

sliced onion and fry gently until onion is reduced and golden brown. (This will take at least fifteen minutes.)

3. Crumble tamarind into a bowl and soften in one-half cup boiling water. When tamarind has cooled enough to handle, rub the fruit with your fingertips to form a puree. Strain the puree to remove seeds and skins.

4. When the dal has softened. Add tamarind puree, chopped tomato, and salt to taste. Remove the chili and for added spiciness, chop the cooked chili and return it to the soup. Add two cups additional water if lentils seem too thick. Simmer five minutes.

5. Add seed-scented oil with fried onion. Taste for seasonings, adding a generous squeeze of lime juice for added tartness, and a pinch cayenne or powdered chili for zest. Simmer a few minutes to combine flavors.

6. Serve the soup in bowls with a spoonful of yogurt and sprinkle chopped cilantro over the top. And think of my good friend Pillay.

—

Mr. Mistry, our Indian science teacher from Gujarat whose wife speaks no English, pops by and invites us to Sunday lunch. We walk about a quarter of a mile along the tall grass-edged dirt path to their somewhat older house that mirrors our own pale yellow cinderblock bungalow. Their two children giggle at the door when I hand them each a balloon. The five-year-old daughter skips about barefoot in a light cotton dress, and the two-year-old boy pads along in a pullover shirt, his bare bottom diaperless.

The family is Hindu: everything is vegetarian, and the meal must have taken all morning to prepare. We four adults sit at the dining room table, each of us facing a wide circular metal tray, a little water glass, and a teaspoon.

Mrs. Mistry places a metal cup of thin yellow soup on each tray and gives us a thick chapati. The soup has a yogurt base seasoned with fresh ginger, green chilis, turmeric, cumin, and garlic. A layer of sweetened lentils fills the chapati. We break off a chapatti segment, dip it in melted ghee and follow the sweet bite with a spoonful of tangy soup. Next, our hostess serves potato and onion *bhujias* (fritters) with coconut chutney.

A lentil stew beside a mound of rice and spicy cooked cabbage fills the center of our trays.

We gather balls of rice with our fingers and scoop the lentils and cabbage into our mouths. As I float on a carpet of enjoyment, I look across the table and see beads of sweat rolling down Bob's cheeks. Thankfully there's no dessert; I couldn't have swallowed another morsel. I chew a cardamom pod from a tray of digestive whole spices.

—

This morning I set off on foot toward town to cook with my Sikh friend, Mrs. Singh. I take the shortcut path for a mile and a half. Soon I shed my raincoat, although the grass is still wet from the night's shower. A white-gowned old man outside his hut greets me, "*Jambo, memsaab,*" as I bow, and four round-bellied children step out to stare. Five- or six-year-old boys bathing in the river giggle with embarrassment as I pass. Younger tots sucking juice from oranges scamper ahead of me, all but blocking my way. When they race away, I fear I've frightened them till I peer down at a solid mat of tiny stinging ants crossing the trail.

Once I join the main Matagoro/Songea road, a schoolboy pedals by, then slows down, and waves me aboard. I hop on his back fender, and the rest of the way is "smooth sailing," even as his bike bounces over the rugged dirt main road to town. In the market square by nine, I bargain and fill my basket with bananas, cucumbers, and sweet potatoes. I join the line waiting at the meat stall where today's hacked up, dark-red beef carcass hangs from a roof beam, and the bloody-aproned butcher with his giant curved *panga* whacks off the next hunk of "steak."

The Singhs live in a whitewashed square house with a flat roof near the market square. Alas, Mr. Singh, our local postmaster, and his family will return to the Punjab in a few months. Like the other Indian kitchens I've been in, the floor is the cooking space. Mrs. Singh brings a bucket of fresh water from the single tap behind the house where her husband just washed his hair and stands on the back cement slab, turbanless with a thin shock of black hair hanging to his knees.

Mrs. Singh's mounds of onions and garlic wait in low baskets while she digs fresh ginger from a damp patch of sand beside the house. She has no fridge, but keeps her jar of curd from morning to evening in a pan of cool water. Into her bowl-like grinding stone still dusted with crushed cinnamon, cloves, and cardamom, she adds handfuls of sliced onions, garlic, ginger, and chilis, which she pounds to a coarse mash with a heavy mahogany pestle.

She likes the steady heat of charcoal, and when she wants a slow simmer, she sets a few glowing coals on the cement floor, places a pot on the coals, and sets more hot coals on the lid for oven-like heat. I'm captivated by the smell of her gingery braised potatoes and nutty, ghee-brushed graham chapatis. I wish I were staying to eat, but on his usual Saturday drive to the post office, Vic comes by to pick me up at noon, and I'm home in time to make Bob an Adolph's Tenderizer-softened steak sandwich for lunch.

Mrs. Singh's Ginger Potatoes, serves 4

4 Tablespoons vegetable oil or pure olive oil
8 oz. (2 cups) peeled, chopped onion
1 chopped green Serrano chili including seeds
(2-3 teaspoons; remove seeds from chili for milder seasoning)
3 large cloves chopped garlic
3 Tablespoons peeled, sliced, and chopped fresh ginger
1 teaspoon ground coriander seed
1/2 teaspoon ground cumin seed
1/4 teaspoon cinnamon
grated fresh nutmeg
1/2 teaspoon turmeric
1/8 teaspoon cayenne chili powder, optional
2 cups peeled, diced potatoes (about 1 pound)
1 cup chopped fresh or canned tomatoes, or 1/2 cup canned crushed tomatoes 1/2 cup water
8 oz. (2 cups) diced zucchini or eggplant for garnish
(2 medium squash or 1 small eggplant)
fresh coriander leaves (cilantro)

1. Heat oil in medium wok or large saucepan. Gently sauté onion until softened and beginning to brown.

2. Combine chili, garlic, and ginger in mortar with generous pinch of salt and grind to a paste. Or place in blender with 2–3 tablespoons water and whiz to a paste. Add ground coriander, cumin, cinnamon, nutmeg, turmeric, and cayenne to ginger mash. This mixture is a masala.

3. When the onion is golden and tender, add the masala or spice mash and continue to fry stirring all the time until the spices smell fragrant and cooked.

4. Add potatoes, tomato, and water. Season with salt. Stir and simmer covered. Add eggplant along with potatoes or add zucchini when potatoes are half cooked.

5. Taste for seasonings. Add more water if needed to make a light sauce. Use a bit of lime or lemon juice to lift the flavor if needed and serve with coriander leaves and yogurt.

And then write a paean to Mrs. Singh.

—

I spend the afternoon watching an Indian man prepare curry. Once in a while Chukla, our local bank manager, comes by the school to cook for our neighbors and included us. I'm learning that real curries are seasoned with a mixture of spices rather than curry powder. Chukla flavors his chicken curry with onion, garlic, chili, turmeric, cinnamon, cloves, tomatoes, and coriander leaves. He makes *poories*, deep-fried unleavened breads. He eats everything neatly with his fingers; Bob opts for a fork. Chukla tells us our fingers bring the warm softness of the food directly to our lips without the intrusion of a cold metal fork.

Months later Chukla guides us through the Indian commercial neighborhood of Dar where I outfit my cook's wares with a lava rock grinding stone, a brass mortar, and a chapati board.

We follow Chukla home for dinner. His extended Indian family of nine seems contentedly cramped in a neat-as-a-pin four room apartment. The tiny kitchen has no cabinets or work boards. A few open shelves line one wall next to a little electric stove and a minuscule sink.

Women squat or sit on the cement floor while they peel vegetables and sweep the peelings into a corner. Pots simmer over low charcoal braziers; the electric stove is used to boil water. I observe the vegetarian dinner of chili-laced lentils, eggplant fried with onions, steamed rice, fiery coconut chutney plus thick curd (yogurt) and chapatis. We feast on a mat-covered floor and lick the spicy oils from our fingers. I learned a lot more about Songea than mere geography. ☐

Bessie and the Cobra
Miles Paul

One night when Bessie, a dog I had inherited from Ben Sensiba, was barking excitedly by the corner of the house next to the kitchen door, our house boy Ali summoned me indicating that I should go outside. I found Bessie confronting a black spitting cobra that was "standing" by the house with its hood fully flared out. I told Ali to go get Brian (Atkinson) next door to help me catch the *nyoka*, and I grabbed my snake stick.

Ali told Brian that I wanted him to help me catch an *ndudu*. As you probably know "*ndudu*" is usually translated as "insect," but to native Swahili speakers more commonly means any creepy-crawly. You can imagine Brian's surprise and trepidation when he saw that I needed his help catching a cobra and not an insect.

We did capture the critter. I later took it down to Mikumi Game Reserve and released it in a safe area. ☐

A Lunchtime Experience

Jerry Schieber

It was a typically beautiful, blue sky, puffy white-clouded day at Mzumbe Government Boys Secondary School, which was nestled in the foothills of the Uluguru Mountains outside of Morogoro, Tanganyika. It was my last math class of the morning, so I grabbed my books and notes and headed back to the little cement block, tin-roofed house that I shared with Rod Hinkle to have lunch. The house was located at the far end of the soccer pitch. It was reachable from the main road and driveway, but I usually chose to walk across the pitch to a little rise behind the goal post and down to the backyard of the house.

A path led past the hot water heater, two fifty-gallon drums built into a brick stand with space underneath for a wood fire to heat the water, past the open carport where my pet monkey would be waiting, knowing that a banana or piece of fruit would soon appear for lunch, and up the stairs of the front porch and inside to something Shabani, our cook, had prepared for lunch. After lunch, a little stretch time, or kip as it was called, and then back to school for afternoon classes. As I approached the backyard, I had a weird sensation that I had seen something move but didn't think much about it. As I approached the house, I noticed there was a hole in the backyard that I hadn't seen before, but dismissed it all and went about the day's activities.

The next day, another gorgeous day, when morning classes were completed, I headed home by the usual route. But this time as I walked through the backyard, something moved and seemed to disappear down the hole. I wondered if maybe we had a guest living in the backyard. For the next couple of days it was quiet, but on the third day, as I came over the ridge, there it was, a snake curled up and enjoying the warmth of the sun. As I started down the slope, it was down the hole and gone in seconds.

At lunch, I told Shabani about what I had seen, and he left no doubt that we would not share our backyard with a snake. So that afternoon, when I returned home after classes and activities, he took me to the backyard, where we devised a trap to catch the snake. First he pounded a stake, something like a horseshoe peg, into the ground about a foot away from the hole. Then he tied a cord to the stake, carefully fashioned a loop around the hole, and then carried the cord to the corner of the house.

The trap had been set; now to see if it would work!

The next day, as I approached the house, sure enough, our "friend" was enjoying the sun completely unaware of what was waiting for him. I called to Shabani, who quickly appeared at the corner of the house with the cord in hand. As I walked down the hill, the snake made a sudden move for the hole. He had slithered about a third of the way in when Shabani pulled the cord. It tightened around the snake and there it was, trapped, one-third in the hole and two-thirds exposed. With one blow from a club, the snake went limp and then one more blow to make sure.

When there was no movement left, we removed the snake from the hole to find that it was a spitting cobra almost six feet long. I was told that they are capable of spitting venom, usually going for the eyes of the perceived meal or threat. Certainly not one you would like living in your backyard! Actually it was longer but not as fast as the puff adder we killed next to the carport, but that's another story. ☐

A Eureka Moment

Joan (Hoffman) Schieber

After spending several months learning teaching methods and British-style curriculum and educational philosophy at Makerere, members of TEA group 1B were dispersed in 1961 to secondary schools throughout East Africa for practice teaching. I was assigned to Kamusinga Friends' Secondary School for boys in western Kenya. Only a few weeks after my arrival, the boys went on strike. Though student strikes were common in the early 1960s and food was often named as one of the reasons, I never really knew the cause of this strike. But practice teaching certainly could not be accomplished if there were no students in the classrooms.

I was quickly transferred to another school, this time a Catholic girls' secondary school close to Lake Victoria. During one of my early math classes there, the students were struggling with the concept of perimeter. This type of problem often involves unusual shapes and a mix of units of measurement. I drew and labeled a problem on the board and then side by side, using colored chalk to mark our progress, translated the dimensions into a common unit of measure and added the parts.

When all sides were accounted for and we had an answer, the class broke out into applause. I was stunned, pleasantly so. This had never happened before, and it never happened again! Naïve young teacher that I was, I assumed they were applauding because they could see that there was a process for problem-solving that worked, a "Eureka Moment."

As I look back, perhaps the students were just surprised and pleased that someone could actually get the same answer as in the back of the book. However it was as happy and encouraging a moment for me as it seemed to be for the students. And it has remained with me as a wonderful memory from practice teaching. □

The Mikado in Morogoro

Joan (Hoffman) Schieber

I spent my TEA teaching tour at Marian College, now Kilakala, in Morogoro, Tanganyika. The school was fairly new, one of the very few secondary schools for girls, and it was staffed, run, and supported by Maryknoll Sisters from the US. It was a positive and nurturing place, beautifully situated at the foot of the Uluguru Mountains. The sisters aimed at instilling the three Rs while enriching their students' school lives with cultural and other broadening experiences. They felt that they were training the wives and partners of future leaders of their country.

One such project was putting on a musical performance. This required school-wide participation. Main characters were selected and parts learned. The chorus learned and rehearsed a number of songs. Costumes were designed and sewn using colorful satiny materials. Wigs were created out of strands of sisal, dyed black, and shaped into geisha styles. Sets were made and backdrops painted. Many after-school practices were held. Eventually it was time for public performances. People from town and the surrounding area as well as students and staff from the nearby boys' secondary school were invited to attend.

As I sat in the audience, I was amazed, in awe. I had come to know these students as individuals, by name: Theobista, Cecilia, Amandina, and Gertrude, to name only a few. But as I watched the performance, I had to pinch myself to realize where I actually was. These were African students, teenagers, putting on a Gilbert and Sullivan opera called *The Mikado* with exemplary skill. This was not music of their culture. They had had no exposure to the background story or this type of musical performance. Nothing about the program had any bearing to where we were. It was completely out of context —and extraordinarily well done. The sisters and our students had pulled off an amazing feat. ☐

Celebrity Contacts

Joel Watne

During our training at Teachers College in the summer of 1961, I attended an all-day hootenanny at the nearby Riverside Baptist Church in New York. At one point, the M.C. introduced an "up and coming" singer songwriter. The guy was skinny, with tousled hair, a guitar that needed the strings trimmed, and a harmonica hanging around his neck. He played the guitar and harmonica quite well, but his singing voice was so bad that I felt he couldn't even get into a third-string choir back at Concordia College in Moorhead, Minnesota. After I returned from Tanzania in January, 1964, it became apparent the skinny guy with the lousy voice had up and come. It had been Bob Dylan, a fellow Minnesotan who was born in Duluth and grew up in neighboring Hibbing, and well known in Eveleth on the Iron Range where I had gone to teach.

While I was teaching in Arusha, the city hosted an international track meet involving Kenya, Tanganyika, Uganda, and Zanzibar. I was signed up as one of the officials for the track meet, which starred Kenya's Kipchoge Keino before he became known worldwide. Among the guests attending was Jomo Kenyatta, soon to be first president of Kenya. During a break in my on-field duties, I took my camera up into the stands and approached Mr. Kenyatta, who was accompanied by several large, burly, and very serious-looking men, presumably his bodyguards.

I asked, "Mr. Kenyatta, would it be okay for me to take your picture?"

He said, "Please do," and posed for me.

—

When leaving Tanzania in January, 1964, I stayed overnight at the New Stanley Hotel in Nairobi where the dress code dictated that gentlemen wore jackets and ties in the dining room. As I breakfasted in jacket and tie, another patron walked in, without jacket and tie, and proceeded to sit down. He appeared bleary-eyed and as hung-over as his reputation would suggest, but the staff ignored his lack of jacket and tie.

It was Robert Mitchum. I refrained from loaning him my spare tie. □

V: Politics and Politicians

Julius Nyerere of Tanzania has attracted the veneration of both his countrymen and TEA-Alumni authors. Jerry Atkin's tender and decidedly honorific tribute is a reminder that Nyerere visited the first group of TEAers at Teachers College, the day before they flew off to East Africa. He was called "*Mwalimu*" because he was a teacher, one who like all teachers had a covenantal relationship with those he served.

A letter home in 1969 recounts an experience in Nairobi so unsettling that it prompted Ted Hoss in 2012, forty-three years later, to state that he could "still feel a sense of horror as I remember the scene as it unfolded."

A gentler approach to governance involves the ballot box. Kay Borkowski's *Voting in Kenya*, in excerpts from letters home written on the eve of Kenya's independence, gives us her assessment of voting in Machakos. "I crossed paths with Idi Amin three times." Those are the opening words of Ron Stockton's *Encounters with Amin*.

In this section:

Jerry Atkin	*Mwalimu* • 351
Kay Borkowski	*Voting in May, 1963* • 352
Hank Hector	*Who Can Be the President of What* • 354
Ted Hoss	*Assassination in Nairobi* • 355
Ben Lindfors	*Amending Nyerere's Julius Caesar* • 357
Clive Mann	*Convocation at Makerere* • 363
	BaHima and BaTutsi in Uganda • 364
	Soviet Doctors in Uganda • 366
	Presidential Visit • 369
David Sandgren	*A Grim Mau Mau Legacy* • 370
	Memories of Kenyan Independence • 371
Ron Stockton	*Nelson Mandela* • 372
	Encounters with Amin • 379
Nola Stover	*JFK Assassination* • 381

Mwalimu

Jerry Atkin

We met with Julius Nyerere before the commencement exercises where we would become certified graduate teachers and he would confer an honorary doctorate on Jomo Kenyatta. We were to be posted to Tanzania and Nyerere would answer questions and frame the task nation building in Tanzania and our role in it.

If *Mzee* fit Kenyatta like a glove, *Mwalimu* was tailor made for Nyerere. He spoke in English, but when he switched to Swahili to tell a story, an amazing transformation took place. Speaking Swahili, he came alive. His voice and gestures grew animated, his eyes flashed and there was a lot of laughter in the room. But even in English, you felt like he was truly there with you in the room, that you were engaged in a common project together.

Unlike Kenyatta, he seemed like one of us. He was only forty-two, educated in Edinburgh, where he rubbed elbows with the Fabian Socialists. I felt the excitement of his vision of a nation making its own way, creating a new and better world for its people, free of tribalism and based on African values. I was hooked and I knew that if he were my president, I would follow him anywhere. There were only six graduate African teachers in Tanzania, and I got it that what we brought to Tanzania was critically important and my vision of my role as a teacher came into focus. Now I knew why I was there.

The following year, Nyerere would make the leaders of Tanganyika African National Union (TANU) walk from Dar es Salaam to Mwanza to help them remember their roots, and a year later he would send all of the students at the University down after they struck to uphold the nation-building principle that they should not be asked to share rooms. He refused aid from the Soviet Bloc because it came with the demand for a naval base on Zanzibar. In 1967, the Arusha Declaration put forward a doomed vision of communitarian African socialism.

When Nyerere came to Tabora, where he had once taught in the school for the sons of chiefs, he was forty-five. His hair had turned gray, there was no sparkle in his eyes, the weight of trying to lead a nation still staggering under the weight of its colonial history, its lack of education and natural resources, had taken its toll. And I still would have followed him anywhere. □

Voting in May, 1963

Kay Borkowski

When my mother died in 2005, it was my job to do the sorting and packing at her home of thirty-plus years. Amid her things was a box of letters I had written from Makerere and later from my posting as maths mistress in Machakos.

On Wednesday 15 May, 1963, I had written in regard to the upcoming Kenyan elections:

> "Internal self government is slowly approaching. Elections are this weekend, next week, and the next weekend. I'm quite interested in seeing what happens. I also thought it would be interesting to be able to visit a polling station to see just exactly how democracy works in Kenya.
>
> "I asked David Roundturner (the district commissioner) about it last night at the Machakos Club and he said that I wouldn't be allowed in the polling area unless I was some kind of election officer. So he's going to fix it up for me to be some kind of election officer on May 25th and 26th! I'm really quite excited about it."

Monday, 27 May, 1963:

> "Elections are over—all but the shouting and rioting (if there is any). I enjoyed seeing how they were run and got some movie films which I hope will turn out. Some of the people where we were felt that they hadn't been allowed to vote because we

wouldn't let them put their cornstalks (symbol of Paul Ngei's African Peoples' Party) in the ballot box!"

As I recall from my 2011 view, someone also wanted to put a rooster in the tin *debe* that was used for a ballot box!

The letter goes on:

"Most of the people disliked having to put their right thumb in red dye to show that they had voted. One man said that it was because he couldn't lick his thumb with the dye on it. The few funny things that happened make it worthwhile; most of the time it was just plain boring. About ninety percent of the people who voted were illiterates—one woman kept saying that she couldn't read the pictures on the ballots."

(Each party and each independent candidate had a picture to represent him on the ballot as well as his name.)

And further:

"At the two places where we worked people would come to vote and then go outside and dance! Most of the pictures that I have are of the dancing."

I also remember the weather:

"It has rained very heavily over the weekend which has made getting to and from places most interesting. The road from the school (Machakos Girls' School) to Machakos is the worst I've ever seen it."

I wonder how many of Wave I remember the Uhuru souvenirs that appeared around the December 12, 1963 Independence date, such as ties, shirts, and the silk scarf worn among first Kenyan cabinet. They're probably very valuable now. □

Who Can Be the President of What

Hank Hector

In 1964 I was in my third year of teaching East African History to my Form 3 students. We were dealing with colonialism and the effects on the people ruled under colonialism. After that we moved on to democracy and self-rule and how it differed. We discussed majority rule and the need for protecting the rights of the minorities.

Suddenly the discussion shifted to the United States. One of my students asked when I thought there would be a black President of the United States. I told them that the majority of the people in the US were white and that it was unlikely that a black President would be chosen for quite a while. The class immediately raised the issue of bias and bigotry, which I admitted did exist in the US.

They became even more vocal and demanded a date when I thought a black President would be elected. I thought about it for a while and finally said it would be at least the year 2000 before this might occur. I knew these students well after three years of teaching them, and they had no inhibitions about pointing out the shortcomings of the US. I let the criticism go on for a while and then I shifted back to the topic of democracy. Again I mentioned that in a democracy the majority picked the leaders of the government and the same was true in Tanzania.

I then asked the class when they thought an Asian would be elected president of Tanzania. Almost with one voice they rose out of their seats and said, "*Never.*" To this day I still smile, recalling when they all sat down and the realization of what they had said dawned on them. The notion that they could have bias had never occurred to them.

By the way, all of these students passed the Cambridge overseas exam in history the following year. ☐

Assassination in Nairobi

Ted Hoss

Note: This letter was written to family and friends in the US shortly after Tom Mboya was assassinated.

On July 5, 1969, a Saturday, Pat and I had taken our son, John, to Nairobi to keep a doctor's appointment. After the appointment we did a little shopping. Because the stores close at 1:00 p.m. on Saturday, we didn't get a chance to do too much shopping. At 1:00 we walked to Government Road where most of the government offices are located. As we crossed Government Road, we saw a government car with P.K. Keiange, the minister of foreign affairs, in it. We thought how interesting.

We walked to Lavarini's, an Italian restaurant, located on Government Road. As we sat down, we heard two loud sounds. I thought it was a car backfiring. Waiters were at the front of the restaurant looking out across the street. After what I thought was a burglar alarm going off, I approached the doorway of the restaurant, which was about 200 feet from our table. I thought someone or some store was being robbed. When I got to the door, the headwaiter was just coming back in. I asked him what had happened.

He said, "Tom Mboya has been shot in the chest."

I was shocked and could not believe what I had just heard. Tom Mboya was the Minister for Economic Planning and Development and was a chief rival of President Kenyatta.

I ran over to the crowd of people who had gathered near the pharmacy. I was one of a few whites, and I was concerned that the crowd would turn on me in their rage.

An African said to me, "You should leave now!"

It seared me, but I wanted to see what was going on. I saw Mboya's white Mercedes parked at the curb. I ran to the drugstore where Mboya had been taken. I peered in, and I could see him lying on his back on the floor with two Asians looking down at him. Blood covered the floor. Mboya just lay there with a vacant look from eyes that stared upwards.

Just then the crowd turned and began running. Some people were knocked down. I ran too. I don't know why they began to run. They just did. Within minutes the police and ambulance were there. It was too late; Mboya was dead. I hurried back to the restaurant, told Pat what had happened, and said it would be wise if we left Nairobi immediately.

I was concerned that roadblocks would prevent us leaving the city. But no such police activity was evidenced. As a matter of fact as we walked hurriedly to our car, the city was quite normal. Word had not gone beyond Government Road. We were able to leave with no difficulty. What was interesting though was the fact that all our servants and most of the population of Nyeri, ninety miles from Nairobi, knew what had happened by the time of our return. Word had spread rapidly.

Very little has been said about his assassination. Police have not caught his killers. Apparently two men had stopped him on the street as he left his car to enter a drug store. As he was talking to these two men, someone in a car shot him. Government Road is one of the main streets in Nairobi. It is the main road that takes you out of town. Most of the shopping traffic had cleared by the time of the shooting. It would be very difficult for a car to escape the area, but it did.

Having gone through three assassinations in the US, I thought about all that I had read in the newspapers and heard on TV about the Kennedy and King assassinations. Being as close as we were to an assassination was a frightening experience. In America, people tend to act in a predictable manner when there is such a tragedy. But in Africa, you're not sure how people are going to react; hence, you tend to be very cautious.

We heard that there was some rioting in some parts of the country. So far nothing has happened in our area. Mboya was a Luo. The Luo tribe is concentrated in the west. We were in Kikuyuland, so people were not as upset as the Luo population around Kisumu. We were supposed to go to a party on the night of the killing, but we stayed home as a precaution.

In America, such actions are serious, but there is continuity. In Africa, these actions cause big waves, and the reactions are highly unpredictable. This was the well-planned act of group of conspirators. Two other attempts on Mboya's life had been made before. What we don't know at the moment is how this is going to affect Kenyan politics in the near or distant future. We'll keep you informed.

Time of the gunshot and shooting 1:10 p.m. Mboya's body was removed in the ambulance at 1:40 p.m. □

Amending Nyerere's *Julius Caesar*
Ben Lindfors

I had wanted to acquire a command of Kiswahili sufficient to read some of the rich literature written in that language, but I found its esoteric alliterative poetry daunting, so I started to search for more accessible texts that I could tackle for my independent studies project.

As it happened, Julius Nyerere had published his translation of Shakespeare's *Julius Caesar* just a year earlier, and the UCLA library had obtained a copy, so I took an unhurried look at it. Nyerere had devised a new type of blank verse for his translation, and this was far easier for me to decode than the earlier traditional forms of Kiswahili poetry. So with my instructor's blessing, I began to work on Nyerere's *Julius Caezar*, translating it back into English and then comparing my translation with the Shakespearean original. It was a fascinating exercise and I learned quite a lot from it.

Here is a portion of my translation of Nyerere's charming foreword to the book:

> "When I was translating this book I did not know what its end would be. First, I did not know that I would translate the entire book. Second, I did not intend the translation itself to be published. My intention was to get something to do in the times when my usual work was tiring me out a great deal and I needed relaxation. But as I translated more and more, my desire of going on to the end increased. Finally, when the rest of my friends discovered that I had this occupation, they urged

me to bring it to completion and I agreed that the translation be published. In saying this it is not that I want my friends to be blamed for any mistakes and deficiencies whatsoever which will appear in this translation. I explain only how this translation was made. I would like to warn the reader. First, this translation is not a scholarly translation. I am not a Kiswahili scholar nor am I an English scholar. But I love both languages. It is evident, of course, that if this book were translated by a person who is a scholar of Kiswahili and English, and in particular a scholar of the writings of Shakespeare, possibly his translation would be better."

Nyerere then speaks of the type of blank verse he developed to simulate Shakespeare's blank verse without violating the norms of Kiswahili poetry. He goes on to say:

"In translating *Julius Caesar*, I have used one law of traditional poetry, that is I have tried to make every line be sixteen syllables. But these lines do not have rhymes nor are they divided into stanzas... I have said that I have tried hard to make every line have sixteen syllables. I did not say that I have succeeded, because it is not an easy matter. First, the syllables of Kiswahili are easy to get if all the words are Kiswahili, or their pronunciation is Kiswahili. For example, if you pronounce Caesar 'Siza,' it will have two syllables without trouble. But how would you pronounce Brutus? 'Burutusi' or 'Brutusi'? 'Cassius' is how many syllables?

"What I have tried hard to do is to make it possible for a person to sing a line having a name of these types by reducing or increasing the syllables on account of the number of the syllables of other words of this line. Second, English poetry is intended to be read; but Kiswahili is intended to be sung. My effort was to make it possible for the reader to sing or to read. It is difficult to sing an entire book. But if a person likes, he can try... Kiswahili is a sweet and very open language, but its sweetness and openness must be used more, then it will increase."

It was this sweetness and openness that could be found on every page of Nyerere's translation. He took a few liberties with the English original when he had to, mainly in order to indigenize the flora, fauna, and phenomena of the play's setting. Shakespeare's "knotty oaks" became Nyerere's "baobabs" (*mibuyu*); a wolf was transformed into a jackal or wild dog ("*mbwa mwitu*," literally dog of the forest); and "winter's cold" became "fierce cold" (*baridi kali*). These were quite natural changes, since they were attempts to introduce local color in place of unfamiliar foreign references.

But a close line-by-line reading also revealed a few changes that seemed unnatural and in fact looked like simple blunders. Curious about these, I decided to write the translator and ask about them. Here is the letter I composed in collaboration with Professor Goodman and sent to President Nyerere on 15 December 1964:

"*Mtaalamu Bwana Nyerere,
Salaam sana.*

Tumesoma tafsiri yako ya Julius Caezar *katika darasa letu la Kiswahili hapa katika chuo kikuu cha California katika Los Angeles. Bwana Edward Mhina kutoka Tanga alitusaidia kufahamu sehemu ngumu fulani, na Bwana* William Shakespeare *alitusaidia kidogo pia. Sasa tunakuandikia kwa maana hatujui kwa sababu gani ulibadilisha maneno machache ya mchezo wa* Shakespeare. *Maswali yetu yote yahusu hesabu.*

1. Kwa sababu gani ulibadilisha "ides of March" *kuwa* "tarehe za katikati ya Machi" (p. 12, 45, 70). *Maana ya* "ides" *ni siku moja hasa katikati ya Machi, yaani, siku ya kumi na tano ya Machi (siku ile ile ufasiriyo katika sehemu nyingine–katika maneno ya Brutus, p. 28–kama* "tarehe ya katikati ya Machi"). *Mpiga ramli alimwambia Caesar kujihadhari na tarehe moja hasa; usawa wa onyo hili waongeza* "irony" *ya mauti ya Caesar siku ile ile. Kwa nini ulitumia* "tarehe za katikati ya Machi" *badala ya* "tarehe ya katikati ya Machi"?

2. Kwa nini ulibadilisha "an hundred senators" (IV, iii, 175) *kuwa* "wakuu wa Baraza/Mia mbili" (p. 76)?

3. *Tena, mahali ambapo* Shakespeare *ameandika* "Two mighty eagles" *(V, I, 80), kwa nini umeandika* "Tai wakubwa watatu" *(p. 85)? Hicho ni kifungo kingine ambacho hatuwezi kufungua.*

Tungependezwa sana ungetueleza sababu za tofauti hizi baina ya mchezo wa Shakespeare *na tafsiri yako, tena kutuambia* "edition" *gani uliyoitumia ulipotengeneza tafsiri hiyo.*

Tena, tafadhali, waweza kutuarifu ya maumbo kama "sintakuwa" *na* "sintaweza" *uliyotumia mara kwa mara badala ya* "sitakuwa" *n.k. Hatukuweza kuyakuta maumbo haya katika vitabu vyetu vya sarufi ya Kiswahili, na twataka kujifunza asili yake na matumizi yake. Tulifurahi sana kusoma* Julius Caezar, *na twatumaini kwamba wakati kazi zako za kawaida zinapokuchosha sana na wataka kiburudisho utaendelea kutafsiri michezo mingine au, bora zaidi, kuandika michezo wewe mwenyewe. Twakutakia furaha ya Sikukuu ya Kuzawiwa.*

Wasalaam,
Bernth Lindfors
Morris Goodman

For those unfamiliar with the niceties and imperfections of third-year level academic Kiswahili (please remember that I had been studying the language for only fifteen months) here is a translation of the letter:

> Honorable Mr. Nyerere,
> Greetings.
>
> We have read your translation of *Julius Caezar* in our Kiswahili class at the University of California at Los Angeles. Mr. Edward Mhina from Tanga helped us to understand several difficult parts and Mr. William Shakespeare helped us a little as well.
>
> We are writing to you because we do not understand why you changed a few words of Shakespeare's play. All of our questions are concerned with numbers.
>
> 1. Why did you change "ides of March" into "dates in the middle of March"? The meaning of "ides" is that one day exactly in the middle of March; that is, the fifteenth of March (which you translate in another place–i.e., Brutus's speech, p.

28–as "date in the middle of March"). The soothsayer is warning Caesar to watch out on one particular day of March; moreover, this warning increases the irony of Caesar's death on that very day. Why did you use "dates in the middle of March" instead of "date in the middle of March"?

2. Why do you change "an hundred senators" to "two hundred senators"?

3. Again, when Shakespeare has only two eagles, why do you have three? This is another knot we have not been able to untie.

We have looked at many different editions of Shakespeare's *Julius Caesar* in English, but we have not found any edition that has these changes. Will you tell us which edition of Shakespeare's *Julius Caesar* you used when you made your translation? Also, please, can you give us some information about the tense "-nta-" which you used sometimes. We have not been able to find it in our grammar books and we want to learn about its origin and use.

We enjoyed reading *Julius Caezar* very much and we hope you will continue to relax from your work by translating more plays or, even better, by writing some of your own. We wish you a Merry Christmas.

Best wishes,
Bernth Lindfors
Morris Goodman

We never had a response from Nyerere to this letter, and we had never really expected one. We knew he had far more pressing matters to deal with in Tanzania at that time. There had been a revolution in Zanzibar and army mutinies in Tanganyika early that year, Tanganyika and Zanzibar had coalesced into the United Republic of Tanzania just six weeks before we sent our letter, and the new nation was busy formulating a constitution and beginning to prepare for elections that were to be held in September, 1965. In such circumstances, it would have been strange indeed for Nyerere to spend his time responding to our pedantic questions instead of remaining focused on matters of state.

It therefore came as a great surprise when Goodman and I discovered that we had been very graciously acknowledged in Nyerere's preface to the second edition of his translation of *Julius Caezar* (now entitled *Juliasi Kaizari*), which was published in 1969. After thanking many others who had responded to the first edition, he added:

> "*Nawashukuru pia Mabwana Bernth Lindfors na Morris Goodman wa Los Angeles, USA, kwa maswali yao ambayo yamenisaidia kuona makosa fulani na kuyasahihisha.*"
> (I thank as well Messrs Bernth Lindfors and Morris Goodman of Los Angeles, USA, for their questions which helped me to see certain mistakes and to correct them.)

This was an exciting moment for Goodman and me, and on checking the new edition we found that all three of the minor bloopers we had singled out in our letter had been amended. The three eagles were now two ("*tai wakubwa wawili*"), the two hundred senators were now one hundred ("*masenata mia moja*"), and, most important, the soothsayer's very precise warning, "Beware the Ides of March," which is repeated three times in the text of the play, was in every instance changed from the plural ("*tarehe za katikkati ya Machi*") to a singular sate ("*tarehe ya katikati ya Machi*"). We felt proud that we had been sable to make these minuscule contributions to a translation that has become a modern classic of Kiswahili literature.

The late Julius Nyerere, known throughout his career simply as "*Mwalimu*" (teacher), had proved once again by his example and practice that he was modest and wise enough to learn from the questions of his pupils, even those from unexpected queries thrown at him from half a world away from Tanzania. He probably would have been the first to admit that "*asiyekjosa ni malaika*" (only angels are free from mistakes), but a better proverb to sum up his approach would be "*elimu haina mwisho*" (education has no end). Quick-witted, level-headed, open-minded, and ready to correct his own mistakes, he obviously was the kind of leader who didn't need a soothsayer to warn him to remain alert.

For more information, see *Swahili Beyond the Boundaries: Literature, Language, and Identity* by Alamin M. Mazrui. http://amzn.com/0896802523

Convocation at Makerere
Clive Mann

At some point during the Dip.Ed. course at Makerere, I think early 1965, I bought my first single-lens reflex (SLR) camera. It was an East German Zeiss sold to me by fellow student Carl Georgeson. Through a shared love of Indian classical music I became friends with Kanti Shah who owned a photography shop, the place where I once met Paul Theroux, and here I bought a Pentax 120mm lens that had a screw thread compatible with East German Zeiss.

One afternoon I was wandering around Makerere taking random black-and-white photos when I noticed a throng of people going into the Assembly Hall. I waited until they had gone in and entered myself. I didn't recognize anyone, and as they were all so well-dressed, complete with mortar-boards or caps and gowns, and I was scruffy and sweaty, I didn't ask what was happening.

Then I looked at the daïs, and I was gob-smacked. Seated upon it were Milton Obote, The Kabaka, Jomo Kenyatta, Julius Nyerere, Kenneth Kaunda, Hastings Banda, and a few others I did not recognize. I later discovered one was the Prime Minister of Mauritius. Others were obviously university and government bigwigs.

No one said a word to me as I made my way and sat on the floor in front of the daïs. I then proceeded to snap away at all these august folk, regretting that my only spare film was another black-and-white. After finishing both films, I quietly got up and left as a series of speeches was going on. It was as if I were invisible.

Could it have been a convocation? No one I asked later had a clue. Why were none of the people who lectured us present? To date I have been unable to unearth those films. Probably fifty percent or more of my black-and-white films were never processed. Over the past five years I have scanned the majority of my huge collection of color slides, checked my black-and-white prints and unprinted film strips. I still occasionally unearth more material in odd places, and I am hoping one day to find this treasure.

In retrospect, the lack of security was amazing, and in a way it reminded me of an old friend in the early 1970s unknowingly entering Nyerere's garden to tape-record birds, and then getting arrested—but that's another story. In those days, one could not get anywhere near any of Kenyatta's residences. ☐

BaHima and BaTutsi in Uganda
Clive Mann

Reading about eastern Africa before arriving there in 1964, it seemed that since the late 1950s there had been mayhem in the eastern Congo), and to a lesser extent Rwanda and Burundi. Hideous acts of inhumanity occurred in Rwanda, and the minority BaTutsi people produced many refugees. I had seen the impressive BaTutsi drummers performing in London, but I now saw these people as refugees begging in Kampala, and later at a camp in Ankole. The men were very tall, increased by their hairstyles. Some would sit against a wall, with their long legs stretched out across the pavement, but unfortunately decreased in some cases where their legs had been chopped off around the knees, and swathed in filthy bandages. It was said that the BaHutu did this because they believed the BaTutsi had been able to dominate them because of their greater height. The women were also tall, and this again was enhanced by their large "beehive" hairstyles.

The social setup whereby two or three different peoples live amongst each other, speaking the same language, but remaining distinct, has been likened to the caste system of India.

I began to wonder who these people really were. They dressed differently from the locals, with long white shirts, some with colorful *kikois*, and carried sticks. About eighteen months later I visited Rwanda, and Goma (DRC). Observing the people I realized that although they were very mixed I could not easily detect BaTutsi, although some people were quite tall, with long, slender faces. But not all people who herded cattle seemed of this type.

The anthropologist in me became really fired up when sometime later I was walking through the bush in Teso District looking for birds when I came across what I realized was a couple of BaHima men herding long-horned cattle. They each wore two *kikois*, one around one shoulder, the other around the waist, they smoked long wooden pipes and carried sticks and short spears. My KiSwahili was poor, but I tried to find out where they came from. I thought they were reluctant to tell me, but later it occurred to me that they probably came from Teso.

The "castes" if we are to call them that are three in this case: BaTutsi/Bahima, BaHutu/BaIru, and BaTwa (including Pygmies). I was told by one rather cynical Rwandan that because there had been a great deal of miscegenation you could tell a MuHutu because he had one cow, but a MuTutsi had ten. One of my top pupils, the late James Bahinguza, a MuHima from Ankole, said the best way was examining their fingers. Long, slender digits indicated BaHima/BaTutsi.

BaHima, BaHororo, BaNyamulenge, and BaTutsi, along with similar peoples from northwest Tanzania of the Karagwe, Sukuma, and Nyamwezi tribes have a somewhat disputed history and origin. The received wisdom is that they are related and have a common origin; that they were long-horn cattle herders, speaking a similar (Nilotic?) language that moved south, perhaps in the fourteenth to fifteenth centuries BCE from the Bahr el Ghazal region of today's South Sudan. They conquered Bantu-speaking tribes in what are now Uganda, DRC, Rwanda,

Burundi, and northwest Tanzania. In the process, they lost their own language, as did the Norsemen when they conquered France, exchanging Norse for French, and again when they conquered England, losing French and acquiring Anglo-Saxon.

There might have been limited miscegenation: BaHima men could only marry BaHima women, but could take others as concubines. BaHima women could more easily marry others to become a "fifth columnist" or because the prospective husband was important. They established kingdoms in Bunyoro, Butooro, Ankole, Rwanda, and Burundi.

Other theories have them as coming from Ethiopia, central Sahara, perhaps even Egypt. One theory is that they were derived from a "white" people called the BaChwezi, but more recently it was found that the BaChwezi were in fact "black," and Bantu speakers.

    To learn more:
    The Bahima: http://bit.ly/myUgHistory
    The Tutsi: http://bit.ly/theTutsi
    The Bahutu Manifesto: http://bit.ly/bahutu57
    ☐

Soviet Doctors in Uganda

Clive Mann

When I lived in Soroti, the chief physician at the government hospital was a rather eccentric Irishman, Barney Seale, who was very good at his job, and enjoyed his drink. At different times there were others under him, including a few Asian doctors, an Ulsterman, and two doctors, a married couple, from the Soviet Union. There were a number of private Asian general practitioners in the town. I gathered that Soviet doctors were highly specialized, and our two were no exception. They were both brain surgeons, and apparently had forgotten, or never learned, more general medicine and surgery as might be required in a small hospital such as ours out in the sticks.

I knew a Soviet doctor in Mbale, sometimes having a few drinks with him when I visited a friend in the town. He had very obvious Mongolian features, and spoke quite good English. He would down a bottle of Stolichnaya Blue Label vodka every evening, encouraging me to do the same, explaining that this would avoid a hangover that you would get from only half a bottle. I never tested his theory, preferring to stick to beer. In his cups, he would weep and say that he hated the USSR and did not want to return, but was forced to otherwise his family would be persecuted.

Our couple was rather different, and they had a small daughter. At the time of the incident I am going to relate I had four Israeli agronomists staying at my house while their accommodation was being prepared at Serere Agricultural Station. Only one of the Israelis was truly kosher, and as luck would have it, he arrived at the start of Shabat, alone, the other three followed in a couple of days. I managed to work things out so that he neither sinned nor starved.

On one occasion I took the four to the government rest house for lunch. I had stayed there a while when I first arrived and found the food good. The Russian couple were newly arrived and put up there. It soon became obvious that the Russians had only their mother tongue, but one of the Israelis, Ali, was a real polyglot and soon got chatting to them. Ali was quite a character and disliked very religious Jews. He used to amuse the locals by doing circus tricks on my motorbike.

A few days later, on a Sunday morning, a neighbor, a matron from the hospital, came to my house and asked if I could speak Russian. I answered in the negative, but said I had a Russian speaker living with me. This was the problem. Barney Seale was in Kampala, and the male Russian doctor was on duty. The police chief had contacted the hospital to say that some Karamojong had raided a village in the north of Teso near the Karamoja border and rustled some cattle, and killed three Ateso. They needed to have a doctor to pronounce the unfortunates dead and make a short report on cause, time, locality, and so on. Problem was the Russian doctor, who would have to go, couldn't communicate in any other language than his own.

To cut a long story short, the police provided a LWB Land Rover with about eight policemen as an escort, and the hospital another Land Rover with driver to take Ali, the Russian doctor, and me to the crime scene. The plan being that I would, with my pathetic KiSwahili talk to the locals, who themselves would not know much of the language. I would turn it into English for Ali to produce Russian for the doctor, and similarly in the opposite direction.

On arrival in the village it appeared at first to be deserted. We could see the bodies. I sometimes wonder if I am going to be squeamish in such situations, but I guess spending time visiting friends in the medical school's dissection room at University College London helped. We got out of the vehicles and then a Karamojong, naked as was their custom then, came from behind a hut carrying a spear.

Suddenly with a great revving of the engine and a cloud of dust, the police vehicle sped off with a couple of constables just about making it into the open back. We looked at each other. Our driver was made of sterner stuff and did not abandon us. The Karamojong indicated he wanted us to go over to one of the bodies with him. I put out my hand to him and said "*Ejoku. Tolai?*" The full extent of my Karamojong vocabulary.

He beamed at me, took my hand and told me he was responsible, using the odd KiSwahili word, for the guy's death and showed us where the spear had entered. Ali and I realized that we were not really much use, nor was the driver who was a westerner. The doctor took photographs of the three corpses, and made notes quickly.

Ali, unbeknown to me, had stuffed four bottles of beer into his rucksack. They were now almost as hot as tea, but they were just what Ali, the driver, and I needed as we drove back to Soroti. ☐

Presidential Visit

Clive Mann

In October, 1969, the president of Kenya, Mzee Jomo Kenyatta, made his last ever visit to Kisumu. It was a few months after the assassination by a Kikuyu of Tom Mboya, a prominent Luo. Also it was the home area of Mzee's arch-rival, the Luo Oginga Odinga, who had recently set up a new political party in opposition to KANU.

It was a Saturday morning and Tom Heaton, friend and fellow teacher at Kabarnet Boys' Secondary School, and I were inspecting the school dormitories and noticed some boys were listening very intently to a radio. There was a live broadcast from Kisumu, and they explained the happenings to us. They became increasingly worried and thoughtful.

As the president's motorcade entered Kisumu, stones were thrown, and the crowd began chanting, "*Ndume! Ndume! Ndume!*" (bull! bull! bull!), the symbol of Odinga's new party. Security forces opened fire. Many of the crowd were injured, some killed, some children trampled in the stampede. When Mzee mounted a dais along with the P.C. of Nyanza and Odinga and others, there was more shouting, stone throwing, and shooting. Kenyatta was reported to have used foul language against Luos in general. He was quickly escorted away, carried apparently by a bodyguard, and the motorcade made its way back to Nakuru along empty roads.

Our school boys were very nervous, and worried that there might be a "civil war" and return to conditions similar to Mau Mau days. Most of the pupils in our school were Tugen, or other Kalenjin, but we had a number of Kikuyu boys, and sometimes they would go home to "the reserve" in Central Province for the weekend.

Later in the afternoon a couple of prefects came to see Tom and myself and said that many pupils believed that the Kikuyu boys went home to swear allegiance to Kenyatta, "oathing" they called it, and believed it was similar to the oaths made to Mau Mau. A couple of Kikuyu boys who had not gone home accompanied the prefects. Some firebrands had collected *pangas* and were planning to meet the bus and *matatus* on Sunday that were bringing the boys back to school and to kill them.

Tom and I were the only teachers around, and told the prefects to remain neutral, unless we needed them, and to lie low so as not to incriminate themselves. We locked the Kikuyu boys in one of our houses.

On Sunday afternoon, Tom and I took a Land Rover with some beers to Kabarnet center and waited, occasionally taking a walk along the roads. Tom had a double-twelve bore shotgun concealed in the vehicle in case of serious trouble. The boys all arrived and were accounted for, and we crammed them into the Land Rover. We took them to our houses, where we kept them under lock and key for a few days.

We went singly at times to the dormitories that night and, with the help of prefects, disarmed a few drunken pupils. One had to be tied to his bed until he sobered up. The anticipated trouble didn't really happen. Most of the tension petered out in probably less than a week, and we allowed the Kikuyu boys back into class. ☐

A Grim Mau Mau Legacy

David Sandgren

Sometime during the fall of 1963, a few months after arriving at Giakanja Secondary School just outside of Nyeri, Kenya, I was looking out over my front lawn and saw row upon row of little mounds or bumps in the grass illuminated by the slanted rays of the late afternoon sun.

When I asked a fellow staff member, he said they were graves, and added that the school had been built on the site of a former Mau Mau detention center (Mau Mau Rebellion or the Kenya Emergency, 1952-60), and those who filled the graves had died under interrogation by the security forces.

When I asked my students if they knew that my front yard was filled with graves, every hand shot up! Upon reflection, I realized that I should not have asked the next question, but it just popped out: did they know anyone buried there? At least half the class raised their hands. None volunteered more, nor did I pursue it, thinking that it was traumatic for them.

But, thirty years later when conducting interviews for my collective biography of Kenya's postcolonial elite (*Mau Mau's Children*), I learned more. Several former students told me that they had relatives or neighbors in those graves. Another said that his mother had been held for a year at the center, where she was forced to be the concubine to the security forces.

I also learned that in 1962, when Giakanja officially opened, local people interrupted the ceremony to point out to the visiting dignitaries that the bright future they were forecasting for Giakanja students was only made possible by people's sacrifices during Mau Mau, some of whom were buried beneath their very feet.

Of course, none of this was known to me when I first sighted those bumps in my lawn eighteen months later. □

Memories of Kenyan Independence

David Sandgren

The evening I spent witnessing the ceremonies that created Kenya into a new nation independent from British colonial rule, December 12, 1963, was one of my most memorable experiences ever. I remember arriving at sundown (about 6:30 p.m.) at the temporary stadium built to hold thousands of people and located just west of Nairobi on the Athi Plains.

During the long wait to midnight I remember seeing displays of ethnic dancing and military and police marching bands. But two things especially stand out in my memory from that evening so many years ago.

First, the conversations that were going on around me were so heartwarming and joyous. I had been apprehensive at first when I realized the size of the crowd and the fact that I could not see any white faces. But as I sat there, I began to hear what people were saying around me, such phrases as:

> "I never thought that I would see this day happen in my lifetime."
>
> "I thought that only my children or grandchildren would witness this event."
>
> "We will alright now; our future will be golden!"

People were awed by the moment, optimistic about the future, and peaceful.

The second memory comes as the very moment of independence drew near. As the crowd counted off the last sixty seconds before midnight the British Union Jack was lowered down the pole at the center of the stadium. As the last couple of seconds ticked off, one could see the flag fall onto the ground into the dust and then all the lights went off.

A moment later when the lights came back on, there was the new Kenyan flag at the top of the pole, flying for the first time ever. Not a sound could be heard in the immense stadium as the army band played the Kenyan national anthem for the first time. Tears streamed down people's cheeks as they listened, and when it was finished, a thunderous roar filled the stadium for many minutes. I too was gripped by emotions, knowing that I had witnessed a special moment in Kenya's history. □

Nelson Mandela

Ron Stockton

Jane and I had two encounters with Nelson Mandela. Neither was a close encounter, but both were memorable. The first was in 1965. We were teaching in Kenya, young, no children, and apparently with little common sense. We got the crazy idea of driving down to Cape Town during our six-week winter break. With two friends, one British, one

American, we set off in our ancient VW Beetle with its 110,000 miles of punishing Kenya road experience.

The timing was awful. This was just a month after Ian Smith of Southern Rhodesia had rejected a transition to majority rule and had proclaimed a Unilateral Declaration of Independence (UDI) for that white-ruled British colony. The US Embassy told us the situation was unstable and we should not go, but we ignored them.

UDI had produced an international boycott, which had the unintended result of cutting off Zambia, Rhodesia's northern neighbor, from its oil supply. The British and other countries began running petrol convoys from Dar es Salaam, through Tanzania, to Lusaka. These convoys ran along the Great North Road, which was originally meant to go from Cape Town to Cairo (although it stopped somewhere in East Africa). The convoys were running on dirt roads barely able to handle normal traffic, much less waves of heavy-duty lorries. The roads were quickly demolished.

By the end of the first day, we had lost all four of our hubcaps. The situation did not improve until we got well into Zambia itself.

Given the oil embargo, the roads were not the only problem. We were also concerned about running out of petrol. We decided to take a five-gallon gas can with us in the car, just in case. It sat in the front, between the knees of the person riding shotgun. I shudder when I think back on this. If we had rolled or crashed that car, it would have become an inferno. Fortunately, everything was okay, and we never crashed or even encountered the feared petrol shortage.

This trip, which was only eighteen inches on the map, turned out to be 7,000 miles on the road. We drove constantly, only twice spending more than one night in the same place. We averaged around 250 miles a day, with me doing almost all of the driving.

One of those two-night stops was in Cape Town. This is a wonderful city, straddling the Indian and Atlantic Oceans. Table Mountain rises sharply out of the ocean for a thousand feet and looms above the city. We took the cable car to the top. (It was not until the year 2000 that I managed to climb it, which is a story of its own). As we stood on top of that mountain on that sunny day, we could see Robben Island, a small barren pile of rocks four miles out into the Atlantic Ocean.

The Rivonia trial had found Nelson Mandela and nine fellow ANC defendants guilty of trying to overthrow the white apartheid regime. Mandela had delivered a defiant speech in response to his conviction, acknowledging his activities and affirming his goals, and acknowledging the fact that he was facing a possible death sentence:

> "This is the struggle of the African people, inspired by their own suffering and experience. It is a struggle for the right to live. I have cherished the ideal of a democratic and free society, in which all persons live together in harmony and with equal opportunity. It is an ideal which I hope to live for and achieve. But, if needs be, my Lord, it is an ideal for which I am prepared to die."

The accused had been given life sentences and sent to that desolate place. Standing on that most beautiful mountain peak, it gave Jane and me pause to realize that this great heroic man was down there breaking rocks or doing whatever it was that prisoners did on Robben Island.

Twenty-seven years after his incarceration, Mandela emerged from prison in 1990 as a triumphant hero. As we watched his release on television that Sunday morning, we were thrilled. No one had seen any image of him since his imprisonment. His black hair had turned white, but his back was straight, and he was as determined as ever to create a multi-racial South Africa with a constitutional democracy. Releasing him and decriminalizing the ANC represented an implicit commitment to create a majority-rule political system.

The inevitable "all races" election occurred in 1994, and Mandela became President of the "New South Africa," as it was called. Very quickly he was the premier world leader, a notch above everyone else. His political instincts were perfect and he had an inner strength that made him unshakable.

I am of that school of political analysis that sees leaders as an outgrowth of the power structures that produce them. Their personal qualities are important but the structures of power are often so strong that the outcomes would not be much different if someone else had been chosen. With Mandela, the models went out the window. I had taught a class on South Africa for some time and had always predicted (along with Nadine Gordimer in her wonderful novel July's People) that the white population would never negotiate and the republic would go up in flames, with enormous human suffering. Mandela and Bishop Desmond Tutu made sure that did not happen. They were indispensable men in the salvation of their country.

Our second encounter with Mandela was when he visited Detroit in 1990. He was an international hero, but not every stop on his six-city American trip went smoothly. Ted Koppel's *Nightline* held a ninety-minute prime-time town meeting. Early on, Koppel recognized two prominent Jewish leaders who said that while American Jews supported the liberation movement, they were concerned that Mandela had received Yasser Arafat, Colonel Khadafi, and Fidel Castro. There was "profound disappointment" at the "amorality" of Mandela's position (These words were met with boos from the audience).

Mandela did not mention the elephant in the room, that Israel, with winks and nods from the Reagan Administration, had maintained a very close security relationship with South Africa (Ariel Sharon was a point man) and had helped South Africa evade the arms embargo. Congressman Howard Wolpe of Michigan, chair of the African Affairs Subcommittee—and my professor one summer—had played a major role in getting the Israelis to stop that transfer.

Mandela looked straight ahead throughout the whole interview, not making eye-contact with Koppel. To say that Koppel was disoriented would be an understatement. To the comments, Mandela responded with his firm but non-confrontational style:

"There are people who think their enemies should be our enemies." Then he continued: "As we struggle for our freedom, they supported us to the hilt with more than rhetoric, and we will not forget them."

When Koppel suggested that Mandela be more nuanced in his words lest he offend America's Jews and Cubans, Mandela's response brought down the house:

"For anybody who changes his principles depending on whom he is dealing with, that is not a man who can lead a nation."

Mandela had been friendly to South African Jews. He had noted once that several had made a "particularly outstanding contribution" to the liberation movement, which was true. He specifically mentioned that as a young lawyer the only law firm that would give him a job was a Jewish firm. On the other hand, he had been critical of Israel, saying that they would never be secure if they clung to "narrow chauvinistic interests."

For a man who had spent his life fighting white domination of his country, there was no authentic alternative to this position. He had also met with Yasser Arafat, then the demonized head of the PLO. Mandela had said to Arafat at their Lusaka meeting, "We live under a unique form of colonialism." The common form to which he alluded was that settler populations had come into the land and become indigenous.

I saw this as a very positive statement, that the settler populations must be accepted, but the Israeli government of Mr. Shamir saw such a comparison as a serious threat. Now, to Koppel, Mandela called Arafat a "comrade in arms" and said that, "We identify with the PLO because like the ANC they are fighting for self-determination." Only his enormous stature saved him from being savaged for his integrity.

An equally difficult situation was in Miami where he was snubbed because he had greeted Castro and made friendly comments about him. City officials would not even welcome Mandela at the airport. He was received by a group of community leaders.

Given these incidents, his triumphant reception in Detroit was a welcome relief. Mandela had been razor-focused on this trip. He was asked once if he had anything to say about the treatment of black people in this country. He said he was here to establish strong relations with America in the ongoing struggle for liberation, but, "It would not be proper for me to delve into the controversial issues that are tearing this country apart." Ouch!

In Detroit, the only place big enough to host him was Tiger Stadium. There was no way that Jane and I were going to miss that event, in spite of the traffic jams. We went down early, paid our ten dollars and got our seats. Everyone was there: Mayor Coleman Young, UAW President Owen Biber, Aretha Franklin, Stevie Wonder, and Isaiah Thomas. Jesse Jackson was in the audience. When he walked in, all eyes turned to look. He had a proud, majestic manner, towering a head above those with him.

Mandela arrived with his strikingly beautiful wife Winnie, the Mother of the Revolution, as she was called. This was before she betrayed him with another man and he divorced her. On that night, they looked like the power couple to end all power couples. During the decades when he had been in prison, Winnie had defiantly stood up for Nelson and spoken the words he could not speak.

Now Mandela delivered a speech designed to inspire and please. He did not mention how the Americans had tipped off the South African secret police as to his location back in 1962 and had enabled them to arrest him. (President Clinton officially apologized for this later, as did the US Congress. John Conyers sponsored that resolution.) He did not mention that the Reagan administration had permitted Israel to transfer American weapons to South Africa to undercut the arms embargo. Instead, he said that the prisoners had been aware of the divestment movements on American campuses and knew that the American people were with them.

I was pleased with that comment since I had been active in the pro-boycott International Defense and Aid Fund, an ANC-support group banned in South Africa. I had published an article in *Transafrica*, the ANC-linked journal and had once even spoken to the UM Regents urging them to sell university stocks in companies that traded with or had facilities in South Africa. One of the Regents explained to me that their investments were building up the black middle class and heading off a bloody revolution. I knew that was a foolish observation on several levels, but was grateful that he did not pat me on the head, which was the spirit of his response.

That evening Mandela also said that the prisoners on Robben Island had been encouraged by the music of Motown. He even quoted from "What's Going On," by Marvin Gaye.

Whatever the reality of life on Robben Island, on that wonderful evening, everything he said received loud cheers.

As Jane and I walked out, we were stopped by a reporter from a local black radio station. I would like to think that we were chosen because we looked wise and insightful, but it may also have been an effort to find a conventional-looking white couple to say something for the record. Jane spoke first:

> "Twenty-seven years ago we stood on top of Table Mountain and looked out into the Atlantic Ocean. We saw Robben Island and realized that Nelson Mandela was there in a cell, serving a life sentence. Now he is a free man and he is here in triumph."

I was stunned at the eloquence of her statement. If I had spent an hour thinking about it, I could not have come up with anything so powerful. I could see no reason to continue the interview and started to walk away, but then the microphone was pushed in my direction. I just mumbled a few words: "Nelson Mandela is the greatest black man of the twentieth century, and as a white person I am proud to be here to honor him."

As we walked away, Jane said to me, "I know what that was. That was a sound bite."

Of course, she was right. The radio station ignored her eloquence and replayed my short comment over and over during the next day. At times, life is just not fair. □

Encounters with Amin

Ron Stockton

I crossed paths with Idi Amin three times. The first was in 1966 when I was living in Machakos, Kenya. Milton Obote, the prime minister in neighboring Uganda, had just crushed his rival, the Kabaka, with General Amin's help. The thought that the military could unleash such violence was frightening. Kenya was very peaceful, and we were forty miles from Nairobi, but still, the headlines were nervous-making.

One Saturday afternoon, I was in my front yard on the school compound. The road twisted through the school grounds with the school in the front and teachers' houses along the road farther in. My house was the very last one. I looked up and saw a large military lorry coming down the one-track road. Fear is irrational, but as that lorry got closer and closer to my house, with nowhere to go after me, I wondered what was going to happen next. It pulled up in front of my house, and a large, uniformed man jumped out.

I was so relieved when he said, "Sir, where is the football match?"

My second encounter was in 1970 when I was returning to Kenya to do doctoral research. I stopped in Kampala to see some friends at the university and to get whatever advice I could on doing field work. This was a time when armed gangs, known as *kondos*, were running wild. They would often close off a street in Kampala or surround a house and do great damage. Many people were killed. I spoke to a Kenyan groundskeeper at Makerere who told me that in Kenya thugs would rob you for your bicycle, but in Kampala, they would kill you for your pots and pans. He was living in fear.

That night I slept on the sofa in my friend Jack's living room. The next morning, he came in from an inspection walk and said there were footprints outside the sofa window.

"Apparently, they saw you and decided to come back another time when the situation was more predictable."

My friends were living in fear.

My third encounter was a year later when my research in Kenya was nearing its end. Jane and I (with our small boys) decided to take a trip to Kampala. We were driving in Jinja, an industrial city on the Nile. Idi Amin had just overthrow Milton Obote. He was rounding up the *kondos* and dropping their bodies into the river. The crocodiles were very happy. In fact, a lot of people were happy. This was a time when Amin was riding high, and the army was riding high. Civil liberties be damned, the *kondos* were getting theirs. But Amin was also rounding up politicians who criticized him and judges who released criminals for lack of evidence. And the army was doing what it wanted.

We were driving through Jinja late in the afternoon, looking for someplace to get a meal. I was paying no attention to the fact that there was a military jeep behind me. Even if I had been paying attention, I would not have known that in that environment anyone with any sense pulled over when a military jeep was behind you. The jeep accelerated around us, pulled sharply in front of me, and forced my Beetle off the road. I was dragged out of the car and interrogated.

"Who are you? What are you doing in Uganda? What are those things in your bags?"

Jane was standing there mute, holding Ted, who was one, while Greg, four, sat in the car. I thought to myself, I am going to be beaten unconscious right here in front of my family. I told the soldier I was looking for a place to eat. He seemed skeptical. He grabbed one of the bags and said, "What is in this?"

When he opened it, he was greeted by a smelly diaper that had been left on top. He threw it down, got in the jeep, and drove away

Years later, a colleague offered a course on the Holocaust. One of the readings said how people in the camps had to learn quickly how to behave around the guards. I told him this observation was wrong. When someone has complete power over you, the power to destroy you, with no consequences, you do not have to learn how to behave. You know instinctively what to do. You become small, deferential, quiet. You lower your voice and your eyes. Your words slow down. You agree to everything.

Groveling is an inadequate word. I knew that if I were beaten, there would be a formal protest from the American embassy, and nothing more. If I disappeared, there would be a short news item in the *New York Times*, and nothing more.

And I learned that in a situation such as this, salvation can come from unexpected quarters. I have always been grateful to my small son for his contribution to our family safety. ☐

JFK Assassination

Nola Stover

With Sputnik and the dawn of the Space Age, I became especially interested in science and mathematics, with a burning desire to be of service to mankind. Racism was very common in those days, but I did not embrace the way most viewed different ethnic groups.

Upon graduation in 1961 with a bachelor's degree in education, I saw an announcement for the Teachers for East Africa Project and became very interested. However, having already applied for a teaching position at the Indiana Soldiers' and Sailors' Children's Home, I did not apply for the project.

Two years passed, and I saw another announcement for TEA. This time I applied and became a part of the 1963 group. The TEA project enabled young Africans to meet Americans and realize that we all have many things in common. They were very passionate about education. And we, young Americans, benefited in a positive way. Not only were we exposed to another language, but also our horizons were broadened and we became more open and accepting of people from other countries and ethnic groups.

I have many memories of this experience. One which stands out is the day I went to the Standard Bank in Mwanza, Tanzania. Every week each teacher had one-half day in the schedule to run errands. That day in November, 1963, I went to the bank and saw a sign on the door: closed in honor of the late president of the United States of America. I rushed from the bank back to Rosary College to see if anyone knew what had happened to our president. That evening we gathered with the Maryknoll nuns to listen to the Voice of America. What a shock when we heard that President Kennedy had been assassinated.

I have a firm belief that projects like TEA are very important for the development of our American youth. Meeting people of other nations can broaden their minds, dreams, and accomplishments. In this way, we lay foundation stones for peace. ☐

VI: Tributes

Jim Blair's *Tribute to Frank Ballance, II* was written in response to Henry Hamburger's tribute to Frank. Henry's *Tribute to Frank Ballance* is, in essence, tribute I, which Jim acknowledges as eloquent. His own tribute exhibits the same quality.

Ann Dickinson's *EA11 Revisited* is a salute to the van travelers through Uganda, Kenya, and Tanzania on the reunion trip to East Africa that followed the alumni reunion at Teachers College in June 2011. It is a light, efficient piece: she likens the two dozen travelers to "AARPers on Survivor, the castaway reality show," commenting, in turn, on the general compatibility and cooperation that were the natural orientation of the travelers and, respectfully, on their eccentricities that made the trip the fine occasion it surely was.

Pat Colby's remembrance of a student and Leal Dickson's of a colleague show strength of character we might not have initially anticipated when posted to our first schools. Bill Jones deftly connects his own Sunday school teacher with a Ugandan elementary school teacher speaking a language he did not understand but with an affect which he certainly did.

In this section:

Jerry Atkin	*In Memoriam: Julius Nyerere* • 385
Betty Coxson	*TEEA Tour Sparks Amazing Art Career* • 390
Pat Colby	*Ruth* • 392
Ann Dickinson	*EA11 Revisited* • 394
Leal Dickson	*Josephat Coelestine, Educator and Colleague* • 396
Brooks Goddard	*Sharifa Zawawi, Mwalimu wa Kiswahili* • 397
Henry Hamburger	*Tribute to Frank Ballance* • 398
Jim Blair	*Tribute to Frank Ballance, II* • 399
Sharon Hepburn	*Headmistress Helen Inkpen* • 400
Moses L. Howard	*Suttee and Mr. Chandra* • 401
Bill Jones	*Eyes Full of Light* • 407
Dagmar Telfer Muthamia	*Meru Names* • 409
George Pollock	*Child of Africa: Story of an Mtoto Mzuri* • 410
Bernard Sauers	*See If You Can Find This Man* • 411
Lee Smith	*Sue Johannot, Special Memories* • 412
Larry Thomas	*Moira Harbottle, Mother to Many* • 412

In Memoriam: Julius Nyerere

Jerry Atkin

Julius Nyerere, the former president of Tanzania and a personal hero of mine, died yesterday, of leukemia, in a hospital in London. He died far from the Africa he had loved and had given his life to. Nyerere was a great man, a man whose name you could mention in the same sentence with Mandela's and not be embarrassed. I met him when he was in his early forties, just a few years after independence for Tanganyika and right after the merger with Zanzibar that yielded the nation of Tanzania.

I was finishing a graduate teaching course at Makerere College in Kampala and Nyerere, as Chancellor of the University of East Africa, was there to confer an honorary degree on Jomo Kenyatta. Those of us who would be teaching in Tanzania met informally with him. I was stunned by his energy and vitality, his sparkling eyes and teasing style of talking to us, especially when he was speaking Swahili.

Two years later I would see him at a town meeting in Tabora. He had aged a decade in the two years that had passed. His hair was gray at the temples and the wrinkles around his eyes were no longer from laughter, they were the badge of exhaustion. Independence always creates expectations far beyond the existing resources to meet them. But, he never gave up. I would have followed him anywhere.

He was trying to create a communitarian socialist state based on tribal values in a sea of neo-colonialism. In those days the US did not view the third world as a giant sweatshop and engine for super-profits. It was viewed as a giant storehouse of raw materials and an engine for super-profits. A few diamonds, a small coffee-growing region, and fields of sisal did not add up to much for Tanzania, a country with six graduate teachers, and no all-weather roads connecting the southern and northern sections of the country.

Working with one of the poorest countries in the world, Nyerere squared off with the US and the old colonial powers to try and create a just society. And he never gave up. Later he would acknowledge that his attempts to collectivize farming were a mistake. Not because it was wrong, but because it wouldn't work without resources. There was no escape from the world economic forces that dictated then, just as they dictate now, what could be allowed to exist and what had to be destroyed as a threat to profit, to progress. And still he tried.

When he felt the members of Parliament, all elected from the single party, TANU (Tanganyikan African National Union), were out of touch with the people, he made them walk the two hundred miles through the countryside to the annual party meeting in Mwanza. Hot and dusty, they stayed with the people in the villages, re-experiencing the real conditions in the country, not those of the city and the educated civil service class, a class called in East Africa, the Wa-Benzi (people of the Mercedes Benz). How they must have hated it!

Later that year, while I was still teaching at a day secondary school (just down the road from the boarding school that had been built for the sons of chiefs by the British), students at the university in Dar es Salaam, influenced by colonial ideas of entitlement, went on strike when they were asked to share rooms. Nyerere thought that perhaps they had forgotten that they were there to help build a nation and not assure their own privilege. He suggested that it would be a good idea if they all went back to their villages to remember why they were there at the university. He sent them down and shut the university for the rest of the year.

In my school, students complained bitterly about the mistreatment of the students. They, after all, like ghetto youth hoping for an NBA contract, saw access to this privileged class as their ticket out of the village. In a totally futile and pointless gesture, I threw them out of my classes for a day.

Nyerere turned down foreign aid when there were heavy political strings attached. He refused the German offer to build a sugar factory in the Kilembero Valley in exchange for a naval base on Zanzibar. A principled stand, but one that hampered development. How much of your soul can you sell before you lose it in a hostile takeover? I have no answer to this question, but I do know that it is a question. This is not a trivial distinction. Julius Nyerere knew that too, and the compromises of governing must have eaten away at him, like bilharzia ate away at the guts of the children in the countryside. Would he have accepted the deal if they were offering health care?

Nyerere was also one of the great Pan-African leaders. The national anthem of Tanzania does not say, "God bless Tanzania, or our noble leader *Mwalimu* (Teacher) Nyerere," it says, "*Mungu ibariki Afrika* (God bless Africa), and another version of the song was sung by the ANC in South Africa. The ties with the South African struggle were close. When I arrived in Africa, Nelson Mandela had only been in jail for a year or two (I grew old as he grew wise) and Tanzania, under Nyerere's leadership, had become a haven for refugees from the underground war against apartheid. Kurasini, a school for the children of these refugees, was set up in Dar es Salaam. One of the few regrets of my life is that I didn't teach there when I had the opportunity.

After Nyerere stepped down as the leader of Tanzania, one of three African leaders (including Mandela) to step down peacefully and voluntarily when the time came, he continued to involve himself in the work of the Organization of African Unity, which he had helped to found, and worked tirelessly for peace and justice on the continent. In the year before his death he was instrumental in negotiating an end to the civil war in Burundi. Until the end, he worked for Africa, for what he loved, for what he believed in.

My years in Africa were like a dream bounded on either side by nightmares. The year before I went to Africa, John Kennedy was assassinated; the year after I returned, Martin Luther King Jr. would draw his last breath alone on a motel balcony in Memphis, Tennessee after marching with garbage workers demanding jobs with justice. In the same year, Robert Kennedy would also die, not alone, seen by millions of people tuned in for news of the California Primary. In the years between 1963 and 1968, while I was in Africa, Malcolm X would also be assassinated. His death passed unnoticed on the high savannah five hundred miles west of Dar es Salaam.

While our country was being torn apart by our own struggle against apartheid, and a burgeoning war that would leave us dazed and confused, Nyerere was trying to bring something new to birth. Inheriting a legacy of poverty and colonialism, the deck was stacked against him. He was naïve, really, to believe that he could he could get out from under the lion's paw. But he knew that if the people of Tanzania and the rest of Africa were to have a good life, it would have to be built out of something other than self-interest and unbridled competition.

I want to know if Nyerere, one of the planet's best and brightest, really died of a broken heart. Had he seen too much murder in the name of tribalism? Too much murder wearing the guise of civil war? Was the genocide in Rwanda the stake driven through his heart? Or did he know that he had done the best he could? That the struggle will last for generations before Africa can throw off the yoke of economic imperialism and the ruling ideas? Did he see the good in the common citizen, however confused, that convinced him that he was on the right side of history, the side of the people? Did he know how much he was loved? How many lives he had touched, including mine? Was it enough? I have selfish reasons for wanting to know this.

If Bill Clinton had died, I don't think I would feel anything. My grief is almost always for the nameless, those whose stories rarely find their way into the papers or onto the television screens. The real heroes of this world who simply take the hand life deals them and do the best they can. In spite of my general immunity to the tragedies of the rich and famous that are served with our morning coffee, when I saw the headline announcing Nyerere's death, I cried. The tears, I think, were for this man whom I had loved and believed in, for the suffering continent of Africa trampled beneath the flashing hooves of three of the Four Horsemen of the Apocalypse (War, Famine, Pestilence), and for my own lost innocence.

I dig through my desk drawer, find the picture taken in late spring, 1965. I am the young, skinny, white guy, wearing tight pants that must have been an embarrassment, even then. Without my glasses, I am squinting toward the camera. I am standing on the verandah of an abandoned army barracks thirty miles outside Kampala. The paint is flaking, and the adobe is falling off around the doors and windows. To my left are a handful of refugees from the civil war in the Sudan, a civil war that continues thirty years later... some of the anonymous grief that touches me more than the death of a princess or the son of an assassinated president. They pose for the camera with knowing smiles, guarded looks.

Trying to read my own prose, I see someone who is very unsure of himself, trying to look cool, and failing. There is just enough distance between me and the refugees to make it clear who is the teacher and who are the students, who can return to America and who can't. The body language speaks volumes. I mean well, but I am ignorant as a stone about the realities of war, of hunger, what is means to piss blood because of intestinal parasites, what it feels like to have an endless future going nowhere.

I taught English once a week in this crumbling building in a clearing at the end of an unpaved washboard road that rattled my teeth when I drove it. Many of these "school boys" were guerilla fighters in exile. They lived on one meal a day and when they were sick... they were sick. No doctor came this far into the bush. Once, when I came to teach, they were playing soccer on a short field, using a dead rat for a ball. This was part of the reality that Julius Nyerere spent his life trying to change, so that young people would have better lives than this, so they would have a chance to go to school, to eat more than once a day, to be treated for their diseases, and never know war. It is something worth living for.

Julius Nyerere is dead of leukemia, or possibly a broken heart, at seventy-seven. We are poorer for his death, richer for his life. □

> Note: Julius Nyerere, first President of Tanzania (1961-1985), known as *Mwalimu* or "teacher," his earlier profession, died in 1999.

TEEA Tour Sparks Amazing Art Career

Betty Coxson

When Byron Birdsall answered TEEA's advertisement in 1966 recruiting teachers with five years of experience plus a master's degree, he could not have imagined the dramatic change that was about to take place in his life and career.

After a brief orientation at Columbia University's Teachers College in New York, a group of about thirty were on their way to teaching posts in East Africa. He and his wife were assigned to Kyambogo Teacher Training College in Kampala, Uganda.

There Byron met Eldon Katter, art professor and fellow TEEA tutor from an earlier year. Eldon and his wife, Adrienne, had signed up with TEEA after returning from a Peace Corps stint in Ethiopia. Through the friendship that developed, Eldon detected such exceptional creative talent in his colleague that he urged Byron to arrange a solo showing of his art work at a gallery in Kampala. That was all the motivation Byron needed to go into town to stock up on all the brushes and paint tubes he could find in Kampala.

By the time set for the showing, Byron had amassed over thirty paintings, mostly of local subject matter. His prodigious work quickly exhausted the art supply in Kampala. Since there was no white paint needed for oil painting, he turned to woodcuts and added another sixteen items to the show.

Needless to say, the Birdsalls never "went home again." Wherever they went, Byron painted. He held more than 150 one-man shows in the following years. The couple sampled life in many parts of the world including South America, American Samoa, Russia, and Hawaii. In 1975, they settled down in Alaska, where he became a master in portraying ice and snow formations so real they could almost inflict frostbite. When I met a couple who had recently moved to Iowa from Alaska, the first question I asked was, "Do you know of Byron Birdsall?" They lit up with recognition. They knew of him, even if not face to face.

Besides Eldon Katter, Byron credits one other person with gently nudging him into a career in art. It was a lady who sat behind him in church where his father was the preacher. Preachers' kids are generally expected to be models of decorum, but little boys are not always mindful of that unreasonable notion. Hoping to head off trouble for the little boy, the lady reached over the pew to hand him a tablet and some colors to keep him quiet. I wonder if that lady ever learned the happy result of her compassionate gesture toward a little boy with an exploding need to create.

Byron's lifelong work is incredibly diverse. Once his reputation was established, he was recruited to do all sorts of projects. In 1992 he was commissioned by the Postal Service to design a stamp commemorating the building of the Alcan Highway. His book entitled *Alaska and Other Exotic Worlds*, published in 1993, contains a collection of 100 full-color images.

In 2006 and 2007, Byron was working for Saltchuk—a conglomerate of member companies delivering goods and services mostly by sea—to gather material for a book. Saltchuk means salt water. He took hundreds of photos showing the work of members in the shipping industry. From the photos, Byron painted copies of the photos in oil. There are over 130 paintings in the book, *People of the Saltchuk*, plus the journal he kept from his photo shoots at designated locations. It was a monumental task and the resulting volume is a work of art in itself.

According to Mike Garvey, retired CEO of Saltchuk,

> "Art inspires us to act on the better angels of our nature. In this book, the art reminds us of the beauty of where we work, the adventure in which we are engaged, the people with whom we are privileged to work, and the importance of the work to the greater society. It calls on us to reject cynicism, to overcome boredom, and to rededicate ourselves to professionalism and a belief in a bright future. And no matter what our particular role, we are an integral part of a team."

> Continuing to address the Saltchuk team, Garvey explained that the book was intended as a thank you gift to all employees

and personnel who were members of Saltchuk. "While one purpose of this book is to encourage you to consider yourself part of a larger group, another purpose is to let you know that we, at Saltchuk, consider ourselves part of your business and have a long-term commitment to its future."

The book was a tribute to the ethics and quality of the men and women of Saltchuk. Of all the artists Saltchuk could have chosen, it was clear from Garvey's explanation that the people of Saltchuk chose Byron, not only for his talent and skill, but also for his character which conformed so well with the stated ideals of Saltchuk. □

Ruth

Pat Colby

Shortly after my appointment to Machakos African Girls' School in Kenya, the headmistress informed me that three Kikuyu girls in the Form 3 to which I had been assigned had bad reputations. Whether these reputations had evolved during their earlier days at the school or had traveled with them upon acceptance into the high school, I do not know. Of the three, Ruth Muwara, was particularly secretive and untrustworthy.

In the weeks and months that followed, I became very close to the Form 3 girls as we interpreted the works of H.G. Wells, Alfred Lord Tennyson, Oliver Goldsmith, and Shakespeare. We examined the complexities of English grammar, wrote compositions, and bonded during the evening prep hours and my visits to each dormitory on Friday nights. We shared the weekends, when once a month, one of the teachers had to provide entertainment by way of guest speakers, film or group activities.

Ruth and her two friends were initially reserved and shy, but as time passed, I found in Ruth a quiet kind of leadership and intellectual curiosity. I saw qualities of behavior that did not match her "bad reputation."

It is true: she was less outgoing than some of her classmates, but I saw they listened to her and admired her. At the end of the year, my girls would lead the school in the roles of prefects and head girl in Form 4.

The headmistress asked for recommendations, and she accepted all my suggestions eagerly, except the naming of Ruth Muwara as one of the prefects. By then, I knew Ruth well and believed strongly in her potential. I argued passionately that she should be given a chance. She was put on the prefects list, and I was elated. A week later, the names of the new school leaders were announced. In her reserved way, Ruth received the news in what must have been considerable surprise. She knew how the headmistress had perceived her in the past.

That afternoon following the end of classes, I walked up the hill to my little house, the big jacaranda trees in glorious bloom on either side of the dirt road. By degrees, I sensed someone was following me. I looked back several times, and finally noted the flash of a red school uniform behind a jacaranda. Tired from a long day, I entered my little house and gratefully closed the door. Yet, I was curious about that uniformed figure. I looked out the window so as not be seen and saw Ruth. She was standing five yards from the house in full view. She did not come to the door nor did she seem to want anything other than what she was doing–making her presence known.

Each time I peeked out the window, she was still there; standing, facing the house, paying a kind of tribute to its resident. Minutes slipped by. Intrigued, I watched as she remained in the same position, unmoving, for a long, long time. Then, as magically as she had appeared, she slipped away into tall grass and purple jacarandas. To this day, it remains the sweetest thank-you I have ever received. □

EA11 Revisited

Ann Dickinson

"It was great to watch how both lion and buffalo worked as teams, with many coordinated moving parts: just like us on the trip, if I remember!" This comment by David Newbury, upon seeing my game park video, reveals the dynamics of our EA11 group.

Imagine two dozen AARPers on *Survivor*, the castaway reality show, where teams actually choose monikers like Lion and Buffalo, and you get the general idea. On *Survivor*, people vote each other off the island (bossy ones first to go), something our group would never do! Okay, it's true I got tossed off the bus for bossiness at the behest of my dear husband, but that doesn't count since it was to my advantage: I got to join lion van to view animals in daylight, while buffalo bus backtracked to watch nighttime roadside welding. In any case, no matter what we had to endure, we all survived...so here's a salute to our group:

To Betty and Sam for hosting a great welcome party, the memory of which sustained us through not-so-great times ahead, i.e., excruciatingly long border crossings. At one crossing Sam had the smarts to head back over the border for necessary paperwork, saving us from languishing forever in no-man's land.

To Mary Ann, on her first African trip, for expressing an enthusiasm that helped the rest of us to see Africa in a fresh light. To Gus for giving new meaning to the word unflappable (Gus would never get tossed off the bus).

To Andrea for proving that lost luggage doesn't preclude being a fashionista. Her Pan Am training (travel in a nice outfit with accessories in your carry on) paid off. As did her stint as her sorority's song leader: her memory of singalong tunes seemed to shorten one of our many long nighttime bus rides.

To Neil for bringing his New York savvy to Africa and for doing the *polepole* with Babu Paul up Mt. Meru.

To David and Kathy, armed with coping skills developed during decades in Africa, for stepping up during hard decision making sessions, and for helping us out of tight spots (like roadside welding).

To Jan and John for being good sports no matter how many inconveniences they encountered.

To Patrick, whose energetic hide-and-seek with Sipi Falls's kids enabled us to get a glimpse of African children in delight mode.

To Eddie, who once befriended a student, who in turn befriended us by arranging housing near the border, which spared us hours of night driving in buffalo bus to Kakamega.

To Pat Gill for being a role model by tirelessly working to improve East African education. With her cane-stool handy, she was up for all adventures and misadventures.

To Nola, my Rosary College-Nganza buddy, for continuing to teach homebound students full time in LV's school system. Her unforgettable trip is bound to come in handy when working with those students who all face difficult situations.

To Bill (*Puleeez!*) for entertaining us with his witty insights and gymnastic feats, and in his more serious moments for encouraging reading... and exhorting roadside kids not to repeat biased words they've learned from rap songs.

To Pat Colby for bringing sunny California to our group with her smile and upbeat nature, and for graciously joining Bill as our spokesperson at the schools.

To Sharon, whose interest in Africa and its people (and the antics of her fellow travelers) kept her constantly at her notebook. We await publication of her travel memoirs trusting that names will be changed to protect the innocent.

To Brooks for taking blame for every mishap, a leader's plight. It follows then that he take credit for our timely presence in Ngorogoro—our arrival much delayed by mishaps—at the exact moment a lion pride decided to take on a buffalo herd, an encounter our guide claimed was the best in his six years of leading safaris.

Finally, hats off to Jerry (Hello...o...oh! the guy whose hat never left his head), to Joan, to Teresa and Ray for arranging suitable transport into Ngorogoro Crater, sparing us from merely peering over its edge and imagining the wonders below. My sense is that the young adults in that team weren't as likely as us AARPers to simply complain and accept; they thought outside the box and Voila! We were all off buffalo bus.

> TEA-Alumni sponsored three trips to East Africa: First, in 2003 starting in Kampala; second, in 2005 starting in Dar es Salaam; and third, starting in Kampala. All were "led" by Brooks Goddard. ☐

Josephat Coelestine, Educator and Colleague
Leal Dickson

My first day on the job at Nyakato Secondary School, Bukoba, Tanzania in March, 1963, was traumatic. The headmaster, J.E.D. Swatman, handed me a timetable of five biology and two chemistry classes and told me the students would be waiting for me at 8:15 the next morning after their return from a short break. He then introduced me to Josephat Coelestine, the education ministry assigned lab assistant who took me around to see the biology, chemistry, and physics classrooms/labs. The state of those rooms was shocking, but Josephat assured me that he could do any preparation needed for my classes.

And true to his word he always did so. Josephat had the materials we needed there and set up. While the first class was progressing he assembled the materials for the second and so on throughout the day. He knew where to gather local plant and animal materials. When we studied kidney structure, he knew just whom to contact at the local butcher shop to get fresh specimens. And he always anticipated the needs well ahead. It did not take me long to realize that Josephat was adept and astute in helping me asses the needs of students in the labs as well. He had been doing this long enough that he could point out what students should be seeing and studying, yet he always deferred to me as the authority. I soon learned to trust him completely.

Josephat was the kind of person who was easy to be around, and we soon formed a close friendship that we have carried for years. When our son was born in 1964, he brought my wife two chickens as a gift. It was a local custom to give a gift of chickens to women after giving birth. He was an invaluable help on the collecting excursions we did together to find materials for use in the lab.

I had an interest in snakes at that time, and Josephat was a great conduit for news of where a certain snake was to be found or one that local villagers had killed. On one occasion I kept a good-sized puff adder in a cage in the empty servant's quarters behind our house and he helped me collect live rodents for feeding it. Another time he brought me a green *momba* that had been killed. And we went together to get a twelve-foot python, which I skinned with his help.

I was not the only TEA teacher who relied on Josephat for help; fellow TEA teacher Richard Lemke also found him to be a great help in setting up physics demonstrations and experiments. Over the many years of his career I know that Josephat assisted many TEA science teachers.

On two recent visits to Nyakato School we learned that Josephat has become a leader in his village, spearheading an effort to build a grade school near Nyakato. He is an inspirational friend who continues to aid TEEA in our work at Nyakato. □

Sharifa Zawawi, Mwalimu wa Kiswahili
Brooks Goddard

Something here should be said of Sharifa Zawawi, who taught many of us Swahili at Teachers College. Myself, I shall never forget her and her energy. And we were learning from a Zanzibari by way of Oman. As

Shakespeare said, "She was short but she was fierce." Fierce in that "I'm going to teach you, you better learn" sense.

I recall that she spotted someone reading the yellow-and-black colored cover of *Teach Yourself Swahili* and told the miscreant to put the book down, that that book was not her equal. Sharifa didn't come into a room, she burst into it. The energy level went way up, and it is by lifelong regret that I never mastered her Swahili, much less the nuances that surrounded the word "*bibi.*"

One of her other students commented:

> "She assured me that I spoke Swahili with an Italian accent for which I loved her. As luck would have it, I was posted to Kampala and Sharifa's excellence as a teacher would not be judged by my ability to speak Swahili in the kingdom of Buganda." □

Tribute to Frank Ballance

Henry Hamburger

Today I visited the first officer of TEA: Reunion Planner Frank Ballance, who brought off the gathering we now call DC01, an event remarkable for having taken place at all, coming as it did nine days after 9/11, 2001. There we were, 130 strong despite chaos in the airlines and there was Frank, rising to the occasion. There too were two ambassadors, a fabulous memorabilia room, and more.

Four years later, when Brooks Goddard so ably organized for us another great event, Dar-05, it was Frank who got Tanzania's President Mkapa, his old Makerere buddy, to address us. The next morning there we all were in the Dar newspapers, in English, in Swahili, even in photos—our Warholian fifteen minutes.

Today's little reunion (June 21, 2014) was not the triumph that these earlier events had been. Frank has succumbed to a stage of life one cannot but dread; he is now diagnosed with sixth-stage Alzheimer's which has made him a round-the-clock responsibility, one bravely assumed by his companion and law partner, Sopon Geramethakul.

The old Frank is largely gone, but when there was talk of eating, out popped "Chakula!" and though I could not elicit any other Swahili, he still has a bit of German. Me: *Habari?* Him: *Wunderbar.*

His grip is strong, but his language is muttered and mostly off-point. Still when I mentioned TEA, he said "Teachers for East Africa," and said we were wonderful people, though with little affect. There was little or no response to talk of the old days in Africa, and none to my mention of the stories written by his students that I know he was saving for a book of then-and-now stories. Sadly, too, he could not react to prompting about his role in the marvelous DC01.

So here's to Frank and the things he did for us. Raise a glass for him sometime soon. ☐

Tribute to Frank Ballance, II
Jim Blair

I was stationed in Lushoto, Tanzania about ninety miles from Tanga where Frank Ballance taught. I often stayed with Frank while visiting Tanga. We both coached track teams at our respective schools. I took a track team to Tanga, and Frank and Quinn Buckner brought their team to Lushoto. Frank had been accepted to Yale law school and encouraged me to apply to law school while still in Tanzania. But for his friendship I would never have applied and my life would have been very different.

When Ed Schmidt "found" me two years ago, I contacted Frank. I wondered why he did not respond to my e-mail. It seemed so unlike him. Now I know why. I wish I had the words to say something profound about Frank's disease (that is, Alzheimer's disease). The best I can do is to thank you for taking the time to visit with Frank. Maybe somehow he appreciates your effort. I know I do. If you see him again, just say *kwaheri rafiki* for me.

When I saw the title, I naturally assumed that Frank had died (as so many of our TEA compatriots have done). I was relieved at first to read that he was still alive, but I was then dismayed to learn that although he is breathing and his heart is beating, he is not really "alive." And yet, he is not suffering and he is not unhappy. He is just unaware. It is indeed sad that a man who was so alive and vibrant and who touched so many people's lives is now just a mere husk of what he once was.

When I compare Frank's condition to Stephen Hawking, whose brilliance remains but whose body is gone, I believe that Dr. Hawking is more fortunate. Most fortunate of all are those of us who were privileged enough to be in the TEA program fifty years past who still retain (nearly) all of our mental and physical faculties. Frank's disease brings two famous quotes to mind: 1) There, but for the grace of God go I; and 2) Omar Khayyam:

> The Moving Finger writes and having writ
> Moves on; nor all your piety nor wit
> Shall lure It back to cancel half a line
> Nor all your tears wash out a word of It.

Frank Ballance died on March 29, 2016. ☐

Headmistress Helen Inkpen

Sharon Hepburn

In 1962, we met our Headmistress from Twickenham, England. Her name, Helen Inkpen, was deemed most appropriate, and she fulfilled our expectations. As newbies to Swahili, we were impressed with her command of the language as she communicated with African staff or helped us tell our *shamba* boys how much we liked roses.

The smile was genuine, her laughter infectious but when, infrequently, her authoritative voice was needed, all of us heeded. On a day safari to the Serengeti, we experienced righteous wrath as her VW sped desperately across the plain. With her voice at top volume, she chastised us for getting out of our car in lion country. She minced no words in noting the stupid and dangerous thing we had done.

Any staff member with genuine issues knew that her help and empathy was freely given. A phone call to Minnesota for Colleen's sister's wedding, an invitation for afternoon tea after a trying week, or special soup for someone feeling poorly were extra perks.

Her innate fairness and ability to lead enabled the staff to focus on teaching assignments and the students. Her radar could detect those trying to use a situation. She seemed to know all the staff as well as their families. Anyone trying to get around the rules was dealt with in plain English. Today she would be accused of "political incorrectness."

Despite battling bilharzia, her energy levels never flagged in front of the students and staff. After her fiancé was killed in Somalia in 1963, she left Africa. Carol Olson Heath, Colleen Peterson, and I realized how much she had given to those of us at Bwiru Girls School in Mwanza, Tanzania. The vibrant energy, the caring protectiveness, the terrific hostess at her parties, her generous welcoming of travelers into her home, and her effective leadership were gone. ☐

Suttee and Mr. Chandra

Moses L. Howard

Mr. Chandra was a slender man whose face was that light brown color of Hindi boiled tea with milk. His wife was a slight shade lighter and tended her profile in every mirror with which she became acquainted. Semidry Chandra loved books and ideas. He had always been a success in school and in the world of ideas. Privately he took pride in being a teacher. He did not like being a trader. In the early years of his marriage to Lila Vital, he had tried a small shop in Fiji.

Lila was a beautiful but uneducated girl who longed to be rich and listened to the schemes of other women who spoke of how clever their husbands were and told of deals that brought their families riches. The daughters of these women went about on parade Sundays in fine clothes after wearing drab green school uniforms all week, while the Chandra daughters wore dresses quickly sewn from cheap but colorful cloth bought by their mother at a higher price in one of the high-end shops.

For a short time Lila had cut and sold bolts of expensive colorful cloth and cheap glittering jewelry. Though Lila loved the shop and the status it gave, she had no head for business and keeping records. And Mr. Chandra worked even harder, studying in the schools wherever they went and viewing teaching as the chosen way for his family to hold on to the tenuous level of affluence he had attained.

He applied himself, hoping Lila would forget grandiose ideas of riches and settle for a steady, hard grind of study to upgrade herself as well. The students chastised her and loved and admired her teacher husband. They talked of the couple often, praising the husband, and wondering at the wife's unhappiness. My students showed their affection for Mr. Chandra, who was head of the science department at the college where we taught.

He and I shared an office, and I heard snatches of conversation between them when his wife visited him while we worked. Her talk was all about opening businesses, which she tried over and over. Each time, as she complained, it was no fault of her own that she failed and lost whatever money they had invested. The students would come to class whispering: "Mrs. Chandra's new shop had just closed." Again and again he told her she did not have the temperament for business: "We care too much about people to succeed in business."

He reminded her of other ventures. "Remember in Fiji, in your shop there: when you let out cloth on credit to those women who made dresses for their daughters and then couldn't pay. You let them off. You are learning over and over that business is not friendship. You mix them and you lose."

"So I must sit and do nothing."

"No, just know it is better to keep a small shop with gum and candy, coffee and aspirins. No involved expense and bookkeeping."

"But that does not give the big return of cloth and expensive jewelry."

"It is true it does not give the big losses either."

But after a time, he supported her in another shop. And soon after it was rumored they could not pay the landlord the rent on their living compound. Mr. Chandra was seen driving a tractor at night, doing road-clearing work.

One Hindi student said, "She's out of control. My grandma said in other times the village women would watch her."

"Watch her?" I said, over the test tubes in science class.

"Yes, she is putting the family in danger."

I did not know what possible danger. "What do they mean?"

"That is far in other times," Dalken said.

"I know he's thinking if anything happens, she will be responsible. "

"But it is not allowed anymore. That's why she is pushing him so hard. She wants her way."

So it went until his wife became adamant. So Mr. Chandra gave in and let her once again open a shop that quickly failed.

It was customary for our science students to have tea one day a week as a kind of review seminar where students asked questions and discussed difficult topics. The students came to tea one day. Mr. Chandra was not yet there, but they said he was closing his wife's shop. He did not show during the afternoon, so when classes ended for the day, I closed the lab office and went home.

The next morning when I arrived at the lab, I was met by the custodian. He emerged from the office wringing his hands, a dreaded look of horror on his face. I saw beyond him into the office. The headmaster and several other staff members were shaking their heads as they contemplated a body stretched out beyond them on the floor. Beside an overturned chair, a chemical bottle lay open with some of its contents spilled about and a spoon nearby. And there was Mr. Chandra lying dead, his body all contorted.

The headmaster, a grey-haired man from Britain, closed the lab and with several assistants waited for the police and talked with them in the closed lab for an hour. He dismissed us and announced to the student body that the school was closed for two days, that there had been a terrible incident that had taken Mr. Chandra away from us and we would get the official details later.

But the news was all over the campus: Mr. Chandra had committed suicide by taking spoonsful of a mercury compound. My students whispered it was his wife's fault. The students mulled about in mixed groups around the teachers' college campus. Usually the students hung about in isolated ethnic groups, but now they mixed, African and Asian students, talking together, trying to make sense of what had happened.

Asian students from my science class congregated on the green near my house and chatted. I also wanted to know what had happened. Phrases they had uttered in class now needed an explanation. I invited them in for tea. The girls got out the tea things, and the boys talked among themselves. One said Mr. Chandra was very smart, but he had behaved stupidly; first, for not controlling his wife's behavior, and, second, for doing harm to himself.

But the girl who made tea said it was the wife's fault. "He was a man of principle. My grandpa says at home, he knows the part of India where Mrs. Chandra came from, and he knows they practiced it."

"Practiced what?" I wanted to know.

"When a husband died like this, what a wife must do."

Another said, "But that was long ago. It's now against the law. But my grandpa knows, knows Mr. Chandra loved knowledge and teaching, and his wife loved money and she goaded him. She didn't like him to be a teacher. She wanted him to make money so she could be rich and show how important she was. And everyone had better watch her, because my grandmother said, 'She will show her feelings after the ceremony.'"

"Yes, only my grandpa said, 'But not her; she doesn't even care he's gone.'"

"But she has to care," said Desai.

"But why must she be watched?" I asked.

Several students started to answer, saying, "The ceremony. You know they cremate him. Maybe…that's when…probably tomorrow."

The girl making tea said, "But my grandpa says that part is long over; it is outlawed. They cannot do it anymore. It's long since over. But if a wife is so saddened, she might…"

A silent girl pulled her sari scarf around her head and then spoke. "You all should not talk of it. She might do it. That's why she should be watched."

One day later, in the early afternoon, Bosni and Peak Patel knocked on my door.

"Sir, the others said you wanted to see."

"See?" I said.

"You know the ceremony of Mr. Chandra, sir."

I knew then he meant the cremation. "Where?"

"You come with us. It's at the edge of town, on a little-used road where no one travels."

We left the campus main road, walking through forest and weeds, and came to a place where there was a little-used path on the edge of the forest, high above the streets of town. The isolated road abutted an abandoned lumber truckway that washed out during heavy rains, with ruts and deep gullies, one not used by regular traffic. To the side of the road was a wooden trailer on tractor tires, the kind of trailer you see on the road usually pulled behind trucks or cars carrying loads of furniture or heavy machinery or old tires. Now it was loaded with a mixture of stacked cords of wood, old truck tires, and dry bales of hay, stacked very high with an empty space in the center.

An open truck with many colored streamers arrived among the waiting men, and as they removed the body and put it in the center of the loaded trailer, the crowd swelled and people covered the hillside.

We were behind it all at the edge of the woods, but we heard constant chanting from the crowd as the flames rose, spreading until the whole trailer was engulfed. People stood some distance away. Even though it was late in the afternoon, the African sun was still hot.

Bosni and Patel recognized some of the people from town, and some teachers were there, but there was no sign of Mrs. Chandra. Maybe they detained her at home. Then they spotted an entourage of women standing away, nearer the road, watching the flaming pyre. Bosni said, "She's there. I see her there." He nodded to point the direction. "They have her surrounded."

We waited in our cover while the flames leaped, burned, and the odor of burning rubber assailed our nostrils, and the whole wooden trailer and tires with the body was consumed.

"What did they expect might happen?" I wondered out loud.

Patel said, "Well, in other times, if a woman had driven her husband to ruin…I mean…in the old India, during cremation…a woman…a wife would dash from among the watchers and throw herself upon the burning pyre and perish on her husband's body."

"That's not done anymore," Bosni hastened to put in.

"No, the British colonialists forbade it. Put a stop to it. But even now, every now and then throughout the world where Indian women are, some woman tries to save face by doing it."

"But not Mrs. Chandra," the girl with the colorful sari said. "I heard she is going to Nairobi where she has relatives."

In the following weeks, in class the students spoke of Mrs. Chandra leaving with her daughters on the train, going to relatives in Nairobi. ☐

Eyes Full of Light

Bill Jones

As part of Makerere's orientation, in August, 1961, I was sent to Fort Portal in northern Uganda for two weeks to Nakasura School, a secondary school at the foot of the Rwenzoris, the Mountains of the Moon. In an effort to get a sense of what early education was like, I observed a local teacher at work with youngsters, students who were first or second graders, nobody older. The teacher, a woman, was clearly skilled. I could see that, even though I could not understand a word she spoke, once she had greeted me and sat me down for the brief observation. The classroom was alive, the students' faces animated, their eyes full of light.

What I knew immediately was that I had been in such a class, had been in the presence of such a teacher. It was remarkable that the woman, except for the language that she spoke, could have been Grace Jones, my Sunday school teacher (not a relative) the person who taught cradle roll classes, Sunday school classes for children up to about the third grade, at Mount Zion Baptist Church in South Hackensack, New Jersey, the township next to Hackensack, the town where I had grown up.

The Ugandan teacher was, in fact, only the second black professional teacher I had ever seen teach. The first was Professor Otieno, the Kenyan who taught Swahili at Teachers College during our orientation. I had had two black colleagues in the English Department at Hackensack High School, where I had taught for a year, but I had never seen them in front of a class. I expect, however, that they would fit into the cultural and political context that I was to construct years later which was inaugurated by the observation I had made that afternoon in that classroom in Fort Portal.

My brothers and sisters, as adults, once in a moment of reminiscence and revelry, agreed with me that Grace Jones was somehow in a category different from the teachers we had had in elementary school. I am the one, now, holding back from the conclusion we came to at that time. We said she was better. We did not linger long on that judgment, but I think we meant that she gave us what other teachers did not, that we felt connected to her in ways that we did not to our public school teachers. But since I have deep affection for all of my teachers and not a single quarrel with a single one of them, that distinction is uncomfortable for me to make.

Still, what I have come to understand is that teaching is a culturally driven socializing activity, and, in the racialized context of the United States, it is a political one as well. The simplest definition of *teacher* is an adult charged with passing on the values and customs of society to youths, intending to prepare youths to live in the world that lies before them. The role of the teacher necessitates a covenantal relationship with the community in which the role is enacted and requires a familiarity with and a respect for those in whose service it is performed.

The best teachers have a profound understanding as well of what the world will demand of students and equip them to deal with that reality however brutal it is. The definition, here, I realize, may now move, inappropriately perhaps, toward overstatement, but it allows me, as a black educator, concerned with the education of black youth, to posit something that is central to teaching, especially to teaching black students: teachers cannot teach those they despise and will miseducate if they as teachers do not understand that the world may find their students despicable even if they do not.

In that regard, only classrooms that produce competent students can stand against the indictment of undervaluing black students, abandoning them to brutalizing indifference. I want to believe that the teacher in the classroom outside of Fort Portal would escape such condemnation and that Grace Jones would too, if it had been my good fortune to have encountered her in a public school classroom. ☐

Meru Names

Dagmar Telfer Muthamia

One of the first things I learned at Kaaga Girls School in Meru District, Kenya, was the rule that each girl had to choose one name and stick to it during her time at Kaaga. The British missionary women who ran the school could not handle the Meru tradition which allows for one to have many names, to choose which ones to use, and to change freely. All the girls had one name that was their "Christian" name. It was in English and usually a Biblical name or positive Christian attribute. Popular names were Jerusha, Agnes, Mary, Tabitha, Sarah, Charity, Mercy, and Faith.

Most of the girls also had one or more names related to personal characteristics, which we might think of as nicknames. Even I acquired additional names. The first time, I was left to supervise the workers during a school holiday. I became known as Kagwiria, which meant I was someone they were happy to work for because I was not a very strict supervisor. A person might also be addressed in a way that referenced their relationship like daughter of, mother of, wife of, e.g., *mwana wa* Josephat, *gina or mama wa* Mutegi or *muka wa* Kimathi. The form might be shortened so it became Faith Josephat instead of Faith *mwana wa* Josephat.

The first name given to a child is the most interesting. Children are named after family members. The first four born in a family are named after grandparents. The next are named after aunts and uncles in birth order. At each level the paternal relative is first, then the maternal. This is similar to the Scottish tradition and many others. A major difference is that the exact name is not used; rather the name is descriptive of the person after whom an individual is named and is given by that person. For example, a girl could be named Kainda, meaning "she who gets up early" by a grandmother who is known to be an early riser. My husband was the second-born son, so he was named after his mother's father. This grandfather was not alive to bestow the name, so my husband had to take the name of an age-set of his maternal grandfather's generation. Muthamia was the one he chose.

Throughout life an individual might be referred to as if he or she actually was the namesake. A daughter named after her paternal grandmother might be addressed as Mama by her own father. When I married, I became the wife of Samuel, but Samuel was named after his maternal grandfather, who was his own father's father-in-law. As his wife, I became my father-in-law's mother-in-law, so he could have called me Muthoni or "in-law," but in Meru tradition all women of your mother's generation are politely referred to as Mama. So I became Mama to my very polite father-in-law. □

Child of Africa: Story of an Mtoto Mzuri
George Pollock

I went to Kenya as a teacher with the Teachers for East Africa program of Columbia Teachers College. Fresh from college and with an intrepid new bride, I was going to save the world. I would do good. I would spread civilization. I would make friends for America. I was young and didn't know any better. I did know enough to bring a camera, however, a little point-and-shoot Instamatic. Everywhere we went, I clicked away with the little Instamatic. Back in the US, we turned the photos into slides and little black-and-white prints and put them in a little box. There they mostly sat for close to a half century.

There sat also the photographic story of how Gregory Francis Pollock started off life in a faraway land and culture that could not be more different from our own. It is certainly an unusual story. Afraid that the story of Greg's African beginnings would vanish forever, I decided to make sure that this would not happen. First, I retrieved the slides, nearly two hundred of them, and had the best of them, about seventy-five, digitized and put on a CD.

> For a longer version of this story, with photos, see http://bit.ly/mtoto-1. □

See If You Can Find This Man

Bernard Sauers

While I was at Butimba (in Tanzania, near Mwanza, on the south shore of Lake Victoria), I had a Maasai student who invited my family and me to visit his home while we were on school vacation. We did, and it was one of the highlights of our time in East Africa.

As I was preparing to come home in 1970, this young student asked if he could have my address in the States. I had just signed a contract, and so I gave him the name and address of the school. It turned out to be the school at which I would spend the next twenty-nine years.

This past Christmas, we received a phone call from a pleasant young lady with an African accent. She asked if I remembered the name of Simon Sitayo. We said we did. She then went on to explain that she was his daughter, and that with the birth of her child the parents were visiting. She then told us the story of her father coming and bringing this piece of paper with a name and address on it and saying, "See if you can find this man." She went on the internet and found the phone number of the school. The school gave her our phone number. It has been forty years since we last saw Simon, now a man of sixty-five, who has retired from teaching and a job as a school inspector in the Arusha region. We traveled to Georgia for a visit, and he and his wife were to fly to be with us a week in Pennsylvania before they returned home in May.

My first question when I met Simon was, "Why would you have kept a piece of paper with an address on it for forty years?"

His simple reply, "I always thought we would meet again."

My other thought is how many other people in TEEA must have touched young African lives and never knew it, nor ever had the opportunity to meet again forty years later to reconnect and to ask what happened after they left. TEEA was a rich experience, but perhaps the richest was meeting my former student and catching up. ☐

Sue Johannot, Special Memories

Lee Smith

Sue Johannot was a special person who following practice teaching in Soroti, Uganda, started her TEA career in April, 1963, on Zanzibar where she taught biology at Seyidda Maastuka Secondary School on the island. Afternoons, she was "seconded" to the sultan of Zanzibar, Sayyid Jamshid bin Abdullah Al Said, for the training of his horses.

In August she was visited by friends Lee Smith and Bill Powell. Lee, the source of this story and your editor the amanuensis, remembers the occasion when he and Sue were out swimming when they got caught in a riptide and started frantically waving to Bill who was obvious to the plight. Sue and Lee dragged themselves over rocks and wicked things and bloodied but surviving crawled onshore. After medical attention and a few beers, they were fine.

Eventually, Sue was caught up in the revolution of January, 1964, and was airlifted to Nairobi where she stayed with Bruce Franklin before being re-posted. She returned to New York City to train to be a doctor and was admitted at the University of Colorado. Sue applied for her internship to be served Alaska where she wanted to assist Inuit people. She was headed to a nearby island when the boat capsized, and she died. Her spirit has lingered long with many of us. □

Moira Harbottle, Mother to Many

Larry Thomas

We were met at Entebbe by a gracious woman who, with sandwiches and welcoming words, greeted us warmly as we entered a new world. We were the first of many to arrive in East Africa, and soon we were scattered to far-away places in a far-away land. But that first taste of Uganda was less strange because of Moira's warm English welcome.

I was posted to Kyambogo, on the edge of Kampala, first to teach at Kampala Technical Institute, later at the teacher training college on the same hill. My academic life as well as my social life brought me in frequent contact with Mrs. Harbottle.

At the TTC, the Tour and Travel Center, Moira was present at the faculty meetings, guiding us deftly into the intricacies of working with the Ministry of Education, and working with me on the problems of running the teacher-practice program. She and I often went on safari together, playing darts in the hotel in Tororo, enjoying the comforts of the English-style hotel in Kitale, Kenya, and showing me around Mbale. We laughed a lot, especially after a demanding day of helping new teachers to establish good educational practices in situations often foreign to them.

My English housemate, Malcolm Maries, introduced me to rugby. The Harbottles were also involved in the games and social life of the KRUFC, the Kampala Rugby Union Football Club. I became entertainments member, arranging dinners of curried lamb and organizing such activities as scavenger hunts. The Harbottles entertained groups of us at their home. Harry, Moira's husband, worked for the water purification ("It's as safe to drink as at home") part of the Uganda government. We had a good old-fashioned Thanksgiving dinner at their home, even though Harry couldn't eat turkey: so he fried up a steak for himself. I remember their daughter mostly through visiting her at her school in Scotland when I was on vacation. She told me she had encountered an ape at an English zoo who recognized her from their days in Uganda.

Moira Harbottle did much for wave after wave of TEA/TEEA teachers. I remember her fondly as a very great help, a buffer in a new and exciting experience, but mostly as a dear friend. □

TEA-Alumni Authors

Donald Adams has had science in the forefront of his adult life, beginning at Malangali Secondary School in southern Tanzania. He then earned an MA and PhD in veterinary anatomy and taught at Michigan State University and Iowa State. Towards the end of his career, Donald produced veterinary anatomy programs for the web and then went to the Caribbean to teach for four years. He lives now in Ashland, Oregon. See http://vetneded.com and http://www.images4u.com.

Gloria Lindsey Aliburaho taught in Moshi in TEA, Georgia in the US for most of her career, married and divorced a Ugandan, and spends Decembers in Entebbe.

Jay Anderson won the Madhvani Prize at Makerere and then taught at Budo in Kampala. He returned to study food and folklore at Plymouth Plantation and then taught his specialty at Penn, Western Kentucky, and Utah State. He is considered the father of living history museums and the author of *Time Machines*.

Jerry Atkin taught in Tabora and returned to Oregon and an activist life on workplace and social issues.

Jerry Barr was dutiful at Sir Samuel Baker SS in Gulu, Uganda. After all those adventures he lies up in Kissimmee, Florida, watching sunsets and gators, especially with a nice glass of pinot noir. His real passion has been fighting with the local governments assisting residents who want to have pet pot belly pigs.

John Beyerle instructed students and Moses Howard at Ntare School in Mbarara, Uganda. He later had a teaching career in science at both the secondary and university levels in Florida.

John Bing taught at Lango College in Lira, Uganda, and then political science at Heidelberg University in Ohio from 1975 to 2016. His PhD dissertation was on Ugandan elections. John is consultant to the president of Madonna University in Michigan.

Jim Blair was posted to Magamba School in Lushoto, Tanzania, and then became a lawyer, ultimately settling in Colorado.

Kay Borkowski taught at Machakos Girls School in Kenya and has continued her teaching career in various parts of the world, currently in Mexico.

Jay Butts, a Teachers College professor, was one of the founding fathers (with Karl Bigelow) of TEA/TEEA and author of *In the First Person Singular*. J. Lindfors's book *The TEA Experience* holds him as our progenitor. He died in 2010 at the age of 99, godfather to the end.

Bill Cahill taught in TEA at Chewoyet SS in Kapenguria, Kenya. His Africa honeymoon with Fran included the birthing of three daughters. The family returned to Kenya with the Ford Foundation, and then Bill had a career at Long Beach (CA) City College. He is an avid astronomer.

Dan Callard called Kamusinga School in Kamilili, Kenya, home long enough to chat up the nearby VSO lovely and then marry her. He had a long career teaching in Philadelphia where he also extended his deep interest in music.

Paul Cant cannot be described. He is and has always been a man of the world and currently resides at Dar Etouta in Raf Plage, Tunisia, when he's not in Europe promoting his books under the nom de plume of Jonathan Bower. He taught in TEA in Mpwapwa in central Tanzania.

Emilee Hines Cantieri taught at Machakos Training College in Kenya which was the focus of her book, *East African Odyssey*. She returned to the US to a writing career and latterly extensive travel.

Betty Castor started her career in Uganda at Kibuli SS. She later served as a legislator, Commissioner of Education, and president of the University of South Florida. She continued her global interest as a member of the Fulbright Foreign Scholarship Board.

Gene Child taught physics at Kenyatta College, Nairobi, Kenya, 1969-71, and retired after thirty-three years teaching science and math in 1990. He has helped organize all the TEEA reunions since the first one in 1999.

Pat Colby was a TEA worthy at Machakos Girls School and travelled extensively on her way home. She has taught English in Switzerland and Los Angeles where she also became a principal and union grievance chair. She is active in the League of Women Voters and at a local library.

Betty Coxson was sent to the best sounding schools, St. Scholastica's Teacher Training College in Fort Portal and at Lady Irene College, Ndejji, Bombo, both in Uganda. She had a long career teaching English and journalism in southern California, and has retired to a small Iowa town where she sustains her love of libraries.

Ann Russell Dickinson taught English, art, religion and geography at Rosary College, Mwanza, Tanzania. She later concentrated on raising seven children and founded two non-profit organizations to aid pregnant women. Her leisure is devoted to oil painting and making iMovies.

Audrey Van Cleve Dickson lived and worked in Bukoba, Tanzania, with husband Leal. Her career included nursing research and management and supervision of family planning services for Seattle. She enjoys writing poetry and short stories.

Leal Dickson taught biology at Nyakato SS, Bukoba, Tanzania. He is retired from the University of Washington, Department of Biology, where he taught and researched Arctic plant physiology. He and wife Audrey have three sons (one born in Bukoba), and they live in Seattle.

Linda Donaldson was an English and science teacher at Loreto Convent SS for Girls in Limuru, Kenya. Then she spent five years in Tanzania, Nigeria, and England teaching part-time before raising a family in Minnesota and working as a writer and democratic activist.

Elaine Durham taught "everything" for the Peace Corps in a school near Lira, Uganda. She married Joe in 1969 in Kampala and became a willing assistant/co-conspirator in various hijinks. She and Joe returned to Seattle where she became a middle school teacher. Elaine is now retired and living near her children.

Joe Durham helped run the TEEA office in Kampala which he closed down in August, 1972. He returned to Seattle where he worked at the University of Washington; he died in 2007.

John Dwyer was a student and teacher of history first in West Nile, Uganda, and later at several universities in the States. Later he worked with the Southern Association of Schools and Colleges to assess the quality of academic programs.

David Evans taught at Makerere College School where he started the school band. After his doctorate at Stanford, he spent forty-nine years as the Founding Director of the Center for International Education at the University of Massachusetts Amherst.

Nat Frothingham was one of the few TEAers to teach at Alliance High School in Kenya. He has lived in Vermont and worked as a local journalist and activist since returning. He edits "The Bridge" in Montpelier.

Brooks Goddard drove his Land Rover first to Kitui SS, then to Kagumo School, and finally to Giakanja SS. He took the Hippie Trail home and returned to Kenya four years later with his wife Jeanie when they were on leave from their teaching. He had a thirty-five-year career teaching high school English in the Boston area and remains an avid traveler and book editor. Brooks is the president of TEA-Alumni.

Charles Good enlivened the faculty at Lubiri SS in the Buganda heartland and then returned to the States to teach at various universities, most recently at Virginia Tech.

Robert Gurney taught French and English at Kitante Senior SS in Kampala. He went on to lecture in Spanish in London and has published several books. He started the TEA-Alumni chapter in the UK in 2012.

Charlie Guthrie found three ways to serve his country. First, he taught with TEA at Malangali High School south of Iringa; second, he served in the US Army in Vietnam; then had a long and admirable career teaching area studies at Indianapolis College in Indiana; third, he taught in the Peace Corps in Rwanda.

Henry Hamburger taught A-level math and physics in Kakamega, Kenya. His thirty-six-year academic career was mainly teaching and research in applications of mathematics. He now tutors math at Washington, DC high schools, serves as DC coordinator in the AAAS STEM classroom volunteers project, and is TEA-Alumni's treasurer, webmaster, and most frequent site visitor.

Sharon Lybeck Hartmann was at Mzumbe Government SS from 1961-63. She was in the first wave of American teachers sent to Tanganyika. Sharon taught high school English for another ten years before becoming a civil rights lawyer.

Carol Heath taught at Bwiru Girls SS in Tanzania. After teaching back in the States for a few years, she went to library school, worked as a librarian, and volunteered for such organizations as Meals on Wheels, the United Way, and in schools. She is a devotee of classical music.

Ted Heaton taught at Bungoma SS in Bungoma, Kenya, and then returned to the States to become an early computer programmer. He retired early and went into age-group running, travel, and sports cars rebuilding.

Hank Hector joined TEA in 1961. He was posted to Tanga SS in Tanga, Tanzania, where he taught English and renewed in 1963. After finishing course work at Columbia he joined TEEA in 1968 and taught at a teacher training college at Marangu, Tanzania. After TEEA he worked at a number of places in higher education in New York, Florida, Alabama, and Georgia.

Ward Heneveld taught and headmastered at Kiangona SS near Nyeri, Kenya. He returned to the US for an EdD and proceeded to work for a number of foundations worldwide ending with the World Bank. He has now retreated to extreme northern Vermont.

Sharon Hepburn taught at Bwiru Girls SS and married Bill while in Tanzania. She returned to various jobs: nursery school teaching and directing, working in libraries, and now calligraphy.

Niall Herriott taught biology at Namilyango College near Kampala and returned to Ireland to set up an ecological consultancy business, worked in shellfish farming and marine biology. He now writes and gardens and visits with Mike and Judy Rainy when they visit Cork.

Rodney Hinkle taught history and geography at Mzumbe SS in Morogoro, Tanzania. He then earned an EdD in International Education at Teachers College and enjoyed a forty-year career in jobs that required travel or residence in Germany, Italy, Nigeria, and China. Rod now lives with his second wife, Kirstin Moritz, on Cape Cod.

Ted Hoss taught at Kagumo TTC in Nyeri, Kenya, and just kept on teaching eighth grade English in Geneva, Illinois. He also worked summers with low-income families for twenty-two years. He has been all over the US and Canada. He rejoices for the White Sox and Blackhawks.

Moses Leon Howard is an American educator who taught in Africa for ten years as a Fulbright Fellow and TEEA teacher, training medical technologists and secondary school teachers. A retired dean of a community college in Washington State, biology teacher, and mentor for at-risk students, Dr. Howard has written four novels, three children's books, and numerous short stories.

Jack Humbles taught at Holy Ghost Boys School in Moshi and Butimba TTC in Mwanza, both in Tanzania. Then he worked at Indiana U, did a stint in Peace Corps in Ecuador, then botanical work at University of Wyoming and Missouri Botanical Garden. He got a MA in linguistics and worked in Saudi Arabia, Yemen, and Japan, also completing twenty-five years of teaching at Ohio University. Now he spends twenty-five hours a week as a volunteer in the botany department at Museum of Northern Arizona and enjoys living in Flagstaff.

David Hummel was at Kenyatta Teachers College. He returned to teaching science at Yuba City High in California, and then in Thailand and Saudi Arabia. He also taught at Yuba Community College. In 1994 he and Jeannette taught, libraried, and coached in Pakistan, Slovakia, Togo, and Namibia. Now they both have their volunteer activities and "work camping."

Clarence Hunter went to Kisubi, Uganda, to teach at St. Mary's College on the Entebbe Road. He returned to various library jobs working largely in the state archives in Mississippi. He currently uses those skills in activist ways in Jackson, Mississippi.

David Imig taught at Nyajato SS in Bukoba, Tanzania, worked for USAID in West Africa, and had a long career with the American Association of Colleges for Teacher Education (AACTE). David is now a faculty member at the University of Maryland and a Senior Fellow at the Carnegie Foundation for Advancement of Teaching.

Charles Irby brought his wife and two children with him to Machakos Boys SS in Kenya. Upon returning to the States, he resumed his forestry profession and retired as forest supervisor of the San Bernardino National Forest in California in 1990. He also worked in Job Corps and Peace Corps (Fiji).

Gary James was first assigned to Mzumbe Secondary School in Morogoro and then Bwiru Boys SS and Mkwawa. Back in the States, he worked at Orange Coast Community College in Costa Mesa, California, teaching biology and eventually serving as dean. He retired in 1993 and went to work for Lindblad Expeditions. Now he organizes trips to Mexico every year to see the gray whales.

Bill Jones has kept Africa always on his mind and in his heart. Bill taught at Kapsabet SS in Kenya. Since the mid-eighties, he has collected contemporary Africa art and has become enamored of African diaspora travel. After thirty years at Rutgers-Newark he retired in 1999 as an associate professor in the Department of Academic Foundations.

Don Knies virtually ran TEA from his Kampala office from 1962 to 1967. He kept us all afloat. He arrived at TEA via twenty-one months of hitchhiking around Africa ending in 1962 (see *Walk The Wide World*, available on Amazon), was hired by Peace Corps, and bird-dogged by TEA. Later he was a history teacher in Plattsburgh, New York, and Modesto, California. He now thrives on beer and jazz in the UK with the lovely Maureen.

Charles Kozoll taught with Frank Ballance at Tanga Boys School in Tanzania, and then had a long career in higher education training at the University of Illinois.

Lucy Larom assisted her husband, Hank, at Nakuru SS in Kenya. After she and Hank were divorced in 1974, she continued her career in social work at institutions for developmentally disabled adults in Oregon and Virginia. Lucy now lives San Diego, California where she is close to family and dabbles in activism. For six years she served as co-chair of Campaign to End Genocide in Uganda...Now! **Hank Larom** followed TEA by serving in the Peace Corps in Asmara, Eritrea, and resumed his teaching career at St. John's College and Eastern Oregon University. He was working on his PhD in English at Idaho State University when he died in 1978.

Marty McCall Lemke taught at Nyakato SS in Bukoba, Tanzania, where she married Dick Lemke. She had a long career in nursing home and hospice care and administration. She has dedicated her life to volunteerism and equity efforts.

Gus Lewis taught at Mzumbe SS in Morogoro, Tanzania and returned to earn a PhD in physics at the University of Illinois. He taught mostly at the high school level until 2005. He and Mary Ann love to travel.

Ben Lindfors and **Judy Lindfors** both taught at Kisii SS in Kisii, Kenya, and then returned to Texas where they had remarkable careers at the University of Texas. Ben became one of the foremost experts on African literature, Judith on child language acquisition. Judy edited *The TEA Experience*. Now they write, grandparent, and travel.

Clive Mann taught in both Uganda and Kenya, later in Brunei and London. He is an author and co-author of numerous books and papers, mostly ornithological. Clive is the TEA-Alumni contact in UK.

Eugene Marschall is a dual UK–Netherlands citizen who taught at Mkwawa High School in Iringa, went back to the Netherlands to establish a business and family, and joined the TEA-Alumni trip to Tanzania in 2005. He is the only TEA-Alumni to have a student under his tutelage create a measurement now with its own Google entry.

Dean McHenry went to Mpwapwa, Tanzania, to teach history and then returned to a career in higher education in politics and policy, most recently at Claremont University in California.

Mary Jo McMillin (aka Wendel) taught on local terms at Songea SS, Songea, Tanzania. Mary Jo's keen interest in local food took her into nearby mission gardens, Indian merchants' kitchens, and back into the pioneering past of preserving. She streams a cooking show and is the author of *Mary Jo's Cuisine*.

Patricia (Schmitt) Mische taught in Kenya at Mukumu Girls SS in Kakamega. She later co-founded Global Education Associates, was a professor of peace and global studies, and wrote several books and more than one hundred articles on global issues.

Eva Murray-Scelzo taught at Gayaza High School in Kampala and for sixteen years in Japan, Greece, and Kenya. Eva also taught and tutored English in New Jersey and Virginia. She died in 2015 in Spotsylvania, Virginia.

Dagmar Telfer Muthamia taught at Kaaga Girls School in Meru, Kenya. She married a Kenyan and taught at Egoji Teachers College and Nairobi International School. She and her family eventually settled in Long Beach, California.

Larry Olds taught in Uganda at the Makerere College School and Teso College/Soroti. He was a strong proponent of a democratic and participatory approach to education in which personal stories move to shared experience and collective understanding. He died in 2016.

Dale Otto taught English and chemistry at Chavakali Secondary School, Maragoli, Kenya, and then had a career at Central Washington University. Dale and his wife Elizabeth have taught in several other international situations.

Jack Paarlberg famously took his family from northeastern Massachusetts to teach math at Bishop Willis TTC in Iganga, Uganda, and back again. He now splits his time between Florida and New Hampshire.

Kate Parry taught at Kigezi High School, in Uganda, and divides her time between teaching at Hunter College in New York and Uganda. She has played a prominent role in the Uganda Community Library Association since being a co-founder of the Kitengesa Community Library near Masaka, her husband's home. See http://bit.ly/kitengesa.

Miles Paul taught at Mzumbe SS in Morogoro, Tanzania, and retired early from teaching biology at the University of Victoria, Canada, to be a full-time amateur astronomer, traditional fiddler, ham operator, back packer, and frequent traveler to Botswana and Namibia where he and his wife Dorothy are resident astronomers at Sossusvlei Desert Lodge.

George Pollock has had at least three lives, and you can read about each on his extensive blog. He taught at Kisumu Day School, became a father, and went to West Africa. Back in the States he wrote and edited for a living, he went into advertising, he remarried. He continues to write and plays competitive tennis in Worcester, Massachusetts. George has a special interest in foster care, himself a product.

Joel Reuben looks back approaching his eightieth birthday in 2017, with warm feelings for the two years at Chadwick TTC in Butere and Eresgi TTC in western Kenya. He appreciated the opportunity to train the students in the New Primary Approach.

Jonatha Stifle to **Jonne Robinson** has had many life changes and is richer for them: four countries, four cultures, three degrees, two wonderful children, two grandsons and sons-in-law, one (now zero) husband. Now, as ever, trying to create meaning from the raw materials given—writing, reading, fighting couch potato-dom. She taught at Mpwapwa SS in Tanzania and resides in the UK.

David Sandgren taught in Kenya at Giakanja SS and then went on to earn a PhD in African history and had a forty-two-year career teaching it to college students in Minnesota.

Bernard Sauers went from Butimba TTC in Mwanza, Tanzania, to Shady Side Academy in Pittsburgh where in his spare time he built the house on a farm in Clymer, New York, where he and his wife now live.

Harold Scheub taught at Masindi SS in Uganda and is Evjue-Bascom Professor of Humanities emeritus at the University of Wisconsin–Madison. He has authored a number of books, including *The Tongue Is Fire*. Harold is the American expert on South African folklore. He spent ten years in Africa.

See "The Harold E. Scheub Collection" in the University of Wisconsin Digital Collections at http://bit.ly/HES-1. See also "...Harold Scheub keeps the storytelling tradition alive" at http://bit.ly/HES-2.

Jerry Schieber started at Mzumbe SS in central Tanzania, served in the US Army in Vietnam, married Joan Hoffman, earned a masters degree, taught high school math and science, left teaching, got involved in real estate, and continued a lifelong interest in baseball.

Joan Hoffman Schieber studied at Makerere and then taught math at Marian College, Morogoro, Tanzania. She returned to California to teach and married Jerry Schieber in 1969. The Schiebers moved to New

York City, where they have lived and worked ever since. Joan has maintained her interest in Africa.

Ed Schmidt taught mathematics and physics at Kakamega High School and continued a career in teaching on his return to the States. In 1999, he began the search for former TEA and TEEA teachers which led to the first reunion and formation of TEA-Alumni in 2001. He has served as scribe and newsletter editor throughout TEA-Alumni's existence. Ed has returned to East Africa seven times to visit and evaluate schools supported by the TEA-Alumni grant program.

Lloyd Sherman taught at Narok SS in Kenya and led a life of adventure. His career was in science education at the Mount Sinai School of Medicine in New York City. Lloyd died in 2012.

Reed Stewart took his whole family back to Africa so learned how wonderful both west (Liberia and five children) and east (Kenya, coaching excellent aspiring teachers at Kenyatta Teacher Training College) coasts are. He is still on a coast in Massachusetts.

Ron Stockton is a professor of political science at the University of Michigan–Dearborn. He grew up in a small coal mining town in southern Illinois. He and Jane both contributed to this book and both taught at Machakos SS.

William Stoever taught at Tabora Boys School and Jangwani Girls School, Dar es Salaam. When his contract was finished, he spent eighteen months hitchhiking through the Middle East and Asia. After graduate school he taught international business, management, and law at Rutgers and Seton Hall for thirty-three years.

Nola Stover taught science and math at Rosary College (now Nganza SS) in Mwanza, Tanzania, from 1963 to 1965. Over the past fifty years, she has taught various middle school, high school, and college courses.

Julie Sulman was the non-teaching spouse of Ron Richardson and the mother of toddlers Andrew and Diane posted to Bungoma SS. She has an AB, MLS, and JD and had a career with the LADA's office. She is married to Michael Sulman.

Mary Ryan Taras taught history and English at Mukumu Girls SS in Kakamega, Kenya. She taught history in Birmingham, Michigan, and ended her career at the National Board for Professional Teaching Standards. In retirement, she teaches history at Oakland Community College.

Beverly Templin taught at Shimo la Tewa in Kenya and Tororo Girls School in Uganda. She studied linguistics at the University of Minnesota, taught, sold real estate, and served in a Chinese-American restaurant. Before retirement, she helped the elderly.

Larry Thomas taught in both TEA and TEEA at Uganda Technical College and National Teachers College, Kyambogo. Back in the US, he lectured on poetry in Arkansas and has published books of poetry, fiction, and humor. He founded the creative arts magazine, *Third Wednesday*.

Brenda Tillberg has spent most of her life teaching in schools, including Tabora Girls, Jangwani, and Marian College/Kilakala, all in Tanzania, and Mt. Abraham Union High School in central Vermont, her homeland. Her hobbies include teaching chemistry, attending NSTA conventions, reading mysteries, and encouraging wildflowers.

George Urch arrived in Kenya in 1964 with his wife Dorothy and two young children. He was assigned to Kenyatta College as a geography tutor. He served as Kenya's national basketball coach and then taught at the University of Massachusetts at the Center for International Education. He worked in about a dozen African nations in both formal and non-formal education for various periods of time.

Jim Wallace taught at Old Kampala SS in Uganda and subsequently spent much of his life on a motorcycle. He lived in Vermont and was one of six from Williams College who joined TEA. Jim died in 2014.

Jim Weikart has been a teacher, an accountant, and a writer. First, in Nyakato SS in Bukoba, Tanzania; second, in New York City; third, in Asheville, North Carolina. He splits his waking time between writing mysteries and drinking the odd bottle of Tusker beer.

TEA and TEEA History

It is instructive to know that TEA was formed in seven weeks, between the Princeton Conference ending on December 5, 1960, to Teachers College signing the contract with Agency for International Development (USAID) on January 26, 1961, one of the first international activities of the Kennedy administration. The Peace Corps was formed by President Kennedy's executive order on March 1, 1961 and authorized by Congress on September 21, 1961.

Three books have been written (one published) on the history, nature, and experiences of people who enrolled in the USAID Teachers for East Africa (TEA) Project and Teacher Education for East Africa (TEEA) Project:

> Sue Nanka-Bruce's doctoral dissertation, *Teachers College Project in East Africa: A History of International Cooperation, 1961–1971* (1988; available only at the Teachers College library).

> *The TEA Experience* of 2002, initially compiled by Emilee Cantieri and produced by Judith Lindfors, contains many individual sketches and photographs not included in this book. It also contains a summary history of TEA/TEEA. Reprinted, it is available from Brooks Goddard, goddard@rcn.com.

> Raymond Gold's 2004 evaluation, *A Teaching Safari: A Study of American Teachers in East Africa*.

Four people have written books on their particular experiences:

> Emilee Hines Cantieri, *East African Odyssey* (2005).

> David Sandgren, *Mau Mau's Children* (2012).

> Moses L. Howard, *A Teacher in East Africa* (2013).

Bob Gurney, *A Night in Buganda* (2014), and *Absurd Tales from Africa* (2017).

Other TEA-Alumni have written about their experiences, and we are all the richer for these accounts. The Teachers College publication, *Teachers College Newsroom*, printed an article in 2002 at http://bit.ly/tea-cu.

TEA-Alumni stories, experiences, and photographs are on the TEA-Alumni website at http://bit.ly/teaaki.

For logistical reasons, not all of the stories from the TEA-Alumni website and none of the pictures are replicated in this book. The website has a second source of stories: TEA-Alumni "newsletter menu," "Earlier issues," every issue starting in 1999, a real trove.

There was a cousin program to TEA, described in *Airlift to America: How Barack Obama, Sr., John F. Kennedy, Tom Mboya, and 800 East African Students Changed Their World and Ours* (2009) by Thomas Shachtman, which tells of bringing of promising university students from six countries in the East African region to the US for higher degrees from 1959 to 1963. See also http://bit.ly/airliftus.

Several Peace Corps volunteers have written about their teaching experiences in East Africa, most notably *An African Season* (1966) by Leonard Levitt. A full list of Peace Corps writings is at: http://bit.ly/pcexpbooks.

If it occurs to you, write your own book—really! Whatever you do, please consult the TEA-Alumni website, where much more information exists in past newsletters: www.tea-a.org.

Acknowledgments

First and foremost, to Bill Jones for the idea; second, to Henry Hamburger for website facilitation; third, to Moses Howard for encouragement; fourth, to Ed Schmidt for compiling newsletters. In 2011 Bill Jones thought to have several people tell their TEA-Alumni stories to the NPR StoryCorps project, but the logistics were daunting.

However, at the NYC11 Reunion, TEA-Alumni members were called to write their stories. Henry organized an online protocol on the TEA-Alumni website for people to enter their stories and suggested that stories be of a single memory, with authors encouraged to write as many stories as they wished.

Bill wrote introductions to the sections and edited each story. Brooks Goddard volunteered to be the project editor and thus acknowledges ownership of the project but not of the stories.

Major kudos to Annie Pearson of the Jugum Press in Seattle, Washington. Moses connected Annie and Brooks. Annie has been the perfect person for bringing our memories into book form.

Institutionally, we are all indebted to Teachers College, Columbia University for having experts who saw in the 1930s that international education could be a major field of study and employed individuals like Karl Bigelow and Jay Butts who seized a strategic opportunity to engage young Americans and Brits with the countries of East Africa at a critical time in the lives of those countries and the lives of those who went to serve the young people of Kenya, Tanzania, and Uganda. Many TEA-Alumni have advanced degrees from Teachers College, so the institution has served many individuals as well.

Elimu haina mwisho

Author Index

Adams, Donald
   Much Forgotten, Much Regained, 12
   Wonderful If Random Memories, 133
Aliburaho, Gloria Lindsey, 415
   Kibo and Paradise, 14
Anderson, Jay, 139, 415
   A Clean Well-Pressed Shirt, 15
   Papa, Martha, and Me, 138
Atkin, Jerry, 57, 415
   In Memoriam: Julius Nyerere, 385
   Mwalimu, 351

Barr, Jerry, 12–13, 17, 415
   A Multi-use Souvenir Found in Northern Uganda and Kenya, 250
   Hiring a Domestic Servant, 142
   Introducing Basketball, 17
   Nile Perch Fishing in Lake Rudolf, 245
   Reporting to Sambaker, 140
   Sambaker and Spare Time in Northern Uganda, 248
   Sambaker School Strike, 141
   Stopping Fires in the Bush, 16
Beyerle, John, 415
   Long Break in Southern Africa, 252
Bing, John, 416
   Testing for a Driver's License, 19
Blair, Jim, 416
   Tanganyikan Tales, 144
   TEA Reflections, 20
   Tribute to Frank Ballance II, 399
Borkowski, Kay, 416
   A Life-defining Experience, 21
   Voting in May, 1963, 352
Butts, Jay, 416
   Career Memories, 22

Cahill, Bill, 416
   A Humbling Experience, 24
   Turbans and Windscreens, 253
Callard, Dan, 263, 416
   Music Alone Shall Live, 145
Cant, Paul, 416
   Crossing Cultures, 147
Cantieri, Emilee Hines, 416
   Students on Strike, 153
Castor, Betty, 416
   Operation Uganda and More, 25
   Scaling Kilimanjaro with Schoolgirls, April 1964, 254
Child, Gene, 417
   Camping in Uganda, 325
   Duncan Kimamu and Electricity, 154
Colby, Pat, 395, 417
   Recipe for Sukuma Wiki (stretch the week), 155
   Ruth, 392
Coxson, Betty, 417
   Africa in My Life, 27
   TEEA Tour Sparks Amazing Art Career, 390

Dickinson, Ann Russell, 417
   EA11 Revisited, 394
   Memories Come in All Sizes, 30
Dickson, Audrey Van Cleve, 417
   Bukoba, Tanzania, 1963, 31
Dickson, Leal, 417
   Josephat Coelestine, Educator and Colleague, 396
Donaldson, Linda, 417
   Visits to My Students' Homes, 32
Durham, Elaine, 417
   Manone's Mercedes: Joe, Joshi, and the East African Safari Race, 326
Durham, Joe, 326, 418
Dwyer, John, 418
   Three Letters Home, 38

Essebaggers, Ted, 103
   School Outing to Lake Manyara, 255
Evans, David, 418
   Practice Teaching, 156
   The Famed Flight to Entebbe via Kano, 53
Frothingham, Nat, 418
   You Are My Son, 54

Gill, Pat
   My English Challenge, 157
Goddard, Brooks, 125, 396, 398, 418, 429
   A Prank Gone Wrong, 327
   Introduction, 1
   My First Christmas in East Africa, 261
   Sharifa Zawawi, Mwalimu wa Kiswahili, 397
   Sports, 56
   That First Night at Makerere, 55
   The Head of a Leopard, 328
Good, Charles, 13, 418
   Life-long Close Connections, 57
Gurney, Robert, 418
   The Hills of Kampala in Three Acts, 58
   Things That Fly, Three Versions, 329
Guthrie, Charlie, 418
   Back to Africa Fifty Years Later via the Peace Corps, 158

Hamburger, Henry, 418, 429
   Culture Gap in Kakamega, 168
   Math, Temba, Adongo, and Pedagogy, 176
   Music at Kakamega, 177
   TEA Successes, Then and Now, 60
   The Cook, 178
   Tribute to Frank Ballance, 398
   Unwelcome, 59
Hartmann, Sharon Lybeck, 419
   Travel during Heavy Rains, 1962, 269

Hayden, Anita
   East African Safari Rally, 260
Heath, Carol, 401, 419
   TEA Time, 62
Heaton, Ted, 419
   Attending a Circumcision Ceremony, 62
Hector, Hank, 419
   Who Can Be the President of What, 354
Heneveld, Ward, 57, 419
   Kiangoma and Student Fees, 180
   Kiangoma Track Meet, 179
Hepburn, Sharon, 419
   Headmistress Helen Inkpen, 400
   Instant Expert at Twenty Years Old, 183
Herriott, Niall, 419
   A Sense of Proportion, 185
   Boys and Their Toys, 184
   Feeding the Crocodiles, 271
Hinkle, Rodney, 344, 419
   Life-changing Event, 64
   Transition to Peace Corps, 65
Hoss, Ted, 420
   Assassination in Nairobi, 355
   Family of Travelers, 272
Howard, Moses Leon, 420, 429
   About Positive and Negative, 186
   A TEEAer Becomes an African Farmer, 332
   David Bruce's Microscope, 65
   Empakos, 68
   Field Trip: Kampala to Mombasa, 273
   Have We Forgotten?, 7
   India and African Life, 69
   My African Students, 198
   No Entry Permit, 66
   O Levels and Me, 187
   Place of the Lions, 331
   Sundowner, 194
   Suttee and Mr. Chandra, 401

Hower, Edward
   Careers Out of Africa, 72
Humbles, Jack, 420
   Female Circumcision, 73
   Student Teaching Practice, 201
   The Cambridge Overseas Exam, 200
   Wildlife but No Elephants, 335
Hummel, David, 420
   Snake Story, 203
Hunter, Clarence, 420
   The Search for Self in the Motherland, 74
Imig, David and Carol, 420
   TEA Memories, 205
Irby, Charles, 421
   Notebooks Have No Accent, 209

James, Gary, 421
   Supporting a Tanzanian's US Education, 210
Jones, Bill, 232, 421, 429
   Eyes Full of Light, 407
   A Kapsabet Gift: A Practical Dictum for Teaching, 211

Knies, Don, 24, 114, 163, 421
   Our First Date, 279
Kozoll, Charles Lucy, 421
   Africa, 1962, 281

Larom, Lucy, 421
   Adventure on the Narok Road, 283
Lemke, Marty McCall, 422
   First Wave Romance, 78
Lewis, Gus, 422
   Strike to Study, 212
Lindfors, Ben, 422
   Amending Nyerere's Julius Caesar, 357
   Boys in the Cast, 213
Lindfors, Judy, 416, 422, 427
   Owing to Underfeeding, 214

Mann, Clive, 422
   Athletics in Nandi Country, 215
   BaHima and BaTutsi in Uganda, 364
   Convocation at Makerere, 363
   Gorillas at Last, 287
   Malaria and Me, 79
   Pets in Kenya, 84
   Pets in Uganda, 82
   Presidential Visit, 369
   Soviet Doctors in Uganda, 366
   Teaching as a Temporary Measure, 216
   The Driving Test, 284
   The Joys of Ajon, 81
   The Kerio Valley, 292
   The Snake in the Toilet, 336
   Total Eclipse of the Sun 30 June 1973, 290
   Travelers' Rest, 285
   Wild Animal Tales from Kapsabet, 87
Marschall, Eugene, 422
   The Mpemba Effect, 89
McHenry, Dean, 422
   Personal Reflections on Tanzania over a Period of Forty Years, 218
McMillin, Mary Jo (Wendel), 422
   Cooking All the Time, 93
   Double, Double, Toil and Trouble, 90
   Indian Friends, Indian Cooking, in Four Parts, 338
   November 1963, Songea, Tanganyika, 91
Mische, Patricia (Schmitt), 422
   From the Minnesota River Valley to the Peaks of Kilimanjaro, 94
   The Time I Gave Away My Watch, 98
Mitchell, Frank
   My East Africa Story, 100
Moock, Peter, 103
   Journey in My Ford Anglia to Visit Maasai Well, 103

Murray-Scelzo, Eva, 423
  Scenes from a Tropical Hiatus, 105
Muthamia, Dagmar Telfer, 423
  Christmas, 1965, 294
  Meru Names, 409

Olds, Larry, 19, 423
  Teaching at Teso College, 221
  Walking on Kilimanjaro, 296
Otto, Dale, 423
  What a Gift It Was, 227

Paarlberg, Jack, 423
  My Greatest Gift, 106
Parry, Kate, 423
  Uganda Voluntary Work Camps, 108
Paul, Miles, 423
  Bessie and the Cobra, 343
Pollock, George, 423
  Child of Africa: Story of an Mtoto Mzuri, 410
  Why Africa is Always on My Mind, 109

Reuben, Joel, 424
  Getting Posted to the Right School, 111
  The New Primary Approach, 228
Robinson, Jonne, 424
  Electricity Too, 230

Sandgren, David, 424
  A Grim Mau Mau Legacy, 370
  Memories of Kenyan Independence, 371
Sauers, Bernard, 424
  See If You Can Find This Man, 411
Scheub, Harold, 424
  TEA Changed My Life, 115
  Two Remarkable Flights, 119
Schieber, Jerry, 252, 424
  A Lunchtime Experience, 344

Schieber, Joan Hoffman, 424
  A Eureka Moment, 345
  Christmas on Kilimanjaro, 299
  The Mikado in Morogoro, 346
Schmidt, Ed, 2, 61, 227, 399, 425, 429
  Dabbling in Swahili, 231
  I Learned as Much as I Taught, 300
Sherman, Lloyd, 425
  Three Hundred TEA Words, 113
Smith, Lee, 114, 412
  Sue Johannot, Special Memories, 412
Stein, Harry
  A Red Pen and Innocence, 232
Stewart, Reed, 425
  Learning from Future Teachers, 121
Stifle, Jonatha. *See* Robinson, Jonne
Stockton, Jane
  To Kilimanjaro and Back, 302
Stockton, Ron, 425
  Encounters with Amin, 379
  Giant Jungle Ants, 236
  Kenya Nostalgia, 122
  Nelson Mandela, 372
  Toad in Stomach, Beetle in River, 239
Stoever, William, 425
  Hitchhiking the Congo, 302
  Kilimanjaro Catharsis, 306
  Murchison Hippos, 307
Stokes, Bob
  When a Student Strike Isn't Really a Strike, 233
Stover, Nola
  JFK Assassination, 381
Sulman, Julie, 425
  Screams in the Night, 308

Taras, Mary Ryan, 425
  Adventures along the Nairobi Road, 310
Templin, Beverly, 426
  Road Trip, 311

Theodore, Yvonne
   The Bees, 240
Thomas, Larry, 425
   Moira Harbottle, Mother to Many, 412
Tillberg, Brenda, 426
   The First Flight to East Africa, 312

Urch, George, 426
   Memories, 124

Wallace, Jim, 426
   Dukas, Dear Dukas, 125
Watne, Joel
   Celebrity Contacts, 347
   The Crazy Dutchman, 316
   Culture Shock, 126
   Diversity in Arusha, 241
   East African Railways Curry, 317
   Mount Meru, 314
Weikart, Jim, 426
   Death Is Just an Option, 317

Title Index

A Clean Well-Pressed Shirt, Jay Anderson, 15
A Eureka Moment, Joan (Hoffman) Schieber, 345
A Grim Mau Mau Legacy, David Sandgren, 370
A Humbling Experience, Bill Cahill, 24
A Kapsabet Gift: A Practical Dictum for Teaching, Bill Jones, 211
A Life-defining Experience, Kay Borkowski, 21
A Lunchtime Experience, Jerry Schieber, 344
A Multi-use Souvenir Found in Northern Uganda and Kenya, Jerry Barr, 250
A Prank Gone Wrong, Brooks Goddard, 327
A Red Pen and Innocence, Harry Stein, 232
A Sense of Proportion, Niall Herriott, 185
A TEEAer Becomes an African Farmer, Moses L. Howard, 332
About Positive and Negative, Moses L. Howard, 186
Adventure on the Narok Road, Lucy Larom, 283
Adventures along the Nairobi Road, Mary Ryan Taras, 310
Africa in My Life, Betty Coxson, 27
Africa, 1962, Charles Kozoll, 281
Amending Nyerere's Julius Caesar, Ben Lindfors, 357
Assassination in Nairobi, Ted Hoss, 355
Athletics in Nandi Country, Clive Mann, 215
Attending a Circumcision Ceremony, Ted Heaton, 62

Back to Africa Fifty Years Later via the Peace Corps, Charles Guthrie, 158

BaHima and BaTutsi in Uganda, Clive Mann, 364
Bessie and the Cobra, Miles Paul, 343
Boys and Their Toys, Niall Herriott, 184
Boys in the Cast, Ben Lindfors, 213
Bukoba, Tanzania, 1963, Audrey Van Cleve Dickson, 31

Camping in Uganda, Gene Child, 325
Career Memories, Jay Butts, 22
Careers Out of Africa, Edward Hower, 72
Celebrity Contacts, Joel Watne, 347
Child of Africa: Story of an Mtoto Mzuri, George Pollock, 410
Christmas on Kilimanjaro, Joan (Hoffman) Schieber, 299
Christmas, 1965, Dagmar Telfer Muthamia, 294
Convocation at Makerere, Clive Mann, 363
Cooking All the Time, Mary Jo McMillin, 93
Crossing Cultures, Paul Cant, 147
Culture Gap in Kakamega, Henry Hamburger, 168
Culture Shock, Joel Watne, 126

Dabbling in Swahili, Ed Schmidt, 231
David Bruce's Microscope, Moses L. Howard, 65
Death Is Just an Option, Jim Weikart, 317
Diversity in Arusha, Joel Watne, 241
Double, Double, Toil and Trouble, Mary Jo McMillin, 90
Dukas, Dear Dukas, Jim Wallace, 125
Duncan Kimamu and Electricity, Gene Child, 154

EA11 Revisited, Ann Dickinson, 394
East African Railways Curry, Joel Watne, 317
East African Safari Rally, Anita Hayden, 259

Electricity Too, Jonne Robinson, 230
Empakos, Moses L. Howard, 68
Encounters with Amin, Ron Stockton, 379
Eyes Full of Light, Bill Jones, 407

Family of Travelers, Ted Hoss, 272
Feeding the Crocodiles, Niall Herriott, 271
Female Circumcision, Jack Humbles, 73
Field Trip: Kampala to Mombasa, Moses L. Howard, 273
First Wave Romance, Marty McCall Lemke, 78
From the Minnesota River Valley to the Peaks of Kilimanjaro, Patricia (Schmitt) Mische, 94

Getting Posted to the Right School, Joel Reuben, 111
Giant Jungle Ants, Ron Stockton, 236
Gorillas at Last, Clive Mann, 287

Have We Forgotten?, Moses L. Howard, 7
Headmistress Helen Inkpen, Sharon Hepburn, 400
Hiring a Domestic Servant, Jerry Barr, 142
Hitchhiking the Congo, William Stoever, 302

I Learned as Much as I Taught, Ed Schmidt, 300
In Memoriam: Julius Nyerere, Jerry Atkin, 385
India and African Life, Moses L. Howard, 69
Indian Friends, Indian Cooking, in Four Parts, Mary Jo McMillin, 338
Instant Expert at Twenty Years Old, Sharon Hepburn, 183
Introducing Basketball, Jerry Barr, 17

JFK Assassination, Nola Stover, 381
Josephat Coelestine, Educator and Colleague, Leal Dickson, 396

Journey in My Ford Anglia to Visit Maasai Well, Peter Moock, 103
Kenya Nostalgia, Ron Stockton, 122
Kiangoma and Student Fees, Ward Heneveld, 180
Kiangoma Track Meet, Ward Heneveld, 179
Kibo and Paradise, Gloria Lindsey Alibaruho, 14
Kilimanjaro Catharsis, William Stoever, 306

Learning from Future Teachers, Reed Stewart, 121
Life-changing Event, Rod Hinkle, 64
Life-long Close Connections, Charles Good, 57
Long Break in Southern Africa, John Beyerle, 252

Malaria and Me, Clive Mann, 79
Manone's Mercedes: Joe, Joshi, and the East African Safari Race, Elaine Durham, 326
Math, Temba, Adongo, and Pedagogy, Henry Hamburger, 176
Memories Come in All Sizes, Ann Russell Dickinson, 30
Memories of Kenyan Independence, David Sandgren, 371
Memories, George Urch, 124
Meru Names, Dagmar Telfer Muthamia, 409
Moira Harbottle, Mother to Many, Larry Thomas, 412
Mount Meru, Joel Watne, 314
Much Forgotten, Much Regained, Donald Adams, 12
Murchison Hippos, William Stoever, 307
Music Alone Shall Live, Dan Callard, 145
Music at Kakamega, Henry Hamburger, 177
Mwalimu, Jerry Atkin, 351

My African Students, Moses L. Howard, 198
My East Africa Story, Frank Mitchell, 100
My English Challenge, Pat Gill, 157
My First Christmas in East Africa, Brooks Goddard, 260
My Greatest Gift, Jack Paarlberg, 106

Nelson Mandela, Ron Stockton, 372
Nile Perch Fishing in Lake Rudolf, Jerry Barr, 245
No Entry Permit, Moses L. Howard, 66
Notebooks Have No Accent, Charles Irby, 209
November 1963, Songea, Tanganyika, Mary Jo McMillin, 91

O Levels and Me, Moses L. Howard, 187
Operation Uganda and More, Betty Castor (Elizabeth Bowe), 25
Our First Date, Don Knies, 279
Owing to Underfeeding, Judy Lindfors, 214

Papa, Martha, and Me, Jay Anderson, 138
Personal Reflections on Tanzania over a Period of Forty Years, Dean McHenry, 218
Pets in Kenya, Clive Mann, 84
Pets in Uganda, Clive Mann, 82
Place of the Lions, Moses L. Howard, 331
Practice Teaching, David Evans, 156
Presidential Visit, Clive Mann, 369

Recipe for Sukuma Wiki (stretch the week), Pat Colby, 155
Reporting to Sambaker, Jerry Barr, 140
Road Trip, Beverly Templin, 311
Ruth, Pat Colby, 392

Sambaker and Spare Time in Northern Uganda, Jerry Barr, 248
Sambaker School Strike, Jerry Barr, 141

Scaling Kilimanjaro with Schoolgirls, April 1964, Betty Castor, 254
Scenes from a Tropical Hiatus, Eva Murray-Scelzo, 105
School Outing to Lake Manyara, Ted Essebaggers, 255
Screams in the Night, Julie Richardson Sulman, 308
See If You Can Find This Man, Bernard Sauers, 411
Sharifa Zawawi, Mwalimu wa Kiswahili, Brooks Goddard, 397
Snake Story, Dave Hummel, 203
Soviet Doctors in Uganda, Clive Mann, 366
Sports, Brooks Goddard, 56
Stopping Fires in the Bush, Jerry Barr, 16
Strike to Study, Gus Lewis, 212
Student Teaching Practice, Jack Humbles, 201
Students on Strike, Emilee Cantieri, 153
Sue Johannot, Special Memories, Lee Smith, 412
Sundowner, Moses L. Howard, 194
Supporting a Tanzanian's US Education, Gary James, 210
Suttee and Mr. Chandra, Moses L. Howard, 401

Tanganyikan Tales, Jim Blair, 144
TEA Changed My Life, Harold Scheub, 115
TEA Memories, David and Carol Imig, 205
TEA Reflections, Jim Blair, 20
TEA Successes, Then and Now, Henry Hamburger, 60
TEA Time, Carol Heath, 61
Teaching as a Temporary Measure, Clive Mann, 216
Teaching at Teso College, Larry Olds, 221
TEEA Tour Sparks Amazing Art Career, Betty Coxson, 390

Testing for a Driver's License, John Bing, 19
That First Night at Makerere, Brooks Goddard, 55
The Bees, Yvonne Theodore, 240
The Cambridge Overseas Exam, Jack Humbles, 200
The Cook, Henry Hamburger, 178
The Crazy Dutchman, Joel Watne, 316
The Driving Test, Clive Mann, 284
The Famed Flight to Entebbe via Kano, David Evans, 53
The First Flight to East Africa, Brenda Tillberg, 312
The Head of a Leopard, Brooks Goddard, 328
The Hills of Kampala in Three Acts, Bob Gurney, 58
The Joys of Ajon, Clive Mann, 81
The Kerio Valley, Clive Mann, 292
The Mikado in Morogoro, Joan (Hoffman) Schieber, 346
The Mpemba Effect, Eugene Marschall, 89
The New Primary Approach, Joel Reuben, 228
The Search for Self in the Motherland, Clarence Hunter, 74
The Snake in the Toilet, Clive Mann, 336
The Time I Gave Away My Watch, Patricia (Schmitt) Mische, 98
Things That Fly, Three Versions, Bob Gurney, 329
Three Hundred TEA Words, Lloyd Sherman, 113
Three Letters Home, John Dwyer, 38
To Kilimanjaro and Back, Jane Stockton, 301
Toad in Stomach, Beetle in River, Ron Stockton, 239
Total Eclipse of the Sun 30 June 1973, Clive Mann, 290
Transition to Peace Corps, Rod Hinkle, 65
Travel during Heavy Rains, 1962, Sharon Lybeck Hartmann, 269
Travelers' Rest, Clive Mann, 285
Tribute to Frank Ballance, Henry Hamburger, 398
Tribute to Frank Ballance, II, Jim Blair, 399
Turbans and Windscreens, Bill Cahill, 253
Two Remarkable Flights, Harold Scheub, 119

Uganda Voluntary Work Camps, Kate Parry, 108
Unwelcome, Henry Hamburger, 59
Visits to My Students' Homes, Linda Lenhardt Donaldson, 32
Voting in May, 1963, Kay Borkowski, 352

Walking on Kilimanjaro, Larry Olds, 296
What a Gift It Was, Dale Otto, 227
When a Student Strike Isn't Really a Strike, Bob Stokes, 233
Who Can Be the President of What, Hank Hector, 354
Why Africa is Always on My Mind, George Pollock, 109
Wild Animal Tales from Kapsabet, Clive Mann, 87
Wildlife but No Elephants, Jack Humbles, 335
Wonderful If Random Memories, Donald Adams, 133

You Are My Son, Nat Frothingham, 54

Topic Index

Abbreviations for schools:
  HS: High School
  SS: Secondary School
  TTC: Teacher Training College
Abbreviations for countries:
  DRC: Democratic Republic of Congo
  KE: Kenya
  TZ: Tanzania
  UG: Uganda

Aba, Nigeria, libraries, 28
Aberdare Mountains, 46, 179
Aberdare National Park, 328
Aberdeen University, 139
Absurd Tales from Africa (Gurney), 427
Achebe, Chinua, 15
Acholi Province, UG, 140, 141, 245
acknowledgments, 429
Adamson, Joy, 295
Addis Ababa, Ethiopia, 261
African Association for Teacher Education, 23
African beers, 80
African National Congress (ANC), 373, 387
African Queen, The, 246
African Season, An (Levitt), 428
African Studies Association, 220
African Wildlife Foundation, 114
Africana Hotel, Dar es Salaam, 220
AFSC (American Friends Service Committee) exchange programs, 225
Aga Khan Hospital, 64
Aga Khan Primary School, Kampala, UG, 206
Agency for International Development. *See* USAID
agricultural students, 12
Ahmet, Ata, 284
AID. *See* USAID
AIDS. *See* HIV/AIDS

Airlift to America: How Barack Obama, Sr., John F. Kennedy, Tom Mboya, and 800 East African Students Changed Their World and Ours (Shachtman), 428
Ajon, 81-82
Al Said, Sayyid Jamshid bin Abdullah, 412
Alaska and Other Exotic Worlds (Birdsall), 391
Albers, Louie, 221, 226
Albright, Neil, 106
Ali, Mohammed, 123
Aliat, Andrew, 225
Allen, Bar, 295
Allen, Bunny, 295-296
Allen, Jim, 296
Allen, Warden, 12
Alliance HS, KE, 417
alumni. *See* TEA-Alumni
American Friends Service Committee (AFSC) exchange programs, 225
Amin, Idi, 23, 75, 119, 187, 379-381
ANC (African National Congress), 373, 387
Angola, 317-318
Animal Farm (Orwell), 151
animal stories, 81-85, 87-89, 201, 203-205, 236-238, 240, 271-272, 275-279, 286-289, 293, 307-309, 311, 316, 328-329, 331-332, 335-336, 343
Ankole, UG, 193, 331, 366
ants, 236-238
Arab people, in Kenya, 50
Arafat, Yasser, 375
Arua, UG, 43-44, 104, 116, 126
Arusha Declaration, 351
Arusha Goan Association, 241
Arusha Indian School, 241, 317
Arusha SS, TZ, 241
Arusha, TZ, 29, 48-49, 73, 232, 241-242, 314, 317
Ashby, Gene, 50, 273-279
Asian people, in East Africa, 69-72; in Mombasa, 50; in Tanzania, 241

441

askari (Muslim Sudanese), 217
Asmara, Eritrea, 421
Assistant Regional Government Agent (ARGA), 262
Aswan River, 246
Ateso people, 367
Athi Plains, KE, 371
Atkinson, Brian, 343
author index, 431
Ayton, George, 232

"baby elephant walk," 126
BaChwezi people, 366
Baganda people, 77, 146
BaHima people, 364-366
Bahinguza, James, 365
BaHororo people, 365
BaHutu/BaIru people, 365
Bahutu Manifesto, 366
Baker, Sir Samuel Baker, 45
Ballance, Frank, 2, 398-400, 421
Banda, Hastings, 28, 363
Bank of Uganda, board of directors, 12
Bantu languages, 365
BaNyamulenge people, 365
baptism ceremony, 172
Basinger, John, 178, 231
basketball, 18, 222, 225, 426
Basoga people, 146
Basutoland, 252
Bateson, Mary, 56
BaTutsi people, 364-366
BaTwa people, 365
Baumgartel, Walter, 285, 287
BBC News, 123, 205
bees, 240-241
Beira, 281
Belafonte, Harry, 115
Bend, John, 201
Berger, Ron and Iris, 301
Biber, Owen, 377
Bigelow, Karl, 1, 416, 429
bilharzia, 184, 387, 401
Birdsall, Byron, 390-392

Birth of a Dream Weaver, and Makerere University, 13
Bishop Willis TTC, Iganga, UG, 106, 423
Blantyre, Malawi, 281
Bleach, Barry, 221
Bombo, UG, 72, 217
Borkowski, Danny, 22
Bower, Jonathan, 416
Brady, Joe, 219
Brett, T. A., 56-57
British teaching standards, 8
Britton, Peter and Hazel, 293
Brothers of the Holy Cross, 282
Brown v. Board of Education-1954, 76
Brown, Pat, 46-47, 52
Brubakers, 52
Bruce, David K., 65-66
Brunei, 81
Buckner, Quinn, 399
Budo, Kampala, UG, 415
Buganda kingdom, Uganda, 58
Bujugali Falls, Lake Victoria, 45
Bukoba, TZ, 20, 31 79, 201, 206, 207, 269, 271, 252, 417
Bukosi, James, 221, 226
Bull, Arthur, 231
Bume, 263
Bungoma SS, KE, 279, 308, 419, 425
Bunyoro kingdom, Uganda, 116, 118, 366
Burundi, 364-366
Burungu, DRC, 267
Busoga College Mwiri, Jinga, UG, 225
Butere, KE, 112
Butimba TTC, Mwanza, TZ, 411, 420, 424
Butooro kingdom, Uganda, 366
butterflies, 330
Butts, R. Freeman (Jay), program launch, vii, 1, 23, 64, 429
Bwama Island, UG, 109
Bwamba Forest, 288
Bwiru Boys SS, Mwanza, TZ, 101, 421

Bwiru Girls SS, Mwanza, TZ, 61, 183-184, 401, 419

Cambridge Overseas Exams, 32, 99, 123, 145, 146, 160, 169-171, 183-184, 200, 209, 212, 223
Cameron, Tom, 114
Campaign to End Genocide in Uganda...Now!, 421
camping in East Africa, 16-17, 226, 246, 248-250, 251-253, 325
Cape of Good Hope, 252
Cape Town, South Africa, 252, 372
Captains' Coup, Portugal, 318
Castro, Fidel, 121
Celebrated Jumping Frog of Calaveras County (Twain), 170
Central African Republic, 126
Chadwick TTC, Butere, 112, 423
Chagga people, 14
Chandra, Semidry, 69, 401-406
Chavakali SS, Maragoli, KE, 423
Chewoyet Boys SS, Kapenguria, KE, 24, 416
Chinese people, in Rwanda, 167
Christensen, Ed, 239
Churchill, Winston, 138
circumcision, female, 73-74, 121
circumcision, male ceremony, 62-63, 172
City Bar, Kampala, 52, 79, 185, 272, 285
City Club, at Makerere University, 13
Claremont Graduate University, 220
Clinton, Bill, 377
Coelestine, Josephat, 396-397
colonial governments, education, 1
Columbia Teachers College, 1, 24, 218
Composing a Further Life, 56
Congo, 268, 302-303
Congo Crisis, 268
Congolese Rail Line, 321
Conyers, John, 377
Cooke, Peter, 146

copyright, ii
cornstalks, symbol of African Peoples' Party, 352
Cowan, Gray, 24, 114
Cowie, Mervin, 114
Crested Crane, Jinja, UG, 337
crocodiles, 271-272
Cry the Beloved Country (Paton), 275
Cuba, hijacked flight, 120
Cuba, missile crisis, 117
culture gap, in Kakamega, 168-175
culture shock, 7-8, 97, 126, 208
Currey, James, 193
Cutler, Alex and Ruth, 325
Cutrules, Alex, 219

dal, recipe, 338
Dar es Salaam, TZ, 220, 269
Dar-05 reunion, 398
Davis, Julia, 306
Dawes, Robin, 190
DC01 reunion, 398
De Beers gold mine, 252
De Chardin, Teilhard, 97
Dean, Pete, 149-150
Dell, Donald, 56
democracy, in Kenya, 352, 371; in Tanzania, 354
Democratic Republic of Congo (DRC), 302
Dilolo, Zaire, 320
Dodoma, TZ, 92, 148-150, 316
Dogs of Fear (Nagenda), 192
driver's license, in Uganda, 19-20, 284-285
Duke of Kent, Uganda independence ceremony, 26
Dylan, Bob, 348

EA11, 394-395
East African Airways (EAA), 269
East African Locust Control, 126
East Africa maps, 3-5
East African Odyssey (Cantieri), 416, 427

East African Railways, 316
East African Safari Rally, 259-260, 326-327
East African Standard, 205, 254
eclipse, 290-291
Educational Services Exchange with China (ESEC), 29
Egoji Teachers College, Meru, KE, 422
Eldoret, KE, 46, 84, 215, 232
elephants, 20, 135, 325
Elgeyo-Marakwet Escarpment, KE, 292, 293
empakos (nicknames), 68-69
Engaruka ruins, 258-259
enguli (alcohol), 185
Entebbe Fisheries Department and Viral Institute, 66
Entebbe, UG, 53-54, 66, 126, 412
Equator Club, Nairobi, KE, 115
Eresgi TTC, KE, 112, 228-229, 423
Esegu, Edward, 225
Experimental Stock Farm, Mbarara, UG, 334

"facing Mount Kenya" (defined), 1
farming, 333-335
Fatiko, UG, 45
Fechtmeyer, Sally, 297
female circumcision, 73-74, 121
Ferguson's Gulf, 262
fishing, 245-248
"Flaming Spear." *See* Kenyatta, Jomo
Flay, Alan, 211
FNLA (National Front for the Liberation of Angola), 319, 320
Ford Foundation, 226, 416
Foreign Service School, Georgetown University, 67
Fort Jesus, KE, 51
Fort Portal, UG, 39, 407
Fox, Allan, 56
Franklin, Aretha, 377
Franklin, Bruce, 412
Frasier, Joe, 123

Freedom Riders, 7
French Equatorial Africa, 126
Friends School Kamusinga, KE, 73, 146, 345
Fulbright Foreign Scholarship Board, 416

Gabiro, 268
Garland, Peter, 260
Garvey, Mike, 391
Gayaza (Girls) HS, Kampala, UG, 12, 105, 422
Gaye, Marvin, 378
Gedi ruins, 51
Geiger, Sue, 13
Gellhorn, Martha, 139
gender equality, in Rwanda, 167
genocide, Rwanda, 164-166
"Genocide Against the Tutsi" (memorials), 165
Georgeson, Carl, 363
Georgetown University, Foreign Service School, 67
Geramethakul, Sopon, 399
Ggombolola structure, 146
Giakanja SS, Nyeri, KE, 370, 417, 424
Gill, Pat, 395
Gilman Point (Kilimanjaro), 254
giraffes, 311
githeri, 34
Glassboro State College, Operation Uganda, 25-26
Global Education Associates, 422
Goan people, in East Africa, 47, 241, 317
Goma, DRC, 268, 365
Goma-Sake-Lubero Road, 267
Gombola people, 191
Gone with the Wind (Mitchell), 275
Goodbye, Mr. Chips (Hilton), 190
Goodman, Morris, 360
Gores, Joe, 227
gorillas, 286-287, 287-289
Gouffini, John, 43

Graham, Carl, 23
Great Expectations (Dickens), 275
Great North Road, 92, 252, 373
Great Rift, 208
Greenwood, Bob, 56
Grieve textbook, 230
Gulu, UG, 16, 52, 117, 140, 226, 248
Gulwe Station, 148-149, 218, 220

Hagberg, Gloria and Gordon, 114
Hall, Mitchell, 13
Harbottle Harry, 413
Harbottle, Harry, 79
Harbottle, Moira, 79, 217, 412-413
Harris, Frank and Elsie, 253
Hatari, 126
Hawking, Stephen, 400
Hawkins, Richard, 13
Haya language, 207
Haya people, 208
Heaton, Tom, 288, 369
Hemingway, Ernest, 139
Henssler, Professor, 113
Hilders, Franz, 81
Hines, Mary, 310
hippos, 201, 307-308
Hitchhike the World (Stoever), 305
HIV/AIDS studies, in Tanzania, 20, 58
Hobkirk, Bob 12-13
Hoefnagels, Franz, 81
Hoima, UG, 117
Holland, Arden, 114
Holy Ghost Boys School, Moshi, TZ, 420
Hooper, Les, 308
Hotel Terminus, 318
Huambo, Angola, 319
Huckabay, Dennis, 147, 262
Human Mandolin, The (Nagenda), 193
hunting, 135-136, 226
Hutchison, Graham, 221
Hutu people, 165
hyenas, 309

Iganga, UG, 106
impala, 316
Impenetrable Forest, 266, 287
In the First Person Singular (Butts), 416
Indalo, Peter, 231
Indian cuisine, recipes, 93, 338
Indian people, in Uganda, 401-406
indigenous musical instruments, 173-175, 177
Ingqumbo Yeminyanya (Jordan), 118
Inkpen, Helen, 400-401
INSEAD, Fontainebleau, France, 90
insects, 330, 335, 343
International Conference on the World Crisis in Education, 23
International Defense and Aid Fund, 377
International Education Act of 1967, 23
Iringa, TZ, 89
Iveti Hills, KE, 123

Jackson, Jesse, 377
Jackson, Mary Ann, 12
Jangwani Girls School, Dar es Salaam, 425
Jarvis, Andrew, 223
Jeffers, Lance, 74
Jinja, UG, 45, 245, 274, 380
Johannesburg, ZA, 252
Johannot, Sue, 412
Johnson, Lyndon, 23
Jones, David, 221
Jones, Grace, 407-408
Jones, Jill and Roger, 308
Jones, Johnny, 221
Jones, Judson, 25
Jordan, A. C., 118-119
Joseph, Gigi, 115
Joshi, D. T., 326
Joshi, Sumitir, 69
Julius Caezar/Juliasi Kaizari (Nyerere), 357-362
Juma, A.C., 102

Junior SS Leaving Examinations, 45, 117, 226

K Hotel, Kitale, KE, 264
Kaaga Girls School, Meru, KE, 294, 409, 422
Kabaka, Daudi, 13, 146, 363, 379
Kabale, UG, 108, 286
Kabanyola, UG, 12
Kabarnet Boys' SS, KE, 369
Kabarnet, KE, 84, 215, 292, 370
Kaberere, UG, 333
Kagame, Paul, 160, 165
Kagera Lodge, TZ, 268
Kagera Province, TZ, 205
Kaggia, Bildad, 24
Kagumo HS, Niyeri, KE, 327, 328, 417
Kagumo School Wild Life Club, 329
Kagumo TTC, Nyeri, KE, 272, 419
Kahawa, UG, 203
Kahororo, UG, 79
Kajubi, Professor Senteza, 206
Kakamega Country Club, 60
Kakamega Forest, 85, 86
Kakamega Hostel, 231
Kakamega, KE, 57, 58-60, 94-95, 126, 168-175, 176, 177, 310, 417
Kakamega School, KE, 177, 231, 424
Kalam, Ethiopia, 263
Kalenjin, KE, 215
Kalenjin people, 369
Kalifi, UG, 294
Kamilili School, Kamusinga, KE, 416
Kampala, UG, 133, 138, 219
Kampala Rugby Union Football Club (KRUFC), 413
Kampala Technical Institute, 413
Kamusinga School. *See* Friends School Kamusinga
Kano, Nigeria, 7, 53-54, 120, 218
KANU (Kenya African National Union), 369
Kanungu, 266
Kapenguria, KE, 24, 263, 264

Kapsabet, KE, 80, 85-88, 211, 232, 290
Kapsabet SS, KE, 219, 421
Kaptagat Forest, KE, 89, 107
Karagwe people, 365
Karamoja District, UG, 80, 116, 218, 251
Karamojong people, 265, 367-368
Karatina, KE, 179, 180
Karuma Falls, UG, 117
Kashongi, UG, 108
Katanga Region, DRC, 207
Katikiro of Bunyoro, 117
Katter, Eldon and Adrienne, 390
Kaunda, Kenneth, 115, 363
Kawumara-Aboowli, Lisa, 68-69
Kayira, Legson, 28
Kehler, Tom, 245-248
Keiange, P.K., 355
Keino, Kipchoge "Kip," 215, 348
Kemoli, Arthur, 177
Kennedy, John F., assassination, 14, 92-93, 105, 110, 209, 356, 381; Peace Corps, 427; TEA program launch, 1, 26, 116
Kennedy, Robert, assassination, 387
Kenya, independence, 371; map, 5; national basketball team, 125
Kenya Emergency, 1952-60, 370
Kenya in Pictures (Reuben), 229
Kenya National Parks, 114
Kenya Primary Education (KPE) exams, 112, 229
Kenyatta College. *See* Kenyatta University
Kenyatta University, Nairobi, KE, 60, 154, 177, 416, 426
Kenyatta TTC, Kahawa, UG, 121, 124, 203, 420, 425
Kenyatta, Jomo, 24, 60, 76, 110, 247, 264, 278, 279, 348, 351, 363, 369, 385
Kericho, KE, 46
Kerio Valley, 292
Kerr, Jan, 39

Key Moments and Experiences (Section I), 9-127
Khadafi, Muammar, 375
Khayyam, Omar, 400
Kiangona Boys SS, Nyeri, KE, 179, 180, 419
Kibaki, Mwai, 115
Kibera, KE, 110
Kibo. *See* Mt. Kilimanjaro
Kibuli SS, Kampala, UG, 26, 254, 416
Kigali, Rwanda, 160
Kiganda music, 145-147
Kigezi district, UG, 266
Kigezi HS, UG, 423, 108-109, 287
Kigoma Region, UG, 219
Kikuyu language, 33
Kikuyu people, 33, 369
Kikuyu Reserve, KE, 54
Kikuyuland, 356
Kikuyu-Luo conflict, 369-370
Kilakala, Morogoro, TZ, 346
Kilembero Valley, TZ, 386
Kilwa Kisiwani, TZ, 137
Kimamu, Duncan, 154-155
Kimilili, KE, 73
King, Martin Luther Jr., assassination, 356, 387
King's African Rifles, 26
Kings College Budo, Wakiso, UG, 138
Kinshasa, DRC, 302
Kinyamasika, Fort Portal, UG, 28
Kinyarwanda language, 159
Kironda, Apollo, 26
Kisenyi, UG, 267
Kishosha, Sam, 102
Kisii SS, Kisii, KE, 213, 214, 422
Kisoro, UG, 266
Kisubi, UG, 75, 420
Kisumu, KE, 57, 112, 109-110, 310, 369
Kisumu Day School, KE, 423
Kiswahili literature, 357-362
Kitahulira, UG, 289
Kitale, KE, 253, 261

Kitante Senior SS, Kampala, UG, 417
Kitengesa Community Library, Masaka, UG, 423
Kitui HS, KE, 417
Kitui, KE, 239
Kiwanuka, Benedicto, 75, 77
Kiwanuka, Mathias, 77
Knies, Maureen, 114, 279
Knirk, Doyle, 221, 222
Koila, Richard, 73-74
Kololo Stadium, 26
kondos (armed gangs), 379-380
Koobi Fora, 290-292
Koppel, Ted, 375
Korogwe, TZ, 260
KPE (Kenya Primary Education) exams, 112, 229
KSPCA in Nairobi, 87
Kujifunza Kiswahili, 123
Kunz, Linda, 13
Kurasini SS, Dar es Salaam, TZ, 387
Kyambogo, Kampala, UG, 413
Kyambogo TTC. *See* Kyambogo University
Kyambogo University, Kampala, UG, 194, 272, 278-279, 390

Lady Irene College, Ndejji, Bombo, UG, 28-29, 417
Lake Albert, UG/DRC, 45, 116, 246
Lake Bunyonyi, UG, 109
Lake Hotel, Bukoba, TZ, 201, 207
Lake Hotel, Mombasa, KE, 79
Lake Kivu, DRC/Rwanda, 267
Lake Kyoga, UG, 226
Lake Manyara Hotel, TZ, 258
Lake Manyara National Park, TZ, 255
Lake Nakuru, KE, 274
Lake Rudolf (now Lake Turkana), KE, 245, 246, 262
Lake Tanganyika, 302
Lake Turkana (formerly Lake Rudolf), 114, 279

Lake Victoria, 14, 31, 45, 61, 147, 201, 206, 245, 296
Lal, Latigo, 225
Lamu, UG, 294
Land Rover stories, 12, 140-141, 246, 249, 258-259, 261, 293-294, 321
Lango College, Lira, UG, 225, 415
Laropi, UG, 44
"laughing sickness", 208
Leakey, Mary and Louis, 97
Lemke, Richard, 269, 397
leopards, 328-329
Levin, Bruce, 102
Lewinger, Joyce, 103
Liberia, 121
Limited Choices, The Political Struggle for Socialism in Tanzania (McHenry), 220
Limuru, KE, 32-34
Lindi, TZ, 144
lions, 331-332
litungu (musical instrument), 173-175, 177
Living in the Village of Ghosts, 275
Livingston, Marius, 26
Lobito, Angola, 317
Lodwar, KE, 246, 261-262
Loitokitok Boys HS, Rift Valley, KE 254
Lokitaung, 262-263
London Institute of Education, 94, 205
Lord Delaware's Plantation, 272, 278
Loreto Convent SS for Girls (now Loreto HS), Limuru, KE, 32-38, 417
Luanda, Angola, 321
Lubiri SS, Buganda, UG, 57, 417
Lucas, Professor, Makerere College, 79, 217
Lugbara people, 44
Lugogo Stadium, 56
Lukumburu escarpment, 92
Lumumba-Katanga-Mobutu affair, 268
Luo people, 311, 356, 369
Lupogo, Herman, 102
Lushoto, TZ, 21, 144, 260
Lybeck, Sharon, 79

Maasai people, 48, 103, 238, 265, 283
Maasiland, KE, 114, 237
Mabira Forest, KE, 330
Macbeth (Shakespeare), 116
MacGregor, Gordon, 139
Machakos, KE, 301, 379
Machakos Boys SS, KE, 209, 239, 420, 425
Machakos Club, 352
Machakos Girls HS, KE, 22, 237, 353, 392, 416
Machakos TTC, KE, 153-154, 416
Machame Girls SS, TZ, 14
MacMaster, Don, 13
Madhvani Prize, Makerere, 415
Madi people, 44
madinda (instrument), 145-147
Magamba SS, Lushoto, TZ, 21, 144-145, 415
Magher, John, 40, 44
Maji Moto hot springs, 256
Maji, Ethiopia, 261
Makeba, Miriam (Xhosa singer), 47
Makerere Demonstration School, 145-147
Makerere University, 12-13, 20, 55, 100, 139, 205, 216, 363, 417, 423
Makerere University Games-1965, 75, 260-261
Makerere University, Institute of Education, 114
Makerere University, sports, 13, 17, 56
Makutano, 253
Makuyuni, TZ, 259
Malangali HS, Iringa, TZ, 417
Malangali SS, TZ, 133, 136, 138, 160-161
Malangali, TZ, 13, 133
malaria, 79, 184, 217
Malcolm X, 387
male circumcision, ceremony, 62-63, 172
Malindi, KE, 50, 51, 294
Malkemes, Fred, 310

Manda Island, KE, 295
Mandela, Nelson, 372-378, 387
Mandela, Winnie, 377
Manone, Carl, 326
Manuell, John, 103
maps, East Africa, 3-5; Kenya, 5; Tanzania, 4; Uganda, 3
Maragoli people, 112, 228
Maralal, KE, 289
Marangu Hotel, TZ, 306
Marangu TTC, Moshi, TZ, 419
March on Washington-1963, 105
Kilakala Girls HS (*was* Marian College), Morogoro, TZ, 64, 424, 426, 346
Marian College (*now* Kilakala Girls HS), Morogoro, TZ, 64, 424, 426, 346
Maries, Malcolm, 296, 413
Marques, Lorenzo, 317
Mary Jo's Cuisine (McMillin), 422
Mary Stuart Hall, Makerere University, 314
Maryknoll Sisters, 346, 382
Masindi SS, Kinyara, UG, 116-118, 424
Matagoro Mountains, TZ, 90
Mau Mau rebellion, 24, 76, 180, 247, 264, 370
Mau Mau's Children (Sandgren), 371, 427
Mauma, Rommel, 102
Mauritius, Prime Minister, 363
Mawenzi SS, Moshi, TZ, 255
Maxon, Bob, 13, 227
Mbale, UG, 45, 79, 226, 413
Mbarara, UG, 40, 67, 68, 117, 266, 333
Mbotella, Walter, 123
Mboya, Tom, 114, 369; assassination, 355-356
McCall, Marty, 269
McCaw, Mel, 115
McDonald, Malcolm, 232
Meder, Elsa, 114
Mehta, Shekhar, 326
Menengai Crater, KE, 46
Mengo (Kampala), UG, 57

Merchant of Venice, The (Shakespeare), 213
Meru District, KE, 409
Meru traditional names, 409
Mhaiki, Paul, 90
Mhina, Edward, 360
Micklethwaite, Daphne, 279
Mikado, The (Gilbert; Sullivan), 346-347
Mikumi National Game Park, TZ, 343
Miller, Bub, 295
Minishi, Oliver, 178
Mitchell, Grace, 100
Mitchum, Robert, 348
Mkapa, Benjamin, 61, 398
Mkwawa HS, Iringa, TZ, 89-90, 421, 422
Mombasa, KE, 49, 51, 124, 277
Monduli, TZ, 73
Morogoro, TZ, 64, 65, 269, 344
Moroto, UG, 226, 246
Moshi, TZ, 48-49, 51, 73, 95, 104, 144, 415
Moshi Government Hospital, 258
Moshi Technical Secondary School, 103
Moshi Trade School, 103
mosquitoes, 329
Moss, Stirling, 260
Mountains of the Moon, 156, 407
Mozambique, 281
Mozambique Liberation Front, 317
Mpemba Effect, 89-90
Mpemba, Erasto, 89-90
MPLA (People's Movement for the Liberation of Angola), 317
Mpwapwa SS, Dodoma, TZ, 148-152, 219, 220, 424
Mpwapwa, TZ, 218, 416, 422
Mso Bay, TZ, 137
Mt. Elgon, 45, 73, 94, 227, 308
Mt. Gulwe, 149
Mt. Kenya, 52, 114, 122, 181, 227, 310
Mt. Kilimanjaro, 14, 48, 94-97, 103, 114, 125, 144, 227, 253, 254-255, 296-299, 301-302, 306-307, 315

Mt. Longonot, 33
Mt. Meru, 92, 314, 394
Mt. Muhavura, 267, 286
Mt. Rungwe, 136
Mt. St. Mary Namagunga, UG, 240
Mt. Stanley, 40
Mtabi, Ven, 102
Mtoto Mzuri, 410
Mto-wa-Mbu, 255, 257
Mtwara Regional Commissioner, 64
Mtwaro, John, 152
Mugisa, C. K., 118
MuHima people, 365
MuHutu people, 365
Mukumu Girls SS, Kakamega, KE, 94, 97-98, 422, 425
Mukwano (friendship) library, 29
Murchison Falls National Park, UG, 16-17, 45, 116, 307
Murchison Falls, UG, 226, 246, 271-272, 325
Murkurweini, KE, 180-181
Museveni, Yoweri, 108, 187, 219
music education, 173-175, 177, 347
musical instruments, indigenous, 173-175, 177
Mutesa II, Kabaka, 75
MuTutsi people, 365
Muwara, Ruth, 392-393
Mwadui, TZ, 201
"Mwalimu." See Julius Nyerere, 351
Mwangi, Harrison, 211
Mwanza Station, 148
Mwanza, TZ, 101, 147, 201, 203, 381
"Mzee." See Kenyatta, 351
Mzumbe (Government) SS, TZ, 65, 210, 212, 344, 417, 419, 421-424

Nairobi International School, 422
Nairobi, KE, 38, 46-47, 52, 54, 57, 72, 182
Nairobi National Park, 114
Nairobi Road, 310
Nairobi School for Boys, KE, 106

Nairobi Snake Park, 203
Naivasha, KE, 36
Nakuru, KE, 46, 283
Nakuru SS, KE, 407, 421
Namilyango College, Kampala, TZ, 272, 419
Namuruputh, 263
Namwamba, Khassogo Owa, 88
Nandi, KE, 215, 232
Nanyuki, KE, 57
Narok Road, KE, 283
Narok SS, KE, 114, 425
Natal, South Africa, 252
National Teachers College, Kyambogo, UG, 425
Ndebele language, 119
New Bristol Hotel, Mombasa, KE, 49
New Life Hotel, The (Hower), 73
New Primary Approach (NPA), 228, 423
New Stanley Hotel, Nairobi, 52, 348
New York Times, advertisement for Teachers for East Africa *vii*, 113
Newbury, David, 262, 394
NFD (Northern Frontier District), 265, 328
Ng'weno, Hilary, 115
Nganza SS, Mwanza, TZ, 425
Ngei, Paul, 352
ngima/ugali (dumpling), 34
Ngorogoro Crater, 396
Ngorongoro Crater, 227
Niblo, Winfield, 114
Night in Buganda, A (Gurney), 427
Nile River, 44, 117; fishing, 245-248
Nilo-Hamitic tribes, 265
Nilotic language, 365
Northern Frontier District (NFD), 262, 265, 328
NPA (New Primary Approach), 112
Ntare School, Mbarara, UG, 67, 68, 185, 187, 253, 415
Nyajato SS, Bukoba, TZ, 420
Nyakasura missionary school, Fort Portal, UG, 156

Nyakato SS, Bukoba, TZ, 206, 396, 417, 421, 426
Nyamwezi people, 365
Nyangan, Paul, 225
Nyanganyi, Mustafa, 220
Nyapea, UG, 40
Nyasaland/Malawi, health care system, 58
NYC11 reunion, 429
Nyerere, Julius, 1, 23, 62, 76, 116, 208, 218, 220, 351, 363, 385-389; *Julius Caezar*, 357-362
Nyeri, KE, 272, 310
Nymatangia Catholic Mission, UG, 333
Nystrom, Brad, 103
Nzalamba, Paul, *The Teacher*, ii

O Africa, Where I Baked My Bread (Jeffers), 74
O'Connell, Colm, 215
O'Dell, Keith, 223
Obama, Barak, Senior, 115
Obare, Clement, 112
Obote, Milton, 23, 26, 75, 119, 142, 363, 379-380
Odinga, Oginga, 369
Ogilut, Justin, 80-81
Okai, Matthew, 12
Okoboi, John, 80-81
Old Kampala SS, UG, 426
Old Moshi SS, 200-201
Olduvai Gorge, 97
O-level exams, 187-193
Olindo, Perez, 114
Oliver Twist, Charles Dickens, 157
Operation Uganda, Glassboro State College, 25-26
Operations Crossroads Africa, 115
Opiga, Francisco, 143
Organization of African Unity, 387
Ostrich Chase, The (Nagenda), 193
Otieno, Professor, 407
Otto, Dale, 13
Outward Bound Program, 254

Owen Falls Dam, 45, 245, 274
Oyuke, Caleb, 177

Paarlberg, Isabel, 106
Pakose, Frank, 221, 226
Paraa Safari Lodge, 16-17
Pasha, Emin, 217
Patel, Geld, 277
Patrician Brothers, 215
Peace Corps volunteers, 421, 428; basketball, 57; community projects, 167
Peace Corps, and TEA program launch, 24; compared with TEA/TEEA, 162-163; founding, 427; in Uganda, 417; in Rwanda, 158-168, 417; teacher training in Tanganyika, 64, 65
Penn, David, 126
People of the Saltchuk (Birdsall), 391
Perkins, James, 23
Peters, Rev. Elvin, 267
Peterson, Colleen, 401
Petley's Hotel, Manda Island, 295
pets, in Kenya, 84-85; in Uganda, 81-83
Phenomenon of Man, The (De Chardin), 97
Playboy, November 1962, 51
PLO (Palestine Liberation Organization), 375
Pokot reserve, 264
Polga, Margaret, 64, 65
Politics and Politicians (Section V), 349
Pollock, Gregory Francis, 410
Pollock, Phyllis, 110
Pomegranate Princess, The (Hower), 72
Pope John Paul II, 211
Port Bell, Kampala, UG, 206
Powell, Bill, 412
Princeton Conference-1960, 1, 427
provincial education officer (PEO), 235
Pygmies people, 365

Queen Elizabeth National Park, UG, 20, 39, 266

Rainy, Mike and Judy, 289
Ramsdell, Dick, 13, 227
recipes, ginger potatoes, 341; Indian, 338; Sukuma, 155-156
Reed, Phyllis, 114
reprint permissions, ii
Resochen (anti-malarial), 80
Reuben, Eva, 111
Revolutionary Front (at University of Dar es Salaam), 219-220
Rhodesian and Nyasaland Federation, 252
Rice, Ted, 114
Rift Valley, KE, 32, 46, 107, 215, 292, 316
Rift Wall, 256
Ripon Falls, UG, 45, 245
Rivonia trial, 373
Robben Island, 374, 378
Robinson, Ian Cameron, 139
Robinson, Reverend James, 115
Rock Hotel, Tororo, 45, 337
Rosary College, Mwanza, TZ, 20, 382, 395, 417, 425
Roundturner, David, 352
Rudisha, David, 215
Ruhizha rest house, 287
rungu (Maasai weapon), 48
Rungwe SS, 136
Russian documentary film crew, 24
Ruti, UG, 191
Rutshuru, 267
Ruwenzori Mountains, UG, 75, 92, 116
Rwanda, 267, 364-366; genocide, 164-166, 388; Peace Corps experience, 159-164

Sacred Heart Brothers, 52
Salazar dictatorship, 318
Sambaker SS. *See* Sir Samuel Baker Senior SS

Saska, Dr., 126
Scanlon, Dave, 23, 24, 64, 232
Schramm, Don, 114
Seale, Barney, 366
Seddon, Tony, 217
Seeger, Pete, 114
Semakula, Latria, 276
Sengawawa, Adawale, 114
Sensiba, Ben, 343
Serengeti Plain, 296
Serere Agricultural Station, 367
servants, 15, 143, 178, 231, 232, 235
Seyidda Maastuka SS, UG, 412
Shah, Kanti, 363
Shankar, Ravi, 292
Sharon, Ariel, 375
Shifta people, 294
Shimo la Tewa, KE, 425
Shriver, Sargent, 65
Sikh people, in Kenya, 253
Silverbeck Hotel, Nanyuki, KE, 57
Singh, Joginder, 326
Singleton, Seth, 219
Sir Samuel Baker Senior SS, 16, 18, 45, 140-141, 142-143, 245, 248-250, 415; sports, 18; student strike, 141-142
Sisters of Notre Dame, 112
Sitayo, Simon, 411
Smart, Bob, 45
Smith, Doug, 307-308
Smith, Ian, 373
snakes, 203-205, 248, 336, 337, 343, 34, 397
Somali Bantu resettlement, Virginia, 58
Songea SS, Songea, TZ, 93, 422
Songea, TZ, 90, 91-93
Soroti Club, 222
Soroti Rest House, 337
Soroti Senior SS, 217, 336
Soroti, UG, 79, 80-81, 88, 116, 366, 412
Sossusvlei Desert Lodge, 423
South Africa, 252, 281

South African oral traditions, 119, 424
Southern Rhodesia, 252, 373
Soviet doctors, in Uganda, 366-368
Sowing the Mustard Seed (Museveni), 187
spiders, 330
sports, 179, 215, 222, 224, 242
Sputnik, 381
Ssematimba, Madoxx, 145
St. Aloysius College, Nyapea, UG, 39
St. Mary's College, Kisubi, UG, 420
St. Patrick's Boys HS, Iten, KE, 215
St. Scholastic's TTC, Fort Portal, UG, 417
Stag's Head Hotel, Nakuru, KE, 46
Standard 8 school-leaving examinations, 239
Stanleyville, 302
Stockton, Jane, 122
Stout, Dr., 222
Streets, Bill, 206
strike, student, 141-142, 153-154, 185, 232-235, 345
strike, teachers, 229
student fees, 180-182
student ratios, boy v. girl, 1
Sudan language, 365
Sudan, 217
Sukuma (recipe), 155-156
Sukuma people, 365
sukuti (drum), 177
Sunday Star Time, 72
sundowner (custom), 194-198
Surprise (Section IV), 323
Swahili Beyond the Boundaries: Literature, Language, and Identity (Mazrui), 363
Swahili stories, 231
Swati language, 119
Swahili translations, *Dunia ni maarifa* (The world is knowledge), 1; *Elimu haina mwisho* (Education never ends), 429
Swatman, J.E.D., 396
Swaziland, 252

Syracuse University, training Peace Corps teachers, 65

Table Mountain, 373, 378
Tabora Boys SS, TZ, 425
Tabora Girls SS, TZ, 426
Tabora, TZ, 352, 385, 415
Tambach, KE, 292
Tanga Boys SS, TZ, 419, 421
Tanga, TZ, 399
Tanganyika African National Union (TANU), 351
Tanganyika (*now* Tanzania), independence, 48, 76, 219, 357
TANU (Tanganyikan African National Union), 386; anti-witchcraft effort, 91
Tanzania in Pictures (Carstens; Reuben), 229
Tanzania, map, 4
Tanzania Studies Association, 220
Tanzanian State Railway, 148-149
Taveta, KE, 102
TEA and TEEA, history, 1, 7, 427; Kampala office, 421; program goals, 28; reunion, 61
TEA and TEEA waves
  Group 1, 12, 23, 78-79, 156, 205, 269
  Group 2, 113
  Group 3, 20, 144
  Group 4, 81
  Group 6, 203
TEA-Alumni, authors, 415; DC2001 reunion, 2; formation, 2; grants to schools in East Africa, 2, 61; Story Project, 2; Tanzania trip-2005, 20; website, 428; wiki, 2
TEA Experience, The (Lindfors), 416, 427
Teacher Education for East Africa. *See* TEA and TEEA
teacher training. *See* Makerere University
Teachers College, Columbia, 1, 427, 429; cultural orientation, 100; International Studies, 23

Teachers College Newsroom, 428
Teachers College Project in East Africa: A History of International Cooperation, (Nanka-Bruce), 427
Teachers for East Africa. *See* TEA and TEEA
Teacher in East Africa, A (Howard), 427
Teaching and School Life (Section II), 129-242
Teaching Safari: A Study of American Teachers in East Africa, A (Gold), 427
Temba, Joseph, 176
Teso College Aloet (TCA), UG, 217-218, 221, 226; Soroti, 81, 423
Teso District, UG, 365
Thant, U, 26
Theroux, Paul, 363
Thika, Kenya, 38
Things Fall Apart (Achebe), 15275
Third Wednesday (Thomas), 426
Thomas, Isaiah, 377
Thompson's Falls, KE, 46
Thorn Tree café, Nairobi, 52
Tickell, Lancelot, 289
Till, Graham, 103
Time Machines (Anderson), 415
Toepfer, Ken, 113
Tom Brown's Schooldays (Hughes), 188, 275
Tom Stetson and the Giant Jungle Ants, 236
Tongue Is Fire, The (Scheub), 424
Top Life Club, at Makerere University, 13
Tororo Boy's HS, UG, 79, 217
Tororo Girls School, UG, 274, 425
Tororo, UG, 45, 52, 79, 413
Train, Russell E., 114
Transafrica journal, 377
Travelers Rest, Kisoro, UG, 266, 285-286, 287
Tributes (Section VI), 383-413
Trips and Travel (Section III), 243-322
Tsavo National Game Park, KE, 49-50, 312

Tugen people, 369
Turkana District, KE, 251
Turkana, famine relief camp, 262
Turkana people, 247, 262, 264, 265, 280, 290
Tutsi people, 165
Tuttlebee, Jack, 318
Tutu, Desmond, 375

Uasin Gishu district, KE, 293
UAW, 377
UDI (Unilateral Declaration of Independence), 373
Uganda Community Library Association, 423
Uganda Open-1965, 56, 269
Uganda Technical College, 65, 425
Uganda Voluntary Work Camps Association, 108
Uganda, Driving Code, 19; map, 3; national anthem, 117
Uhuru souvenirs, 353
Ujamaa Villages, UG, 219
ujamaa vision, 221
UK involvement (in TEA), 1
Uluguru Mountains, TZ, 344, 346
UNESCO, Uganda Technical College, 65
Unilateral Declaration of Independence (UDI), 373
UNITA (National Union for the Total Independence of Angola), 319-321
United Nations (UN), Tanzania's independence, 23
University College London, 216
University Farm, Kabanyola, UG, 12
University Games-1965, at Makerere, 260-261
University of Calibar, Nigeria, 220
University of Cambridge Examination Syndicate, 169
University of Dar es Salaam, TZ, 219
University of East Africa, 148, 261, 385
University of Kenya, 154

University of Wisconsin-Madison, Dept. of African Languages and Literature, 118
Urch, Dorothy, 125
US African Affairs Subcommittee, 375
US involvement (in TEA), 1; *see also* USAID
US Navy, books to Mombasa, 26
USAID, and TEA program launch, 24, 427; in West Africa, 209; library grants in Uganda, 29; West Africa, 420
Uvira, 302

Victoria Falls, 252
Victoria Nile River, 325
Virunga Volcanoes, 285
Voi, KE, 51
Voice of America, 123
Voice of Kenya (VOK), radio, 123; TV, 72, 327
Voices in the Water (Hower), 73
volcanoes, 267, 314
voodoo, 137-138
VSO (Voluntary Service Overseas), 184-185, 223, 416

Wa-Benzi (people of the Mercedes Benz), 386
Wafford, Harris, 115
Wagogo people, 150
walimu (teacher), defined, 1
Walk The Wide World (Knies), 421
Walton, Brian and Kathryn, 194
wanafuzi (students), defined, 1
Warford, Jim, 279
Washington, DC, 2001 reunion, 61

Weep Not, Child (Thiong), 190, 275
Wendel, Robert, 91-93
West Nile, UG, 44, 218-219, 417
White Highlands, KE, 46
White Horse Inn, Iringa, TZ, 92
White Nile source, 245
White Nile, The, at Makerere University, 13
Wigglesworth, Margaret, 81
Wigglesworth, Roger, 81, 284
Wild Life Education Center, KE, 114
Wild, Bill, 114
Wildlife Clubs of Kenya, 329
Wildlife Society, 271-272
Wilkins, Robin, 57
Williamson's diamond mine, 201-202
Wills, Denis, 192
witchcraft, 90-91, 137-138, 239
Wolpe, Howard, 375
Womeldorf, Anne, 222
Wonder, Stevie, 377
Woodson, Carter G., 77
Wyatt, Martin, 84

Xaverian Brothers, 112
Xhosa language, 119

Young, Coleman, 377

Zaire (*now* DRC), 318
Zambia, 115, 373
Zanzibar, 252; revolution, 360
Zawawi, Sharifa, 25, 397-398
Zenani, Nongenile Masithathu, 119
Zimbabwe, 252
Zulu language, 119
Zululand, 252

About Jugum Press

Jugum Press, an independent publisher, presents an eclectic collection of fiction, historic monographs, memoirs, and the *Opera en Español* series.

Nzinga, African Warrior Queen by Moses L. Howard

> Nzinga, in history and legend, is a brilliant leader during a time of violent upheaval. This fictional biography brings to life the Angolan culture in a flourishing seventeenth century African kingdom, where early explorers' maps of West Africa call out: "Here reigned the celebrated Queen Nzinga!"

A Boy from Wannaska by Marjorie W. Mortensen

> Sparkling tales of life in a tiny northern Minnesota town amidst first-generation Scandinavian immigrants in the early twentieth century.

Journey Into Gold Country: Memories of a Forty-Niner
by Ralph Buckingham; foreword by Charles Barker

> Three wild years in the California Gold Rush, remembered in tranquility sixty years later by a New England younger son of a youngest son who went to seek his fortune.

Jugum Press titles are available at online stores,
and you can request these books from your local bookseller.
Find print and eBook editions
and sign up to receive notice of new books at:
www.jugumpress.com

Made in the USA
Middletown, DE
08 June 2017